ENCYCLOPEDIA
OF THE
CONFEDERACY

ENCYCLOPEDIA
OF THE
CONFEDERACY

KEVIN J. DOUGHERTY

THUNDER BAY
P·R·E·S·S

San Diego, California

Thunder Bay Press
An imprint of the Baker & Taylor Publishing Group
10350 Barnes Canyon Road, San Diego, CA 92121
www.thunderbaybooks.com

All notations of errors or omissions should be addressed to Thunder Bay Press, Editorial
Department, at the above address. All other correspondence (author inquiries, permissions)
concerning the content of this book should be addressed to:

Amber Books Ltd.
Bradley's Close
74–77 White Lion Street
London, N1 9PF
United Kingdom
www.amberbooks.co.uk

ISBN-13: 978-1-60710-107-9
ISBN-10: 1-60710-107-6

Library of Congress Cataloging-in-Publication Data available on request

Printed in China

1 2 3 4 5 14 13 12 11 10

Project Editor: Michael Spilling
Picture Research: Terry Forshaw
Design: Joe Conneally

CONTENTS

THE CONTENTS FOR THE *ENCYCLOPEDIA OF THE CONFEDERACY* INCLUDES SOUTHERN MILITARY AND POLITICAL LEADERS, SOCIO-ECONOMIC FACTORS RELEVANT TO THE CONFEDERACY, AND MORE GENERAL TOPICS SUCH AS BATTLES AND NATIONAL POLITICAL EVENTS THAT WERE IMPORTANT TO BOTH NORTH AND SOUTH. IN THE CASE OF THESE BROADER TOPICS, THE ENTRIES ATTEMPT TO PLACE PARTICULAR EMPHASIS ON THE IMPACT OR PERSPECTIVE OF THE SOUTH AND THE CONFEDERACY.

CONTENTS

CONTENTS

ADAMS, WILLIAM WIRT (1819–88)

❖ RANK: Brigadier General

❖ PLACE OF BIRTH: Frankfort, Kentucky

❖ MILITARY CAREER:
1839: Private for the Republic of Texas
1861: Formed "Wirt Adams" Cavalry Regiment; fought at Battle of Shiloh
1863: Promoted to brigadier general
1864: Adams's brigade attacks Sherman's advance on Meridian, Mississippi

Wirt Adams was a Confederate cavalryman who operated primarily in and around Mississippi. He was born in Frankfort, Kentucky, but later moved to Mississippi, where he served as a district court judge. After serving in the army of the Republic of Texas, Adams returned to Mississippi and began a series of successful business ventures. He was an active advocate of Mississippi's secession, raised the First Mississippi Cavalry, and was commissioned a colonel on October 15, 1861.

Adams served as Major General Earl Van Dorn's chief of artillery at Corinth in the spring of 1862 and then fought at Shiloh, Iuka, and Corinth. On April 17, 1863, Major General Ulysses S. Grant dispatched Colonel Benjamin Grierson on a raid from La Grange, Tennessee, into Mississippi to divert Confederate attention away from Grant's crossing of the Mississippi River as he began his Vicksburg Campaign. Adams led seven cavalry companies from Port Gibson to try to locate and defeat Grierson. Adams attempted to ambush Grierson near Union Church, but the plan was foiled when one of Grierson's reconnaissance elements, a small force known as the "butternut

guerrillas," learned of the plan and alerted him. Grierson ultimately eluded his pursuers and escaped into Louisiana.

NEW APPOINTMENT
Adams was appointed brigadier general on September 23, 1863, and in 1864 he operated in northern Alabama, Mississippi, and western Tennessee. With Confederate resistance collapsing throughout the South, Brigadier General James Wilson launched a raid from the upper northeast corner of Alabama to the industrial and manufacturing center of Selma. Adams joined Lieutenant General Nathan Bedford Forrest in an unsuccessful attempt to bring Wilson to bay. Adams surrendered his command on May 4, 1865. After the war he lived in Mississippi until he was killed in Jackson in 1888 in a private argument with a local newspaper editor.

AFRICAN AMERICAN SOLDIERS IN THE CONFEDERATE ARMY

From the opening days of the war, African Americans were active in the Confederate war effort. Many wealthy Southerners brought an African American body servant with them when they joined the army. The servant's duties included taking care of his master's personal and cooking needs while in camp or serving a group of four to eight soldiers who had formed a mess, and all contributed to the servant's costs. During the fighting, most body servants remained in the rear, but occasionally one would be caught up in the battle. A few even fired weapons at the enemy. After the battle, the servant would move

forward to locate his master and resupply him with food and water. If the soldier had been wounded, the servant would help get him to medical care, and if he had been killed, the servant would escort the body home. In many cases, there was an intimate bond between these masters and their body servants that was based on a childhood association. While there were obviously some cases of abuse, the shared hardships of military life almost always resulted in a more positive master-slave relationship in the army than on the plantation.

SLAVE LABOR
By the second year of the war, labor shortages on the home front greatly reduced the practice of body servants accompanying their masters into the army. Much more common was the military use of African Americans to construct fortifications or perform other manual labor. At first, masters were fairly generous in loaning their slaves to the government. For example, when Major General George B. McClellan threatened Richmond in his 1862 Peninsula Campaign, General Robert E. Lee ordered Major General D. H. Hill to "get all the free black and slave labor you can" to help prepare defenses. As the war dragged on, however, war-weariness and labor shortages made owners less willing to share their slaves. In 1864 the Confederate government was forced to pass an Impressment Act authorizing the secretary of war to conscript 20,000 African Americans for military labor. The measure met stiff resistance from opponents of strong centralized government and also suffered because, once impressed, many African Americans deserted their posts. Owners also complained that the slaves were mistreated, and in April, the government was forced to appropriate over $3,000,000 to

compensate owners whose slaves had died or escaped.

Racial prejudice and fear of revolt made Southerners much less willing to arm African Americans and use them as actual soldiers. In February 1864, Major General Patrick R. Cleburne raised a proposal to enlist African Americans, but governmental authorities quickly suppressed the matter. However, by early 1865, the emergencies of war and the real possibility of defeat led to drastic action. In January, Lee said, "Under good officers and good instruction I do not see why they

Below: *African American Confederate soldiers, 1865. The emergencies of war compelled the Confederates to allow African Americans to enlist, but too late in the conflict to have any real impact.*

[slaves] should not become good soldiers." On March 6, Virginia enacted legislation allowing for the enlistment of African Americans, and a week later the Confederate government followed suit with a law authorizing President Jefferson Davis to call as many as 300,000 slaves into military service. There was no provision made for freedom after the war for those slaves who joined the army. While a few companies were formed, the war ended before the enlisted African Americans could see any meaningful service.

HOLT COLLIER

One of the more famous African American Confederate soldiers is Holt Collier. Born into slavery in Jefferson County, Mississippi,

Collier followed his masters, Howell and Thomas Hinds, into the Confederate army. At the age of fourteen, Collier joined Company I of the Ninth Texas Cavalry and served as a sharpshooter and spy. He gained national attention in 1902 when he served as a guide for President Theodore Roosevelt on a black bear hunt in Mississippi. It was as a result of this trip that "teddy bears" came into production. The Sons of Confederate Veterans Camp 2018 in West Point, Mississippi, is named after Collier, and in 2004 his grave was honored with a Confederate headstone.

AGRICULTURE

Agriculture formed the basis of the antebellum South. Southerners produced ample supplies of sugar, rice, tobacco, hemp, and assorted grains. Most importantly, in any given year after 1845, the region provided an estimated two-thirds of the world's cotton supply. Most of this produce, however, was exported in raw form. As a result, capital flowed out of the South and into the more industrialized North. What capital Southerners did acquire was routinely invested in land or slaves, a practice that did little to broaden the region's economic base. The South's agrarian nature impacted more than just its economy. It brought with it the social implications of both the planter class and slavery.

In spite of the South's emphasis on agriculture, there were still serious wartime food shortages. Southern cotton and tobacco were not food sources, and Federal armies early in the war occupied or threatened key rice-growing areas such as the South Carolina lowlands. Military

Above: *Southern social, political, and economic life revolved around vast plantations that harvested crops such as cotton, rice, tobacco, and sugarcane (as illustrated).*

operations forced many farmers to abandon their property, and those that remained were forced to contend with broken fences, foraging armies, and trampled crops. Much of General Robert E. Lee's motivation for his two invasions of Northern territory was the hope of relieving some of the pressure on Virginia's farmers.

A WAR ECONOMY

Agricultural production also suffered when Southern farmers left their fields to become soldiers. Wives, children, and older people attempted to fill the void, but efficiency obviously suffered. Moreover, by becoming a soldier, the farmer changed his status from being a producer of food to a consumer of it. Although overseers were exempted from military service, slave productivity was reduced as supervision lessened and slaves became less beholden to authority.

Even in those parts of the Confederacy relatively untouched by the war, the weak Southern transportation hindered getting the crops to where they were needed. For example, the Trans-Mississippi Confederacy offered remarkable potential. Texas led the nation in cattle, with an estimated 3.5 million head. As a point of comparison, Virginia and Georgia, the next largest Confederate cattle-producing states, counted slightly more than one million each. Texas ranked second in the number of horses and mules, fourth in the number of sheep, and seventh in the production of swine. It was a significant source of livestock for armies in the west. Most of these Texas resources traveled east on a railroad that crossed the Mississippi River at Vicksburg and then connected with other lines at Jackson and Meridian. The loss of Vicksburg in July 1863 and Federal control of the Mississippi River isolated this important agricultural source from the rest of the Confederacy. In many ways, the Confederacy's agricultural problem lay in distribution rather than production.

ALABAMA

Although Governor Andrew B. Moore was a strong secessionist, Alabama's departure from the Union was not a foregone conclusion. Southern Democrat John C. Breckinridge had carried the state in the election of 1860, but the more moderate candidates, John Bell and Stephen A. Douglas, combined for a respectable total of 41,526 votes compared to Breckinridge's 48,831. Much of the disunity was caused by Alabama's geographical conditions and political heritage. North Alabama was traditionally the home of small farmers and Jacksonian Democrats with a penchant for cooperation. In Mobile and Montgomery, however, a large population of slaveholding planters took a more radical stance. It was in south and central Alabama that the plantations, cotton fields, and slaves created the conditions necessary to breed secessionist fervor. After Fort Sumter, preliminary polls showed the Alabama convention split fifty-four to forty-six in favor of secession. In the final count on January 11, 1861, the secession ordinance passed sixty-one to thirty-nine. When Alabama joined the Confederacy, it brought with it important industrial capacity at Selma, the state's agriculturally rich Black Belt, and the key port of Mobile.

The state also hosted the Montgomery Convention in February, at which delegates from the states that had thus far seceded adopted a provisional constitution and elected Jefferson Davis president. Montgomery served as the capital of the Confederacy until it was moved to Richmond on May 20, 1861, after Virginia seceded. Famous Alabamians who served the Confederacy include the fire-eating politician William L. Yancey and Lieutenant General James Longstreet. In addition to the naval Battle of Mobile, the state was the site of Brigadier General James Wilson's cavalry raid from the extreme northwest corner of the state to Selma.

ALCORN, JAMES L. (1816–94)

James L. Alcorn owned a small plantation, practiced law, founded the Mississippi levee system, and served in the Mississippi state legislature before the war. He personally opposed secession, but voted in favor of it with the other Whigs at the Mississippi secession convention. He was elected brigadier general of state troops in 1861, and his subsequent military service was undistinguished.

When Federal forces overran northern Mississippi, Alcorn urged arming slaves as soldiers. He then became involved in a lucrative cotton black marketeering operation that netted him considerable

Above: *James L. Alcorn was a Mississippi planter who benefited from the cotton black market during the war and became a scalawag after it.*

wealth. He was a consistent critic of President Jefferson Davis. After the war, Alcorn became Mississippi's Republican governor from 1870 to 1871 and U.S. senator from 1871 to 1877. Although skilled at manipulating the African American vote, he resisted Federal efforts to enforce social equality.

ALEXANDER, EDWARD PORTER (1835–1910)

Edward Porter Alexander graduated third of thirty-eight in the West Point class of 1857. He was commissioned as an engineer and served as an instructor at West Point. In 1859 he worked with Albert J. Myer, future chief signal officer in the Union army, on the "wigwag" system that used flags to relay line-of-sight messages. Alexander resigned from the army when his native Georgia seceded and was appointed a captain of engineers in the Confederate army on June 3, 1861. He served as Brigadier General Pierre Gustave Toutant Beauregard's engineer and signal officer at First Manassas, where Alexander used his wigwag system to warn Colonel Nathan Evans of a Federal flank attack.

In November 1862, Alexander was given command of an artillery battalion under Major General James Longstreet. He was promoted to colonel in December and served at Fredericksburg and Chancellorsville. At Gettysburg he superintended the massive but ineffective artillery barrage that preceded Pickett's Charge. He fought with the Army of Northern Virginia against Lieutenant General Ulysses S. Grant's Overland Campaign in 1864–65 and surrendered with General

Robert E. Lee at Appomattox. Alexander's *Military Memoirs of a Confederate*, published in 1907, remains a classic account of the Confederate effort.

AMENDMENTS, CONSTITUTIONAL

The Federal victory in the Civil War did not end the sectional differences between the North and the South. Throughout the Reconstruction era, the struggle to either maintain the status quo of the antebellum South or to exert Federal authority continued. Three constitutional amendments helped reshape the United States in the postwar era. The first of these was the Thirteenth Amendment, which was passed in 1865 and abolished slavery. The Emancipation Proclamation had declared an end to slavery only in those states then in rebellion. It was the Thirteenth Amendment that ended slavery throughout the United States. The Fourteenth Amendment was passed in 1868. It extended citizenship to all people born or naturalized in the United States, overturning the Dred Scott case. It also prohibited states from denying "any person of life, liberty, or property, without due process of law." This provision was extremely useful in guaranteeing civil rights for African Americans. It also prohibited any state from paying any debt incurred in aid of insurrection or rebellion against the United States. Finally, the Fifteenth Amendment of 1870 prohibited states from denying a citizen the right to vote based on "race, color, or previous condition of servitude." While these amendments were strongly resisted by many Southerners and Democrats, they became the bedrock of Reconstruction, and accepting them became a precondition for a state's readmission into the Union.

ANDERSONVILLE PRISON

Andersonville has the distinction of being the most notorious of the Civil War prisons. In fact, its commandant, Captain Henry Wirz, was the only Confederate to be executed after the war for official wartime conduct.

The prison was built in February 1864 in order to relieve Richmond of its dangerously large population of Federal prisoners. Located northeast of Americus, Georgia,

Below: *This dramatic illustration of the notorious Andersonville Prison, drawn in September 1865 after the war's end, shows a wagon full of dead Federal prisoners in the foreground.*

the site commonly called Andersonville bears the official name of Camp Sumter. It originally consisted of 16.5 acres but was later enlarged to 26 acres. A log stockade detained the prisoners.

Living conditions in the facility were abysmal, and the stream running through the prison quickly became contaminated by the unsanitary habits of some inmates and by pollutants dumped into the swampy area that fed into the stream. Poor sanitation, meager rations, exposure to the elements, and disease took an incredible toll. Overcrowding was also a problem. By the summer of 1864, some 32,899 Federal enlisted men were housed at Andersonville. As Major General William T. Sherman approached on his March to the Sea, all prisoners who could be moved were evacuated to Charleston, South Carolina. The national cemetery at the site today contains 12,912 graves, but the total casualties were no doubt much higher.

In spite of the postwar outcry against Wirz, rations for Federal prisoners at Andersonville were the same as those of Confederate soldiers in the field. When Lieutenant General Ulysses S. Grant assumed overall command of the Federal armies, he virtually ceased the exchange of prisoners in order to drain Confederate manpower resources. By this time, the South could hardly feed its own soldiers adequately, let alone care for prisoners properly. Under the circumstances, Wirz probably had done the best he could.

ANTIETAM CAMPAIGN

- ❖ DATE: September 4–20, 1862
- ❖ LOCATION: Hanover County, Virginia
- ❖ ARMY OF NORTHERN VIRGINIA (C): 45,000
- ❖ ARMY OF THE POTOMAC (U.S.): 75,500
- ❖ CASUALTIES: 10,316 (C); 12,401 (U.S.)

Antietam was one of the pivotal battles of the Civil War, and one that ended as a severe setback for the Confederacy. Building on his recent victories in Virginia, General Robert E. Lee hoped that a successful campaign in Maryland might convince the state to secede or cause Europe to recognize the Confederacy. At a minimum, taking the battle to Northern soil would allow the Virginia countryside a brief respite from the ravages of war. Although the battle itself ended in a stalemate, Lee was forced to withdraw back to Virginia, giving President Abraham Lincoln enough of a victory to justify issuing his Emancipation Proclamation, an event that changed the course of the war.

Following his decisive victory at the Battle of Second Manassas,

Below: *During the Battle of Antietam, McClellan piecemealed his forces in a series of uncoordinated attacks that allowed Lee to rush defenders from one threatened point to another.*

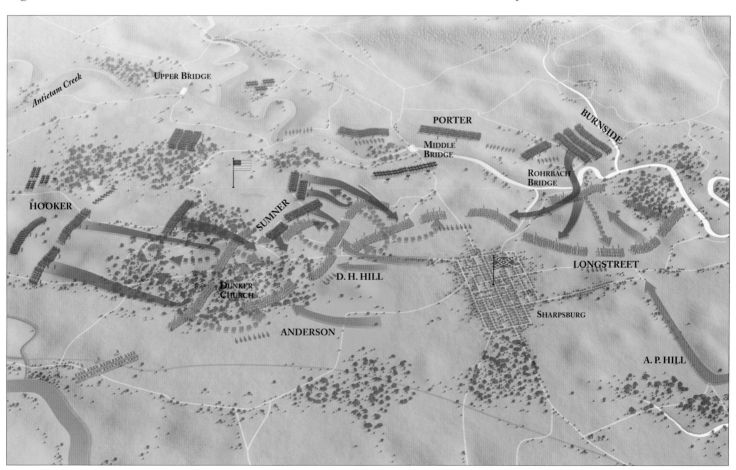

Lee was confident in the superiority of the Confederate soldier. In spite of having just 45,000 men, much less than a large-scale offensive would normally require, Lee counted on Major General George B. McClellan's characteristic caution to offset the disadvantage the Confederates had in numerical strength. On September 3, 1862, Lee wrote to President Jefferson Davis, "The present seems to be the most propitious time since the commencement of the war for the Confederate army to enter Maryland."

FIRST ENCOUNTERS

In the preliminary actions, Lee escaped a close call when he was forced to divide his army and send Major General Stonewall Jackson to deal with the Federal garrison at Harpers Ferry. While Jackson was thus occupied, two Federal soldiers stumbled upon three cigars wrapped in a sheet of paper that turned out to be a copy of Special Orders 191, Lee's campaign plan. With this intelligence, McClellan had everything he needed to destroy Lee's dangerously scattered army.

Instead McClellan delayed, giving Lee precious hours to react. Thus as the Federals finally advanced on South Mountain early on September 14, they found strong Confederate positions waiting for them. In fierce fighting, the Federals worked their way through the gaps, but the delay was enough to allow Lee to concentrate at Sharpsburg and wait for Jackson to arrive at Harpers Ferry.

Lee established a defensive line that stretched across the angle formed by the junction of the Potomac River and Antietam Creek. The natural terrain gave Lee both protection and the opportunity to use interior lines to securely move reinforcements from one part of the battlefield to another.

Above: *A contemporary illustration showing the difficulty faced by Burnside's corps as it tried to push across the Rohrbach Bridge over the Antietam Creek. Just one unit at a time could cross the bridge, meaning Burnside could only launch piecemeal attacks.*

McClellan's plan was to attack both Confederate flanks in a risky double envelopment and then use his reserve to attack the center. On September 17, the Federals launched what became a series of piecemeal and uncoordinated attacks that allowed Lee to send reinforcements from one threatened sector to another. By failing to mass his force, McClellan wasted his overall numerical advantage.

FAILED ATTACK

The inefficiency of the Federal attack was nowhere more apparent than at the Rohrbach Bridge, where Major General Ambrose E.

Burnside's Ninth Corps was to cross Antietam Creek and assault Lee's right. Instead, Burnside remained in position, allowing Lee additional freedom to reposition forces to more contested areas. By the time Burnside finally attacked at 10:00 a.m., Lee had moved so many forces from in front of Burnside that his 11,000 men were opposed by a brigade of just 550 Georgians. Nonetheless, Burnside's attack was so uninspired that it was not until early afternoon that his men used a ford downstream to turn the Confederate position. By then, the Federals had suffered 500 casualties, compared to just 160 for the Confederates. More

Right: The Battle of Antietam, 1862 *by Thure de Thulstrup depicts the charge of the Iron Brigade near the Dunker Church, which was the focal point of several Federal attacks against the Confederate left.*

importantly, the already-delayed Federal attack on the Confederate right had been stalled for three full hours. The debacle resulted in the Rohrbach Bridge being rechristened "Burnside's Bridge."

Still Burnside delayed, calling up his reserve division and then slowly

Above: *The inexcusable Federal delay in crossing Antietam Creek at the Rohrbach Bridge gave Major General A. P. Hill time to march to the battle from Harpers Ferry.*

funneling it across the bridge rather than using the recently discovered ford as an additional means of

crossing. Traveling along the same route Jackson had used a few days earlier, Major General A. P. Hill marched his men the seventeen miles from Harpers Ferry in eight hours and arrived just in time to force Burnside to retreat.

By 5:30 p.m., the Battle of Antietam was all but over. After twelve hours of fighting, 12,400 Federals and 10,300 Confederates were casualties. It was the bloodiest single day in American military history. On the night of September 18, Lee was forced to abandon his invasion of Maryland.

While the battle itself was a tactical draw, the fact that Lee was forced to withdraw back to Virginia made it a strategic victory

Below: *Lee's surrender occurred in the home of Wilmer McLean, who had moved his family to Appomattox from Manassas to escape the heavy fighting in northern Virginia.*

for the Federals, and that was enough to give President Lincoln the opportunity he had been waiting for to issue the Emancipation Proclamation. This made the Federal war objective not merely to restore the Union but also to free the slaves in the Confederate states. This new development made European recognition nearly impossible for the Confederacy. Indeed, the real significance of Antietam occurred not on the battlefield itself, but in the issuance of the Emancipation Proclamation that the battle made possible.

APPALACHIAN MOUNTAINS

The Appalachian mountain chain runs from Pennsylvania through Maryland, Virginia, and the Carolinas to northern Georgia

and Alabama. With few passes to accommodate rail or even significant foot movement, this natural barrier served to create eastern and western theaters of war. The divide was so prominent that in many ways the two theaters were fought independently of each other. Lacking the large plantations found elsewhere, the Appalachians were also home to a number of pro-Union Southerners who had little stake in the region's slave-based society.

APPOMATTOX COURT HOUSE, SURRENDER AT

After his supplies were destroyed at Appomattox Station and any chance of opening a route to the south had evaporated, General

Robert E. Lee realized surrender was inevitable. On April 7, 1865, he received a note from Lieutenant General Ulysses S. Grant stating that "the results of the last week must convince you of the hopelessness of further resistance . . . I feel that it is so, and regard it as my duty to shift from myself the responsibility of any further effusion of blood, by asking of you the surrender of . . . the Army of Northern Virginia." After additional exchanges of correspondence, the two generals met on April 9 to finalize the terms of surrender.

The great commanders presented a stark physical contrast at the meeting. Grant wore a mud-spattered uniform that, with the exception of the shoulder straps, resembled that of a private. Lee, on the other hand, was immaculately dressed with sword and sash.

Grant offered Lee gracious terms, allowing Lee's officers to retain their sidearms as well as their private horses and baggage. At Lee's request, Grant then extended the concession to allow private soldiers as well to keep personally owned horses and mules so that they could

"work their little farms." Grant even went so far as to supply Lee's hungry army with rations.

In one of the war's most interesting coincidences, the surrender occurred at a house owned by Wilmer McLean. Originally a farmer in Manassas, McLean had moved his family to Appomattox to escape the heavy fighting in northern Virginia. In the process, he forever tied his name to the war he sought to avoid.

ARISTOCRACY, SOUTHERN

Although aristocratic planters represented just a small fraction of the overall population in the South, they enjoyed power and influence well beyond their numbers. As slavery became inseparably intertwined with the Southern way of life, the upper class of the social structure came to dominate the political, social, and economic landscape in the South. Because of this influence, the manners, customs, and values of the aristocracy filtered down, creating a

Above: *This illustration shows the room in the McLean house, at Appomattox Court House, in which General Lee (seated left) surrendered to General Grant (seated center).*

certain shared consensus in Southern society.

Young Southern aristocrats received a classical education intended to prepare them for assuming the role of a leader. They enjoyed abundant leisure time that allowed for reading and hunting. Military service was considered admirable, and many fine Southern families sent their sons to West Point, the Citadel, or the Virginia Military Institute. By the time of the Civil War, the Southern aristocracy was well positioned to play a major role in all aspects of the Confederacy.

ARKANSAS

Arkansas's turbulent debate over secession was decided after President Abraham Lincoln called for volunteers in the wake of Fort Sumter. Facing what many in the state considered coercion, the convention voted sixty-five to five in favor of secession on May 6, 1861. In spite of this resounding sentiment, Arkansas's geographic position on the frontier of the Confederacy left it vulnerable to Federal attack and in many ways isolated from the rest of the Confederacy.

Many Arkansans hoped to increase their security by swaying Missouri to join the Confederacy, but the Federal victory at Pea Ridge on March 6–8, 1862, in northwest Arkansas dashed this possibility. After the defeat, Richmond ordered Major General Earl Van Dorn to withdraw his forces into Mississippi, which to many seemed to represent a decision to abandon the state. However, the Confederates mounted another effort led by Major General Thomas C. Hindman to drive the Federals from the state, only to be defeated at Prairie Grove on December 7, 1862. The Federals then expanded into other parts of the state, and without adequate troops for protection, Arkansans turned to partisan and guerrilla warfare and raids on Federal supply lines to try to resist occupation.

In addition to Pea Ridge and Prairie Grove, smaller battles in Arkansas were fought at Marks' Mills and Jenkins' Ferry. In related fighting at Poison Spring, Texan troops were accused of massacring surrendered African American Federal soldiers whose bodies were then mutilated by Confederate Choctaws. Arkansans who fought for the Confederacy include Hindman, adopted son Brigadier General Albert Pike, and Brigadier General Albert Rust.

ARKANSAS POST, BATTLE OF

- ❖ DATE: January 4–12, 1863
- ❖ LOCATION: Arkansas County, Arkansas
- ❖ FORT HINDMAN GARRISON (C): 4,500
- ❖ ARMY OF THE MISSISSIPPI (U.S.): 30,000
- ❖ CASUALTIES: 5,500 (C); 1,047 (U.S.)

Arkansas Post, also known as Fort Hindman, was a strongpoint fifty miles up the Arkansas River, from which the Confederates could send gunboats into the Mississippi River and threaten Major General Ulysses S. Grant's efforts to capture Vicksburg. While Major General William T. Sherman was in the process of returning north from his failed battle at Chickasaw Bluffs, Major General John A. McClernand reclaimed troops he considered Sherman had "borrowed" from him and proceeded to lead an expedition up the Arkansas River to capture Arkansas Post.

Fort Hindman was defended by about 4,500 Confederates under Brigadier General T. J. Churchill. He was opposed by McClernand's 30,000 men, supported by fifty transports and thirteen gunboats belonging to Admiral David D. Porter. After a bungled attack on January 10, the Federals launched a coordinated land and naval attack that forced Churchill to surrender on January 11.

RETREAT TO VICKSBURG

However, as McClernand planned further operations in the interior of Arkansas, Grant ordered him to return with his force to the Vicksburg area. McClernand, who disputed Grant's authority over him, reluctantly complied, and subsequent orders from Major General Henry W. Halleck compelled McClernand to bring his force under Grant's command. Tensions continued between Grant and McClernand, and Grant would eventually find an opportunity to relieve his troublesome subordinate on June 18, 1863.

Left: *The Federal victory at Arkansas Post (Fort Hindman) showed the Confederates' vulnerability to coordinated land and naval attacks.*

ARLINGTON HOUSE

Arlington House was the home of George Washington Parke Custis, George Washington's adopted grandson. When Robert E. Lee married Custis's daughter Mary, he became master of this stately mansion across the Potomac River from Washington. Lee must

Below: *One consequence of Lee's decision to side with the Confederacy was the personal loss of his majestic Arlington House across the Potomac River from Washington.*

have known that his decision to side with his native Virginia would put this beautiful property in jeopardy. Indeed, using a wartime taxation measure, the Federal government confiscated Arlington House and offered it for public sale on January 11, 1864. A tax commissioner purchased it for "government use, for war, military, charitable and educational purposes." Brigadier General Montgomery C. Meigs, commander of the garrison at Arlington House, appropriated the grounds on June 15 for use as a military cemetery, intending to render the house uninhabitable

should the Lee family ever attempt to return.

After the war, Mary Lee requested that the Arlington House relics, many of which had originated in Mount Vernon, be restored to her. President Andrew Johnson, with his characteristic conciliatory attitude toward the South, agreed, and the items were returned. In 1882 the Supreme Court declared the original seizure to be invalid, and Lee's heirs were awarded $150,000 compensation, but the property remained in government hands. Today, more than 300,000 people are buried at Arlington National Cemetery.

ARMISTEAD, LEWIS A. (1817–63)

Lewis A. Armistead attended West Point but did not graduate. He served with distinction in Mexico, winning two brevets and helping storm the citadel at Chapultepec. On the eve of the Civil War, Armistead was serving in California. His good friend Winfield Scott Hancock hosted a farewell party in Los Angeles for the many comrades departing for service with either the Confederate or Federal army. Armistead was among those in attendance, and he entrusted Hancock's wife with a satchel of personal items and mementos to be opened only in the event he was killed.

Armistead resigned from the U.S. Army on May 26, 1861, and was commissioned a major in the Confederate army. By April 1, 1862, he was a brigadier general,

Above: *Lewis Armistead led a brigade in Pickett's Charge at the Battle of Gettysburg that reached the "high water mark of the Confederacy." He was mortally wounded in the action.*

and he commanded his brigade from the Peninsula Campaign to Gettysburg. He is most famous for his role in Pickett's Charge on the third day of the Battle of Gettysburg. Cheering his brigade forward with his hat on his sword, Armistead briefly reached the Federal lines commanded by his old army friend Hancock. Armistead was mortally wounded in the attack, but the position he reached is commemorated as the "high water mark of the Confederacy," acknowledging the idea that Gettysburg was the turning point of the war.

ARMY, CONFEDERATE

The "Army of the Confederate States of America" was established by the Provisional Congress on March 6, 1861, but never really came into existence.

The organization that fought the Civil War on behalf of the Confederacy was the volunteer or Provisional Army established by the Confederate Congress on February 28 and March 6. Under these acts, President Jefferson Davis assumed control of military operations and received state forces and 100,000 volunteers for a one-year term of service. Under this authority, Davis had called for 82,000 men by April. On May 8, the Confederate Congress voted to extend enlistments for the duration of the war. On August 8, they authorized 400,000 additional volunteers for periods from one to three years. All of these troops entered the army via the states.

On April 16, 1862, the Confederate Congress passed legislation conscripting men between the ages of eighteen and thirty-five. This marked the first time soldiers directly entered the Provisional Army rather than passing first through the states. Conscription was expanded in September and then again in February 1864. Regardless, most men who entered the army did so as volunteers.

Confederate territory was organized into departments that generally gave their names to the field armies operating within their boundaries. The Confederate armies were the Army of Central Kentucky, East Tennessee, Eastern Kentucky, the Kanawha, Kentucky, Louisiana, Middle Tennessee, Mississippi, Missouri, Mobile, New Mexico, Northern Virginia, the Northwest, the Peninsula, Pensacola, the Potomac, the Shenandoah, Tennessee, the Trans-Mississippi, Vicksburg, the West, and West Tennessee; there was also the Southwestern Army. The Army of Northern Virginia was the principal army in the eastern theater, and the Army of Tennessee was the principal army in the western theater.

ARMY OF NORTHERN VIRGINIA

After General Joseph E. Johnston was wounded at the Battle of Seven Pines, General Robert E. Lee assumed command. In his assumption of command orders dated June 1, 1862, Lee gave his command the name Army of Northern Virginia.

Although the unit was the same one Johnston had previously commanded, the Army of Northern Virginia is almost exclusively associated with Lee. In fact, Lee was its animating force. His men

Right: The First Virginia Cavalry at a Halt *by Alfred R. Waud, published in* Harper's Weekly, *September 1862. Especially during the war's early years, Lee's Army of Northern Virginia enjoyed an advantage over the Federals in the quality of cavalry.*

became intensely loyal to him, calling him "Uncle Bob" and "Marse Robert," and Lee returned the affectionate bond.

When Lee assumed command, the Confederate army did not authorize the designation of corps. Instead, Lee's army consisted of two wings, commanded by Lieutenant Generals James Longstreet and Stonewall Jackson. Corps eventually became authorized on September 18, 1862, and on November 6, Lee assigned Longstreet command of the First Corps and Jackson the Second Corps. Major General Jeb Stuart led the Cavalry Corps.

NEW FORMATIONS

After Jackson was killed at Chancellorsville, Lee did not feel he had a suitable subordinate to take command of Jackson's large corps, so he reorganized the Army of Northern Virginia into three corps commanded by Longstreet, Richard S. Ewell, and A. P. Hill. On May 29, 1864, Major General Jubal A. Early replaced Ewell as commander of the Second Corps after Ewell's wounds rendered him unfit for active field service. In late October 1864, a Fourth Corps was formed under the command of Lieutenant General Richard Anderson. In December, Early stayed in the Shenandoah Valley with 3,000 men and the rest of the Second Corps was placed under the command of Major General John Brown Gordon.

The Army of Northern Virginia was the principal Confederate force in the eastern theater. Its strength varied as a result of reinforcements and losses. Lee took less than 50,000 men with him on the

Antietam Campaign. At Chancellorsville, he had about 60,000. For the Gettysburg Campaign, he had some 89,000. At Appomattox Court House, he surrendered 26,765.

LEE AGAINST GRANT

In spite of being routinely outnumbered, the Army of Northern Virginia under Lee was characterized by audacity and offensive action. It made short work of a succession of Federal commanders until Lieutenant General Ulysses S. Grant arrived to use his superior numbers to relentlessly bludgeon the Army of Northern Virginia into submission. Grant understood the importance of this army to the Confederacy, ordering Army of the Potomac commander Major General George G. Meade, "Lee's army is your objective point. Wherever Lee goes, there you will also go."

ARMY OF TENNESSEE

The Army of Tennessee was the Confederacy's principal army in the western theater. It lacked the reputation and power of its eastern counterpart, the Army of Northern Virginia, and definitely suffered from a Confederate strategy that placed primacy in the east.

One problem that plagued the Army of Tennessee was its lack of a strong commander. The army traces its origins to the state of Tennessee's Provisional Army of Tennessee, which was transferred to Confederate service in July 1861 and placed under the command of Albert Sidney Johnston. Many touted Johnston as the South's best general, but his performance during the Forts Henry and Donelson Campaign and at Shiloh did not live up to these expectations. When Johnston was killed at Shiloh, General Pierre Gustave Toutant Beauregard assumed command. Beauregard also failed to justify the reputation he had won at Fort Sumter and First Manassas, and his quarrels with President Jefferson Davis led to his being replaced by General Braxton Bragg when Beauregard went on sick leave in June 1862. It was under Bragg that the Army of Tennessee was officially designated as such in November 1862.

Under Bragg, the army reached its nadir. The costly victory at Chickamauga was more than offset by defeats and poor showings in Kentucky, Murfreesboro, and Chattanooga. Soon Bragg's corps commanders were petitioning for his relief, and General Joseph E. Johnston finally replaced him on December 27, 1863. Johnston led the army in an effort to delay Major General William T. Sherman's Atlanta

Campaign until Davis grew tired of Johnston's defensive tactics and replaced him with Lieutenant General John Bell Hood on July 17, 1864.

Hood assumed the offensive, only to lose Atlanta and have the Army of Tennessee all but destroyed in the Franklin and Nashville Campaign. After this debacle, the army withdrew to Tupelo, Mississippi, and Johnston again became its commander on February 23, 1865. Johnston vainly led the army against Sherman's Carolinas Campaign, surrendering on April 26.

ARSENALS AND FORTS AT THE OUTBREAK OF SECESSION

When a Southern state seceded, it usually took the Federal property within its borders

with it. Gaining control of arsenals that manufactured and stored weapons was a tremendous boost to the Confederacy's weak industrial base and need to equip its fledgling army. For example, machinery captured when Federal authorities abandoned the Harpers Ferry arsenal in Virginia became the core of the Confederate ordnance effort.

In some cases, however, the Federal forces refused to withdraw. Fort Sumter, South Carolina, is the most famous case, and Federal efforts to maintain the beleaguered garrison eventually led to the opening rounds of the Civil War.

FORT MONROE
While Fort Sumter ultimately succumbed to Confederate bombardment, the Federals

Below: *This map shows the division between the Federal and Confederate states, and the key positions of the forts that remained in Federal hands.*

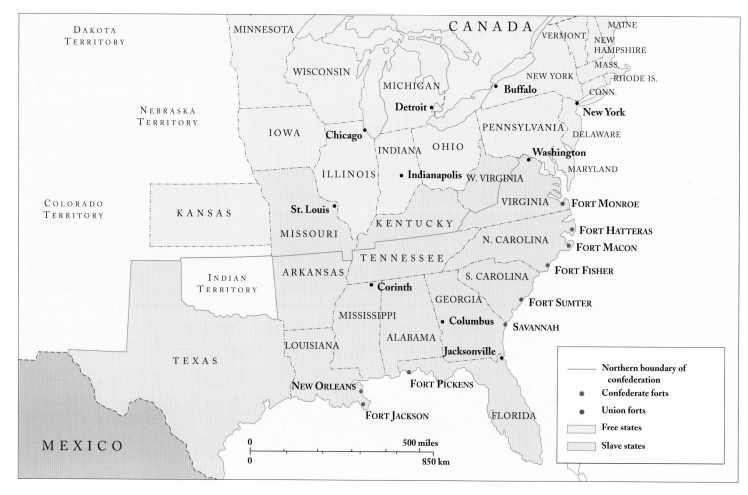

successfully held on to other forts in Southern territory. In Virginia, Fort Monroe's size and land connection made it more easily defendable than Fort Sumter, and indeed it proved too powerful for Virginia's militia to overcome. The Virginians seemed to accept this reality, striking an informal agreement with Colonel Justin Dimick, Fort Monroe's commander, by which if Dimick did not encroach on Virginia soil, they would not deny him access to his water supply. Thus, the strategic fort remained in Federal hands and played a critical role in Major General George B. McClellan's Peninsula Campaign.

The Federals also hung on to Fort Pickens, Florida. On January 10, 1861, the day Florida seceded, Lieutenant Adam J. Slemmer consolidated the Federal position at Fort Pickens and resolved to hold on until reinforcements could arrive. Florida senator Stephen R. Mallory, the future Confederate secretary of the navy, arranged a truce with President James Buchanan that promised the Confederates would not attack Fort Pickens if the Federal troops being sent there did not land. An uneasy freeze in the situation followed, just one of the many unresolved issues Buchanan left for Abraham Lincoln to handle upon assuming the presidency.

ARTILLERY AND MORTARS

The Confederacy began the Civil War at a tremendous disadvantage in terms of artillery. By seizing the various coastal forts early in 1861, the South acquired acceptable numbers of large siege guns, but none of the captured arsenals had yielded sufficient quantities of light artillery. The pieces in possession of the Southern states were often antiquated smoothbores from the War of 1812, and state governors were even reluctant to relinquish these to the Confederate government.

To alleviate the immediate shortage, President Jefferson Davis's purchasing agent in Europe, the enterprising Caleb Huse, was able to procure a total of 129 pieces during the first two years of the war. Nearly half of these were bronze six-pounder smoothbores, but he also obtained Blakely

rifles, Whitworth rifles, Armstrong rifles, small-caliber bronze howitzers, and twelve-pounder steel-rifled cannons. Still other pieces were added to Confederate holdings by capture. It was not until after 1863 that the Confederacy began to produce its own artillery in anything close to the necessary numbers thanks to the tireless efforts of ordnance chief Josiah Gorgas. Contracts were written for foundries in Rome and Columbus, Georgia; New Orleans; and Nashville, and the government began developing its own works in Augusta, Georgia, and Selma, Alabama. Patriotic citizens even donated everything from candlesticks to church bells in order

Below: *Confederate and Federal forces used many of the same models of artillery pieces, including this 3.4-inch (86 mm) caliber boat carriage gun. The gun had an effective range of around a mile.*

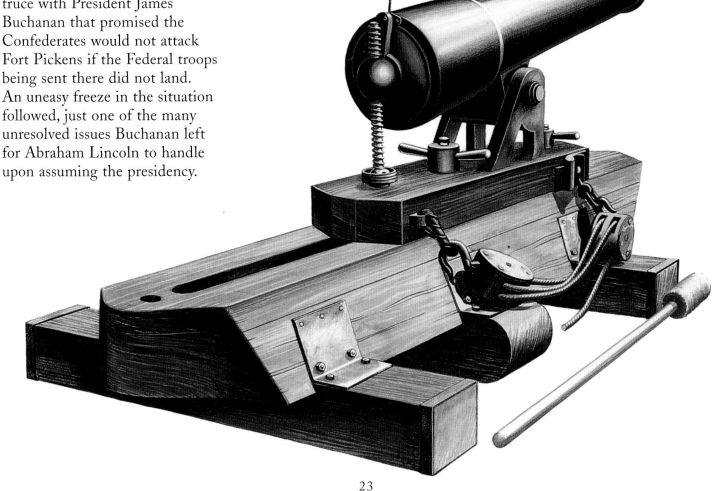

to provide the brass needed to manufacture cannons.

The workhorse of Confederate artillery production was Richmond's Tredegar Iron Works. From July 1861 to January 1865, Tredegar

Below: *These Confederate cannons were captured by Federal forces during the Peninsula Campaign. The limited Confederate resources made losses like these very costly.*

produced 341 large siege guns and 1,306 pieces of field artillery, as well as many caissons, gun carriages, fuses, and other accessories. However, much of the South's domestically produced artillery was of substandard quality. Limited resources, shortages of skilled labor, inadequate transportation, and interference from state governors conspired against the process. During the Peninsula Campaign,

Above: *This collection of munitions at a facility in Charleston includes both shot and shell. Shell contained a bursting charge of powder, while shot contained no explosives and was most commonly used to batter down fortifications.*

Major General D. H. Hill was so frustrated by repeated artillery malfunctions that he said, "There must be something very rotten in our Ordnance Department."

Quality improved during the last two years of the war as Gorgas built his capabilities, but by then shortages of horses and accessories were serious problems. While the Confederacy had talented artillerymen such as Brigadier General E. Porter Alexander and Major John Pelham, its deficiency in equipment prevented it from competing on anywhere near equal terms with the Federal artillery.

Terms associated with artillery are often used

interchangeably, but there is a difference between a gun and a howitzer. Guns have a relatively flat trajectory while howitzers have a greater arc. Mortars fire at an even greater arc, making them very useful in sieges.

Just before the outbreak of the Civil War, the Model 1857 was introduced as a multipurpose twelve-pounder gun-howitzer that was designed to replace existing guns and howitzers, firing canister and shell like the twelve-pounder

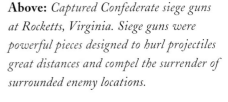

Above: *Captured Confederate siege guns at Rocketts, Virginia. Siege guns were powerful pieces designed to hurl projectiles great distances and compel the surrender of surrounded enemy locations.*

howitzer, and solid shot at an effective range of 1,680 yards like the twelve-pounder gun. The Model 1857, along with most pieces in the Confederate inventory, was a smoothbore. Although rifled artillery pieces had been developed, they did not have the dramatic impact that rifled muskets did.

While rifled artillery provided greater range and accuracy, it proved somewhat less reliable and slower to load than smoothbores. More importantly, even the

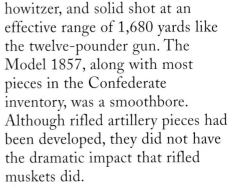

Left: *Although sources conflict, this heavy siege mortar, used at Petersburg, appears to be manned by a Confederate crew. The Federals were known to have deployed heavy mortars of this type.*

additional range of rifled artillery did not allow it to get close enough to protected defenders to produce the desired effect without exposing the gunners to the long-range fire of the defenders' rifles. Thus, most of the war's famous artillery actions were defensive rather than offensive.

Furthermore, the increased range of cannons provided no real advantage in the broken and wooded terrain common to so many Civil War battlefields. Indeed, in places like the Wilderness, General Robert E. Lee consciously chose to give battle in restricted terrain that would negate Lieutenant General Ulysses S. Grant's artillery advantage.

WHISTLING DICK

Among the famous Confederate artillery pieces are the Whistling Dick and the Widow Blakely, both of which saw service at Vicksburg. The Whistling Dick—named for "the peculiar whizzing noise the projectiles made when fired"—was an eighteen-pounder smoothbore that had been rifled and reinforced by a jacket at the breech.

The Widow Blakely was a 7.44-inch (189 mm) rifled cannon so named because of its uniqueness among the Confederate artillery.

Blakely rifles were cast at the Low Moor Iron Works in England according to specifications established by Captain Alexander T. Blakely.

Some 400 Blakely rifles were exported during the Civil War era, many of which made their way to the Confederacy. Two other Blakelys were purchased for the defense of Charleston.

Also notable was the colossal 150-pounder Armstrong rifled cannon that guarded Wilmington, North Carolina, from Fort Fisher.

ASHBY, TURNER
(1828–62)

Turner Ashby was a wealthy planter and local politician who, in spite of his lack of military background, served well as Major General Stonewall Jackson's cavalry commander in the Shenandoah Valley. Ashby began his service to the Confederacy by raising a private army and assisting with the defense of Harpers Ferry. This private command was incorporated into the Seventh Virginia Cavalry in 1861.

Ashby was a natural leader and a skilled horseman. He was extremely popular with his troops and well known for his nontraditional approach to military decorum. In the early spring of 1861 he traveled in disguise to Chambersburg, Pennsylvania, on a reconnaissance. In general terms, he had little interest in military discipline. Ashby was promoted to brigadier general on May 23, 1862, and maintained a semi-autonomous command. Throughout the Valley Campaign, he fought well, screening Jackson's

Left: *Turner Ashby was one of the many dashing cavalrymen who served the Confederacy. He provided Stonewall Jackson valuable service throughout the Shenandoah Valley.*

force and providing the command with valuable intelligence. He was killed fighting a rearguard action near Harrisonburg on June 6, 1862. After his death, his name was often used as a rallying cry to spur troops forward.

ATLANTA CAMPAIGN

- ❖ DATE: May 1–September 8, 1864
- ❖ LOCATION: Northern Georgia
- ❖ ARMY OF TENNESSEE (C): 62,000
- ❖ MILITARY DIVISION OF THE MISSISSIPPI (U.S.): 100,000
- ❖ CASUALTIES: 32,000 (C); 37,000 (U.S.)

The Atlanta Campaign was one part of Lieutenant General Ulysses S. Grant's coordinated strategy for the spring of 1864 that involved simultaneous advances designed to press the Confederacy on all fronts. Grant's orders to Major General William T. Sherman were "to move against [Confederate general Joseph] Johnston's army, to break it up, and to get into the interior of the enemy's country as far as you can, inflicting all the damage you can against their war resources." The campaign represented a marked step in the North's willingness to prosecute "hard war" in an effort to crush Confederate resistance.

Atlanta was a vital supply, manufacturing, and communications center that was second only to Richmond in its industrial importance to the Confederacy. Thus far it had escaped the ravages of war. By capturing Atlanta, Sherman would not only interrupt supplies that were helping keep General Robert E. Lee's Army of Northern Virginia in the field, he would take the war to the Confederate people. But

capturing Atlanta would not only dispirit the Confederate population, it would also silence those peace advocates in the North who considered Grant to be hopelessly deadlocked with Lee in Virginia with no end to the fighting in sight. With President Abraham Lincoln facing a tough challenge in the 1864 election from a Democratic peace platform, capturing Atlanta would have as much political importance as it would military.

After his defeat in the Chattanooga Campaign, General Braxton Bragg retreated twenty-five miles south to Dalton, Georgia, and dug in his forces. Amid a public outcry for Bragg's removal, President Jefferson Davis replaced Bragg with General Joseph E. Johnston, a defensive fighter by

Right: *As the Confederates retreated during the Atlanta Campaign, they made use of natural obstacles such as rivers and creeks as well as man-made obstacles such as these chevaux-de-frise.*

nature. With only 62,000 men compared to Sherman's 100,000, Johnston set out to use the terrain to his advantage and trade space for time to slow Sherman's advance.

Sherman, on the other hand,

Above: *While Lee and Jackson gave the Confederates a leadership advantage in the eastern theater, the Federals had the upper hand in the west. James McPherson was a capable Federal corps commander until he was killed during the fight for Atlanta.*

Above: *Sherman's capture of Atlanta and subsequent March to the Sea exposed the Confederacy to "hard war." Railroads and depots were among Sherman's favorite targets for destruction.*

thrived on the offensive. He began his march on May 7, just a few days after Grant began his offensive in Virginia. Sherman quickly engaged Confederates around Rocky Face Ridge, but Johnston fell back without becoming decisively engaged. More fighting occurred at Resaca on May 13–16, but as Sherman threatened an envelopment from the west, Johnston again withdrew.

On May 19, Johnston was unable to execute his offensive plan to descend on Sherman's divided army at Cassville. The forces clashed at New Hope Church on May 25 and Pickett's Mill on May 27, and then Johnston retired to Kennesaw Mountain. On June 27, Sherman launched a costly frontal attack against Johnston's strong defenses at Kennesaw and was repulsed with great losses. Undeterred, Sherman resumed his efforts to turn Johnston on July 2, and Johnston withdrew to a previously prepared position at Smyrna. His new line was built along the Chattahoochee River, which represented the last major obstacle between Sherman and Atlanta. In fighting on July 4–9, Sherman again turned the Confederates, and Johnston withdrew to Peachtree Creek. By this time, President Davis was exasperated by Johnston's failure to make a stand and replaced him with Lieutenant General John Bell Hood.

As Sherman closed in on Atlanta from the north and east, Hood, true to his combative reputation, ordered an attack on July 20. The Confederates launched a series of assaults, but ultimately were forced to withdraw to the defenses of Atlanta after suffering 2,500 casualties compared to about 1,600 for the Federals.

As Hood withdrew, Sherman kept up the pressure and by July 25 he had invested Atlanta from the north and east. Hood still had an open railroad to the south, which Sherman tried unsuccessfully to sever with two raids between July 26 and 31 and the Battle of Ezra Church on July 28. Hood finally evacuated Atlanta on September 1, and the Federals moved in to occupy the city the next morning.

Hood marched north into Tennessee, hoping to compel Sherman to abandon Atlanta in order to protect his line of communications. Sherman refused to pursue Hood in force and instead expelled all the citizens from Atlanta and turned the city into an armed camp that could be held with the smallest possible force. Thus freed to maneuver, Sherman cut loose from his base in Atlanta in November and began his March to the Sea.

ATROCITIES

Although Andersonville Prison commandant Captain Henry Wirz was the only man executed for war crimes commited during the Civil War, numerous atrocities went unpunished. These took the form of reprisals, bushwhacking, massacres, and mistreatment of civilians.

Federal authorities were greatly frustrated in their efforts to bring to bay guerrillas and partisan rangers such as Colonel John S. Mosby and his men. Unable to catch the partisans, some Federal commanders resorted to reprisals against the civilian population.

Brigadier General Adolph von Steinwehr arrested five citizens in Luray, Virginia, and held them hostage, vowing to kill one of the

Above: *Both sides accused each other of atrocities on and off the battlefield. This print is entititled* The Confederate Atrocities in Texas. *Many accusations against the Confederates involved mistreatment of African American soldiers serving in the Federal army.*

citizens for every Federal soldier killed by a guerrilla. Mosby became involved in his own tit-for-tat escalation of reprisals when six of his men were captured and executed in Front Royal in 1864.

Mosby blamed Brigadier General George Armstrong Custer for the incident, and on October 29, Mosby wrote General Robert E. Lee to inform him, "It is my purpose to hang an equal number of Custer's men whenever I capture them." In November, Mosby made good his promise, hanging three captured Federals at Berryville on November 6. On one of them was pinned a note that said, "Measure for measure."

Bushwhackers perpetrated horrific atrocities, especially in border areas such as Missouri. These included William C. Quantrill's raid at Lawrence, Kansas, and "Bloody Bill" Anderson's gruesome attack at Centralia, Missouri. Anderson took great pleasure in his killings,

marking each with a knot on his sash and hanging Yankee scalps from his bridle.

RACIAL TENSIONS
As more African American soldiers began entering the Federal ranks, tensions often flared when they battled Confederates. Confederates allegedly massacred wounded and surrendered African Americans at Fort Pillow, Tennessee, and Poison Spring, Arkansas, but African American Federals are accused of retaliating at Jenkins' Ferry, Arkansas.

Perhaps most terrifying to the Southern population were the "hard war" tactics of Major General William T. Sherman in his March to the Sea and Major General Philip H. Sheridan in his Shenandoah Valley Campaign. These tactics made destruction of civilian property a matter of formal policy. Sherman vowed to "make Georgia howl," and he did.

BAHAMAS

Some 570 miles off the coast of Wilmington, North Carolina, and even closer to Charleston, South Carolina, and Savannah, Georgia, the islands of the Bahamas were a popular destination for

Confederate blockade-runners. Although Florida was the closest Confederate state to the Bahamas, its lack of ports limited its utility in blockade running.

In many cases, cargoes of European goods would be transferred from larger ships at the convenient port of Nassau. For example, on January 11, 1862, Lieutenant John N. Maffitt ran the *Cecile* through the blockade at Wilmington with a cargo of 700 bales of cotton. Three days later he arrived at Nassau and exchanged his cotton for 900 barrels of gunpowder, which he then brought back through the blockade to Wilmington.

BALLOONS

While the Federal army, led by the ambitious efforts of Thaddeus Sobieski Constantine Lowe, established a much more robust Balloon Corps, the Confederates also attempted to avail themselves of this pioneering intelligence-gathering tool. However, the South simply lacked the resources necessary to mount anything more than a halting attempt at military ballooning.

Probably the first Confederate flight was made south of Richmond by Lieutenant John Randolph Bryan. Bryan received large volumes of enemy fire and quickly descended. Upon returning to earth, Bryan offered his resignation from ballooning, to which General Joseph E. Johnston replied, "Absolutely not! You're the only experienced balloonist in the Confederate army."

This, however, would not be the end of Bryan's misadventures with ballooning. On what would prove to be his final flight, Bryan's balloon escaped and floated over Federal lines. Facing capture, he destroyed his notes and his identification papers. When the wind changed and blew him over water, Bryan threw his clothing overboard and prepared to swim for his life.

Still another breeze brought Bryan back over a Confederate camp, where he landed, unknown and without identification. Only after some quick talking did he avoid being shot as a spy.

Other Confederate balloons were sent up over Fort Pulaski, Georgia, and Charleston, South Carolina, but perhaps the best-known Confederate balloon story centers around the Seven Days Battles. Without the Federals' resources, the Confederates reportedly constructed a balloon out of silk dresses donated by Southern belles. The dresses were sewn together and coated with varnish to make the surface airtight. The result must have been quite a fantastic sight. Lieutenant General James Longstreet described it as "a great patchwork ship of many varied hues."

BATTLE BALLOON
The only available source of gas was in Richmond, so the balloon was inflated there, tied to a locomotive, and transported down the York River Railroad as far as possible. The balloon was then placed on a steamer and floated down the James River, ready for battle. Unfortunately, along the way the

tide went out, leaving the boat and the balloon hopelessly grounded, and the Federals captured both. Longstreet was heartbroken. Describing the loss of the balloon, he wrote, "The Federals gathered it in, and with it the last silk dress in the Confederacy. This capture was the meanest trick of the war and one that I have never yet forgotten."

BALL'S BLUFF, BATTLE OF

❖ DATE: October 21, 1861

❖ LOCATION: Poolesville, Virginia

❖ CONFEDERATE FORCES: 1,700

❖ UNION FORCES: 1,700

❖ CASUALTIES: 149 (C); 921 (U.S.)

Colonel Edwin Baker bumbled into a Confederate force led by Colonel Nathan Evans on October 21, 1861, at Poolesville, Virginia. The Federals suffered 921 casualties, including Baker, who was killed. The Confederates lost only

Below: *Ball's Bluff was a disastrous defeat for the Federals. Colonel Edwin Baker was killed in the fighting, leaving Brigadier General Charles Stone to become the scapegoat for the mismanaged battle.*

149 men. Coming hard on the heels of the defeat at First Manassas, the debacle had serious political repercussions in the North.

In a politically charged investigation by the Joint Committee on the Conduct of the War, Brigadier General Charles Stone became the Federal scapegoat.

BARKSDALE, WILLIAM (1821–63)

William Barksdale resigned from Congress on January 12, 1861, when Mississippi seceded. He then served as quartermaster general of the Army of Mississippi until he entered the Confederate army as colonel of the Thirteenth Mississippi Regiment. He commanded the regiment at First Manassas and during the Peninsula Campaign until he was given a brigade on June 29, 1862. "Barksdale's Brigade" consisted of the Thirteenth and three other Mississippi regiments. It saw particularly tough fighting during the Battle of Fredericksburg, withstanding a furious artillery bombardment to delay the Federal advance through the town.

Barksdale also fought at Antietam, Chancellorsville, and Gettysburg, where he was mortally wounded.

BATTLES, NAMING OF

Many Civil War battles are known by two names, reflecting the Southern tendency to associate the battle with the closest town while Northerners usually named the battle after a nearby body of water. Historian Shelby Foote hypothesizes that the reason for the difference is that the largely rural Confederates were more impressed by a population center

while the more urban Federals were more impressed by water. Whatever the reason, the convention has led to a duplication of names for many common battles. For example, Confederates use Manassas, the railroad junction town near the battlefield, to describe the same fight that Federals named Bull Run after the small creek that flowed through it. In the same way, Confederates often use Shiloh, Sharpsburg, and Murfreesboro to refer to the battles many Federals may call Pittsburg Landing, Antietam, and Stones River respectively.

BEAUREGARD, PIERRE GUSTAVE TOUTANT (1818–93)

❖ RANK: General

❖ PLACE OF BIRTH: St. Bernard Parish, Louisiana

❖ EDUCATED: West Point

❖ MILITARY CAREER:
1846–48: Engineer, Mexican War
1861: Captures Fort Sumter; Battle of First Manassas; promoted to full general; takes command at Battle of Shiloh
1862: Successfully withdrew his troops at the Siege of Corinth
1864: Bermuda Hundred Campaign; Battle of Petersburg

Pierre Gustave Toutant Beauregard graduated second in the West Point class of 1838 and performed excellent service as an engineer during the Mexican War, including superb reconnaissance at Cerro Gordo. Unlike most of his fellow junior officers, Beauregard was less than impressed by the Mexican War generalship of Winfield Scott. Beauregard was especially suspicious of Scott's use of the turning movement. In fact, of all the Civil War's important generals, Beauregard was the one

who most steadfastly preferred the frontal attack.

Beauregard has the distinction of serving the shortest tenure as superintendent of West Point. He was reassigned on January 28, 1861, after less than a week in office, because of his Southern sympathies. Beauregard resigned from the U.S. Army on February 20 and was appointed brigadier general in the Confederate army.

Beauregard gained rapid fame as the "Hero of Sumter" when he shelled the Federal garrison there into surrender and was heralded as one of the Confederacy's military geniuses. He was given command of the Confederate forces at Manassas Junction and cooperated with General Joseph E. Johnston there to win another victory. Beauregard was promoted full

Above: *The Confederates' high expectations of Pierre Gustave Toutant Beauregard after his heroic roles at Fort Sumter and First Manassas were never fully realized.*

general on August 31, 1861, but never lived up to his early reputation. He was transferred west and served as General Albert Sidney Johnston's second-in-command at Shiloh. When Johnston was killed, Beauregard assumed command. His penchant for the frontal attack led him to develop an unimaginative scheme of maneuver that squandered the Confederacy's initial surprise. Many Confederate sympathizers fault Beauregard for the great "lost opportunity" of Shiloh.

After Shiloh, Beauregard went on sick leave and turned his command over—temporarily, he thought—to

General Braxton Bragg. Instead, President Jefferson Davis relieved Beauregard for abandoning his post. Beauregard next commanded the coastal defenses of the Carolinas and Georgia. He thwarted Major General Benjamin F. Butler's attack up the James River–Appomattox River Peninsula in early 1864 by "bottling him up" in Bermuda Hundred. Beauregard ended the war as second in command to General Joseph E. Johnston during the Carolinas Campaign.

After the war, Beauregard declined commands in the Romanian and Egyptian armies. Instead, he served as a railroad president and as the controversial supervisor of the Louisiana Lottery, where he drew a large salary for a small amount of work with the corruption-plagued enterprise. He wrote several military works, including volumes on his roles at Charleston and First Manassas.

BEE JR., BARNARD E.
(1824–61)

Above: *South Carolinian Barnard Bee was killed at First Manassas after providing Stonewall Jackson with his famous nickname.*

Barnard E. Bee Jr. graduated from West Point in 1845 and served on the frontier and in Mexico. He resigned from the U.S. Army on March 3, 1861, and on June 17, 1861, he was appointed brigadier general in the Confederate army. He led a brigade at First Manassas, where he told his men, "There stands Jackson like a stone wall. Rally behind the Virginians." This declaration gave Thomas Jackson his immortal nickname of "Stonewall." Bee was mortally wounded during the fighting.

BENJAMIN, JUDAH P. (1811–84)

Judah P. Benjamin was among the most accomplished and versatile members of the Confederate cabinet. He resigned as a United States senator on February 4, 1861, and became the attorney general of the provisional Confederate government, a position he held until September 17. He then succeeded Leroy P. Walker as secretary of war, but became the scapegoat for the Confederate defeat at Roanoke Island. Although he was relieved as secretary of war, Benjamin was too valuable not to be reassigned to other duties. On March 18, 1862, with the establishment of the permanent government, Benjamin became the secretary of state. He served in that capacity for the duration of the war, but President Jefferson Davis's scant emphasis on diplomacy caused Benjamin's considerable talents to be largely wasted.

After the surrender, Benjamin fled to England, where he began a distinguished law practice. He is often remembered for being the most prominent Jew in the Confederate government, although this distinction caused many in the solidly Protestant South to view him with suspicion.

Above: *Judah Benjamin was one of the Confederacy's most accomplished cabinet members, but his Jewish faith caused many to view him with suspicion.*

BENTONVILLE, BATTLE OF

- ❖ DATE: March 19, 1865
- ❖ LOCATION: Johnston County, North Carolina
- ❖ ARMY OF THE TENNESSEE (C): 21,000
- ❖ GRAND ARMY OF THE WEST (U.S.): 60,000
- ❖ CASUALTIES: 2,606 (C); 1,646 (U.S.)

Major General William T. Sherman ended his March to the Sea by reaching Savannah, Georgia, on December 10, 1864. From there he turned north for his Carolinas Campaign, advancing on February 1, 1865. General Pierre Gustave Toutant Beauregard had divided his force to protect Charleston, South Carolina, to the east, and Augusta, Georgia, to the west. This measure left a wide gap

Above: *The Battle of Bentonville marked the end of Joseph E. Johnston's feeble resistance to Sherman's Carolinas Campaign. President Davis wanted Johnston to continue to wage guerrilla war.*

BERMUDA HUNDRED, BATTLE OF

As part of his strategy to isolate General Robert E. Lee's Army of Northern Virginia in the spring of 1864, Lieutenant General Ulysses S. Grant ordered Major General Benjamin F. Butler and his Army of the James to conduct an amphibious operation via the James River against the Richmond–Petersburg area. Butler's objective was to cut the Richmond and Petersburg Railroad to both interdict Lee's supply line and weaken Lee's own force by causing him to send reinforcements to stop Butler.

Butler disembarked from navy transports at Bermuda Hundred, a small town outside Richmond, on May 5 and fought a series of battles against a motley force commanded by General P. G. T. Beauregard. Midshipmen from the Confederate

Below: *Instead of cutting Lee's supply line, Butler was bottled up at Bermuda Hundred. His headquarters is shown here, after it was eventually captured by Federal troops.*

for Sherman to pass through against almost no opposition. As Sherman cut his path of destruction through South Carolina, General Joseph E. Johnston gathered a force of just 21,000 men to establish some resistance in North Carolina.

After a small skirmish near Averasboro on March 16, Johnston established a position at Cole's Plantation on March 19 to block the Goldsboro Road near Bentonville. Sherman's left flank under the command of Major General Henry Warner Slocum ran into Johnston that morning, and Johnston launched several counterattacks but was unable to destroy the isolated Slocum. The fighting ended in a tactical draw, and Johnston then withdrew to Mill Creek.

There was a small amount of fighting on March 20, but by the next day Sherman had united his entire 60,000-man force to confront Johnston. Sherman attempted to envelop Johnston, but Johnston succeeded in blocking the maneuver with his reserves and held his main position. That night Johnston retreated toward Smithfield, having lost 2,606 men. The Federals suffered 1,646 casualties. Sherman did not vigorously pursue Johnston, knowing he would eventually bring his outmatched opponent to bay. Indeed, Bentonville was the last time Johnston could muster the strength to fight. He asked for an armistice on April 14 and surrendered on April 26.

Naval Academy at Drewry's Bluff helped resist the Federal advance. At the May 20 Battle of Ware Bottom Church, Beauregard succeeded in constructing a line across the peninsula formed by the Appomattox and James rivers that effectively bottled up Butler at Bermuda Hundred. Instead of weakening Lee, Butler's mismanagement of the operation actually allowed Beauregard to send Lee reinforcements to help battle Grant.

BIBLE SOCIETIES

Shortly after the Civil War began, Southern affiliates of the American Bible Society severed their ties with the parent organization and formed the Bible Society of the Confederate States. This institution was energetic in supporting religion in the Confederate army by the publication and distribution of Bibles, religious literature, and tracts. Nonetheless, the organization was challenged by the fact that before the war, few Bibles were printed in the South and obtaining copies was difficult. Most Northern Bible societies stopped sending religious literature to the Confederacy, but the American Bible Society proved the exception. This organization contributed many Bibles to the Confederacy, including one shipment of 100,000. The British and Foreign Bible Society also made large contributions and extended unlimited credit without interest for the purchase of Bibles. By 1863 the efforts of these groups had reached large proportions. Many credit the easy access to religious materials made available by the various Bible societies as being a great contributor to the revivals that swept the Confederate army.

BIG BETHEL, BATTLE OF

❖ DATE: June 10, 1861

❖ LOCATION: York City and Hampton, Virginia

❖ FORCE UNDER MAGRUDER AND D. H. HILL (C): 1,400

❖ FORCE UNDER BUTLER (U.S.): 3,500

❖ CASUALTIES: 8 (C); 76 (U.S.)

Big Bethel Church was the site of a Confederate outpost northwest of Newport News, Virginia. On June 10, 1861, Major General Benjamin F. Butler launched an attack from the Federal garrison at Fort Monroe that was easily repulsed by Confederates in what is often considered the first land battle of the Civil War.

Big Bethel was an extremely small affair. Not more than 300 of the 1,400 Confederates led by colonels John B. Magruder and D. H. Hill

Left: *"Federal troops driving the rebels from one of their batteries at Great Bethel." Big (or Great) Bethel was an early Southern victory that helped buoy hopes of a quick end to the war.*

were engaged simultaneously. There were only seventy-six Federal and eight Confederate casualties in what amounted to a twenty-minute encounter.

Later in the war, such a small skirmish would barely attract notice, but at this early juncture, Big Bethel was considered a significant battle. Primarily from the reputation he gained at Big Bethel, Magruder was promoted to brigadier general on June 17, 1861, and reached the rank of major general on October 7, 1861.

At the time, many Confederates considered him second only to General Pierre Gustave Toutant Beauregard, the "Hero of Sumter," in fame. Magruder would not live up to these early laurels.

BLACK MARKETEERING

Direct trade between the Federal and Confederate states was prohibited, but, especially as far as cotton was concerned, a certain amount of surreptitious trade was conducted. Northern industries that were deprived of cotton found common cause with Southern growers who needed a market. Among the most notorious locations of this highly profitable but illegal trade were Memphis, Tennessee, and northern Mississippi when Major General Ulysses S. Grant advanced during his Vicksburg Campaign. One of the most unashamed participants in cotton black marketeering was James L. Alcorn, Mississippi's future Republican governor.

BLOCKADE, IMPACT OF

On April 19, 1861, six days after Fort Sumter, President Abraham Lincoln issued a proclamation declaring a blockade of the coastline from South Carolina to Texas. On April 27, the blockade was extended to Virginia and North Carolina. The purpose of the blockade was to isolate the Confederacy from European trade. Historians have long debated the overall effectiveness of the blockade, but most agree that while not alone decisive, the blockade certainly contributed to the overall Federal victory.

The Federal blockade effort was planned by the Navy Board (also called the Blockade Board) created by Secretary of the Navy Gideon Welles in June 1861. This very effective body was largely successful in providing a road map for a coordinated strategy between the army and the navy.

Through a series of joint operations, the two services achieved a synergistic relationship in which the army held key ports and harbors that allowed the navy to maintain a fairly continuous blockade supported by a network of secure bases of supply. As a result, important Confederate sites such as Port Royal Sound, South Carolina, on the Atlantic and New Orleans, Louisiana, on the Gulf of Mexico fell into Federal hands early in the war.

The exact effectiveness of the blockade is hard to measure and a subject of much historical debate. On the one hand, numerous ships successfully ran the blockade. In the first year of the war, up to nine out of ten blockade-running ships were able to elude capture. Even in 1865, as many as half of the ships that tested the blockade succeeded.

On the other hand, these statistics do not reflect the number of ships that never attempted to run the blockade because they were deterred by its presence. Accounting for these passages that never occurred helps explain why in the twelve months before the war some 20,000 ships entered or left Southern ports, but the average yearly traffic during the war was just 2,000 ships, a reduction of 90 percent.

To be sure, the Federal blockade was just one of many factors that contributed to the outcome of the Civil War. While not decisive in and of itself, the blockade certainly took its toll. It denied the Confederacy the purchasing power it would have gained from unfettered exports, raised costs throughout the South, reduced the volume of imported goods, and disrupted traditional trade and transportation networks. As a result, the blockade had a cumulative deleterious effect on the Confederate economy, quality of life, daily routine, and ability to prosecute the war.

BLOCKADE-RUNNING

With 189 harbor and river openings along the 3,549 miles of Confederate shoreline between the Potomac and the Rio Grande, the Federal blockade was certainly not seamless. The vast Confederate coastline, often punctuated by various shallows, barrier islands, and inlets, offered promising opportunities for blockade-runners to avoid the Federal dragnet. Consequently, hundreds of enterprising individuals took their chances running the blockade in order to bring cargoes in and out of the Confederacy. Their efforts helped satiate the South's dependence on overseas goods and also produced handsome profits for the blockade-runners.

Blockade-runners possessed several advantages. Blockade duty was monotonous and dreary, and it was hard for the Federals to be constantly vigilant. Blockade-runners could exploit this weakness using the element of surprise to

Above: *The combination of Federal naval strength and capture of key points on the Confederate coast made blockade-running difficult. Here Federal shore batteries repulse blockade-runners off Newport News, Virginia.*

take advantage of a momentary Federal lapse in attention. Blockade-runners also often had local knowledge of the intricacies of the Confederate coast and knew how to use the geography to their advantage. The Federal ships could obviously not be everywhere, and the blockade-runner needed to find just one seam to avoid detection.

RIFLES FROM BRITAIN

These opportunities for success and the potential for huge profits attracted a wide variety of blockade-runners. A few were Confederate navy officers such as John Maffitt who commanded ships owned or leased by the government

and devoted a significant portion of their cargoes to items of military necessity. One European item most needed by the Confederate army was rifles. In fact, President Davis dispatched Caleb Huse to Britain to secure rifles, and Huse ended up purchasing more than 100,000 Enfields for the Confederacy. Although Huse's efforts were in part hamstrung by a limited amount of specie and the Federal blockade, Confederate blockade-runners still delivered some 600,000 stands of arms to the South, most of which were British Enfields.

More common than these government-organized runners, however, were civilian captains who sailed their own vessels and specialized in luxury goods such as wine, perfume, and cigars, fetching huge profits. A round-trip between Wilmington, North Carolina, and Nassau could net as much as $425,000 for such entrepreneurs.

Rhett Butler represents this type of blockade-runner in the movie *Gone With the Wind*. One criticism of the Confederate blockade-running effort is that so many of the cargoes contained civilian consumer goods rather than wartime essentials. The Confederate Congress responded to this situation in February 1864 by passing a law "to prohibit the importation of luxuries, or of articles not necessaries or of common use." Still, the government was slow to exert complete authority over blockade-running, requiring ships to reserve only half their cargo space for government shipments.

In addition to bringing European goods to the Confederacy, blockade-runners also exported Confederate products, particularly cotton. Throughout the course of the war, some 1.25 million bales of cotton safely reached Great Britain. Sales of this commodity gave the Confederate government some

Above: *Before the Federals improved their blockade, many blockade-runners were willing to run the risks of capture. Here the CSS* Sumter *eludes the USS* Brooklyn *in July 1861.*

access to much-needed specie, but early reliance on the power of "King Cotton" was clearly misplaced.

While the lure of great payoffs was enticing, blockade-running was certainly not for the faint of heart. Seaworthiness of vessels was often sacrificed for speed and maneuverability. Ships' profiles were kept low to avoid detection and crews' quarters were Spartan in order to maximize cargo space.

Furthermore, as Federal victories closed one Confederate port after another, the blockade tightened, and it became more difficult for runners to advance undetected. Nonetheless, blockade-running continued until Wilmington, the last Confederate port, was closed in January 1865. Even then blockade-runners descended on the coast, only to be captured or to escape to safe havens such as Bermuda.

Below: *Confederate blockade-runners, including the CSS* Teaser *shown here, came in all shapes and sizes, but all were designed to carry cargo and elude capture.*

BONDS AND NOTES

One of the Confederacy's most pressing problems was a shortage of hard currency. Some hard money specie was raised by the sale of bonds, and in the first year of the war, when secessionist fervor was high, this was an effective source of income. On February 28, 1861, the Confederate Congress authorized a $150 million loan in the form of 8 percent bonds. The loan was to be repaid by levying an export duty on Confederate cotton. Another piece of legislation on May 16 authorized the Treasury Department to issue $50 million worth of 8 percent bonds and

Right: *The Confederacy tried to raise funds by the sale of bonds. Initially promising, results were eventually disappointing. One of the Confederacy's greatest shortcomings was its failure to develop an effective financial policy.*

Below: *A $5 Confederate States of America banknote, dated September 2, 1861. An overreliance on paper money led to rampant inflation in the Confederacy, with some $2.2 billion in paper money entering circulation.*

immediately print $20 million worth of treasury notes to circulate in lieu of specie. By the late fall of 1861, bonds had generated $15 million worth of specie for the

Confederacy. However, sales soon slackened, and by April 1862 the government resorted to offering bonds that could be purchased with farm produce rather than

Above: *A $100 Confederate States of America banknote, dated December 22, 1862.*

increasingly scarce cash. This proved to be an ineffective policy because, although the government acquired vast stores of cotton and tobacco, the Federal blockade prevented the Confederacy from readily selling these items to Europe for cash.

INFLATION

Moreover, the attempt to finance the war by issuing bonds and notes produced rampant inflation. In Richmond in January 1863, a gold dollar bought three dollars of treasury notes. Nonetheless, the Confederate government still needed money to sustain its existence. As a solution, Secretary of the Treasury Christopher G. Memminger proposed removing as much as two-thirds of the paper money in circulation by offering to exchange non-interest-bearing notes for interest-bearing bonds. On March 23, 1863, the Confederate Congress approved Memminger's plan and authorized the Treasury Department to issue each month up to $50 million in treasury notes that could be exchanged for thirty-year

bonds bearing 6 percent interest. Under this policy, the Confederate government printed more than $500 million worth of notes, but because the inflation rate made bonds an unattractive investment, only $21 million worth of notes were withdrawn from circulation. The plan failed to stem inflation, and in January 1864, a gold dollar in Richmond was worth $18 to $20 in Confederate notes.

With the economy in crisis, the Confederate Congress enacted a Compulsory Funding Measure on February 17, 1864, designed to force the exchange of notes for bonds in order to reduce the amount of paper money in circulation. Note holders who failed to make the exchange would suffer devaluation of their notes by as much as one-third of their value. Still, many note holders refused to exchange their notes in part because the long stream of fiscal manipulations had undermined confidence in both the Confederate economy and its government. Desperate acts such as the Compulsory Funding Measure, as well as the Confederate

Right: *The Bonnie Blue flag symbolized the Confederacy—as a single-starred flag and a popular patriotic song.*

citizenry's failure to embrace it, were indications that the Confederacy was in trouble.

BONNIE BLUE FLAG

The "Bonnie Blue Flag" was a popular Confederate song first performed in Richmond and New Orleans theaters in 1861. The single-starred first flag of the Confederacy inspired the piece, which is set to the music of an old Hibernian song entitled the "Irish Jaunting Car."

Scholars disagree on the authorship of the lyrics and the exact date of composition, although Harry McCarthy is often credited with having written them. "Hurrah! Hurrah! For Southern Rights Hurrah!" the song proclaims. "Hurrah! For the Bonnie Blue Flag that bears a single star!"

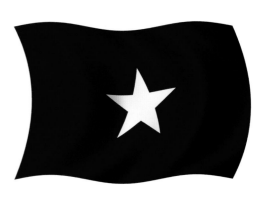

BOOTH, JOHN WILKES (1838–65)

John Wilkes Booth assassinated Abraham Lincoln while the president attended a showing of *Our American Cousin* at Ford's Theatre on April 14, 1865. Booth leaped into Lincoln's box, shot him, and then jumped to the stage shouting, "*Sic semper tyrannis!* [Thus always to tyrants!] The South is avenged!" During the jump, Booth caught his spur on an American flag draped over the box, fell, and broke his leg. He escaped to a waiting horse, only to be found on April 26 in a barn near Bowling Green, Virginia. The barn was set on fire, and Booth was shot trying to escape.

Booth's action was part of a larger plot to kill several key Federal officials. Coconspirator George

Above: *John Wilkes Booth failed to receive the hero's welcome throughout the South that he anticipated after assassinating President Lincoln. Instead, many saw his act as one of cowardice.*

Atzerodt was supposed to assassinate Vice President Andrew Johnson but lost his nerve and made no attempt. Lewis Paine shot Secretary of State William H. Seward and seriously wounded him. Prior to this incident, Booth had been a successful Shakespearean actor and had previously developed a plot to kidnap Lincoln.

BORDER STATES

The states of the upper South and the slaveholding Northern states were absolutely critical to the outcome of the Civil War. Before the fall of Fort Sumter and President Abraham Lincoln's subsequent call for volunteers, only South Carolina, Mississippi, Florida, Alabama, Georgia, Louisiana, and Texas had seceded. Both President Lincoln and President Jefferson Davis made securing the border states a critical part of their strategies.

Lincoln's first subtle outreach to the border states was his policy decision to openly resupply Fort Sumter with an unarmed relief effort. This nonbelligerent measure ensured that any backlash against the side that fired the first shot would fall on the South. Nonetheless, when Lincoln called for the states to place 75,000 militia at the service of the Federal government after Fort Sumter, the states of Virginia, North Carolina, Tennessee, and Arkansas opted to secede rather than fight against their fellow Southerners. Davis had helped lay the groundwork for this decision by earlier dispatching envoys to the upper South states in a pioneering Confederate effort at diplomacy.

Even after this second wave of secession, four slaveholding states—Maryland, Kentucky, Missouri, and Delaware—remained in the Union. If these states

decided to secede, the Confederacy's population would grow to over 12,000,000, the Federal capital of Washington would be surrounded, the Ohio River would provide the Confederacy with a natural line of defense, and the cause of the continuance of slavery would stand undivided. Lincoln could not accept such developments, and he moved swiftly and effectively to secure the upper tier of slave states.

CRUCIAL KENTUCKY

Kentucky, with its command of the Ohio River, was of special concern to Lincoln, who felt "to lose Kentucky is nearly the same as to lose the whole game." The state was intensely divided with a secessionist governor and a Unionist legislature. It had declared itself neutral, an assertion that Lincoln and Davis initially respected, but that everyone knew could not last.

Lincoln proved more adept at walking this fine line by patiently resisting neighboring governors' demands to send troops into Kentucky. Davis, however, let Major General Leonidas Polk occupy Columbus. Polk felt he was acting to preempt Brigadier General Ulysses S. Grant from doing the same thing, but the Kentucky legislature saw the Confederate move as an invasion. With the neutrality issue no longer standing in the way, Grant moved Federal forces into Paducah and proceeded to gain control of the state.

In Maryland, Lincoln acted with much less nuance. When a Massachusetts regiment marched through Baltimore en route to Washington, a volatile pro-Confederacy crowd accosted the soldiers. Lincoln responded by sending Federal troops to occupy Baltimore and by throwing various secessionist leaders in jail until the problem was under control. Lincoln's actions were clearly extralegal, but he could not afford to have Maryland join the Confederacy and isolate Washington. With his opponents in jail, Maryland's pro-Union governor was able to thwart any action on secession.

Missouri was also a sticky situation for Lincoln. The state had a pro-Southern governor who maintained a camp of state troops outside St. Louis. Many Unionist-leaning Missourians feared the governor would order the troops to seize the weapons held in the arsenal at St. Louis and arm the secessionists. To prevent this action, Captain Nathaniel Lyon, an impulsive favorite of the Radical Unionists, arrested the state troops, took away their weapons, and dispersed their camp. When Lyon's men marched back to their barracks, they were met by the same sort of crowd that had threatened the Massachusetts soldiers in

Below: As the Sixth Massachusetts Regiment marched through Baltimore, a pro-Southern crowd attacked it with epithets and projectiles. President Lincoln responded with a strong show of force to safeguard Maryland for the Union.

Baltimore. Lyon opened fire on the crowd, killing at least twenty-eight civilians.

GUERRILLA WARFARE
Lyon's erstwhile superior, Brigadier General William Harney, worked out a truce with the governor that Lyon quickly disavowed. He neutralized the governor and then marched his men into southwest Missouri in an effort to remove all armed Confederates from the state. Lyon was killed in the Battle of Wilson's Creek, and his army was forced to retreat. The Confederates maintained an active presence in the southwestern part of the state, and Lyon's mismanagement of the situation no doubt contributed to the bitter partisan and guerrilla warfare that plagued Missouri for the next four years.

With just 1,800 slaves, Delaware was never really likely to secede, but the strong Union sentiment in the western counties of Virginia posed an interesting possibility for Lincoln. He sent Major General George B. McClellan into the region, and he succeeded in defeating the small Confederate

force there. Buoyed by the presence of Federal troops, Unionist sentiment grew strong enough for West Virginia to separate from Virginia and be admitted to the Union as a new state in 1863. This action in effect created a border state within a border state and ensured that the Ohio River would not be the northern boundary of the Confederacy. It also gave the Federals control of the Baltimore and Ohio Railroad, which served as an important connection between the eastern and western theaters.

The final result was that the Union won the struggle for the border states. Nonetheless, the victory merely meant the North had held on to what it already had and saved itself from disaster. To win the war, the Federals would have to move south of the border states and defeat the Confederacy. The border states also remained battlegrounds throughout the war, with the South launching significant offensives into Maryland and Kentucky and numerous raids and guerrilla activities elsewhere.

BOWIE KNIFE

The Bowie knife was immortalized when Jim Bowie used it to great effect during the famous Maddox–Wells duel fought on September 19, 1827, on a sandbar on the Mississippi River. The exact origin or design of the knife Bowie wielded that day is a matter of conjecture, but it soon became widely copied throughout the Southwest. In an era when pistols frequently misfired, the Bowie knife was a reliable backup weapon with a variety of uses. Hunters and pioneers used it for skinning game, cutting meat, digging holes, eating, and fighting. It was strong enough to cut firewood or hack a trail through dense undergrowth.

Imaginative users found its handle suitable for everything from hammering nails to grinding up a bag of coffee beans. The popularity of the Bowie knife reached its peak in the 1850s, and the knife was

Below: A modern, highly decorative replica of the famous Bowie knife. Today, the term has become a generic label for almost any type of large sheath knife.

carried by many Confederate troops during the Civil War. Typical Bowie knives had large blades and a guard to prevent the user's hand from slipping forward from the handle.

BOYD, BELLE
(1843–1900)

Belle Boyd was a seventeen-year-old Confederate spy who used her local knowledge of the countryside and her feminine virtues to provide intelligence support to Major General Stonewall Jackson during the Shenandoah Valley Campaign. Boyd reportedly had beautiful ankles and she was greatly aided in her intelligence acquisitions by her attractiveness to men.

Boyd's champions argue that her information convinced Jackson to attack the Federal forces at Front Royal, but some historians claim Boyd's reports merely confirmed what Jackson already knew. Either way, Boyd's exploits won her wide acclaim. However, her lack of discretion and her penchant for self-promotion limited her effectiveness as a spy. She was arrested twice, although she was

Above: *Belle Boyd's shapely figure made her quite attractive in her day, and she used her feminine charms to spy for the Confederacy.*

released both times. In 1863 she fled to England, where she performed onstage. In 1865 she wrote her memoirs, and after the war she toured as a one-woman show depicting her adventures. She died while on tour in Wisconsin.

BRAGG, BRAXTON
(1817–76)

Braxton Bragg graduated fifth in the West Point class of 1837 and obtained some fame as an artilleryman in the Mexican War before resigning from the U.S. Army in 1856. He was appointed as a brigadier general in the Confederate army on March 7, 1861, and his first important command was defending the coast between Pensacola, Florida, and Mobile, Alabama. Considering this territory to be untenable, Bragg asked to be sent to Kentucky. He was promoted to major general on September 12 and fought as a corps commander at Shiloh.

Above: *Braxton Bragg was a martinet who was very unpopular with his men and many fellow officers. President Jefferson Davis, however, was among Bragg's loyal supporters.*

Bragg made full general on April 6, 1862, and on June 27 he assumed command of the Army of Tennessee. He led an ill-fated invasion of Kentucky that included the Battle of Perryville. Preliminary to the campaign, Bragg showed logistical and administrative expertise in moving his force, but failed to achieve unity of effort with Major General Edmund Kirby Smith during the actual fighting. Bragg withdrew from Kentucky and ordered a concentration at Murfreesboro, Tennessee. In the ensuing battle there, Bragg gained a minor tactical victory, but was unable to destroy the larger Federal army or drive it from the field. Instead, Bragg withdrew to block a Federal advance to Chattanooga. Bragg commanded poorly at Chattanooga, and the loss of that key city was a critical blow to the Confederacy.

By this point, several of Bragg's subordinate commanders were calling for his relief. Although

President Jefferson Davis was a staunch supporter of Bragg, he had to bow to the pressure, and when Bragg asked to be relieved, Davis recalled him to Richmond, where he served as Davis's military adviser. Bragg actually performed rather well in this capacity, using his abundant skills as a planner and logistician. In fact, his ability to tend to myriad details made him an excellent administrator. However, he lacked a broad strategic vision, and his abrasive personality helped make him an unsuccessful army commander.

BRANDY STATION, BATTLE OF

❖ DATE: June 9, 1863

❖ LOCATION: Culpeper County, Virginia

❖ ARMY OF NORTHERN VIRGINIA (C): 9,500

❖ ARMY OF THE POTOMAC (U.S.): 11,000

❖ CASUALTIES: 523 (C); 936 (U.S.)

After his victory at Chancellorsville, General Robert E. Lee pushed north for his Gettysburg Campaign behind Major General Jeb Stuart's cavalry screen. In order to determine Lee's dispositions, Major General Joseph Hooker dispatched a cavalry reconnaissance led by Major General Alfred Pleasonton. Stuart and Pleasonton clashed on June 9, 1863, at Brandy Station, Virginia, in the biggest cavalry battle of the war.

Although Stuart was initially surprised, he managed to maintain control of the battlefield, suffering 523 losses compared to 936 for the Federals. However, Pleasonton had succeeded in learning Lee's whereabouts, and Stuart had failed in his screening mission. It was a humiliation for Stuart, and many consider his ill-advised extended reconnaissance at Gettysburg to have been an attempt to repair his reputation after this setback.

Below: *Like many battlefields, Brandy Station has been encroached upon by urbanization. Several preservationist groups work to protect such historic sites.*

Above: *The May 23, 1863, edition of* Frank Leslie's Illustrated Newspaper *depicted the women of the Richmond Bread Riot in a harsh and unglamorous way.*

BREAD RIOT
(APRIL 2, 1863)

In the spring of 1863, a rash of civil disorder spread throughout the Confederacy. Led primarily by white women, these events protested high prices, hoarding of food, and speculation in commodities by launching bread riots against bakeries, groceries, and government facilities. Protests broke out in Atlanta, Macon, Columbus, and Augusta, Georgia; and Salisbury and High Point, North Carolina; but the most famous incident was the Bread Riot of April 2, 1863, in Richmond, Virginia.

Transporting food and produce to Richmond was a tedious process with the city under martial law. For security purposes, a passport system required local farmers to wait in line while their credentials were inspected. This already stressed procedure was overloaded on March 19 and 20, 1863, when a nine-inch snowfall rendered travel nearly impossible.

On April 2, a group of women, mostly wives of workers at Richmond's Tredegar Iron Works, gathered at a Baptist church near their homes to lament the high prices and low supply of food. They resolved to seek redress from Governor John Letcher, and they began walking to the governor's mansion on Capitol Square. As they marched, their numbers grew, and by the time they reached their destination the crowd had grown to several hundred and included men and boys as well as the women.

Letcher listened to their complaints and offered his sympathy but no solution. When he went back inside his mansion, the crowd turned angry and headed for Richmond's commercial district, where the protestors ransacked an area of ten square blocks, taking not only bread and food, but in some cases jewelry, clothing, and hats as well.

Letcher hurried to the scene, and he and Mayor Joseph Mayo tried to no avail to disperse the mob. As the crowd pressed on to one of the city's two marketplaces, it was met by a company of reserve soldiers drawn from workers at the Confederate armory. Before tragedy ensued, President Jefferson Davis arrived and got the group's attention by reaching into his pockets and throwing what money he had into the mob. He then pulled out his pocket watch and, with a glance at the troops behind him, cautioned, "We do not desire to injure anyone, but this lawlessness must stop. I will give you five minutes to disperse, otherwise you will be fired upon."

For a few tense minutes no one moved, but when the captain in command of the troops gave the order "Load," the crowd scattered. The next day, cannons guarded the riot scene, and the War Department kept two infantry battalions on alert in case there was further trouble.

BREASTWORKS

The development of the rifle gave the defense a marked advantage over the offense during the Civil War. This phenomenon was especially pronounced when breastworks protected the defender. Because the nature of the war often placed the Confederate forces in a defensive posture, they became especially adept at constructing these protections.

Companies prepared breastworks of earth and logs to cover their fronts. The procedure was to fell and trim trees and then roll the logs into a line to form a timber revetment usually four feet high. This structure was then banked with earth from a ditch dug to its front. The result was a sloping parapet about seven to ten feet thick at the top and an additional three feet at the bottom. On top of the revetment was a line of head logs positioned to leave a horizontal loophole about three inches wide through which to fire. The trees and bushes in front of the breastwork were then felled outward to create an obstacle that sometimes was augmented by a cheval-de-frise or sharpened palisades. The drill became such a matter of routine that a company could cover itself within an hour of halting, even without engineer support. Defending from behind breastworks greatly aided General Joseph E. Johnston in the Atlanta Campaign.

BRECKINRIDGE, JOHN C. (1821–75)

Although he served in the Mexican War, John C. Breckinridge was most notably a politician, serving as a congressman and as vice president to James Buchanan. Breckinridge ran against Abraham Lincoln as the Southern Democrat nominee for president in 1860. After his defeat he returned to his native Kentucky and served in the U.S. Senate from March to September 1861. When his efforts on behalf of the Crittenden Compromise to avoid war failed, he helped organize Kentucky's provisional Confederate government. Breckinridge fled Kentucky on October 2 to avoid arrest and was appointed as a brigadier general in the Confederate Army on November 2. This led to his expulsion from the Senate.

Breckinridge fought well at Bowling Green and Shiloh and was promoted to major general on April 14, 1862. He unsuccessfully attacked Baton Rouge, Louisiana, in August and withdrew to Port Hudson. He commanded a division at Murfreesboro and Chickamauga. From Tennessee he moved to take command of the Department of Western Virginia on March 4, 1864. Breckinridge distinguished himself in this command, repelling Major General Franz Sigel's threat to the Shenandoah Valley at the Battle of

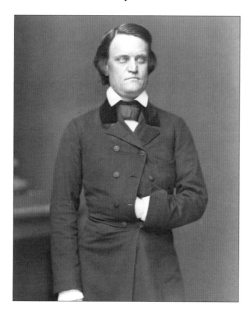

Above: *In spite of his prewar role as a politician, John Breckinridge proved a capable general during operations in the Shenandoah Valley.*

New Market on May 15. He also participated in Major General Jubal A. Early's Washington raid later that summer.

On February 5, 1865, Breckinridge became President Jefferson Davis's sixth and final secretary of war. By this point in the war there was little Breckinridge could do to affect military affairs, but he did assist with the surrender negotiations of General Joseph E. Johnston's army. After the war, Breckinridge went to England and Canada before returning to Kentucky, where he remained immensely popular.

BRICE'S CROSS ROADS, BATTLE OF

❖ DATE: June 10, 1864

❖ LOCATION: Prentiss and Union counties, Mississippi

❖ DEPARTMENT OF ALABAMA, MISSISSIPPI, AND EAST LOUISIANA (C): 3,500

❖ MILITARY DIVISION OF THE MISSISSIPPI (U.S.): 8,100

❖ CASUALTIES: 2,240 (U.S.); 492 (C)

As Major General William T. Sherman set out on his Atlanta Campaign, Lieutenant General Nathan Bedford Forrest recognized the opportunity to raid into middle Tennessee and Kentucky to cut Sherman's line of communications. However, Sherman, well aware of this threat, dispatched Brigadier General Samuel D. Sturgis to occupy Forrest. The two met at Brice's Cross Roads on June 10, 1864.

TWO-PART PLAN
Forrest developed a plan to defeat the Federal cavalry first and then

Above: *Brice's Cross Roads National Battlefield Site. At Brice's Cross Roads and elsewhere, Nathan Bedford Forrest used mobility and audacity to get the optimal effect from his artillery.*

deal with the slower-moving infantry later. The battle began when Sturgis's cavalry routed a Confederate patrol about a mile and a half from Brice's Cross Roads. Forrest then rallied his men behind a heavy rail fence that enclosed a field surrounded by dense undergrowth. Still, Forrest did not assume an exclusively defensive posture. He ordered Brigadier General Hylan B. Lyon to charge dismounted as a feint, and the ruse worked, causing the Federals to dismount and remain in position. Lyon then used the hiatus to prepare his own position with rails, logs, and whatever else he could find. As more Confederates arrived, Lyon launched another attack. In a desperate fight, Forrest's determined men succeeded in defeating the Federal cavalry before the infantry could arrive. But by early afternoon Sturgis's infantry reached the field and drew themselves up in a close semicircle around the crossroads. Now Forrest proceeded to the second part of his plan—defeating the Federal infantry. To do so, he ordered Brigadier General Tyree H. Bell to charge on the left, and the entanglements of blackjack and brushwood there soon reduced the fight to hand-to-hand combat. Captain John Morton brought forward four brass six-pounder artillery pieces that he double-shotted with canister and fired at musket range, ripping great holes in the Federal ranks.

Forrest then launched a bold charge on the heels of Morton's artillery fire that succeeded in breaking the Federal line. Sturgis's men took flight with Forrest in hot pursuit. Forrest maintained his pressure into the next day, and by the time Sturgis limped back to Memphis, 223 of his men were killed, 394 were wounded, and 1,623 were missing. In addition to the personnel losses, the Federals lost numerous weapons to the Confederates. Forrest reported capturing sixteen cannons and 1,500 stands of small arms. While Brice's Cross Roads was a brilliant tactical victory for Forrest, Sturgis could take some consolation in having accomplished his chief object of distracting Forrest from Sherman's communications.

BROWN, JOSEPH E.
(1821–94)

Joseph E. Brown was the wartime governor of Georgia. He was an ardent secessionist and advocate of states' rights. He repeatedly opposed President Jefferson Davis's attempts to strengthen the central government. However, Brown's actions cannot be generalized. While he was a strong opponent of conscription and tried to control the disposition of state troops, he also encouraged Georgia farmers to reduce their cotton crops and instead grow food for the Confederate army. His overall frustration with Davis led to an eventual anti-administration alliance with Vice President Alexander H. Stephens.

After the war, Brown became a Republican and served as chief justice of the Georgia Supreme Court from 1868 to 1870. In 1871 he returned to the Democratic Party and served as a U.S. senator from 1880 to 1891.

BUCHANAN, FRANKLIN
(1800–74)

Franklin Buchanan was one of the Confederacy's most seasoned sailors. He began his naval career as a midshipman in 1815 and became instrumental to the founding of the U.S. Naval Academy. Known as the "Father of Annapolis," he served as the first superintendent there from 1845 to 1847. He fought in the Mexican War and served with Commodore Matthew Perry during his expedition to China and Japan from 1852 to 1855. Buchanan was a captain serving as commander of the Washington Navy Yard when the Civil War broke out.

Buchanan resigned from the Federal navy on April 22, 1861, but tried to withdraw his resignation when his native state of Maryland did not secede. The Navy Department denied his request and dismissed him from the service in May. He was commissioned as a captain in the

Above: *Franklin Buchanan was one of the Confederacy's most seasoned sailors. He figured prominently at the battles of Hampton Roads and Mobile Bay.*

Confederate navy and took command of the Chesapeake Bay Squadron in early 1862.

MISSES FAMOUS DUEL
Buchanan served as the first commander of the ironclad *Virginia* (formerly the USS *Merrimack*) but was wounded during action on March 8, 1862, and relinquished command to Lieutenant Catesby ap Roger Jones for the famous duel with the *Monitor* the next day. Buchanan was made admiral on August 21, 1862, and commanded the Confederate naval forces, including the ironclad *Tennessee*, against Admiral David G. Farragut during the August 1864 Battle of Mobile Bay. After the war, he served as president of Maryland State Agricultural College.

BUCKNER, SIMON BOLIVAR
(1823–1914)

Simon Bolivar Buckner graduated from West Point in 1844 and served in the Mexican War, at West Point, and on the frontier. He resigned from the army in 1855 and became active in the Kentucky militia. He refused commissions in both the Confederate and Federal armies until it became obvious that Kentucky could not maintain its neutrality. Then he joined General Albert Sidney Johnston in Bowling Green and was commissioned as a brigadier general on September 14, 1861. Buckner was left to surrender the

Above: *Simon Bolivar Buckner labored under the incompetent leadership of Gideon Pillow and John Floyd at Fort Donelson and was forced to surrender after his two superiors fled.*

Confederate forces at Fort Donelson after his seniors, Brigadier Generals John B. Floyd and Gideon J. Pillow, passed command to him and fled. He was promoted to major general on August 16, 1862, and participated in General Braxton Bragg's Kentucky Campaign.

In May 1863 he assumed command of the Department of East Tennessee and West Virginia and later served as a corps commander at Chickamauga. Buckner was given command of the District of Louisiana and promoted to lieutenant general on September 20, 1864, but he saw little additional fighting.

After the war, he was Democratic governor of Kentucky from 1887 to 1892. He was a lifelong friend of Lieutenant General Ulysses S. Grant, dating back from their days at West Point, and Buckner served as a pallbearer at Grant's funeral. Buckner's son of the same name was a general in World War II.

BULLOCH, JAMES D. (1823–1901)

Before the Civil War, James Dunwoody Bulloch served in the U.S. Navy and the commercial mail service. He followed his native Georgia in secession and was commissioned as a commander. Bulloch requested a line position, but was instead sent to England as a naval agent to arrange for ships to be built for the Confederacy.

Bulloch operated out of Liverpool, a British shipyard city and site of considerable Confederate sympathy. He carefully maneuvered around both the British Foreign Enlistment Act, which forbade the equipping and arming of ships in British ports for use by belligerents with whom Britain was at peace, and the watchful eye of Thomas Haines Dudley, the U.S. political consul. As a result of his tireless efforts, Bulloch furnished the Confederacy

with the British cruisers *Florida*, *Alabama*, and *Shenandoah*, as well as the French ram *Stonewall*. Unable to procure more ships because of increased scrutiny and a shortage of funds, Bulloch assisted with Confederate diplomatic efforts.

Bulloch was refused a pardon after the war, so he remained in Liverpool, where he worked in the mercantile business, practiced maritime and international law, and published *The Secret Service of the Confederate States in Europe*.

BUSHWHACKERS AND GUERRILLAS

Bushwhackers and guerrillas were irregular Confederate bands that operated outside the Partisan Ranger Act of 1862 and had loose or no official sanction

Below: *William C. Quantrill was one of the Confederacy's most notorious and deadly bushwhackers. His August 1863 raid on Lawrence, Kansas, is depicted in this illustration.*

from the Confederate government. Bushwhacking predated the Civil War during the brutal period of Bleeding Kansas. It was in response to a bushwhacker raid on Lawrence, Kansas, in May 1856 that John Brown launched his Pottawatomie Creek massacre. As opposed to "partisan ranger," the terms "bushwhacker" and "guerrilla" usually connoted brutality, lawlessness, and plunder. Their targets were most often nonmilitary ones, and there was a fine line between many bushwhackers and common criminals. William C. Quantrill was the most famous bushwhacker during the war, but after the war, Jesse and Frank James, as well as Cole and Jim Younger, made careers plying some of the same skills they learned as bushwhackers.

BUTTERNUTS

Although the color most associated with Confederate uniforms is gray, as the war dragged on the effects of the Federal blockade forced the South to resort to domestic dye options. After 1862 Confederates increasingly used a dye made of copperas and walnut hulls to produce a yellowish-brown hue that was dubbed "butternut." By extension, Confederate soldiers came to be known as "butternuts."

Right: *A Confederate cavalryman dressed in a butternut tunic fires his carbine. The style of dress was the consequence of economic necessity—after 1862, the Confederates simply could not afford new uniforms for their troops.*

CALIFORNIA, ARIZONA, AND NEW MEXICO

The vast expanse of America's Far West offered intriguing possibilities for the Confederates to open up a new theater of war. In Santa Fe, New Mexico, the population was largely neutral toward the war, but farther south, the Arizona settlers were more pro-Confederate. In 1861 Brigadier General John Baylor was sent to Arizona to secure the territory for the Confederacy. Baylor declared himself governor and proved to be a nuisance to the Confederate authorities in Richmond. Regardless, the Arizona Territory was

represented in the Confederate Congress as a nonvoting member.

Brigadier General Henry H. Sibley commanded the Department of New Mexico, and in December 1861 he led a 3,700-man army north from El Paso, Texas, toward Fort Craig and Albuquerque, New Mexico. Sibley's attempt to draw Colonel Edward Canby into battle failed, and he tried to bypass Fort Craig to the east.

On February 20, Canby intercepted Sibley's column, but the Confederates scored a victory at Valverde. However, Sibley was often drunk and his men were reduced to half rations. As the Confederates pressed on toward Santa Fe, Colorado, volunteers marched from Denver and met Sibley at Apache Canyon on March 26. A series of skirmishes erupted into a battle near Pigeon's Ranch on March 28 in which Sibley won a tactical victory but lost his supply trains. Without provisions, the Confederates were forced to retreat south to San Antonio, Texas.

OUT WEST
In California, Brigadier General Edwin Vose Sumner replaced Brigadier General Albert Sidney Johnston as commander of the Department of the Pacific when Johnston left for the Confederacy. Sumner proceeded to eliminate the Confederate presence in California. His decisive action and Sibley's failed campaign ended any Confederate designs for California.

CAMP LIFE

The Confederate army occupied camps when not actively involved in campaigning. Camps allowed the army to train, drill, reorganize, prepare, or weather the harsh winter until the spring campaigning season arrived. Camp

Left: *Both sides generally suspended campaigning during the winter and went into winter quarters, such as these that fell into Federal hands when the Confederates abandoned Yorktown, Virginia.*

soldiers in Sibley tents, a prewar invention of future Confederate brigadier general Henry H. Sibley. The Sibley tent was a canvas structure eighteen feet in diameter and twelve feet tall with a pole in the center that gave the tent a conical shape.

A hole in the top allowed ventilation for a stove that was placed in the center of the tent. The tent could sleep twelve men comfortably, but by regulation it could accommodate up to twenty. The occupants slept in a wheel-spoke fashion around the stove with their feet pointing inward. The close quarters and inadequate ventilation often made life in a Sibley tent intolerable.

Below: *This set of Confederate winter quarters at Manassas, Virginia, shows the typical construction of chinked log sides. Board roofs such as these were a luxury. Expedient materials such as canvas and branches were common.*

life was relatively ordered, with a routine schedule, its own set of regulations, and a physical layout designed to facilitate administrative control. Early Confederate camps housed the

As time passed, the Sibley tent was surpassed by simpler versions. Lucky Confederates were issued or captured "pup tents." Each soldier carried half of this tent, and pairs of soldiers connected their individual pieces to form a small shelter that soldiers felt was big enough only for a small dog.

More often, shortages of canvas compelled soldiers to fabricate their own crude shelters of brush or oilcloths draped over a framework of poles.

WINTER QUARTERS

In periods of winter inactivity, armies built winter quarters consisting of small log cabins or other structures made out of available materials. The more solid winter quarters were built by first digging down a floor some twelve inches below the surface, laying logs around the perimeter, and chinking them with mud. Roofs were built of shingles, boards, or canvas. Some cabins had a fireplace, and most had crude furniture made of boxes and crates.

Camps laid out according to regulation formed a grid pattern with prescribed street widths and specified locations for officers' quarters, kitchens, and trains. Pickets were posted on the outskirts of the camp to provide security.

GAMES

In addition to ubiquitous guard duty and drilling, soldiers in camps amused themselves by playing cards, forming improvised theatrical and musical groups, and socializing and cooking with their messmates.

Maintaining discipline in the idle periods in camp sometimes posed a challenge for officers. On the other hand, great spiritual revivals also broke out among armies in camps.

Above: *C. W. Chapman, an ordnance sergeant in the Fifty-ninth Virginia Regiment of Wise's Brigade, depicted this idyllic camp scene that highlights the shared mess for cooking.*

CAROLINAS CAMPAIGN

- ❖ DATE: February 1–April 26, 1865
- ❖ LOCATION: South and North Carolina
- ❖ ARMY OF TENNESSEE (C): 22,500
- ❖ GRAND ARMY OF THE WEST (U.S.): 60,000–80,000
- ❖ CASUALTIES: 7,188 (C); 4,800 (U.S.)

After completing his March to the Sea, Major General William T. Sherman left Savannah, Georgia, on February 1, 1865, and turned north to converge with other Federal forces to destroy General Robert E. Lee's Army of Northern Virginia. Sherman had an army of 60,000 compared to the some 22,500 scattered Confederate forces commanded by General Pierre Gustave Toutant Beauregard. To make matters worse for the Confederates, Sherman maneuvered so as to threaten both Augusta, Georgia, and Charleston, South Carolina. The result was that the Confederates left a wide gap between the two locations through which Sherman passed virtually unopposed.

SOUTH CAROLINA

On February 16, Sherman reached Columbia, South Carolina. The Federal troops harbored particularly hard feelings against South Carolina, considering it the birthplace of secession and the instigator of the war. After the Federals entered Columbia the next day, a massive fire broke out that destroyed over half the city.

President Jefferson Davis brought General Joseph E. Johnston out of retirement on February 23 and placed him in command of the Army of Tennessee. Johnston moved to concentrate the Confederate forces at Fayetteville, North Carolina, but Sherman continued to disguise his true line of march, advancing in three separate columns. Johnston attempted to strike Major General Henry Warner Slocum's isolated corps at Bentonville on March 19, but Sherman was able to unite his force on March 21 and compel Johnston to withdraw. By now, Sherman's strength had grown to 80,000.

North Carolinians showed little of the blatant animosity to the advancing Federals that had been the order of the day in South Carolina, and the Federals inflicted much less gratuitous damage in North Carolina than they had done previously. Nonetheless, Johnston was forced to admit that resistance was futile, and on April 26 he surrendered.

CARPETBAGGERS

Carpetbaggers were Northerners who came south during Reconstruction, carrying their belongings in inexpensive suitcases called "carpetbags." The carpetbaggers were a mixed lot. To be sure, there were countless numbers of cads, motivated by greed and selfish aggrandizement, who exploited the freedmen and white Southerners alike. Horace Greeley, editor of the *New York Tribune*, said these carpetbaggers were intent on "stealing and plundering, many of them with both arms around Negroes, and their hands in their rear pockets, seeing if they cannot pick a paltry dollar out of them." On the other hand, many Northern idealists went south as teachers, clergymen, officers of the Freedman's Bureau, or members of benevolent societies who were motivated purely by a

Below: *Carl Schurz was a Republican senator from Missouri who supported Horace Greeley in the 1872 presidential election. This decision earned Schurz the disfavor of Thomas Nast, who negatively depicted him in this cartoon in* Harper's Weekly.

desire to help the former slaves. Still others viewed the post–Civil War South as so many nineteenth-century Americans viewed the West—as a field ripe for personal advancement. Indeed, most of the Northerners who came south were talented and educated and came to the South before 1867, when African Americans lacked the right to vote and prospects of gaining political office were remote.

But the type of carpetbagger that is most prevalent in the popular imagination is the conniving scoundrel who operated in collusion with "scalawags"—native white Southerners who also saw an opportunity to exploit the postwar chaos. Typical of this breed is Milton S. Littlefield, a colonel from Indiana who moved to North Carolina in 1867 and earned the title "Prince of Carpetbaggers." Littlefield made a fortune speculating on state bonds and lobbying for railroad interests, but he was greatly aided in the process

by William Woods Holden, who was made provisional governor of North Carolina by President Andrew Johnson in late 1865 and then elected as a Republican in 1868. Woods's administration was so scandal-ridden that he was impeached on charges of corruption in 1870. Many white Southerners roundly vilified carpetbaggers like Littlefield and their scalawag counterparts.

Politically, carpetbaggers tended to be Republicans, whether for ideological reasons or to protect their economic investments. Therefore, carpetbaggers played a pivotal role in the congressionally mandated state conventions of 1867 and 1868, comprising between a fourth to a half of all delegates in most states. Carpetbaggers who aspired to political office or were otherwise viewed as threats to the traditional Southern order eventually found themselves common targets for white vigilante groups, including the Ku Klux Klan.

CASUALTIES, CONFEDERATE

In military terminology, a casualty is any loss in numerical strength due to death, wounds, capture, or missing status. Incomplete records create some problems in determining Confederate troop strength and casualties, and estimates vary. A commonly cited set of statistics places Confederate troop strength at 750,000 and total casualties at 450,000. Of these, 94,000 died in battle, 162,000 died from disease and nonbattle causes, and 194,000 were wounded. Casualties among Confederate generals were especially high, with seventy-seven of a total of 425 dying, a ratio of one out of five.

Below: *This casualty at Gettysburg was one of the many losses that forever blunted the offensive capability of the Army of Northern Virginia.*

Especially in the war's early years, the Confederacy enjoyed a marked superiority in the cavalry arm. The cavalry conducted numerous screens, reconnaissance operations, and raids, but traditional cavalry charges with sabers were rare because of the increased effectiveness of infantry defending with rifles.

Instead, effective cavalry leaders like Lieutenant General Nathan Bedford Forrest learned to use their cavalry as mounted infantry. Horses and mules would provide the mobility to get men to the decisive point, but once there they would dismount and fight. In the Civil War, the dominant weapon of the cavalry was no longer the saber—it was the rifle.

The cavalry was also the principal intelligence-gathering organization during the Civil War. The advantage of the cavalry in this area was not just in its speed and

Above: *Confederate dead are lined up along the roadside after the Battle of Spotsylvania Court House, in May 1864. The Confederates lost a quarter of their force at Spotsylvania.*

with Grant suffering 17,000 casualties compared to 10,000 for Lee. Grant, however, could replace his losses while Lee could not—a reality Grant knew and exploited.

Although Federal casualty figures were higher (a total of 640,000), some 2 million Northern soldiers and sailors served. Thus Federal losses amount to over a fourth of their total strength, while the Confederates lost well over half. Given the Confederacy's limited manpower, these losses were irreplaceable.

Lieutenant General Ulysses S. Grant took advantage of this Federal numerical superiority to bludgeon General Robert E. Lee in a relentless war of attrition. For this reason, casualty figures are often deceptive indicators of a battle's strategic significance. For example, the Wilderness was a lopsided tactical victory for the Confederates,

Right: *A graveyard near Richmond, Kentucky, holds the remains of Confederate soldiers following the Confederate victory there in 1862.*

mobility to gather information, but also its ability to return rapidly to friendly lines to report its findings promptly. Cavalry also provided a counterintelligence function by screening friendly movements from enemy observation. In these areas, the Confederacy enjoyed a tremendous initial advantage with Major General Jeb Stuart providing valuable and timely reconnaissance for General Robert E. Lee.

GLAMOUR

The cavalry was perceived as a less dangerous, more glamorous, and easier service than the infantry. "If you want to have a good time," Stuart sang, "jine the cavalry." Such taunts naturally solicited disdain from the infantrymen, who often considered their cavalry

counterparts to be both soft and prone to thievery. One Alabamian felt that every cavalryman should have a board tied to his back with the word "thief" on it to warn innocent people to be on their guard. Another complaint among the infantry was that "you never see a dead cavalryman," implying that the mounted arm avoided the dangerous fighting. In spite of—or because of—these sentiments, many infantrymen found ways to leave their ranks and follow Stuart's advice to join the cavalry. The efforts to transfer many others were refused. Major General D. H. Hill disapproved one such request with the annotation, "Shooters are more needed than tooters."

In addition to Forrest and Stuart, Lieutenant General Wade

Hampton III, Brigadier General William Wirt Adams, Brigadier General John Hunt Morgan, and Major General Fitzhugh "Rooney" Lee distinguished themselves as cavalrymen for the Confederacy. Celebrated Confederate cavalry actions include Stuart's ride around Major General George B. McClellan's army during the Peninsula Campaign, Forrest's victory at Brice's Cross Roads, and Major General Earl Van Dorn's raid on Major General Ulysses S. Grant's supply depot at Holly Springs.

Below: *In this modern painting, Confederate cavalry led by Colonel Nathan Bedford Forrest gallop through woods near Fort Donelson in February 1862.*

CEDAR CREEK, BATTLE OF

- ❖ DATE: October 19, 1864
- ❖ LOCATION: Frederick, Shenandoah, and Warren counties, Virginia
- ❖ ARMY OF THE VALLEY (C): 15,680–21,102
- ❖ ARMY OF THE SHENANDOAH (U.S.): 31,610
- ❖ CASUALTIES: 3,360 (C); 5,355 (U.S.)

As a result of Major General Jubal A. Early's raid on Washington in the summer of 1864, Major General Philip H. Sheridan was dispatched to the Shenandoah Valley, assuming command on August 7, 1864. Sheridan practiced "hard war" tactics, and by October thought he had sufficiently eliminated Confederate resistance. He withdrew to Middletown and was preparing to join Lieutenant General Ulysses S. Grant in his campaign against General Robert E. Lee. Early followed the withdrawing Federals, and on October 13 was at Fisher's Hill. On October 16, Sheridan went to a conference in Washington. On the night of October 18, Early crossed the Shenandoah River at Fisher's Hill and attacked the surprised Federals along Cedar Creek the next morning. The Federals were unprepared, believing Early had withdrawn up the valley, and the Confederates enjoyed tremendous initial success. Nonetheless, Early failed to

continue his attack, thinking the Federals would abandon the field. Instead, Sheridan hastily returned from Washington, rallied his men, and had strengthened his line by the time Early finally attacked. Sheridan then counterattacked and drove Early back to Fisher's Hill with heavy losses.

CEDAR MOUNTAIN, BATTLE OF

- ❖ DATE: August 9, 1862
- ❖ LOCATION: Culpeper County, Virginia
- ❖ ARMY OF NORTHERN VIRGINIA (C): 16,868
- ❖ ARMY OF VIRGINIA (U.S.): 8,030
- ❖ CASUALTIES: 1,338 (C); 2,353 (U.S.)

Cedar Mountain was a preliminary action to the Battle of Second Manassas. Major General Stonewall Jackson planned to attack Federal forces as they slowly moved toward Culpeper, hoping to eliminate the lead

elements and then use his central position to defeat subsequent units as they arrived. Unfortunately, Jackson's penchant for secrecy slowed his movements, and Major General Nathaniel P. Banks attacked him at Cedar Mountain on August 9, 1862. The timely arrival of Major General A. P. Hill saved the day for Jackson, who suffered 1,338 casualties among his 16,868 engaged. Banks lost 2,353 of his 8,030-man force.

CENSORSHIP

The commitment of the Confederate government and President Jefferson Davis to Democratic ideals and individual liberties made the idea of censorship anathema. Although several Southern newspapers were vehemently critical of the administration, none were suppressed during the Civil War. The unchecked freedom of the

Below: *This unsupported attack by Samuel Crawford's brigade at Cedar Mountain had initial success, but was driven back with heavy losses by a Confederate counterattack.*

press made Southern newspapers an excellent source of intelligence for the Federals. In January 1862 the Confederate Congress tried to alleviate this breach by passing a law that prohibited unauthorized publication of information concerning troop movements. Nonetheless, even this modest measure was vigorously protested and roundly ignored.

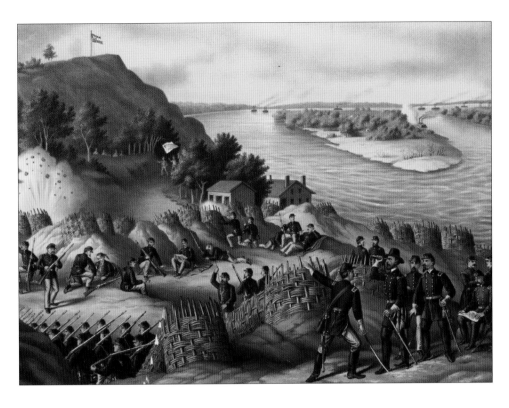

Above: *After the defeat at Champion Hill, the Confederates withdrew to the defenses of Vicksburg and were subjected to a Federal siege.*

CHAMPION HILL, BATTLE OF

❖ DATE: May 16, 1863

❖ LOCATION: Hinds County, Mississippi

❖ DEPARTMENT OF MISSISSIPPI AND EAST LOUISIANA (C): 23,000

❖ ARMY OF THE TENNESSEE (U.S.): 32,000

❖ CASUALTIES: 4,300 (C); 2,457 (U.S.)

Champion Hill was the decisive battle of the Vicksburg Campaign. Major General Ulysses S. Grant's victory there on May 16,

Below: *Grant's attack at Champion Hill pushed the Confederates back into Vicksburg, virtually sealing their fate and Union control of the central Mississippi Valley.*

1863, forced Lieutenant General John C. Pemberton back to his defenses within the environs of Vicksburg. With no freedom to maneuver nor any outside force to relieve him, he was subjected to a siege that resulted in Vicksburg's surrender.

After capturing Jackson on May 14, Grant left Major General William T. Sherman there to finish the destruction of industrial and transportation assets. Grant then sent Major Generals John A. McClernand and James B.

McPherson west toward Vicksburg. By this point Pemberton was in an advanced state of confusion and broken confidence. On May 16 he had begun to march east in hopes of uniting with General Joseph E. Johnston near Clinton when Grant's forces surprised him in the vicinity of Champion Hill.

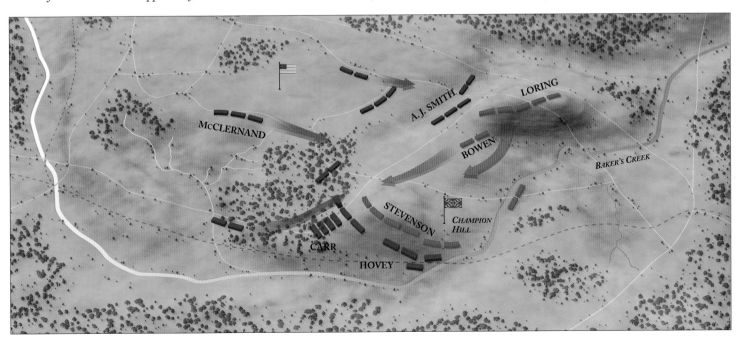

Grant's preparations allowed him to converge from three directions with a force ratio advantage of 3:2 over the Confederates. Outmaneuvered, Pemberton was forced to order a general retreat, leaving Brigadier General Lloyd Tilghman to act as rearguard.

TO VICKSBURG

Pemberton withdrew the rest of his army to the east side of the Big Black River, where he waited for the rearguard to join him. While Pemberton lingered, McClernand struck the dejected Confederates on May 17. Pemberton escaped thanks to some well-placed infantry and artillery on the west bank of the Big Black and the burning of the railroad bridge across the river.

The Confederates had now reached their considerable defenses at Vicksburg, and, with Grant close on his heels, Pemberton prepared to meet the Federal attack. He was safe for the time being, but his defeat at Champion Hill had cost him the ability to maneuver and had given Grant the advantage of time.

CHANCELLORSVILLE, BATTLE OF

❖ DATE: April 30–May 6, 1863

❖ LOCATION: Spotsylvania County, Virginia

❖ ARMY OF NORTHERN VIRGINIA (C): 59,500

❖ ARMY OF THE POTOMAC (U.S.): 134,000

❖ CASUALTIES: 13,000 (C); 17,000 (U.S.)

The Battle of Chancellorsville was perhaps General Robert E. Lee's most impressive Civil War victory. He daringly divided his force in the face of a much larger Federal army commanded by Major

General Joseph Hooker and sent Lieutenant General Stonewall Jackson on a flank attack that decimated the Federal ranks. Although a brilliant Confederate victory, it was a costly one in which Jackson was mortally wounded.

Hooker had originally planned to use his 134,000 troops on a turning movement against Lee. Soon after Hooker began his movement on April 28, Lee began receiving reports that the Federals had crossed the Rappahannock River, not just to his front, but also some twenty-five miles to the northwest at Kelly's Ford. With just 59,500 troops, Lee found himself in the middle of two wings of an army over twice his size. However, rather than withdrawing, Lee saw this as an opportunity to strike Hooker's divided army.

DASH TO CROSSROADS

Lee left just 10,000 men to watch what he sensed was a diversion by Major General John Sedgwick in front of Fredericksburg and rushed the rest of his army west to the tiny crossroads of Chancellorsville. Hooker had a day's head start on Lee, and by midafternoon on April 30, the Federals had reached Chancellorsville. Once there,

Hooker made a costly mistake. Instead of pressing forward and clearing the dangerous Wilderness, he decided to halt and await the arrival of additional troops. While Hooker remained stationary, Lieutenant General Stonewall Jackson was fast marching in Hooker's direction. Upon reaching Zoan Church, a small building on a commanding ridge on the edge of the Wilderness, Jackson ordered his men to dig in.

Jackson's decisive action was critical in shaping the Battle of Chancellorsville, because when Hooker finally got moving again, he collided with the small but aggressive Confederate force. The unexpected stiff resistance caught the Federals off guard, and the initial reports seem to have created an unwarranted panic on Hooker's part. He quickly ordered his generals to fall back to the Wilderness and assume a defensive posture. The decision was the turning point of the battle and was the beginning of Hooker's loss of nerve.

Below: *The Chancellorsville House stood at the intersection of the Orange Turnpike with the Orange Plank Road, Ely's Ford Road, and River Road in the Virginia Wilderness.*

Right: *Dead soldiers from William Barksdale's Mississippi Brigade line the Sunken Road during the Second Battle of Fredericksburg, a part of the Chancellorsville Campaign.*

Around midnight on May 1, Lee received a report from Major General Jeb Stuart that Hooker's "flank was in the air." By that, Stuart meant there was no obstacle to protect this vulnerable point of attack. Lee and Jackson turned their attention to figuring out how to use this new information.

Closely studying the map, Lee asked Jackson, "How can we get at those people?" and then traced a general direction of advance that would put Jackson beyond the right flank in Hooker's rear. With this concept in mind, Jackson dispatched his topographical engineer, Major Jedediah Hotchkiss, and his chaplain, Tucker Lacy, to locate a route that would accomplish Lee's intent. With the help of Colonel Charles Wellford, a local resident, they determined that a road existed that could support Jackson's maneuver.

In a brief exchange, Lee and Jackson devised a plan to send

Below: *Unconventional tactics gained Lee an unlikely victory at Chancellorsville against superior numbers, severely denting the morale of the Union Army of the Potomac.*

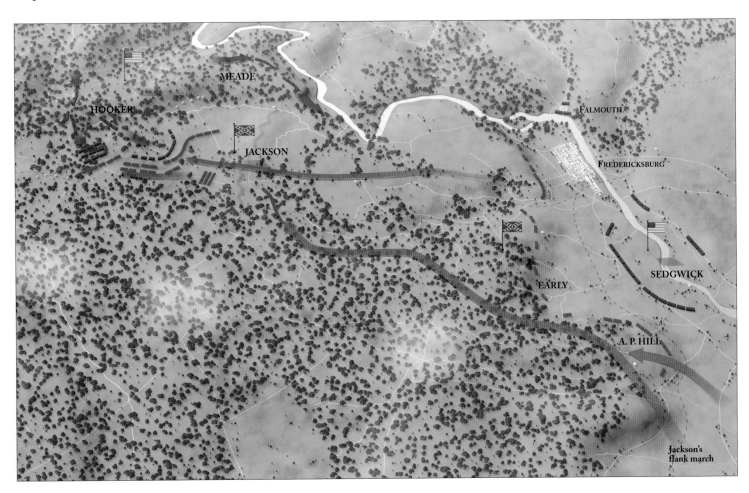

Jackson's flank march

Above: *This romanticized painting is one of many that depict the last meeting between Lee and Jackson before Jackson departed for his flank march during the Battle of Chancellorsville.*

Jackson's entire corps along this route, leaving Lee just two divisions to hold the line against Hooker. Jackson's men began moving at about 8:00 a.m., and by around 4:00 p.m. they had completed the 10.5-mile route. Before 6:00 p.m. Jackson was in attack formation with six of his fifteen brigades astride the Orange Turnpike, west of Chancellorsville, facing east toward the exposed Federal flank.

Jackson gave the order to attack, and with the blood-curdling rebel yell, the Confederates poured into Hooker's flank, completely

overwhelming the Eleventh Corps. A few Federal units rallied and attempted to make a stand, but the overall situation was hopeless. As new units arrived, Jackson fed them into the battle, and within three hours, the Confederates had surged forward two miles. Hooker's line was folded into a U centered on the large house at the Chancellorsville crossroads. There Federal resistance stiffened, and the Confederate onslaught slowed.

With darkness falling, Jackson was desperate to press his victory. By now, however, the rapid advance had left him uncertain of the exact disposition of his troops, so, with a group of staff officers accompanying him, he rode forward to reconnoiter the situation. In the darkness and confusion some North Carolina

troops mistook him for the enemy and opened fire. Jackson was hit in the left arm. Major General A. P. Hill, Jackson's senior division commander, was also struck.

At about midnight Stuart arrived and assumed command of Jackson's troops. With no idea of Jackson's plans, Stuart mounted several weak attacks against Hooker's main body throughout May 3, but without great success. After being knocked senseless when Confederate artillery struck his headquarters at the Chancellorsville House, Hooker withdrew north of Chancellorsville on the night of May 5–6.

Lee inflicted 17,000 casualties on Hooker at Chancellorsville while suffering 13,000 himself. Still Lee's losses represented 20 percent of his force, and even great victories such as Chancellorsville sapped the Army of Northern Virginia of manpower it could ill afford to lose. Of all Lee's losses, the most critical to the Confederate cause was Jackson. Jackson's left arm was amputated as a result of his wound, and it at appeared that he would recover. Complications developed, however, and Jackson died. When Lee learned of the amputation, he said Jackson "has lost his left arm, but I have lost my right." With Jackson gone, Lee would be without his most capable general.

CHARLESTON, SOUTH CAROLINA

For many, Charleston, South Carolina, represented the very center of rebellion. The state's secession convention had been forced to relocate there from the state capital at Columbia because of a smallpox epidemic. Newspaper editor Robert Barnwell Rhett used the pages of his *Charleston Mercury* to do much to advance the agenda of the fire-eaters. The war's first shots were fired at Fort Sumter in Charleston's harbor. For these reasons, the city remained a very important political objective for both Confederates and Federals throughout the war.

Charleston was a model Old South city in terms of the very visible presence of the aristocracy, architecture, and arts and culture. It was also a city where slavery thrived. In 1820 three-fourths of all heads of households in Charleston owned at least one slave. As points of comparison, in that same year just two-thirds of the whites in New Orleans owned slaves and just 50 percent did in Savannah.

However, the dense population of slaves made control difficult, and white Charlestonians were horrified when Denmark Vesey's slave revolt conspiracy was uncovered in 1822. After this brush with insurrection, the white population imposed a series of rigid controls to keep the slaves in check. Charleston became the center of proslavery apologists, which partially explains the city's vehement secessionist rhetoric.

Charleston was also important for practical reasons. It was a good-sized Southern city with a population of 40,552 in 1860. It had a vibrant economy based on rice, cotton, slave trading, and shipping. Its industrial activity included manufacturing steamship engines, locomotives, and steamship

Below: *By 1865 this Confederate depot in Charleston showed the destruction wrought by four years of war.*

machinery. Although other ports were surpassing it as a shipping center, Charleston's important rail link to Savannah, Georgia, made it a transportation hub. Along with Wilmington, North Carolina, it would become a popular Atlantic coast blockade-running port during the war. The city also contained the Citadel, an important training ground for Confederate military leaders.

Assistant Secretary of the Navy Gustavus V. Fox captured the views of many Federals when he wrote, "The fall of Charleston is the fall of Satan's Kingdom." However, as the Confederates had withdrawn from other coastal areas, Charleston's defenses had developed into a series of formidable belts. An abortive Federal land attack failed at Secessionville on June 16, 1862, and a combination of land-based artillery, torpedoes, the CSS *Hunley* submarine, obstructions, and prepared positions had made Charleston even more able to withstand an assault from the sea. Admiral Samuel F. Du Pont was reluctant to risk his fleet against this defense in depth, but he

succumbed to pressure from the Navy Department and made an all-out attack on April 7, 1863. Du Pont was repulsed and then replaced by Admiral John A. Dahlgren who, along with Major General Quincy A. Gillmore, launched at least twenty-five unsuccessful assaults from July to September.

The capture of Charleston did not occur until Major General William T. Sherman's Carolinas Campaign. On February 17–18, 1865, the Confederates evacuated, and Charleston succumbed to Federal occupation.

CHATTANOOGA, BATTLE OF

- ❖ DATE: November 23–25, 1863
- ❖ LOCATION: Hamilton County and Chattanooga, Tennessee
- ❖ ARMY OF TENNESSEE (C): 46,000
- ❖ MILITARY DIVISION OF THE MISSISSIPPI (U.S.): 56,000
- ❖ CASUALTIES: 6,700 (C); 5,800 (U.S.)

After his defeat on September 19–20, 1863, at Chickamauga, Major General William S. Rosecrans withdrew to Chattanooga, Tennessee. General Braxton Bragg placed the city under siege. Expecting Rosecrans to evacuate the city, Bragg took no further action until October 1, when he launched several cavalry raids that disrupted Rosecrans's communications and severely threatened his ability to feed his men.

The Federal high command, however, responded strongly to the situation, rushing two corps under Major General Joseph Hooker west from Virginia and appointing Major General Ulysses S. Grant commander of the newly created Military Division of the Mississippi. Grant arrived in Chattanooga on September 23 and replaced Rosecrans with Major General George H. Thomas.

Grant quickly restored morale among the Federals. Within days, they had broken out of their besieged position enough to establish a "cracker line" by which rations could be delivered through the Tennessee River Valley. Grant's transformation of the army was dramatic, and by the end of November they were strong enough to attack.

Grant sent Major General William T. Sherman on a march to cross the Tennessee River, envelop Bragg's right, and push the Confederate flank toward Tunnell Hill. When Bragg saw Sherman moving, he guessed Sherman was headed to relieve Major General Ambrose E. Burnside's besieged force at Knoxville. Bragg sent two divisions to reinforce Lieutenant

Left: *George Thomas's charge near Orchard Knob on November 24 at the Battle of Chattanooga surprisingly paved the way for Joseph Hooker's decisive attack on Lookout Mountain the next day.*

Left: *Lookout Mountain, stormed by Joseph Hooker on November 24, 1863. The Federals won the fight for Lookout Mountain, also called the "Battle Above the Clouds," in part because of poor Confederate positions.*

Johnston. The gateway to the heartland of the Confederacy was now opened and, before long, Sherman would launch his Atlanta Campaign.

CHESNUT, MARY (1823–86)

Mary Boykin Chesnut was the wife of James Chesnut Jr., a South Carolina politician and brigadier general in the Confederate army. Her position as wife of a high-placed Confederate official and her prominence in the social circles of Charleston gave her impressive access to wartime information. Articulate, opinionated, and passionate, Chesnut recorded her observations in a diary that C. Vann Woodward edited and published as *Mary*

Above: *Diarist Mary Chesnut authored one of the most informative and candid views of the Confederate war effort to be written by a woman.*

General James Longstreet at Knoxville, but recalled one when Thomas attacked on November 23.

Thomas's attack seized part of Bragg's center in front of Missionary Ridge. The next day, when Bragg tried to shift forces to oppose Sherman's crossing, Thomas ordered Hooker to attack to fix Bragg in position. When Hooker encountered only limited opposition, he pressed the attack and seized Lookout Mountain in what became known as the "Battle Above the Clouds."

Hooker's incredible success had been aided by the fact that the Confederates had positioned their forces poorly. Some were too high up the slope, and their shots flew over the Federals' heads. Others were too far down, and when they fell back they blocked the firing of their fellow soldiers further up. By the morning of November 25, the Federals were in firm control of the mountain.

For such a pivotal battle, casualties were relatively low. The Federals lost 5,800 and the Confederates 6,700. Bragg retreated some twenty-five miles to Dalton, Georgia. By now, the outcries against his mismanagement of the Army of Tennessee had become unbearable. On November 29, Bragg asked to be relieved, and President Jefferson Davis eventually replaced him with General Joseph E.

Chesnut's Civil War in 1981. The book provides an invaluable resource to those seeking an aristocratic woman's view of the war that is candid and free from many of the era's social inhibitions. Chesnut regularly expressed her disgust at what she viewed as incompetence or inertia on the part of Confederate officials, often lamenting, "Oh that I were a man!"

CHICKAMAUGA, BATTLE OF

❖ DATE: September 19–20, 1863

❖ LOCATION: Catoosa and Walker counties, Georgia

❖ ARMY OF TENNESSEE (C): 66,000

❖ ARMY OF THE CUMBERLAND (U.S.): 56,000

❖ CASUALTIES: 18,454 (C); 16,170 (U.S.)

Below: Battle of Chickamauga—*a color lithograph by Kurz and Allison, produced in 1890.*

The Tullahoma Campaign of June 1863 forced General Braxton Bragg to retreat from his positions north of Chattanooga, Tennessee, opening that key rail junction to attack by Major General William S. Rosecrans. Bragg withdrew without a fight on September 9, a move that alarmed Confederate authorities. Lieutenant General James Longstreet was dispatched with two divisions from Virginia to help shore up the Confederate situation. In a twelve-day rail movement, two-thirds of Longstreet's force arrived in time to help seal a Confederate victory at Chickamauga.

Rosecrans had concentrated his command near West Chickamauga Creek, about twelve miles south of Chattanooga. On September 19, Bragg attacked with the unusual benefit of a 66,000 to 56,000 numerical advantage. The rugged terrain made control difficult, and during the first day of battle, Bragg largely piecemealed his attack. Late in the evening, however, he reorganized his army into one wing commanded by Longstreet and another by Lieutenant General Leonidas Polk.

On September 20, Bragg launched a series of sequential attacks echeloned from north to south. This technique made little progress, and by 11:00 a.m., Bragg discarded it for a concerted push of four divisions by Longstreet. This force happened to find a gap left as Rosecrans had previously shifted forces to meet earlier attacks. Some 20,000 Confederates poured through the opening, and the Federal defense collapsed. Rosecrans personally abandoned the field, and two of his corps commanders did the same. Only Major General George H. Thomas stood his ground in the center of the battlefield at Snodgrass Hill, earning him the nickname "the Rock of Chickamauga."

Rosecrans lost 16,170 men and fell back to Chattanooga. Bragg lost 18,454, but instead of offering vigorous pursuit, elected

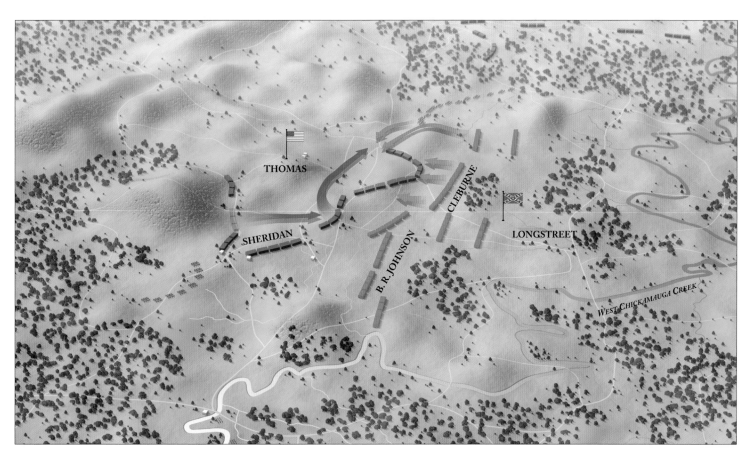

SHERIDAN

THOMAS

B. R. JOHNSON

CLEBURNE

LONGSTREET

WEST CHICKAMAUGA CREEK

to lay siege to Rosecrans. Although Chickamauga was the Army of Tennessee's greatest victory, Bragg's failure to press the matter resulted in numerous complaints from his subordinates. President Jefferson Davis, however, stubbornly continued to support Bragg.

CHICKASAW BLUFFS, BATTLE OF

❖ DATE: December 27–29, 1862

❖ LOCATION: Warren County, Mississippi

❖ DEPARTMENT OF MISSISSIPPI AND EAST LOUISIANA (C): 15,000

❖ ARMY OF THE TENNESSEE, EXPEDITIONARY FORCE (U.S.): 32,000

❖ CASUALTIES: 187 (C); 1,776 (U.S.)

The Battle of Chickasaw Bluffs was part of a two-pronged attack that constituted Major General Ulysses S. Grant's first

attempt to gain control of the Mississippi River. In November 1862 Grant personally led 45,000 troops southward from near La Grange in western Tennessee while Major General William T. Sherman conducted a riverborne expedition from Memphis to the Yazoo River just above Vicksburg. Ultimately, the two axes were to converge in the Vicksburg–Jackson region.

FLANKING THREAT

However, the plan began to unravel after Grant's column was forced to turn back when Confederate cavalry raids threatened his line of communications. Grant's operation had been designed to distract Lieutenant General John C. Pemberton from Sherman's attack, but its failure instead allowed Pemberton to bolster his lines at Chickasaw Bluffs. The Confederates were still outnumbered, but the terrain was such that the defenders had a significant advantage, especially in

Above: *The Battle of Chickamauga had the potential to be a great Confederate victory, but Braxton Bragg failed to properly exploit Southern gains on the battlefield.*

front of the Walnut Hills, where they had established a strong line reinforced by natural water barriers and man-made abatis.

The climactic day of the battle was December 29. Sherman knew the long odds he was up against, but he stoically resolved, "We will lose 5,000 men before we take Vicksburg, and may as well lose them here as anywhere else." Sherman's dim prediction proved correct, and he suffered a severe repulse. On January 1, 1863, he loaded his men on transports and withdrew from the Vicksburg area. The expedition had cost him 1,776 casualties, including 208 killed. The Confederates had suffered just fifty-seven killed and 130 wounded. For the time being at least, it appeared that the Confederate defenses at Vicksburg were sound.

CITADEL

On January 28, 1861, the South Carolina General Assembly combined the Corps of Cadets at the Citadel in Charleston and the Arsenal in Columbia into the Battalion of State Cadets. The two institutions were designated as the South Carolina Military Academy, and the Battalion of State Cadets was made a part of the state's military organization. By 1864 there were 296 cadets enrolled at the South Carolina Military Academy.

Below: *Citadel cadets contributed to the Southern war effort both as trainers and fighters. Their most notable action was firing on the* Star of the West *as it neared Fort Sumter, forcing it to turn back.*

The Citadel's most famous involvement in the Civil War occurred on January 9, 1861, when cadets manning an artillery battery on Morris Island fired the first hostile shots of the growing sectional crisis, repulsing the supply ship *Star of the West*, which had been sent to reinforce the isolated Federal garrison at Fort Sumter. Officers of the Citadel helped establish artillery positions and direct fire during the bombardment of Fort Sumter, and some cadets attached themselves to various military units that participated in the action.

Routine activities of Citadel cadets during the Civil War included training recruits, performing guard duty, and escorting prisoners. However, some cadets actively participated in several campaigns and engagements in defense of Charleston and South Carolina during the war. Of special note is the December 1864 engagement at Tulifinny Creek when the entire Battalion of State Cadets deployed as an independent military unit and suffered eight casualties, including one killed. In all, the Battalion of State Cadets earned nine battle streamers for its service in the war.

Some cadets left the school to join the fighting, including those that formed the Cadet Rangers, a cavalry unit that participated in the Battle of Trevilian Station, Virginia. Citadel alumni such as Brigadier General Micah Jenkins, class of 1854, also provided valuable leadership in the Confederate army. Of some 224 graduates living during the Civil War, 209 served in the Confederate armed forces, including four who, like Jenkins, became generals.

The Citadel continued to serve the Confederacy until February 18, 1865, when Federal troops entered Charleston and occupied the site. Federal troops in Columbia burned the Arsenal. Today a memorial on the Citadel campus commemorates the cadets who fired on the *Star of the West*.

CIVIL WAR, ALTERNATIVE NAMES FOR

Although most commonly called the Civil War, the sectional conflict that occurred between 1861 and 1865 has many alternative names. All are intended to emphasize a point or support an agenda—for example the "War for States' Rights" or the "War Against Slavery."

During the war, the Confederate government avoided the term "civil war" and referred in official documents to the "War Between the Confederate States of America and the United States of America." This distinction emphasized the Confederate point of view that the Confederacy after secession was its own sovereign nation, rather than merely a region of the United States in rebellion. This interpretation gives rise to the most popular alternative name, the "War Between the States." Some Northerners, on the other hand, chose to emphasize the rebellious nature of the conflict. To this end, the U.S. War Department's seventy-volume collection of official war correspondence is called *The War of the Rebellion: A Compilation of the Official Records of the Union and Confederate Armies.*

CLEBURNE, PATRICK R.
(1828–64)

Patrick R. Cleburne came to the United States from Ireland after unremarkable experiences as a druggist and soldier. He settled in Arkansas and organized a volunteer company called the Yell Rifles on the eve of the Civil War. With this unit he seized the Little Rock Arsenal. He was made a brigadier general on March 4, 1862, and fought at Shiloh, Richmond, and Perryville.

Cleburne was promoted to major general on December 20, 1862, and given command of a division, which he led at Murfreesboro, Chickamauga, and Chattanooga. He excelled during the Atlanta Campaign and was elevated to corps command. In this capacity, Cleburne suggested to General Joseph E. Johnston that slaves should be freed to serve as soldiers. Cleburne's proposal was rejected, although as the Confederacy became increasingly desperate, Congress belatedly

Above: *Irish-born Patrick Cleburne was known as the "Stonewall of the West." He was one of the earliest advocates of enlisting African Americans into the Confederate army.*

authorized this measure on March 13, 1865.

Cleburne was killed during the Battle of Franklin on November 30, 1864. His reputation for discipline and efficiency led to his being called the "Stonewall of the West."

COASTAL DEFENSE

The Confederate States' 3,549 miles of coastline were a mixed blessing. On the one hand, they offered nearly eighty safe harbors for blockade-runners, but on the other hand they presented a great vulnerability to attack by the vast Federal navy. At first, the Confederacy tried to defend far too much of its coastal area. This attempt not only diverted troops from other critical locations, it also proved fruitless against the overwhelming Federal naval advantage.

The Federals developed an admirable strategy of seizing critical ports that could serve as logistical bases for the blockade fleet and then securing those locations with army

troops. Steam power and superior ordnance made easy work of the masonry forts the Confederacy had inherited and the earthen ones they often built. After the loss of Port Royal, South Carolina, in October 1861, the Confederacy realized that it was impossible to defend the entirety of its coast and instituted a new policy to focus its limited resources. Thereafter, the Confederacy abandoned many less strategic areas and strengthened its defenses at key locations such as Charleston, South Carolina, and Wilmington, North Carolina.

COBB, HOWELL
(1815–68)

Howell Cobb was a lawyer, governor of Georgia, and secretary of the treasury who originally spoke out in favor of loyalty to the Union and compromise on slavery. Abraham Lincoln's election convinced Cobb of the need to secede, and he was influential in building support for secession in Georgia. He served as the chairman

Above: *Georgian Howell Cobb served the Confederacy as a politician and general. He was the chairman of the Montgomery Convention, where his moderate views helped counter those of the fire-eaters.*

of the Montgomery Convention and president of the Provisional Congress. In both cases he was a voice of moderation.

Cobb was appointed as a brigadier general in the Confederate army on February 13, 1862, and fought during the Peninsula Campaign, Second Manassas, and Antietam. He was promoted to major general on September 9, 1863. As commander of the District of Georgia, he played an important role in mediating between Governor Joseph E. Brown and President Jefferson Davis. He helped defeat Brigadier General George Stoneman Jr. at Macon on July 30, 1864.

After the war Cobb was a successful lawyer and planter, but did not reenter politics. His brother, Thomas Reade Rootes Cobb, was also a Confederate politician and general.

COLD HARBOR, BATTLE OF

- ❖ DATE: June 3, 1864

- ❖ LOCATION: Hanover County, Virginia

- ❖ ARMY OF NORTHERN VIRGINIA (C): 59,000

- ❖ ARMY OF THE POTOMAC (U.S.): 108,000

- ❖ CASUALTIES: 4,595 (C); 12,737 (U.S.)

After the Battle of Hanover Junction, Lieutenant General Ulysses S. Grant resumed his tireless pressure on General Robert E. Lee in front of Richmond, Virginia. On May 27, 1864, Grant crossed the Pamunkey and then turned northwest and west to threaten Lee's railroad

communications. Grant then moved to Totopotomoy Creek, where Lee blocked him again. After that engagement, both forces began moving to the vital road junction at Cold Harbor. The battle fought there on June 3 was an overwhelming Confederate victory, but only served to temporarily slow the relentless Federal advance.

As both Lee and Grant rushed forces to secure the Cold Harbor crossroads, elements of Major General Fitzhugh Lee's cavalry division clashed with those of Major General Philip H. Sheridan on May 31 and continued to struggle for the next two days.

Below: *The Battle of Cold Harbor was a lopsided Confederate victory, but even such devastating losses could not stem Ulysses Grant's relentless pressure on Robert E. Lee.*

Grant planned a general assault for June 2, but later delayed it until the next day. By then, the Army of the Potomac numbered 108,000 men against Lee's 59,000.

FACING UP TO THE WORST

The odds were somewhat narrowed by the defender's advantage Lee had gained by positioning his men in strong zigzag trenches that afforded interlocking fires. The Confederates had also expertly blended their positions in with natural folds of the ground to avoid detection.

The Federal soldiers knew it would be a hard fight. As they prepared for the attack, many wrote their names and addresses on slips of paper and pinned them on the backs of their coats. These precursors to the dog tags familiar to today's soldiers would be used to identify dead bodies and help in notifying loved ones back home.

As was often the case, Grant gave no instructions about the specifics of the attack, leaving those decisions to the individual corps commanders. There had been no substantive reconnaissance of the Confederate lines, and the Federals lacked a true picture of the objective, leading Major General William Smith, commander of the Eighteenth Corps, to complain of "the utter absence of any military plan." Nonetheless, on June 3 at 4:30 a.m., 35,000 infantrymen of the Second, Sixth, and Eighteenth Corps began moving toward the Confederate defenses several hundred yards away.

The Confederate officers had trouble convincing their men to hold their fire against such a tempting target, and when the order was finally given, the results were devastating.

The attackers were helplessly exposed, and one Confederate confessed, "It seemed almost like murder to fire." The Federal line quickly broke, and the battle took on the nature of a series of isolated individual struggles.

LOSSES BY THE THOUSANDS

Enfilading fire from the carefully prepared trenches tore the attack to pieces. An hour into the attack, the hapless Federals were hugging the ground just trying to stay alive. In spite of the carnage, Grant remained remarkably aloof. He did not ride out to the corps headquarters until around noon and only then learned the attack was a failure. Between 5,600 and 7,000 Federals had become casualties, most in the first fifteen minutes of the attack. Lee lost less than 1,500. One Confederate concluded that Cold Harbor was "perhaps the easiest victory ever granted to the Confederate arms by the folly of the Federal commanders."

Federals were quick to criticize the attack as well. One captain called it "the greatest and most inexcusable slaughter of the whole war." Colonel Emory Upton wrote his sister that he was "disgusted with the generalship displayed; our men have, in many instances, been foolishly and wantonly sacrificed." Even Grant confessed, "I regret this assault more than any one I ever ordered."

Below: *Gaines' Mill lay about ten miles northeast of the Confederate capital of Richmond, which was McClellan's objective during the Peninsula Campaign.*

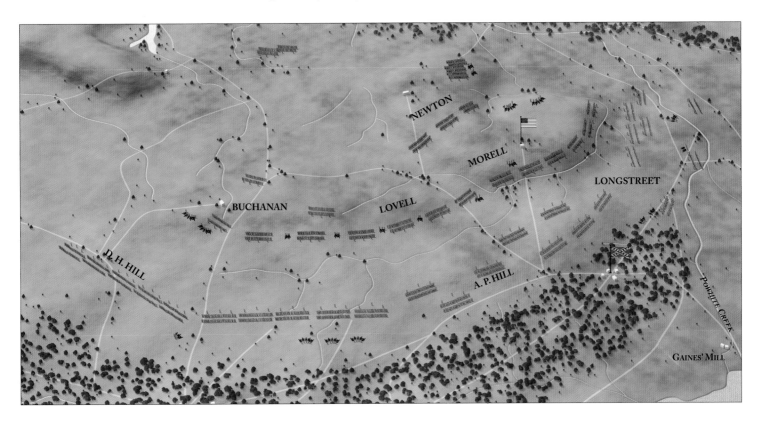

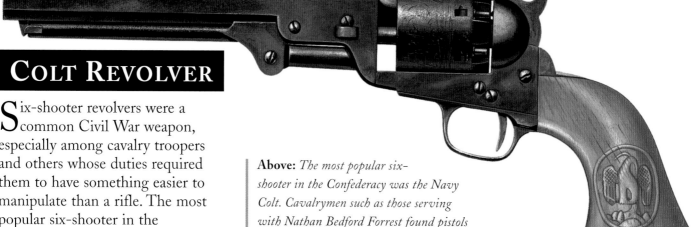

COLT REVOLVER

Six-shooter revolvers were a common Civil War weapon, especially among cavalry troopers and others whose duties required them to have something easier to manipulate than a rifle. The most popular six-shooter in the Confederacy was the Colt Navy Model 1851. While some Southerners had original models, many had copies that became known as "Confederate Colts." These variations closely resembled the original except for a "dragoon-type" barrel that was partially rounded rather than fully octagonal. This modification made the revolvers easier to make and therefore cut production times. Thomas Leech and Charles H. Rigdon manufactured the premier Confederate Colts.

COMMUNICATION SYSTEM

The Confederate Signal Corps was established on May 29, 1862, and operated in a semi-independent status under the general direction of General Samuel Cooper's Office of the Adjutant General. By the end of the war, the corps numbered some 1,500 members.

Strategic and operational communications in the Civil War were greatly facilitated by the telegraph, which connected field headquarters with rear areas. Line-of-sight communications for both armies were based on Albert J. Myer's "wigwag" system that used five separate, numbered movements of a single flag to communicate messages. Myer became the first

Above: *The most popular six-shooter in the Confederacy was the Navy Colt. Cavalrymen such as those serving with Nathan Bedford Forrest found pistols to be easier to use than rifles while riding.*

Chief of the Federal Signal Corps while one of his prewar assistants, E. Porter Alexander, went on to organize the Confederate Signal Corps. In an early example of the system's utility, Alexander signaled Colonel Nathan Evans that a Federal force was turning his flank at the Battle of First Manassas.

COMPROMISE OF 1850

The Compromise of 1850 reflected growing concern in the South that the balance of power in the United States was dangerously shifting to the free states. At the heart of the issue was the status of territory gained in the Mexican War. In the midst of this debate, the Southern champion John C. Calhoun made his final appearance on the Senate floor but was too weak to read his passionate argument that a constitutional

Below: *A symbolic group portrait eulogizing legislative efforts, notably the Compromise of 1850, to preserve the Union. The figures pictured here are (front row, left to right): Winfield Scott, Lewis Cass, Henry Clay, John Calhoun, Daniel Webster, and (holding a shield) Millard Fillmore. Calhoun and Webster stand with their hands resting on the Constitution, a bust of George Washington between them.*

amendment be written to secure equal representation for the South. James Murray Mason, a future Confederate diplomat, read the declaration for the dying Calhoun, and Jefferson Davis emerged from the crisis as the leading Southern spokesman in Calhoun's stead.

With the assistance of Daniel Webster and Stephen A. Douglas, the "Great Compromiser" Henry Clay proposed a solution that, among other things, would admit California to the Union as a free state, abolish the slave trade in Washington, D.C., and enact a tough new fugitive slave law.

While abolitionists such as William H. Seward argued that slavery was a moral evil that could not be compromised with, and fire-eaters such as William Lowndes Yancey demanded explicit recognition of slavery in the western territories, moderates eventually secured the measure's

enactment into law in September 1850. As with the earlier Missouri Compromise, an immediate disaster had been averted, but the tension had long- lasting effects. The debate over the compromise resulted in severe splits in both major parties. Northern antislavery Whigs were now suspicious of Southern Whigs, and Southern Democrats and Free-Soil Democrats were both at odds with the national Democratic Party.

CONFEDERATE CABINET

The Confederate Cabinet was largely ineffective in formulating the comprehensive policies that the Confederacy needed to build the institutions of a nation. In many ways, President Jefferson Davis appears to have ensured this outcome by his

selections for his cabinet. Davis's leadership style discouraged disagreement, so he often picked cabinet members who shared his views. The resultant groupthink failed to produce the dialogue needed to create a holistic war effort. Davis also believed it was important to maintain a broad state representation in his cabinet, so he tended to distribute positions based on this consideration rather than qualifications of the individual. In the final analysis, the Confederate Cabinet was an organization that

Below: *A group portrait of the Confederate Cabinet, including President Jefferson Davis, Vice President Alexander H. Stephens, Attorney General Judah P. Benjamin, Secretary of the Navy Stephen R. Mallory, Secretary of the Treasury Christopher G. Memminger, Secretary of War Leroy P. Walker, Postmaster General John H. Reagan, and Secretary of State Robert A. Toombs.*

had been built to fail, and it did.

Davis's cabinet suffered from personnel turbulence. Only Secretary of the Navy Stephen R. Mallory and Postmaster General John H. Reagan held their posts for the duration of the war. On the other hand, Davis had three secretaries of state, a remarkable six secretaries of war, two secretaries of the treasury, and four attorneys general. Judah P. Benjamin personally served as attorney general, secretary of war, and secretary of state. Mallory, Reagan, and Benjamin were all competent officials whose accomplishments were limited by the scarce resources available to them and the narrow role Davis assigned his secretaries, rather than by their personal talent and effort.

On the other hand, Secretary of the Treasury Christopher G. Memminger and Secretary of War Leroy P. Walker proved less adept at fulfilling their responsibilities. Memminger showed little imagination in pursuing a ruinous fiscal policy based on paper money. Walker was simply ill-suited for his post and had been selected for political reasons.

Many observers believe that the compliant Walker had been chosen because Davis, confident in his own military expertise, intended to be his own secretary of war. The fact that six people held this seemingly critical office does suggest that Davis was a difficult man to work for.

CONFISCATION ACTS

In 1861, and then again in 1862, the Federal government issued Confiscation Acts that addressed the delicate issue of how to handle slaves in areas the Federal army had occupied. In May 1861 Major General Benjamin F. Butler had initiated a policy in which he declared that slaves were contraband, just like any property seized during time of war. Although Butler's action was contrary to official Federal policy, it continued informally until August, when Congress enacted the first Confiscation Act. This law allowed Federal authorities to confiscate slaves used by Confederates for military purposes. Although the act was a small step on the long road toward emancipation, its purpose was focused more on harming the master than helping the slave. Its primary intent was to deprive the Confederacy of the military and economic benefit of slaves who were being used to erect fortifications, dig trenches, transport supplies, and for other activities that aided the Confederate war effort. The law did not attempt to address any rights of the freed slaves or to even guarantee their freedom when the war ended.

A second Confiscation Act was passed in July 1862 that expanded the subject slaves from those being used to support the Confederacy to all slaves owned by a Confederate master. Owners who had taken a loyalty oath were allowed to keep their slaves. Again, the focus of the act was not primarily emancipation but rather weakening the Confederacy. The two Confiscation Acts are significant moments in the gradual Federal shift from a policy of conciliation to one of total war.

CONGRESS, CONFEDERATE STATES

On February 4, 1861, delegates from the seceded states met in Montgomery, Alabama, to organize a Confederate government. The states chose their delegates in various ways, but each state sent the same number of delegates to Montgomery as had been its number of representatives in the U.S. Congress. These delegates formed the provisional Confederate Congress, which conducted five sessions, lasting until February 17, 1862. Elections for the First Confederate Congress were held on November 6, 1861, and this body held four sessions between February 18, 1862, and February 17, 1864.

The Second Confederate Congress convened on May 2, 1864, after elections in 1863. The Confederate voters had used the elections to express their dissatisfaction with the course of the war. In this congress, the number of openly anti–Davis administration members among the representatives rose from twenty-six to forty-one out of 106 districts and in the senate from eleven to twelve out of twenty-six members. It held two sessions, adjourning for good on March 18, 1865.

THE MEMBERSHIP

The total number of members in the Confederate Congress was 267, a figure made up of thirty-six senators and 231 congressmen who served in either the provisional or permanent Congress, or both. In addition to the eleven seceded states, Missouri and Kentucky also had full members in the congress. Nonvoting members represented the Arizona Territory and the Cherokee, Choctaw, Creek, and Seminole Native Americans. Most Confederate congressmen had some political experience from serving in the state legislature, the U.S. Congress, the state courts, or a secessionist convention, and they tended to know their colleagues either personally or at least by reputation. Most were also fairly well off financially and were unlikely to have served previously in the military.

The Confederate Congress represented varied interests, and in many ways lacked the resolve to

Above: *Howell Cobb presides over a meeting of the Confederate Senate in Montgomery, Alabama, in February 1861.*

make the sacrifices necessary to fight a war. A key problem was a lack of strong leadership. Vice President Alexander H. Stephens rarely appeared before the congress after 1862, and many of the South's most able leaders felt their place of duty was with the army in the field, rather than in political office. Absenteeism became an increasing problem as members whose districts had been overrun by Federal troops felt little obligation to continue their duties. High turnover presented another difficulty. Of the 146 legislators who sat at one time or another in the First Confederate Congress, only forty-six had been in the Provisional Congress, a change of over 68 percent. Turnover

between the First and Second Confederate Congresses was also a significant 39 percent.

The congress was also divided in its support for either strong central authority or states' rights. However, although many of its members opposed Davis, only one of his thirty-nine vetoes was overridden. Still, Davis lacked the political skill to manipulate the congress's lack of unity and instead became overly reliant on his generals. For its part, the Confederate Congress failed to make any dramatic contribution to the Confederate war effort.

CONSCRIPTION

Even before he became secretary of war on March 22, 1862, George W. Randolph had been considering how to address the

personnel problem the Confederacy would face when its initial enlistments expired. On March 28, President Jefferson Davis acted on Randolph's recommendations and requested the Confederate Congress pass the first military draft on the North American continent. Although the measure posed a challenge to the traditional Southern characteristics of states' rights and individualism, the congress approved the legislation on April 16. Under its provisions, all white males between eighteen and thirty-five years of age were obligated to three years' service, or less if the war ended sooner. A second law in September raised the upper age limit to forty-five. Those already in the service would remain in it, and the twelve-month volunteers received a sixty-day furlough. In a major concession to

manpower by assigning military details. Under this practice, if the government considered a man to be more valuable in his civil capacity, he could be drafted and then detailed back to his previous job. This new act was poorly implemented and only 15,820 conscripts joined the army between January 1 and April 1. About the same number volunteered, but the Conscription Bureau exempted 26,000 and detailed another 13,000 to critical wartime industries. The result was a net loss of personnel in the military ranks.

While conscription was no doubt an imperfectly executed system, it did serve to mobilize almost the entire Southern military population. At one time or another, about 750,000 of the approximately 1,000,000 white Southern men between the ages of eighteen and forty-five served in the Confederate army. About 82,000 of these were drafted. Facing the much larger population of the North, it is hard to imagine the Confederacy being able to fight as it did without conscription.

Above: *A facetious view of the Confederate States' early efforts to man a volunteer army during the Civil War. While this cartoon depicts a Confederate soldier being enlisted at bayonet point, most Southerners joined the army as volunteers rather than conscripts.*

individualism, soldiers were given the privilege of electing officers at the company level. The act also allowed men eligible for the draft to obtain a qualified substitute to serve in their stead. On April 21 procedures were added to cover those exempted from service based on the possession of special skills or the holding of important positions that made the individual more valuable in a civil than a military capacity. Classes of exemption included national and state officers, railroad workers, druggists, professors, school-teachers, miners, ministers, pilots, nurses, and iron-furnace and foundry employees. The War Department was authorized to grant other exemptions as necessary.

Initially the Adjutant and Inspector General's Office enforced the law, but in December a Conscription Board was created. In a major expansion of central authority, the national government,

rather than the states, was given responsibility for recruiting and organizing units. The Davis administration used its discretionary power to channel exempted workers into manufacturing establishments critical to the war effort and away from nonessential activities.

While the Conscription Act motivated many Southerners to volunteer rather than suffer the stigma of being drafted, others resisted. The substitute and exemption systems were especially rife for abuse. For example, some state governors created superfluous state offices to facilitate exemptions. Georgia governor Joseph E. Brown was particularly resistant to conscription in his state. Class tensions were also exacerbated in October when an exemption was created for owners and overseers of twenty or more slaves, a measure that alienated many Southern yeomen.

As the war dragged on, Davis identified the need for additional manpower. A new Conscription Act was passed on February 17, 1864, that drastically limited exemptions and expanded the age limits to between seventeen and fifty. It also allowed the government to allocate Southern

CONSTITUTION OF THE CONFEDERATE STATES

The Constitution of the Confederates States was hammered out by hardworking delegates at the convention that opened in Montgomery, Alabama, on February 4, 1861. Members of the drafting committee both worked on the document and attended sessions of congress. By February

28, a draft was ready for debate. On March 11, the constitution was unanimously adopted.

Fire-eater Robert Barnwell Rhett had served as the chairman of the drafting committee, but the final version was much more moderate than Rhett had hoped for. In fact, the Confederate Constitution was remarkably similar to the United States Constitution and seemed to indicate its framers did not want a country radically different from the one they left. The document struck a finely tuned balance that reflected the South's constitutionalist background. The preamble spoke of states acting in their "sovereign and independent character," but also of establishing a "permanent federal government." The radical rhetoric that had helped fuel secession seemed to subside once it had accomplished its original purpose. Instead, the moderate voices of Alexander H. Stephens and Robert A. Toombs had the most influence

Below: *As the Federal army occupied Southern territory, the North had to establish a policy for treating the former slaves. Part of this effort was this contraband school, or freedman's village, at Arlington, Virginia.*

during the ten days the draft constitution was debated.

The major difference found in the Confederate Constitution was an explicit protection of slavery, which included the right to take slave property into the territories. Otherwise, changes from the United States Constitution were mainly small details that reflected the Southern way of life. As a largely agricultural society, duties for the protection of special industries were prohibited. Reflecting a tight economy, the Confederates provided for a post office that had to operate using only the income it generated. Being wary of centralized power, they limited the presidential tenure to one six-year term. On the other hand, the president had the power of item veto, and the congress was restricted from making appropriations not specifically requested by the executive unless the appropriations received a two-thirds majority in both houses. In many ways, in theory anyway, President Jefferson Davis had more constitutional power than his Federal counterpart.

CONTRABAND POLICY

In May 1861 Major General Benjamin F. Butler put into place a policy in which he declared that slaves were contraband, just like any property seized during time of war. Butler's terms required a master to pledge loyalty to the Union in order to get his slave back. If the master refused, Butler would free the slave.

CONTRABAND VILLAGES
Subsequent Federal commanders began adopting this policy, and numerous contraband villages sprung up in occupied areas of the Confederacy.

Although Butler's declaration was in conflict with the official Federal position that slaves be returned to their owners, for political and practical reasons, President Abraham Lincoln quietly allowed the contraband policy to continue.

In August, the U.S. Congress took action to formalize the procedures for handling contraband slaves by enacting the first Confiscation Act.

COOPER, SAMUEL (1798–1876)

Above: *Although not as well known as the commanders of the field armies, Samuel Cooper was the highest-ranking officer in the Confederacy.*

Samuel Cooper graduated from West Point in 1815. He was born in Hackensack, New Jersey, but his marriage into an aristocratic Virginia family soon led him to adopt Southern ways and join Virginia in secession. He was named as a full general on May 16, 1861, becoming the highest-ranking officer in the Confederate army.

Cooper's prewar experience had largely been high-level staff and administrative work, and this background made him valuable in helping raise and organize the new Confederate army. His efforts in this regard made a marked contribution to the Confederate success at First Manassas. Although too old for field command, Cooper served throughout the war as an "adjutant and inspector general." He was very close to President Jefferson Davis and was one of the few advisers whom Davis regularly consulted for strategic counsel.

COOPERATIONISTS

Cooperationist was a rather ambiguous title for a variety of Southerners who in one way or another favored exploring all avenues of obtaining Southern rights before resorting to secession. They tended to adopt a relatively conciliatory approach to the sectional crisis and generally favored unified action. They considered options ranging from devout Unionism through unified secession to delay. Delegates to the state secession conventions were often categorized as secessionists, cooperationists, or Unionists. Christopher G. Memminger, who became the Confederacy's secretary of the treasury, was a cooperationist, as was South Carolina governor William Henry Gist.

COPPERHEADS

Copperheads were Northern antiwar Democrats who all had some degree of sympathy for the Confederacy. Their name comes from their habit of wearing lapel pins of Native American heads cut from copper pennies. Overall, the strong executive action taken by President Abraham Lincoln, including arrests, suspension of habeas corpus, and censorship of the press, served to suppress meaningful copperhead activity. Alexander Long and Fernando Wood were notable copperheads, but Clement L. Vallandigham was the most famous.

Copperheads were an

Right: *Clement Vallandigham was expelled from the North as a result of his advocacy of negotiation with the Confederacy.*

important part of the Confederate effort to direct a "fifth column" operation to exploit Northern war weariness. Largely based in Canada and well financed by cotton sales, Confederate agents worked with copperheads and other sympathizers to create an amorphous secret society known variously as the Knights of the Golden Circle, the Order of American Knights, and the Sons of Liberty to help further a pro-Confederate peace. The organization was most active in the Midwest, where it claimed to have hundreds of thousands of members ready to take up arms against the Federal government. Such a grandiose action never took place, but there were lesser attempts to burn New York City, capture a warship on the Great Lakes, destroy railroad bridges, and steal money from Northern banks. While the fifth column showed little tangible success in its direct operations, its mere existence had a demoralizing effect in some Northern circles.

Copperheads were a powerful force at the Democratic convention

Above: *This cartoon shows three caricatured copperheads advancing on Columbia. It depicts how many in the North viewed the copperheads as insidious threats to the Union.*

in Chicago in August 1864. They succeeded in dictating a platform that declared the war a failure and sought to restore the Union based on the prewar status quo. With their backing, George B. McClellan, still holding the rank of major general in the Federal army but without a command, was nominated as a peace candidate. With war weariness besieging the Union, it seemed as if McClellan might be a viable candidate, but the successful conclusion of Major General William T. Sherman's Atlanta Campaign helped ensure President Abraham Lincoln's reelection.

CORINTH, BATTLES OF

❖ DATE: May 29–30 and October 3–4, 1862

❖ LOCATION: Alcorn County, Mississippi

❖ ARMY OF WEST TENNESSEE (C): 22,000

❖ ARMY OF THE MISSISSIPPI (U.S.): 23,000

❖ CASUALTIES: 4,467 (C); 3,090 (U.S.)

The importance of Corinth, Mississippi, lay in the fact that it was the junction of the Memphis and Charleston Railroad and the Mobile and Ohio Railroad. Control of Corinth meant control of railroads from Columbus, Mississippi, and Memphis, Tennessee, as well as those running south into Mississippi and

eastward to connect with Nashville and Chattanooga, Tennessee. So long as the Confederates controlled Corinth, it was possible for them to send reinforcements between Mississippi and Tennessee, a risk the Federals could not tolerate.

After the April 6, 1862, Battle of Shiloh, General Pierre Gustave Toutant Beauregard withdrew to Corinth and began preparing a deliberate defense. On April 29, Major General Henry Halleck began a slow march toward Corinth that gave Beauregard plenty of time to study the situation. By the time Halleck reached Corinth after a month, Beauregard was in no mood to give battle to the much larger Federal force. During the night of May 29, the Confederates withdrew and Halleck took possession of the town.

On July 11, 1862, President Abraham Lincoln ordered Halleck

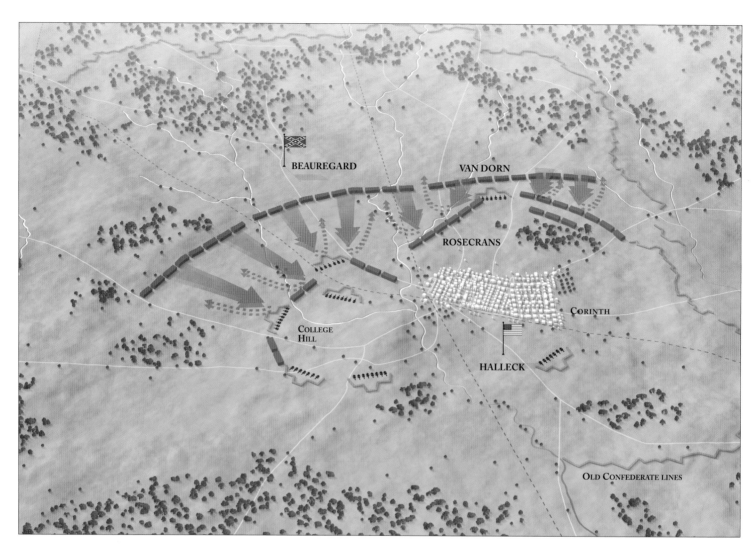

Above: *Corinth was a small railroad junction that gained huge strategic significance as a key to operations in Tennessee. The Federals eventually established permanent control over the town following Van Dorn's failed attack in October 1862.*

to Washington to become the general in chief. Major General Ulysses S. Grant replaced Halleck and inherited a widely scattered army that included Major General William S. Rosecrans's force at Corinth. Confederate major general Earl Van Dorn considered Rosecrans to be isolated and developed a plan to defeat him, seize the railroad junction at Corinth, and use it to support a campaign into western Tennessee.

Right: *Federal troops defend earthworks against Confederate attack at Corinth, on May 30, 1862.*

On October 3–4, Van Dorn attacked. He experienced some local success, but as the Federal defenses contracted, they became stronger and held. Van Dorn was forced to withdraw after suffering 4,467

casualties, compared to 3,090 for the Federals. While Grant was disappointed Van Dorn had not been destroyed, securing Corinth was still a major victory for the Federals, because the Confederates

in Mississippi could no longer send reinforcements to Tennessee. Grant was now free to explore greater opportunities in Mississippi, and he began planning his Vicksburg Campaign in earnest.

CORPS

Corps are military organizations consisting of two or more divisions. Corps in the Confederate army were not authorized until September 18, 1862, and not actually formed until November 6. Prior to that, groups of divisions were commonly called "wings." The creation of corps helped improve tactical flexibility and helped army commanders effect greater coordination and cooperation. Sometimes corps were designated by numerals and sometimes by the name of their commander. Corps in the Confederate army were commanded by lieutenant generals.

(In the Federal army, corps were commanded by major generals.) As the war dragged on and the Confederacy suffered increased leadership casualties, it became difficult to find qualified corps commanders. For example, when Lieutenant General Stonewall Jackson was killed, General Robert E. Lee felt compelled to reorganize his army from two to three corps because he did not feel he had an officer capable of replacing Jackson directly. The leadership shortage resulted in several division commanders being promoted to corps commands that were beyond their leadership skill.

COTTON

In 1792 Eli Whitney Jr. left his native Massachusetts to become a private tutor on a plantation in Georgia. The type of cotton that grew in the interior of Georgia had

sticky green seeds that were difficult to separate from the cotton bolls. With the support of his employer, Catherine Greene, Whitney invented a cotton gin to expedite this time-consuming part of the cotton processing cycle.

Britain's cotton mills had an enormous appetite for raw cotton, and Whitney's invention allowed cotton production to accelerate to meet this demand. In 1800 America was producing 156,000 bales of cotton. By 1860 this amount had skyrocketed to more than 4,000,000. This increase in production necessitated an increase in slaves, and the number of slaves in America grew from 700,000 in 1790 to 4,000,000 in 1860.

Below: The First Cotton Gin *from* Harper's Weekly, *December 1869. Eli Whitney's cotton gin helped streamline the processing of cotton, which resulted in an increased demand for slaves.*

On the eve of the Civil War, cotton was America's leading export and the economic backbone of the South. A significant part of Britain's industry was cotton textiles, and the South provided 75 percent of the cotton that fueled Britain's mills. The result was that cotton was a critical component of the social, economic, and diplomatic fabric of the Confederacy.

Socially, cotton production created the need for large numbers of slaves. Economically, it allowed the new nation to generate revenue. Diplomatically, it created the "King Cotton" strategy through which the Confederacy hoped to attract European intervention in the war.

Below: *A contemporary illustration shows Confederate forces attacking Federal infantry at the Battle of the Crater. Although of no strategic significance, the battle resulted in huge losses for the Union.*

CRATER, BATTLE OF THE

❖ DATE: July 30, 1864

❖ LOCATION: Petersburg, Virginia

❖ ARMY OF NORTHERN VIRGINIA (C), ELEMENTS: not known

❖ NINTH CORPS (U.S.): not known

❖ CASUALTIES: 1,032 (C); 5,300 (U.S.)

On July 30, 1864, in an attempt to break the stalemate at Petersburg, Federal soldiers detonated four tons of black powder in a mine they had dug under the Confederate position. The explosion created a hole 175 feet long, sixty feet wide, and thirty feet deep. For at least 600 feet on either side of the crater, the Confederate line was thrown into havoc. However, this initial Federal advantage of surprise gave way to mismanagement and delay, and the Confederates recovered. The Federals then were largely trapped in the crater. In what became known as the Battle of the Crater, the Federals lost about 5,300 soldiers. Seemingly impervious to the losses and concerned only with the bungled attack, Grant considered the fiasco to be "the saddest affair I have witnessed in the war. Such opportunity for carrying fortifications I have never seen and do not expect again to have." Confederate losses were just 1,032.

CRITTENDEN COMPROMISE

The Crittenden Compromise of 1860 was a last-ditch effort to avoid civil war. It was proposed by Senator John J. Crittenden, a Kentuckian who opposed secession and supported President Abraham

Lincoln. Under the plan, the terms of the Missouri Compromise would be extended to the Pacific Ocean by an unamendable amendment to the U.S. Constitution. Crittenden's proposal was poorly received in both the North and the South.

NO DEAL

Radical Republicans wrote privately to Lincoln asking him for his advice and found Lincoln was against it. As many in the South were beginning to believe, the balance of power was shifting to the non-slave states, and there seemed little motivation to compromise from a position of power.

At the other end of the spectrum, Southern fire-eaters had already committed themselves to secession, so the Crittenden Compromise was a failure.

Above: *John J. Crittenden was a senator from Kentucky whose last-ditch effort at a compromise failed to prevent the Civil War.*

Above: *A thirty-two-pounder cannon from the wreck of the Confederate sloop of war CSS* Alabama *is seen at the U.S. Naval History and Heritage Command laboratory warehouse in Washington.*

CSS *ALABAMA*

The CSS *Alabama* was the most famous and effective of the Confederate commerce raiders, sinking, burning, or capturing sixty-nine ships valued at $6 million in its impressive career. The *Alabama* was a 1,050-ton steam screw sloop of war built at Birkenhead, England, as part of James D. Bulloch's efforts to surreptitiously obtain ships for the Confederacy. John Laird Sons and Company built the ship, and it was launched as *Enrica*, under the guise of being a merchant ship. It then rendezvoused with supply ships and was outfitted at sea as a cruiser and commissioned as the CSS *Alabama* on August 24, 1862. Captain Raphael Semmes was its flamboyant and driven commander.

The *Alabama* cruised in the North Atlantic and West Indies throughout 1862, capturing over two dozen Union merchant ships. Most of the prizes were burned, with the notable exception of the mail steamer *Ariel* taken off Cuba on December 7 with hundreds of passengers on board. On January 11, 1863, Semmes descended on Galveston, Texas, planning to harass a Federal force he thought was assembling there. In reality,

Confederate forces had recently recaptured the city, and Semmes took advantage of the changed situation to sink the USS *Hatteras*. He then sailed the *Alabama* into the South Atlantic, stopping at Cape Town in August, continuing on to the East Indies, and making a call at Singapore in December. Throughout 1863, the *Alabama* seized nearly forty more merchant ships and created panic in the U.S. maritime trade.

As Semmes pressed the *Alabama*, heavy usage began to take its toll. The ship's speed was slowed, and the *Alabama* captured only a few ships in 1864. Realizing a major overhaul was needed, Semmes brought the *Alabama* to Cherbourg, France, on June 11 for repairs. The USS *Kearsarge* soon arrived off the port, and on June 19 the *Alabama* steamed out to meet the challenge. In an hour of intense combat, the *Kearsarge* sunk the *Alabama*. The *Kearsarge* rescued most of the Confederates, but others, including Semmes, escaped to the English yacht *Deerhound*.

The French navy mine hunter *Circe* discovered the *Alabama*'s remains while conducting operational exercises off Cherbourg, in 1984. Since then, French and American researchers have conducted archaeological investigations of the site.

CSS *ALBEMARLE*

The CSS *Albemarle* was a relatively small ironclad ram built on the Roanoke River at Edwards Ferry, North Carolina. It was commissioned in April 1864 under the charge of Commander James Cooke, and saw its first action on April 19 as part of a joint army–navy operation against Plymouth, North Carolina. The *Albemarle* sank the USS *Southfield* and drove off the USS *Miami* and two other gunboats, isolating the Federal garrison from its waterborne communications. A

Below: *The USS* Sassacus *was badly damaged when it rammed the Confederate ironclad* Albemarle *in May 1864.*

Confederate brigade commanded by Brigadier General Robert F. Hoke then surrounded the town and used infantry attacks as well as fire from his artillery and the *Albemarle* to compel the Federals to surrender. The stunning victory earned Hoke a promotion to major general.

The *Albemarle* was back in action on May 5, joining the *Cotton Plant* and *Bombshell* in an attack against seven Federal blockade ships in the mouth of the Roanoke. The battle ended in a draw, but the *Albemarle*'s presence was rapidly becoming a threat to the Federal position on North Carolina's coastal rivers. Lieutenant William Cushing finally silenced the *Albemarle* in a daring raid on the night of October 27–28. Cushing took the torpedo boat *Picket Boat Number One* upriver to Plymouth and sank the *Albemarle* with a spar.

Once the Federals recaptured Plymouth, they refloated the *Albemarle* and took it to the Norfolk Navy Yard in April 1865, where it remained until it was sold in October 1867.

CSS *ARKANSAS*

The CSS *Arkansas* was an ironclad ram that was still under construction at Memphis, Tennessee, as Federal forces closed in on the city in May 1862. To escape capture, the *Arkansas* was towed up the Yazoo River to Yazoo City, Mississippi, where work was resumed. On July 15, 1862, Lieutenant Isaac Brown took it down the Yazoo, where it encountered the Federal gunboats *Carondelet* and *Tyler* and the ram *Queen of the West*. The *Arkansas* badly damaged the two gunboats and continued on into the Mississippi River, where it fought its way through the Federal fleet around Vicksburg. While at Vicksburg, the *Arkansas* was attacked by the *Queen of the West* and the ironclad *Essex*, but not seriously damaged. It was then ordered to assist Confederate forces under Major General John C. Breckinridge who were attempting to retake Baton Rouge, Louisiana. In the process, the *Arkansas* suffered a

Above: *The CSS* Arkansas *helped the Confederates defend Vicksburg, but was ultimately destroyed to prevent capture after fighting around Baton Rouge.*

severe machinery breakdown on August 6 while battling the *Essex*. Brown ran the *Arkansas* ashore and blew it up to prevent capture.

CSS *FLORIDA*

The CSS *Florida* was one of the Confederate ships built in England as the result of efforts by James D. Bulloch. It was a steam screw cruiser of about 700 tons. It was built under the name *Oreto*, and sailed in March 1862 for the Bahamas as a merchant ship. There it was fitted as a naval vessel and commissioned in August 1862. Its commander was Lieutenant John N. Maffitt, who led it first to Cuba and then through the Federal blockade into Mobile, Alabama, where it completed its outfitting.

The *Florida* ran the blockade on January 16, 1863, and began an eight-month cruise in the Atlantic and West Indies. It captured twenty-two prizes before going to Brest, France, in August 1863. In February 1864 it took to sea again, this time commanded by Lieutenant Charles Morris. It took another eleven prizes before arriving in Bahia, Brazil, in October 1864. On October 7, the USS *Wachusett* attacked it while it was anchored in port, captured it, and towed it out to sea. This act was a violation of Brazilian neutrality and, after the *Florida* was taken to the United States, a court ordered it returned to Brazil. On November 28, 1864, it was accidentally sunk off Newport News, Virginia, before it could make the journey.

Below: *The CSS* Florida *was built in England and first commanded by the capable John Maffitt. All told, the vessel captured thirty-three prizes.*

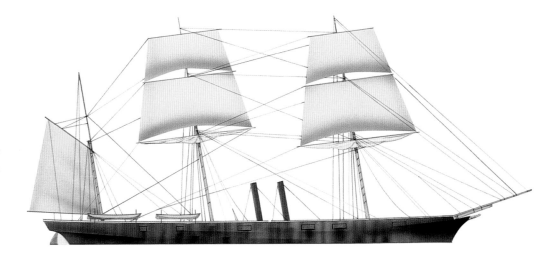

CSS *HUNLEY*

The CSS *Hunley* was a cigar-shaped submarine forty feet long, three and a half feet wide, and four feet deep, and was one of the many imaginative devices employed by the Confederates in the defense of Charleston, South Carolina. The *Hunley* was designed for a crew of nine: one man to steer and the other eight to power the vessel by hand-turning a crankshaft that moved the propeller. In spite of sinking twice and drowning thirteen men, including its builder, Horace Hunley, an intrepid third crew of volunteers stepped forward. On the night of February 17, 1864, this crew approached the 1,934-ton Federal screw sloop *Housatonic*.

Below: *The CSS* Hunley *made history by sinking the USS* Housatonic *off the coast of Charleston in February 1864.*

The *Housatonic* spotted the *Hunley* and engaged it with small arms and tried to escape, but it was too late. The *Hunley* exploded its 130-pound spar torpedo, and the *Housatonic* became the first ship in the history of naval warfare to be sunk by a submarine. The blast, however, likely damaged the *Hunley* as well, and it sunk while returning to shore.

The wreckage of the *Hunley* was discovered off of Sullivan's Island in 1995 and recovered in 2000. DNA was used to identify eight crewmen who were later buried in Magnolia Cemetery in Charleston in 2004.

CSS *SHENANDOAH*

The CSS *Shenandoah* was a 1,160-ton steam screw cruiser purchased in Britain by Confederate naval agent James D. Bulloch. The ship was launched at Glasgow, Scotland, in August 1863 as the civilian steamer *Sea King* and then secretly purchased by the Confederacy in September 1864. It put to sea in October 1864, under the cover story that it was headed for India on a commercial voyage. Instead, the *Sea King* rendezvoused at sea off Madeira with another ship bearing Confederate navy officers, a partial crew, and the heavy guns and other equipment needed to refit it as a warship. Lieutenant James I. Waddell superintended this work and became the vessel's commander when it was commissioned as the CSS *Shenandoah* on October 19, 1864.

Waddell sailed the *Shenandoah* through the South Atlantic and into the Indian Ocean. By the end of the year, he had captured nine U.S.-flagged merchant vessels,

sinking or burning all but two. In late January 1865, the *Shenandoah* arrived at Melbourne, Australia, where it underwent repairs, took on provisions, and added forty crew members. After three celebratory and relaxing weeks in port, the *Shenandoah* returned to sea.

Waddell initially planned to attack the American South Pacific whaling fleet, but could not find sufficient targets. Instead, he headed for the North Pacific and, in early April, he seized four Federal merchant ships in the Eastern Carolinas. He resupplied his ship from the captured stocks and was cruising northward when the Civil War ended. Unaware of the Confederacy's collapse, Waddell continued his mission. Between June 22 and 28, the *Shenandoah* captured two dozen more vessels. Waddell then plotted a course for San Francisco, California, which he believed would be weakly defended.

On August 2, Waddell encountered a British ship that had left San Francisco less than two weeks before. The crew of this vessel informed Waddell that the war was over. Waddell then disarmed his ship and set sail for England. The *Shenandoah* rounded Cape Horn in mid-September and arrived at Liverpool in early November. Only then did Waddell haul down the Confederate ensign and turn the *Shenandoah* over to the Royal Navy.

Above: *The commerce raider CSS* Shenandoah *circumnavigated the globe and did not surrender until November 6, 1865.*

During its storied career, the *Shenandoah* captured or destroyed thirty-six vessels worth $1.4 million. It was the only Confederate navy ship to circumnavigate the globe. In 1866 the *Shenandoah* was sold to the sultan of Zanzibar and renamed *El Majidi*.

CSS *STONEWALL*

The CSS *Stonewall* was the last warship purchased by the Confederacy, although it reached America too late to see wartime service. By the fall of 1863, James D. Bulloch, the Confederacy's naval purchasing agent in Liverpool, found Britain to be much less willing to support Confederate shipbuilding operations than before. In fact, on September 3, Britain's foreign secretary, Lord John Russell, ordered three rams earmarked for the Confederacy to be seized. Bulloch was forced to look elsewhere for support and, using money from the Erlanger loan, he signed two contracts with Lucien Arman, the biggest shipbuilder in France.

To avoid his government's watchful eye, Arman developed a ruse that the ships were being built for Egypt. Although the charade was soon exposed, Napoléon III allowed construction to continue, surmising that he could release or detain the ships upon completion, depending on the circumstances.

As the Federals achieved more battlefield victories throughout 1863, Napoléon decided it would be ill-advised to connect France to the Confederacy. In February 1864, Bulloch informed Secretary of the Navy Stephen R. Mallory that France had forbidden the departure of the ships. France urged Arman to sell the ships elsewhere and one, the ironclad *Sphinx*, was contracted

Below: *The Confederacy obtained the CSS* Stonewall *only after a series of deceptions. The delays caused it to miss any meaningful service during the war.*

to Denmark, which was then at war with Prussia. However, when this war ended, the Danes were eager to unload the *Sphinx*. Arman regained possession and secretly resold it to the Confederacy.

By late 1864, construction was complete. The *Sphinx* was a 1,390-ton ironclad ram that proved sluggish and of dubious seaworthiness. Nonetheless, it was commissioned at sea as the CSS *Stonewall* in January 1865 and then sailed for Madeira, en route to America, where it was intended to attack Federal naval forces and commercial shipping. The USS *Niagara* and USS *Sacramento* confronted it in March off Ferol, Spain, but these wooden ships avoided contact with the more powerful *Stonewall*.

The *Stonewall* continued on to Havana, Cuba, arriving in May after the Civil War had ended. It was turned over to Spanish authorities, who delivered it to the United States government in July.

After spending the next two years laid up at the Washington Navy Yard, it was sold to Japan.

CSS *TENNESSEE*

The CSS *Tennessee* was a 1,273-ton ironclad ram built at Selma, Alabama, and launched in February 1863. It sailed to Mobile to complete its outfitting and was commissioned in February 1864, the most costly ship built by the Confederacy and the one that took the longest to complete. It had six inches of armor on its casemate, five inches on its sides, and two inches on its deck, along with firepower provided by six Brooke rifles. Under the experienced command of Admiral Franklin Buchanan, the *Tennessee* posed a serious threat to wooden ships planning to attack Mobile. To counter the *Tennessee*, Admiral David G. Farragut's Federal fleet was reinforced by four monitors. Even so, Farragut respected the

Tennessee. He wrote his son, "Buchanan has a vessel which he says is superior to the *Merrimack* with which he intends to attack us . . . So we are to have no child's play."

Farragut attacked Mobile on August 5, 1864. Famously ordering "Damn the torpedoes. Full speed ahead!" he steamed past Forts Morgan and Gaines into Mobile Bay, where the *Tennessee* awaited him. The *Tennessee* was inadequately powered for its weight and therefore hard to maneuver. Though it was able to inflict some damage on the Federal ships, it was quickly surrounded, and was rammed and shelled into submission.

The Federals repaired the Confederate ship, rechristened it

Below: *Franklin Buchanan valiantly commanded the CSS* Tennessee *during the Battle of Mobile Bay, but the ironclad was forced to surrender against overwhelming odds.*

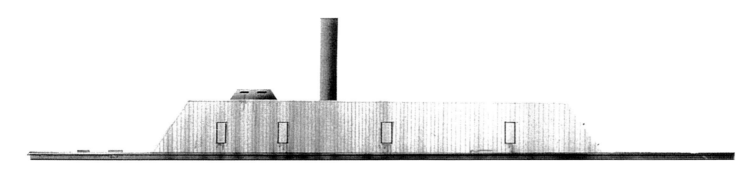

Above: *The CSS* Tennessee *was representative of the manufacturing difficulties that plagued the Confederacy's ironclad production efforts.*

the USS *Tennessee*, and used it to help capture Fort Morgan later in August. It was then sent to New Orleans, Louisiana, for further repairs and served with the Mississippi Squadron until after the end of the Civil War.

CSS *VIRGINIA*

The CSS *Virginia* began its life as the *Merrimack*, a 350-ton, forty-gun U.S. steam frigate that the Federals burned and scuttled when they abandoned Gosport Navy Yard on April 20, 1861. Confederate engineers raised the hulk and found it to be in good shape, except for the upper works that had been destroyed by the fire.

Confederate secretary of the navy Stephen R. Mallory had to be imaginative with the limited Confederate naval resources, and he proposed equipping the *Merrimack* with armor and using it to break the ever-tightening Federal blockade. Naval constructor John Luke Porter and Lieutenant John Mercer Brooke pursued Mallory's idea and designed an ironclad ram that changed the face of the Civil War on the water.

Workers cut the hull down to the berth deck and built a casemate with slanting sides and ports for ten guns. The casemate walls contained twenty-four inches of oak and pine timber with four inches of armor plating. An open grating covered the top of the casemate in order to admit light and air to the gun deck.

Brooke armed the ironclad with two 6.4-inch and two seven-inch Brooke rifles and six nine-inch Dahlgren smoothbores. In addition, the casemate had a thirty-six-degree slope and was covered down to two feet below the waterline with overlapping plates of two-inch armor. An armored pilothouse was forward, and protruding from the bow was a four-foot iron ram.

The major shortcomings of the *Merrimack*'s conversion were a draft of twenty-two feet and inadequate engines from the scuttled warship. This and its great size severely limited the vessel's maneuverability, but such a beast could still wreak havoc with any Federal flotilla.

On March 8, 1862, the *Merrimack*, now rechristened the *Virginia*, sailed down the Elizabeth River into Hampton Roads on what was supposed to be a trial run. Its guns had not yet been fired, and workmen were still making last-minute adjustments. The vessel had a 300-man crew, largely recruited from the army, and was under the able command of Commodore Franklin Buchanan.

As the *Virginia* entered Hampton Roads, Buchanan saw five Federal blockade ships lying at anchor. The *Minnesota*, the *Roanoke*, and the *St. Lawrence* lay off of Fort Monroe, and the *Congress* and the *Cumberland* lay off of Newport News. Buchanan was faced with an opportunity he could not resist.

First the *Virginia* went after the fifty-gun *Congress* and the thirty-gun *Cumberland*, making short work of them both. Shells from the *Congress* as well as from Federal coastal batteries bounced off the *Virginia*'s sloped armor with little effect. When he was as close as he wanted, Buchanan opened the *Virginia*'s ports and delivered a starboard broadside against the *Congress*. Then he rammed the *Cumberland*, leaving a hole one of its officers said was large enough to accommodate "a horse and cart."

When the *Virginia* swung clear, its iron ram-beak broke off in the *Cumberland*, and the Federal ship began to fill with water. Called upon to surrender, its captain replied, "Never! I'll sink alongside." The *Cumberland* continued to fire as long as a gun remained above water, but inevitably sank, leaving its mainmast flag still flying defiantly above the water after the ship itself had struck bottom.

In the meantime, the wounded *Congress* had slipped its cable and had run aground trying to escape. The *Virginia*'s deeper draft forced it to remain 200 yards away, but it nonetheless mercilessly raked the helpless *Congress* from end to end. After confusion between Federal naval and land forces over surrender, the *Virginia* dropped back and set the wooden *Congress* on fire with red-hot cannonballs.

Above: *The CSS* Virginia *took a pounding in its famous Hampton Roads duel with the USS* Monitor, *as this battered smokestack indicates.*

By now the three frigates from Fort Monroe had entered the fray, but the *Virginia* caused them to run aground as they rushed to the battle. The tide, however, was beginning to ebb, and executive officer Lieutenant Catesby ap Roger Jones, who had assumed command after Buchanan was wounded, broke off the *Virginia*'s attack against the *Minnesota* and withdrew toward the deeper waters of the Elizabeth River.

The next day the Federal ironclad *Monitor* arrived on the scene, and the two ironclads battled to a tactical draw during the Battle of Hampton Roads.

Later, when the Confederates evacuated Yorktown and withdrew up the peninsula toward Richmond, Norfolk fell into Federal hands.

This left the *Virginia* without a home port. Its draft was too deep for it to withdraw up the James River, and finally, on May 11, the vessel was abandoned and blown up.

CUBA

Cuba had long enjoyed a special relationship with the South. In 1850 Mississippi governor John Quitman had supported a failed filibuster expedition there led by Narciso Lopez. Southerners saw the acquisition of Cuba as a way to expand slavery, but their high hopes that Franklin Pierce would pursue this policy after he was elected president in 1852 ended in disappointment. Still, the issue, to include talk of an invasion by Quitman and others, continued to be close to the hearts of Southerners.

During the Civil War, Havana was a popular destination for blockade-runners in the Gulf of Mexico. It also played a role in the *Trent* affair as the place that Confederate diplomats James Mason and John Slidell boarded the *Trent*. Several Confederates, such as Robert A. Toombs, fled to Cuba after the war to avoid capture.

DAVIS, JEFFERSON (1808–89)

Jefferson Davis graduated from West Point in 1828 and served in the dragoons for seven years. After leaving the army, he purchased a plantation in Mississippi and entered national politics. Elected to the House of Representatives in 1845, he resigned one year later to fight in the Mexican War.

During the Battle of Buena Vista, Colonel Davis's First Mississippi Rifles halted a Mexican cavalry charge and prevented an American defeat. The battle won Davis national fame, and in 1847, he was offered an appointment as brigadier general in the U.S. Army, but declined. Instead he returned to his political career, serving in the U.S. Senate and as secretary of war for President Franklin Pierce. Davis was an able secretary of war and helped prod the army into adopting the Model 1855 rifled musket.

COMMANDER IN CHIEF

Davis served in the Senate until Mississippi seceded in January 1861. In February, he was chosen to be president of the Confederate States of America. Despite his political and military experience, Davis proved to be a much less effective commander in chief than his seemingly less-qualified Federal counterpart, Abraham Lincoln. Perhaps the problem was that Davis was too comfortable with his qualifications. He had little use for the counsel of his advisers and frequently argued with his military commanders. He went through six secretaries of war in four years.

Davis has also been criticized for focusing on administrative details at the expense of grand strategy. He has been accused of fixating on tasks that could have been handled by a clerk, while ignoring matters that properly belonged to the president.

RELATIONSHIP WITH LEE

Davis did enjoy an effective relationship with General Robert E. Lee, both when Lee was Davis's military advisor and later as the commander of the Army of Northern Virginia. Again, however, Davis is accused of being too beholden to Lee's Virginia-centric strategic views and ignoring the western theater.

In spite of these criticisms, any

analysis of Davis must be weighed against the daunting task he was required to perform. To build a nation in the midst of a war against an opponent who commanded a sizable resource advantage is a tall order. Davis's job was made harder by several governors and his own vice president, who often challenged his authority, as well as by the general individualism of the Confederate population.

IMPOSSIBLE TASK

Davis was hesitant to challenge these forces and build the central authority needed to prosecute the war. While Davis is often criticized, many historians argue that he was the most qualified man in the South for the near-impossible task of governing the Confederacy.

As Federal troops closed in, Davis fled Richmond and toyed with the idea of a government in

Above: *Jefferson Davis served as the Confederacy's first and only president. He faced the daunting task of building a nation while it fought a war for its survival.*

exile. He was captured near Irwinville, Georgia, on May 10, 1865. On May 24, Davis was indicted for treason and sent to prison at Fort Monroe, Virginia, where he was subjected to much hardship while in confinement. He was released on May 14, 1867, never having faced trial. He did not seek restoration of his citizenship.

FINAL YEARS

Davis settled in Biloxi, Mississippi, at his home, Beauvoir, and pursued several unsuccessful business ventures. His most noted postwar achievement was the publication of the two-volume *The Rise and Fall of the Confederate Government*. This memoir helped shape the "Lost Cause" tenet that the South seceded to protect states' rights.

DAVIS, JEFFERSON, CAPTURE OF (MAY 10, 1865)

News that General Robert E. Lee had been forced to abandon Petersburg and withdraw west reached President Jefferson Davis while he was worshipping at St. Paul's Church in Richmond on April 2, 1865. He dispatched his wife and children to Charlotte, North Carolina, and began preparations to move the Confederate government to Danville, Virginia, near the North Carolina border.

Davis assembled his cabinet and instructed them to pack their most valuable papers and deliver them to the Richmond and Danville Depot, where the group would rendezvous that evening to depart. He directed that the $528,000 worth of gold, silver, and other funds the Confederacy had on hand be loaded

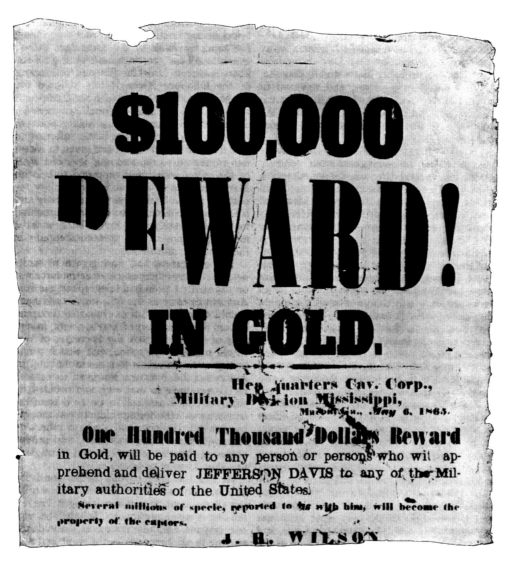

$100,000 REWARD! IN GOLD.

Hea quarters Cav. Corp.,
Military Division Mississippi,
Macon Ga., May 6, 1865.

One Hundred Thousand Dollars Reward

in Gold, will be paid to any person or persons who will apprehend and deliver JEFFERSON DAVIS to any of the Military authorities of the United States.

Several millions of specie, reported to be with him, will become the property of the captors.

J. H. WILSON

Above: *Reward posters such as this one offering $100,000 in gold helped motivate the pursuit and capture of Southern leader Jefferson Davis.*

in a special train to be guarded by sixty midshipmen from the Confederate Naval Academy. Throughout these meetings, Davis displayed an outward calm that belied the actual chaos.

After putting his office in order, Davis rode his horse Kentucky through the now panic-stricken and lawless streets of Richmond to the rail station. His cabinet members met him there, except for Secretary of War John C. Breckinridge who was to remain behind to superintend the final stages of the evacuation and then join the group in Danville. Davis arrived in Danville on April 3 and established a headquarters in a residence

provided to him on Main Street.

At that point there was no news from Lee, but the next day Captain Raphael Semmes arrived with 400 sailors after completing his mission to destroy what was left of the James River Squadron. Davis made Semmes a brigadier general and ordered him to prepare to defend Danville.

Davis then issued a proclamation calling upon the Confederacy to continue the fight by means of guerrilla warfare. A few, such as Lieutenant General Wade Hampton III, concurred with Davis's proposed course, but most Southerners, including Lee, preferred peace. Davis had hoped Lee would reach Danville on his way to join forces with General Joseph E. Johnston. Instead, on April 9, Lee surrendered.

Amid a flurry of vague reports of

Lee's surrender, Davis left Danville on the night of April 10 and reached Greensboro, North Carolina, the next morning. His reception there was a cool one. The northern part of North Carolina had always been mild in its support for the war, and pro-Union sentiment was especially high based on news of Major General William T. Sherman's advance. Undeterred, Davis wired Johnston to come to Greensboro for a strategy session. When Johnston arrived on April 12, he was amazed by Davis's plans to raise a large army by rounding up deserters and men who had previously avoided conscription. Even after Breckinridge arrived from Richmond with firm news of Lee's surrender, Davis remained in favor of continuing the fight. Finally, he acquiesced to allowing Johnston to initiate a discussion of surrender terms with Sherman, though he said he was "not sanguine as to ultimate results."

By April 19, Davis had continued his flight and was now in Charlotte. On April 20, Lee sent Davis his objections to what Davis had described as "a new phase" of the war. Still Davis clung to this hope, and on April 25 he telegraphed Johnston orders to disband his army and prepare to continue fighting as partisans. Johnston personally was to gather as many mounted soldiers as he could and join Davis. Instead, Johnston followed Lee's example and surrendered on April 29. Davis had left $39,000 in Greensboro for Johnston to distribute to his soldiers, which he did, giving each soldier $1.15 to help them on their way home.

DWINDLING SUPPORT

By this point, everyone but Davis seemed to understand the cause was lost. Davis, however, carried on as if he had come to personify the Confederacy. His cabinet was still with him, seemingly unwilling to shake Davis from his delusion. However, as Davis continued his flight, one by one his cabinet members left him. Attorney General George Davis dropped off in North Carolina on April 26, Secretary of the Treasury George A. Trenholm in South Carolina on April 28, and Secretary of the Navy Stephen R. Mallory and Secretary of State Judah P. Benjamin in Georgia on May 3 and 4 respectively. On May 5, in an effort to increase his speed of travel, Davis ordered Secretary of War Breckinridge to leave the group with the five brigades of cavalry that had been serving as

an escort. Most went home to await capture, but Benjamin and Breckinridge both fled abroad.

By this time Davis's flight was mere escapism, made all the more desperate by a $100,000 reward being offered for his capture. His only hope of rallying troops was to reach the Trans-Mississippi, and to that end Davis pressed on. Now only Postmaster General John H. Reagan, three personal aides (Colonels John Wood, Preston Johnston, and Francis Lubbock), and a handful of scouts, teamsters, and quartermasters accompanied Davis. His wife and the children had fled ahead of the renegade government, but they joined

together at a camp at Irwinville, Georgia, fearful that a group of disbanded soldiers was planning to attack and rob them.

END OF THE LINE
Early on May 10, a small Federal cavalry force descended on Davis's party. Davis tried to escape, accidentally grabbing his wife's raincoat in his haste. As he departed, his wife also threw her shawl over his head. When Davis was captured after running just a few yards, his possession of his

Below: *In a gross exaggeration, Federal drawings depicted Jefferson Davis as being disguised as a woman when he was captured at Irwinville, Georgia.*

Above: *Jefferson Davis was held prisoner at Fort Monroe, Virginia, for two years, and never faced trial.*

wife's garments led to rumors he was trying to flee disguised as a woman. Having been led to believe Davis had "several millions of specie" with him and promised by the reward notice that this prize would "become the property of the captors," the Federal soldiers rifled through the luggage in search of gold. They were disappointed, because most of it had been dispersed along the escape route. All that was left was $10,000.

Davis was moved to Brigadier General James Wilson's headquarters in Macon, Georgia, in an ambulance along with his wife and two guards. His sister Margaret and the children followed in another. The other captives were allowed to ride their horses. They arrived in Macon on

May 13 and were moved by prison train to Augusta the next day. While Davis waited at Augusta, masons were converting a gunroom at Fort Monroe, Virginia, into his prison cell. He boarded a ship for this location on May 22 and remained captive there for two years without being brought to trial.

DAVIS, SAM
(1842–63)

Sam Davis served as a scout for General Braxton Bragg in Tennessee. When the Federals captured Davis near Pulaski, he was in possession of maps and papers describing Federal troop dispositions and plans. The Federals questioned Davis about Bragg's chief of scouts, but Davis refused to offer any information. He was sentenced to hang, but the Federals offered to commute his sentence if he would provide them

the information they demanded. Davis refused and was executed on November 27, 1863.

DEBT, CONFEDERATE

When the Civil War ended, the Confederate Government owed some $700 million in debt and the state governments were responsible for another $54 million. Few argued that the Confederate debt should not be repudiated, but there were some demands for repayment of the state debts, especially in Georgia and South Carolina. When repudiation of state debt became a condition for readmission into the Union, Georgia and South Carolina reluctantly acquiesced. The logic behind this repudiation was that those who had loaned money had loaned it to a disloyal cause and did not deserve to be repaid by taxes coming from loyal citizens.

DECORATION DAY

After the Civil War, several communities, usually led by various ladies' associations, began the practice of decorating the graves of fallen soldiers with flowers. One of the first of these events occurred in Columbus, Mississippi, on April 25, 1866. Columbus had served as a hospital site after the nearby Battle of Shiloh, and there were numerous Confederate and Federal graves in the town. The women set out to lay flowers on the Confederate graves, but became saddened by the bare Federal graves and decorated them as well. Columbus claims that this event inspired the declaration by Major General John A. Logan, commander in chief of the Grand Army of the Republic, an organization of Union veterans, that designated May 30, 1868, as a day "for the purpose of strewing with flowers or otherwise decorating the graves of comrades who died in defense of their country during the late rebellion." Originally known as Decoration Day, the day became commonly referred to as Memorial Day after World War II.

HOLIDAY'S BIRTHPLACE

In 1966 Congress and President Lyndon B. Johnson attempted to quiet the debate over which city inspired the popular holiday by declaring Waterloo, New York, as the birthplace of Memorial Day, based on a ceremony held there on May 5, 1866. The city of Columbus, Mississippi, chooses to respectfully disagree. It should be noted that several other Southern cities such as Macon and Columbus, Georgia, and Petersburg, Virginia, as well as a few Northern cities, also claim the distinction of initiating this tradition.

Memorial Day gradually expanded to honor all war dead, not just those from the Civil War. In 1971 Memorial Day was declared a national holiday by an act of Congress, and designated as being the last Monday in May.

Many Southern states also have their own days honoring Confederate war dead. Mississippi, Alabama, and Georgia celebrate Confederate Memorial Day on various days in April. Virginia, North Carolina, and South Carolina observe it in May and Louisiana in June. Tennessee celebrates Confederate Decoration Day in June. Texas recognizes Confederate Heroes Day on January 19, another common day of celebration in the ex-Confederate states because it is Robert E. Lee's birthday.

Below: *Decoration Day stemmed from the custom of decorating Civil War graves with flowers. The tradition eventually grew into the Memorial Day national holiday.*

DEPARTMENTAL SYSTEM

The Confederacy had a vast amount of territory that needed to be somehow organized militarily, but the South's strong adherence to the principle of states' rights impeded efforts to form an efficient, centralized command system. The result was a departmental organization of regional commands that was largely founded on state lines and geographic features. Such an organization lent itself to efficient peacetime administration, but it often failed to provide the unity of effort and flexibility needed in wartime.

An officer of appropriate rank commanded each department, and most operational decisions were left to these departmental commanders. Theoretically, this arrangement allowed the Confederate government to focus on only the most important strategic decisions. In reality, the departmental commanders tended to operate in isolation from each other, with little interdepartment cooperation.

Each departmental commander reported directly to President Jefferson Davis, and this sense of autonomy tended to make the commanders think almost exclusively in terms of their own regional responsibilities. This sentiment caused some commanders to feel that if they lent forces to another department in response to a threat there, they were dangerously exposing their own department to attack. Thus, for example, Lieutenant General John C. Pemberton was largely frustrated in his attempts to gain help from his fellow departmental commanders across the Mississippi River in defending Vicksburg.

Instead of shifting forces from one department to another, some commanders argued that they could best assist a threatened department by going on the offensive in their own department. This concept was based on the idea that the new offensive would compel the Federals to release forces from in front of the originally threatened department in order to meet the new development. This argument was used by General Robert E. Lee to support launching his Gettysburg Campaign rather than sending forces to help Pemberton at Vicksburg.

What the departmental system did was to preclude any other means of strategic direction. By delegating authority and resources to the department commanders from the outset, President Davis left himself very little ability to later influence the situation. He was also reluctant to go against the judgment of a local commander in whom he had entrusted so much authority. Therefore, the system was based on a tremendous reliance on the departmental commanders—some of whom warranted such trust while others did not. For this reason, much of the military history of the Confederacy is biographical, being highly influenced by the personalities of men like Generals Lee, Braxton Bragg, and Joseph E. Johnston.

DESERTIONS

In February 1865, Superintendent of the Bureau of Conscription John S. Preston offered what many thought was a conservative figure in estimating some 100,000 Confederate soldiers had deserted the ranks. The Confederacy could ill afford this loss of manpower in its struggle against the more heavily populated North. Soldiers had several reasons for deserting, and incidences increased markedly as the war progressed.

Some soldiers deserted because of the hardships they personally experienced, such as danger, shortages of food and clothing, and irregular or insufficient pay. Some had always been pro-Union or at least lukewarm to the Confederate cause and had been conscripted against their will. When the opportunity presented itself to desert, these soldiers acted on their sentiments.

Increasingly, soldiers deserted not on their own behalf, but out of concern for their loved ones at home. Shortages, marauders, and approaching Federal armies led many Confederate soldiers to desert as a

Left: *This drawing of a Confederate deserter coming into the Federal lines at Munson's Hill appeared in the December 1861* Illustrated London News.

response to letters from home that described the deteriorating situation on the home front. This phenomenon may in part explain why desertions were noticeably higher among soldiers of the lower classes.

Another motivation was the difficulty in returning home by a legitimate leave or pass. Military necessity caused many promised furloughs to go unfulfilled, and as the war progressed soldiers found themselves being stationed further and further from home, making return difficult. Once soldiers did get an authorized leave, they were tempted to extend their stay, often accompanying their late return with a concocted story of broken-down transportation or a sickness incurred while at home.

Some deserters, especially in the more mountainous areas, would organize themselves into armed bands and collectively resist efforts of the authorities to return them to their units. In many cases, these groups received comfort and support from loved ones in the community. In other cases, deserters preyed upon the vulnerable women and children left behind by soldiers still serving at the front.

Toward the end of the war, desertion became endemic. In a single day in February 1865, 400 men deserted from Major General Sterling Price's command, and an entire brigade deserted from the Army of Northern Virginia the next month. While most Confederates bravely soldiered on to the war's end, a significant number decided their war was over before the official surrender.

DIPLOMACY, CONFEDERATE

Historically, the position of secretary of state is one of the most powerful offices in an administration. This was not the

case in the Confederacy, where President Jefferson Davis cycled through three secretaries—Robert A. Toombs from February to July 1861, Robert Hunter from July 1861 to March 1862, and Judah P. Benjamin from March 1862 to April 1865—none of whom felt particularly empowered to conduct meaningful diplomacy on the Confederacy's behalf. The result was a disjointed and ineffective Confederate diplomatic effort.

Toombs accepted the original post only reluctantly. He had wanted to be president and feared the secretary position would amount to nothing given Davis's resistance to delegation. After getting the initial diplomatic effort in motion, Toombs grew restless and resigned to become a brigadier general. His case illustrates two points about the Confederate

Above: *Robert Hunter was one of three Confederate secretaries of state. Like Robert Toombs before him and Judah Benjamin after him, Hunter had little diplomatic success.*

approach to diplomacy: the secretary of state position was in many ways an idle one, and there was a preference among many Confederates to emphasize fighting rather than diplomacy.

WASTED TALENTS
Hunter too found the position to be frustrating. The conventional wisdom that "King Cotton" would in and of itself solve the Confederacy's problems left the ambitious Hunter with nowhere to devote his energy. He gradually migrated to the Confederate Senate, although he maintained his interest in diplomacy as a

participant in the failed Hampton Roads Peace Conference of February 3, 1865. The highly capable Benjamin was a complete wasted asset in the nominal position as head of Confederate diplomacy. In his previous duty as secretary of war, Benjamin had been made the scapegoat for the loss of Roanoke Island. Davis bowed to public pressure and fired him, but he wanted to retain Benjamin's considerable talents, so he assigned him to the secretary of state position. Benjamin languished in the highly ceremonial position when he could have contributed much more elsewhere.

The underlying message of all Confederate diplomacy was that the Confederacy existed as a de facto nation and deserved the right to stay that way. The Confederacy presented itself to the United States as a fait accompli and avowed its willingness to use force to resist reunion as long as necessary. From its very beginning, the Confederacy treated itself as a fellow sovereign nation. The United States, however, never recognized the legitimacy of secession and refused to deal with the Confederacy as an equal. Thus on February 25, 1861, when Davis sent three commissioners to Washington as representatives of the Confederacy, President Abraham Lincoln's secretary of state, William H. Seward, took no official notice of their presence. Forced to deal through intermediaries, the Southerners got nowhere.

The original group of Deep South states that seceded before Fort Sumter wasted no time in exercising diplomacy toward the border states, dispatching representatives to Delaware, Maryland, Virginia, North Carolina, Tennessee, Kentucky, Missouri, and Arkansas. The diplomatic message to these states was not just the shared institution of slavery, but also some degree of commitment to Southern ideological values. Although Lincoln's call for volunteers after Fort Sumter led to the secession of Virginia, North Carolina, Tennessee, and Arkansas, a combination of heavy-handedness in some places and patience in others allowed Lincoln to save the other four states for the Union.

THE COTTON CARD

In foreign diplomacy, the Confederacy offered its standard argument of actual independence, but also plied more nuanced approaches to appeal to the potential ally's national interests. The Confederacy's most obvious strategy rested on the belief in the importance of cotton and the ability to leverage this resource to win recognition and normal trade relations. To this end the Confederacy focused its efforts on Great Britain and France, countries that possessed both great navies and large demands for cotton. In March, William L. Yancey, Pierre Rost, and A. Dudley Mann were sent to Europe to visit first Britain and then France. The trio was to emphasize that the Confederacy was a true nation, requesting only de jure sanction.

President Davis and Secretary of State Hunter had little appreciation for the difficult task before the three commissioners, and by September 1861 the administration declared the mission a failure. Yancey was ordered home, and Rost and Mann were sent to Spain and Belgium respectively. James Mason and John Slidell were then selected to continue the mission with Britain and Paris. This pair was probably the most well known of the Confederate commissioners, largely because of the *Trent* affair rather than for any diplomatic accomplishment.

While the Confederacy did have some small diplomatic triumphs with France and Britian, namely in the areas of shipbuilding and loans, it never won the prize of recognition. British sentiment against slavery and France's insistence upon not acting unilaterally derailed the Confederacy's efforts with these two countries.

With their formal efforts stymied, the Confederacy also waged a subtle diplomatic effort through the propaganda of Henry Hotze, a Swiss-born Alabama journalist who traveled to London in 1861 as a commercial agent. In May 1862 Hotze began publishing the *Index,* a weekly newspaper that reported the Civil War from a Southern point of view. Hotze also shared his perspective with British journalists, thus widening his impact. His efforts soon attracted the attention of Hunter's replacement as secretary of state, Judah P. Benjamin, who began subsidizing Hotze's work. Benjamin also appointed Edwin DeLeon, a South Carolinian who had been living in France when the war began, to coordinate Confederate public-relations efforts, including those of Hotze, in Europe. While the efforts of Hotze and DeLeon represent a more nuanced approach to diplomacy than the blunt message of Yancey, Rost, and Mann, they still failed to secure British or French recognition.

MEXICO AND RUSSIA

The Confederacy also reached out to smaller countries, including sending John Pickett to Mexico. Its most significant diplomatic effort involving Mexico was its attempt to exploit the French presence there initiated by Napoléon III, but again France was willing to only follow Britain's lead.

The Confederacy had little hope of gaining recognition from Russia, which favored a powerful United States as a counterweight to its competitor Great Britain. France, however, helped draw Russia into the equation in July 1863 by sending a simultaneous mediation proposal to Britain and Russia. Both parties rejected the plan. Sensing the limited chance of gaining Russian support, the Confederate Congress later refused to send L. Q. C. Lamar on a mission there.

The failure of Confederate diplomatic efforts can best be explained in a statement Napoléon III made to Confederate commissioner to France John Slidell. "The policy of nations," Napoléon said, "is controlled by their interest and not their sentiments." While several foreign powers had some degree of sympathy for the Confederate cause, Confederate diplomats were unable to overcome the reality of politics and transition that sentiment into active support. If the Confederacy was to gain international recognition, it would have to be won on the battlefield.

DISCIPLINE IN THE CONFEDERATE ARMY

The typical Southerner was proud of his independence, and many new soldiers had difficulty adjusting to the discipline of army life. Other soldiers became bored in camp and violated regulations as they sought diversions. Still others suffered lapses in loyalty or bravery that led to infractions. Insubordination and disrespect to superiors were remarkably common offenses, while other soldiers were found guilty of fighting, drunkenness, selling whiskey, or abandoning one's post. Acts of

desertion or cowardice were considered very serious.

Accused soldiers were tried before either a general or a special court-martial. The jurisdiction of general court-martials included not just soldiers but sutlers, drivers, and any others receiving pay from the Confederate army. The general court-martial was composed of from five to thirteen officers and could be appointed by general officers in the field and any other officer in charge of a separate department. Special court martials were limited to noncapital offenses involving privates and subalterns. They consisted of three officers who were appointed by commanding officers. The maximum punishment authorized by a special court-martial was a fine of one month's pay and hard labor or imprisonment of thirty-one days. Capital offenses required a two-thirds majority to convict while other charges required only a simple majority. The findings and sentences of both types of court martials were subject to review by the convening authority.

Originally, the authority of court-martials extended to only those offenses alleged to have occurred within areas of military encampments and formations.

However, extended campaigns such as Antietam generated offenses by stragglers that were outside these traditional boundaries. On October 9, 1862, this problem was rectified by the authorization of special military courts whose jurisdiction encompassed both that of the courts-martial and crimes covered by civil laws. These courts consisted of three judges with the rank of colonel and one judge advocate general captain who were assigned to each corps.

In addition to fines, hard labor, confinement, and reductions in rank, disciplinary actions were often quite imaginative. A common humiliation was the "barrel shirt," which required the guilty party to wear a barrel with openings for his head, arms, and legs. Convicts were often forced to carry an appropriate sign identifying their offense, such as "thief" or "AWOL." Marking time on the head of a barrel for hours at a time was another popular punishment.

Punishments for serious offenses were often physical. Bucking, the practice of tying a soldier's hands

Below: *A common punishment for both Confederate and Federal soldiers, such as this member of the Army of the Mississippi, was the "barrel shirt."*

together, slipping them over his knees, and then running a stick through the space between his hands and knees, was common, as was gagging a soldier by tying a stick or bayonet in his mouth. Some offenders were suspended by their thumbs with their feet barely touching the ground, forced to wear a ball and chain, or whipped (until this punishment was banned in April 1863). Deserters were sometimes forced to shave their heads or be branded with a "C" for "coward."

In spite of these seemingly harsh penalties, most commanders were reluctant to issue the death penalty. In a sample of 245 cases of desertion that occurred during the last six months of the war, only seventy were sentenced to the death penalty, and of these thirty-one were invalidated by President Jefferson Davis's general amnesty of February 1865. In those cases in which the death sentence was carried out, commanders sought to make an impression by performing the execution before the assembled brigade or division.

DISENFRANCHISEMENT OF EX-CONFEDERATES

Military commanders during Reconstruction had broad powers, including the authority to determine eligible voters. Because there were no standardized procedures, Reconstruction-era disenfranchisement of ex-Confederates varied from state to state, largely because of differing Republican strategies to court the white vote. Moderate voices in Georgia, Florida, and Texas demanded few disenfranchisements. The large population of African American voters in South Carolina was strong enough to dominate the electorate without numerous disenfranchisements, and in North

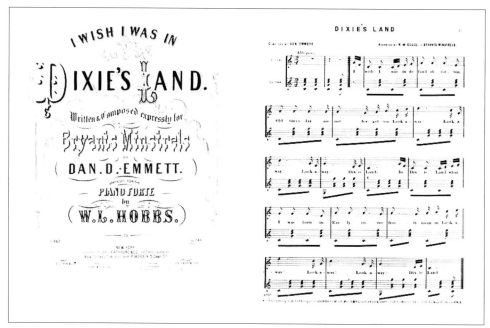

Carolina the party base was also secure enough to result in leniency. Alabama and Arkansas barred from voting anyone who was disqualified from holding office under the Fourteenth Amendment, as well as those who had "violated the rules of civilized warfare" during the Civil War. Additionally, prospective voters had to take an oath acknowledging African American civil and political equality. Disenfranchisements were common in Louisiana and included disloyal newspaper editors and ministers as well as those who had voted in favor of secession. Exemptions were granted for those willing to swear an oath favoring Radical Reconstruction. Mississippi and Virginia also barred large numbers of ex-Confederates from voting.

DIXIE

Dixie is both a common name for the South and a song that came to be the unofficial anthem of the region. Theories abound about the word's origin. One suggests that the term grew out of the predominantly French area in Louisiana where the French word for ten, *dix*, was printed on $10 bills. Louisiana then became known as "Dix's Land," which was later

Above: *An early copy of sheet music for "I Wish I Was in Dixie's Land."*

amended to "Dixie Land." Eventually the phrase spread to refer to the entire South. A more likely explanation is that Dixie comes from the Mason and Dixon Line, the symbolic border between the North and South.

Minstrel David Emmett, author of such early American standards as "Turkey in the Straw" and "Blue-Tail Fly," composed the song "Dixie." Ironically, Emmett was a native of Ohio and first sang the song that would become inexorably associated with the South in New York in 1859. Originally, "Dixie" was a minstrel tune, performed in blackface. Its line "I wish I was in the land of cotton" was a reference to minstrels who would like to tour the North in the summer, but then head south to escape the dreary Northern winters.

"Dixie" enjoyed immediate popularity, especially in the South. It was first used in an official capacity by the Confederacy on February 18, 1861, as a march during Jefferson Davis's presidential inauguration in Montgomery, Alabama. Regiment bands and glee clubs, both North and South, would play the song for soldiers during the Civil War. At a celebration of General Robert E. Lee's surrender on April 9, 1865, President Abraham Lincoln asked a band to play "Dixie." Lincoln explained, "I have always thought 'Dixie' was one of the best tunes I have ever heard. Our adversaries over the way attempted to appropriate it, but I insisted today that we fairly captured it. I presented the question to the attorney general, and he gave me his legal opinion that it is our lawful prize. I now request the band to favor me with its performance. It is good to show the rebels that with us they will be free to hear it again." Lincoln no doubt intended his jocular remarks to be a gesture of reunification. In more recent years, the use of the song has been accompanied by a certain amount of racial tension.

DRED SCOTT CASE

On March 6, 1857, the U.S. Supreme Court handed down its decision in what became known as the Dred Scott case. Scott was a slave who originally belonged to Peter Blow of Virginia. Blow moved to Missouri and took Scott with him. Sometime around 1834, Blow sold Scott to Dr. John Emerson, an army surgeon. When Emerson was assigned first to Rock Island, Illinois, and then to Fort Snelling in what was then the Wisconsin Territory, he took Scott with him. Eventually Emerson was ordered back to Missouri. Again, he brought Scott with him. In 1844 Emerson died, and in 1846 Scott sued Emerson's widow for his freedom, arguing that his trips to the non-slave areas of Illinois and the Wisconsin Territory had resulted in his freedom. The case eventually reached the Supreme

Above: *Dred Scott was the subject of a Supreme Court decision in 1857 that considered slaves to be property.*

Court, which decided against Scott, determining that slaves were property and that Congress had no right to deprive citizens of their property without due process. Scott's travels had no bearing on his status as a slave.

The decision was heralded in the South as a great victory, and it represented a stunning blow to the abolitionist cause.

DREWRY'S BLUFF, BATTLE OF

When General Joseph E. Johnston evacuated Yorktown on May 3, 1862, and

---

- ❖ DATE: May 15, 1862
- ❖ LOCATION: Chesterfield County, Virginia
- ❖ CONFEDERATE BATTERY GARRISON: Numbers unknown
- ❖ FIVE U.S. NAVY GUNBOATS: 5
- ❖ CASUALTIES: 41 (total)

---

withdrew up the Virginia Peninsula, the ironclad *Virginia* was left without a home port. Its draft of twenty-two feet was too deep for it to travel up the James River, and on May 10, it was abandoned and blown up. Without the *Virginia*, the only obstacle to a Federal naval advance up the James to Richmond was Drewry's Bluff, sometimes called Fort Darling. On May 15, the Federal navy tried to push past this position, only to be turned back by a stout Confederate defense.

DREWRY'S BLUFF

Ninety feet high, Drewry's Bluff lies on the south bank of the James River less than eight miles south of Richmond. There the river bends sharply to the east for a short distance and then turns again to the south. At the time Major General George B. McClellan launched his Peninsula Campaign, the earthwork there was only partly finished and lightly defended, but the Federal advance gave the workers a new sense of urgency. The Confederates improved the natural obstacle created by the bend in the river by sinking several stone-laden hulks and driving piles at critical points to narrow the channel. Now, any gunboats making the turn would expose their flanks to the fort.

The Confederates also placed guns from the scuttled *Virginia* and other weapons nearly 100 feet above the water level, knowing that the Federal gunboats would be unable to elevate their guns high enough to hit them. In all, the Confederates had four smoothbore and four rifled cannons trained on the river.

On May 15, Commander John Rodgers and a Federal squadron of five vessels—the ironclads *Monitor* and *Galena* as well as the wooden *Aroostook*, *Port Royal*, and *Naugatuck*—advanced on Drewry's Bluff. In a four-hour

Above: *From an elevation of ninety feet, the fort at Drewry's Bluff commanded the James River approach to Richmond. Columbiad artillery pieces like this one had elevating ratchets that allowed accurate long-range firing.*

engagement, the Federal fleet proved no match for the defenders, largely because the Confederates were able to deliver plunging fire down on the ironclads' thin deck armor, while the Federal shells were unable to reach the Confederates high on the bluff. After the repulse, the Federals would not get so close to Richmond until 1864.

DRUNKENNESS IN THE CONFEDERATE ARMY

Drunkenness was a serious problem in the Confederate army, especially during long periods of inactivity in camp. In December 1861, General Braxton Bragg complained from his headquarters at Pensacola, Florida, "We have lost more valuable lives at the hands of whiskey sellers than by the balls of our enemies."

Commanders tried to curb the temptation by keeping camps as far away from cities as possible and issuing a host of prohibitive orders, but the problem continued at alarming rates, in no small part because of the poor example set by many officers. Colonel Nathan "Shanks" Evans and Brigadier General Henry H. Sibley were among the several Confederate commanders who were infamous for their consumption of alcohol.

EARLY, JUBAL A. (1816–94)

Jubal A. Early graduated from West Point in 1837 and received a commission in the Third U.S. Artillery. As a second lieutenant he

◆ **RANK:** Lieutenant general

◆ **PLACE OF BIRTH:** Franklin County, Virginia

◆ **EDUCATED:** West Point

◆ **MILITARY CAREER:**

1837–38, 1846–48: U.S. Army; Seminole War; Mexican War; rising to rank of major

1861: Commissioned as brigadier general in the Virginia militia; led three regiments at First Manassas

1862: Fought at Second Manassas and Antietam, where he led a division

1863: Chancellorsville, Gettysburg

1864: Corps commander at Battle of the Wilderness and Valley Campaign

fought in the Second Seminole War, but resigned his commission a year later to pursue a law career. Despite voting against secession, Early was eager to defend his native

Below: *Jubal Early rose to corps command in the Army of Northern Virginia and became a key figure in shaping the "Lost Cause" after the war.*

Virginia and was commissioned as a colonel of the Twenty-fourth Virginia Infantry. He served as a brigade commander at First Manassas and was subsequently promoted to brigadier general. During the Peninsula Campaign, he entered into an argument with Major General James Longstreet about the conduct of the Battle of Williamsburg, and a feud between the two developed. The tension continued long after the war as Early championed the generalship of General Robert E. Lee at Longstreet's expense.

DIVISIONAL COMMAND

Early fought at Second Manassas, Antietam, and Fredericksburg and was promoted major general on March 23, 1863. He led a division at Chancellorsville, Gettysburg, the Wilderness, and Spotsylvania until May 29, 1864, when he took command of the Second Corps. In this capacity he conducted a raid on Washington from the Shenandoah Valley to divert Federal strength from in front of Lee. The raid caused much consternation among the Federal authorities, but Major General

Philip H. Sheridan ended any threat posed by Early at the Battle of Cedar Creek on October 19. Early continued to be bested by Sheridan throughout the Shenandoah Valley, forcing Lee to bow to public pressure and relieve Early on March 2, 1865.

After the war, Early went to Mexico and then Canada before returning to Lynchburg, Virginia, to practice law. As president of the Southern Historical Society, he vociferously defended Lee's actions at Gettysburg, remaining vehemently anti-Longstreet in the process.

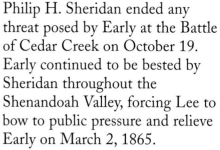

EARLY'S WASHINGTON RAID
(JUNE 27–AUGUST 7, 1864)

Major General Jubal A. Early was in the Shenandoah Valley at Staunton while General Robert E. Lee was blocking Lieutenant General Ulysses S. Grant's approach to Richmond in the summer of 1864. In order to relieve pressure on Lee, Early assumed the offensive. He organized his command of 10,000 men into two corps. Major General Robert E. Rodes commanded one, and Major General John C. Breckinridge commanded the other.

Early attacked Major General Franz Sigel near Martinsburg on July 3–4 and then was forced to bypass the strong Federal defenses around Harpers Ferry. Early crossed the Potomac River at Shepherdstown and reached Frederick, Maryland, on June 9. He levied a $200,000 fine against the town. Brigadier General John McCausland Jr. had levied a $20,000 fine against Hagerstown three days earlier.

The Federal high command was slow to acknowledge the

Above: *President Abraham Lincoln watches Confederate forces under Major General Jubal Early assault Fort Stevens on July 11, 1864.*

Confederate threat, but on June 7 they began hurrying reinforcements to the area. Early defeated Major General Lew Wallace at the Battle of the Monocacy on July 9, but Wallace succeeded in slowing Early down long enough for reinforcements to reach Washington. Early threatened Baltimore and then proceeded toward Washington. He reached Silver Spring, Maryland, on July 11 but determined the place was too strong for a general assault. There was, however, heavy skirmishing around Fort Stevens, where President Abraham Lincoln was on hand to observe the situation and encourage the defenders.

Early withdrew on the night of July 12, crossing the Potomac at Leesburg, Virginia, on the morning of July 14. He continued to retire until the Federals caught up with him at Winchester on July 20 and

dealt him a defeat. He recovered and defeated the Federals at Kernstown on July 23–24, wrecked the railroad facilities at Martinsburg, and then raided Chambersburg, Pennsylvania, on July 13. In reprisal for Major General David Hunter's destruction of private property in the Shenandoah Valley, Early demanded Chambersburg pay a levy of $100,000 in gold or $500,000 in U.S. dollars. When his demands were not met, Early ordered the town's 3,000 residents evacuated and the town burned. Approximately two-thirds of the town was destroyed. Early then sent his cavalry to raid Hancock, Maryland, and threaten Cumberland before suffering a defeat at Moorefield, West Virginia, on August 7.

Early's success had been facilitated by the fact that the four separate Federal military subdivisions opposing him failed to achieve unity of effort. Grant rectified this problem by placing Major General Philip H. Sheridan in charge of the reorganized

Middle Military Division on August 6. Sheridan then proceeded to launch his successful Shenandoah Valley Campaign, which eliminated Early as a threat.

EASTERN THEATER

The Appalachian Mountains, for all practical purposes divided the Civil War into eastern and western theaters. The eastern theater consisted primarily of a 100-mile stretch of land between Washington and Richmond bounded to the east by the Chesapeake Bay and to the west by the Allegheny and Blue Ridge mountains. The way the mountains ran resulted in the theater narrowing in northern Virginia, a phenomenon compounded by the fact that that region held mainly small farms and had not been cleared of timber on a large scale. The result was that eastern theater commanders had limited opportunities to maneuver. The Battle of the Wilderness is a good example. This condition favored the smaller Confederate army and facilitated defense.

THE VALLEY

Of great importance in this theater was the Shenandoah Valley, a rich agricultural region that lay between the Allegheny and Blue Ridge mountains. The valley provided a natural avenue of approach into Maryland and Pennsylvania.

While the Chesapeake Bay provided the Federal navy easy movement along the coast, the rivers in the eastern theater generally ran east to west, which again favored the Confederates by offering ready-made defensive lines.

The presence of the capitals of Richmond and Washington helped ensure the relevance of this theater, as did the influence of General Robert E. Lee, whose strategy was largely based on defending and protecting Virginia.

ELECTION OF 1860

By 1860 the Democratic Party had become increasingly divided. Its presidential convention, held in April at Charleston, South Carolina, was presented with two platforms. One, reflective of proposals by Jefferson Davis, was aggressively proslavery and demanded Federal support of slavery. Stephen A. Douglas led the other. Although it was very sympathetic to the South, it was also much more conciliatory, supporting the Dred Scott decision but also favoring the slave subject be decided by popular sovereignty. After fiery debate, the large number of Northern Democrats at the convention carried the day and the Douglas platform was adopted. With that,

almost all the delegates from South Carolina, Georgia, Florida, Alabama, Mississippi, Louisiana, Texas, and Arkansas walked out. Their departures left Douglas unable to poll the required two-thirds of the delegates necessary to secure the nomination, and after eleven days, the convention adjourned, resolving to meet again in Baltimore, Maryland, in June. The seceding delegates also decided to reconvene, in Richmond, Virginia.

When the majority of the delegates reconvened in Baltimore, they amended the rules to require only two-thirds of those present to be necessary to secure a nomination. Under these new procedures, Douglas was nominated on the second ballot. The dissenters who had walked out at Charleston proceeded to nominate John C. Breckinridge of Kentucky as their candidate.

With the Democratic Party split in two, a third party, the Constitutional Unionists, emerged, drawing chiefly from former Whigs and Know Nothings. This party nominated John Bell of Tennessee.

With the opposition split in thirds, Republican candidate Abraham Lincoln's election was nearly guaranteed. In the final tally, Lincoln drew 1,866,452 votes, Douglas 1,376,957, Breckinridge 849,781, and Bell 588,879. In the electoral college, Lincoln had a decisive 180 votes compared to seventy-two for Breckinridge, thirty-nine for Bell, and just twelve for Douglas.

Many in the South saw Lincoln's victory as a harbinger for continued opposition to slavery and an increase in the power of the North at the expense of the South. Rather than wait around for this expectation to become a reality, South Carolina voted to secede from the Union on December 20, 1860.

Below: *As a crowd watches, Abraham Lincoln is inaugurated as president on March 4, 1861. Lincoln inherited a growing sectional crisis from his predecessor, James Buchanan.*

EMANCIPATION PROCLAMATION

When President Abraham Lincoln issued the Emancipation Proclamation on September 22, 1862, he changed the very nature of the war. No longer was the Federal objective merely to restore the Union, it was also to free a race. This development thwarted Confederate hopes for recognition from European countries that had already ended slavery and could not now support a cause dedicated to perpetuating it.

While the Battle of Antietam itself was a tactical draw, the fact that General Robert E. Lee was forced to withdraw back to Virginia made it a strategic victory for the Federals, and that was enough to give President Lincoln the opportunity he had been waiting for to issue the Emancipation Proclamation. A few Federal generals, such as Ben Butler, John Frémont, and David Hunter had already been pushing for such a move. Hunter, for example, had issued an order after the capture of Fort Pulaski, Georgia, on April 11, 1862, that liberated all the slaves then in Federal hands. On May 9,

Hunter issued another order freeing all the slaves in his Department of the South. Such a move was too much, too fast for Lincoln, and he nullified the orders on May 19 on the grounds that Hunter had exceeded his authority.

While Hunter and others were pressing Lincoln to act more aggressively toward the Confederacy, there were also strong advocates of a more measured approach called "conciliation." This policy assumed that it was only a minority of slaveholding aristocratic fire-eaters that had misguidedly led the South into secession and that popular support for the Confederacy was lukewarm at best. If the Federals treated the Southerners mildly, they would soon return to their senses and the Union would be restored. Adherents to the limited war tradition modeled by Winfield Scott in the Mexican War, including Major General George B. McClellan, favored this approach.

At the outset of the war, Lincoln followed this conciliatory approach, being careful not to interfere with slavery for fear it would alienate the border states, stoke Confederate resistance, and fracture support for the war in the North. Increasingly, however, Lincoln realized that the issue of slavery and the war were inseparable. Aside from any moral considerations, slave labor was sustaining the Confederate economy and even being used to construct military fortifications. Gradually, Lincoln moved away from the policy of conciliation, and on July 22, 1862, he showed his cabinet a preliminary draft of the Emancipation Proclamation.

Left: This postwar lithograph shows President Abraham Lincoln and his Emancipation Proclamation, a document which among other things marked the steady progress of the Civil War toward total war.

Secretary of State William H. Seward advised Lincoln that prematurely issuing the proclamation would appear desperate without an accompanying military victory. Lincoln agreed and waited for the battlefield victory that would give him an opportunity to make the proclamation public.

Antietam provided that opportunity and on September 22, 1862, Lincoln announced, "That on the first day of January, in the year of our Lord one thousand eight hundred and sixty-three, all persons held as slaves within any state or designated part of a state, the people whereof shall then be in rebellion against the United States, shall be then, thenceforward, and forever free . . ." Significantly, in order to not threaten Federal support in the border states, the proclamation did not free slaves in the slave states of Missouri, Maryland, Kentucky, and Delaware that had remained in the Union. Slavery in the entire United States was not abolished until the Thirteenth Amendment was adopted in 1865.

The Emancipation Proclamation changed the very nature of the war, giving it a completely new objective. Conciliation was no longer an option, and the war would take on an increasingly total nature. The move redefined and reinvigorated the Federal cause. The North was no longer merely fighting to restore a union it thought was never legitimately separated. Now it was fighting for a higher moral purpose. By the same token, the South was no longer fighting just for independence. It was fighting for survival of its very way of life.

In addition to these changes generated on the American continent, the Emancipation Proclamation had a profound effect in Europe. The Confederacy had long hoped for European

recognition and intervention, and Confederate sympathies in Britain were especially strong. Indeed, the hopes that a significant victory would seal European support had been one of the rationales for Lee's advance into Maryland. Now, however, the Emancipation Proclamation made it virtually impossible for Europe to recognize the Confederacy. Britain had abolished slavery in 1833 and France in 1848. They could hardly now pledge their support for a cause devoted to defending slavery. Indeed, after the Emancipation Proclamation was issued, Confederate politician William L. Yancey lamented, "The feeling against slavery in England is so strong that no public man there dares extend a hand to help us . . . There is no government in Europe that dares help us in a struggle which can be suspected of having for its result, directly or indirectly, the fortification or perpetuation of slavery. Of that I am certain." The real significance of Antietam occurred not on the battlefield, but in the social, political, and diplomatic developments it made possible through the Emancipation Proclamation.

ERLANGER LOAN

While the Confederacy made numerous efforts to gain European support, the Erlanger loan was its only success in obtaining a foreign loan. Buoyed by its early battlefield victories, the Confederacy contracted with Emile Erlanger and Company of Paris in January 1863 to float a twenty-year loan of £3 million in the markets of Europe. The bonds would bear an annual interest rate of 7 percent and would be convertible into certificates representing cotton priced at six pence per pound.

THE MODERN "CAR OF JUGGERNAUT."
JOHN BULL (*who has his new French cap on, to* MR. SEWARD). "'Old 'ard, SEWARD; you ar running over that £180,000 chap!"
MR. SEWARD. "I can't help it, JOHN; he must be sacrificed."
CHORUS OF ENGLISH SUBSCRIBERS. "Hear! hear!"

Above: *This cartoon depicts the defiant attitude of the U.S. government, represented by Secretary of State William Seward, to the South's effort to use cotton to raise capital through European loans.*

The bonds went on sale on March 19 and at first were well received. John Henry Schroeder and Company were especially active subscribers. By March 23, however, sales began to drop off. Erlanger and Company and other Confederate supporters bought bonds to try to shore up the price, but by April 5, Erlanger decided it could not afford to buy any more. Fearing the loan's failure would demonstrate Europe's lack of support for the Confederacy, the Davis administration agreed to an Erlanger proposal to allow the company to secretly buy bonds using the Confederate loan money. Under this scheme, sales continued, fluctuating with the outlook of war news from America.

Attempts to measure the proceeds generated from the Erlanger loan have yielded various results, but a 1970 study by Judith Gentry placed the figure at £1,760,989, which equated to $8,535,486 in 1863. Gentry's estimate differs sharply from Frank Lawrence Owsley's number of $2,599,000 because Owsley considered only cash transactions while Gentry also included the loan's debt liquidation measures. Regardless of the exact amount of the proceeds, the Erlanger loan generated income for the Confederacy during the critical years of 1863 and 1864. It allowed the Confederacy to purchase the arms, ammunition, ships, and other European supplies that were essential to its survival.

EWELL, RICHARD S. (1817–72)

❖ RANK: Lieutenant general

❖ PLACE OF BIRTH: Washington, D.C.

❖ EDUCATED: West Point

❖ MILITARY CAREER:
1840–61: U.S. Army; Mexican War, rising to rank of captain
1861: Commissioned as colonel in Confederate army; commanded brigade at First Manassas
1862: Promoted to major general; Shenandoah Valley Campaign; Battle of Cedar Mountain; Second Manassas; loses a leg at Groveton
1863: Promoted to lieutenant general; commanded Second Corps at Gettysburg
1864: Wilderness and Spotsylvania Court House

Richard S. "Dick" Ewell graduated from West Point in 1840 and served on the frontier and in Mexico. He resigned from the U.S. Army on May 7, 1861, and was commissioned as a colonel in the Confederate army. He commanded a cavalry camp of instruction and was promoted to brigadier general on June 17. He commanded a brigade at First Manassas and was promoted to major general on January 23, 1862. In April, he reinforced Major General Stonewall Jackson in the Shenandoah Valley and fought at

Above: *Richard Ewell was one of many Confederate commanders who performed better at division than at corps level. This illustration shows why Ewell's nickname was "Old Baldy."*

Winchester and Cross Keys. He went with Jackson to the Virginia Peninsula and fought in the Seven Days Battles. Ewell fought at Cedar Mountain, Second Manassas, and Groveton, where he lost his leg. He was outfitted with a wooden replacement, but he had to be strapped into his saddle.

When General Robert E. Lee reorganized the Army of Northern Virginia after Jackson's death, Ewell was promoted to lieutenant general on May 23, 1863, and elevated to corps command. Bold and wily as a division commander, Ewell had difficulty transitioning to the corps level. His failure to act on Lee's discretionary order to capture Cemetery Hill on the first day at Gettysburg allowed the Federals to strengthen their line. Ewell was wounded again at Kelly's Ford and fought at the Wilderness and Spotsylvania until a fall from his horse rendered him unfit for active field duty. He was then given command of the Department of Henrico and responsibility for the defenses of Richmond. He was captured at

Sayler's Creek on August 6, 1865, and confined for four months. After the war he lived on a farm near Nashville, Tennessee.

FASTING AND PRAYER

The strong presence of Christianity in the South made it natural for the Confederate government to often invoke the Almighty in both thanksgiving and supplication. For example, after the victory at First Manassas, the Confederate Congress officially praised "the Most High God, the King of Kings and Lord of Lords" for the battle's fortuitous result. President Jefferson Davis was raised a Baptist, but became an Episcopalian in 1862 and was very public in his faith. As Lieutenant General Ulysses S. Grant closed in on Richmond, Davis declared April 8, 1864, to be an official day of prayer and fasting. Governor Joseph E. Brown of Georgia, Davis's nemesis when it came to central authority, ignored Davis's declaration but proclaimed his own fasting day a week later.

In addition to this well-known day of April 8, 1864, other days of fasting were held on June 13 and November 15, 1861; February 28, May 16, and September 18, 1862; March 27 and August 21, 1863; November 16, 1864; and March 10, 1865.

FIRE-EATERS

Fire-eaters were radical Southerners noted for their vehement advocacy of secession before the war. Edmund Ruffin, William L. Yancey, and Robert Barnwell Rhett were prominent fire-eaters. They played a major role in organizing the Montgomery Convention of seceded states on February 4, 1861, but at the actual convention they were forced to compromise with more moderate Southerners who formed the majority of the delegates. These moderates wanted to largely preserve what they saw as the Southern status quo rather than radically expand Southern nationalism as favored by the fire-eaters. For example, when a prohibition against the Atlantic slave trade was included in the Confederate Constitution, South Carolina fire-eater L. W. Spratt lamented, "Our whole movement is defeated." Such radical attitudes put the fire-eaters outside the mainstream of the new Confederate nation, and few, if any, were given important governmental positions. Instead, most were relegated to irrelevant roles as elder statesmen.

FIRST SHOT

The most substantive claim to having fired the first shot of the Civil War goes to Captain George James who, at 4:30 a.m. on April 12, 1861, fired a high-arcing shell from a ten-inch mortar to signal the start of the Confederate bombardment of Fort Sumter. James had previously offered the distinction to Virginia fire-eater Roger A. Pryor, who had traveled to Charleston to observe the proceedings.

Pryor, who had earlier urged the bombardment of the fort, declined James's offer. According to lore, after James's signal, Edmund Ruffin, a sixty-seven-year-old ardent Virginian secessionist who had attached himself to the Palmetto Guard, South Carolina Battery, was given the honor of firing the first shot from Columbiad No. 1 of the Iron Battery.

Another line of reasoning credits George Edward Haynesworth with the distinction. Haynesworth was part of a battery of Citadel cadets located on Morris Island under the command of Major Peter Stevens. When the *Star of the West* attempted to relieve the beleaguered Federals at Fort Sumter on January 9, 1861, Stevens gave the order to fire, and Cadet Haynesworth, manning the battery's No. 1 gun, sent a warning shot across the ship's bow.

The day before the *Star of the West* incident, another action occurred that some credit as being the true first shot. In this scenario, the honor belongs to an unknown U.S. soldier under the command of Lieutenant Adam J. Slemmer at Fort Barrancas in Pensacola Harbor, Florida. A group of Floridians attempted to seize the Federal garrison and Slemmer's men repelled the would-be attackers with rifle fire. Two days later, Florida seceded.

FIVE FORKS, BATTLE OF

- ❖ DATE: April 1, 1865
- ❖ LOCATION: Dinwiddie County, Virginia
- ❖ FORCE UNDER PICKETT (CS): 19,000
- ❖ FORCE UNDER SHERIDAN (US): 22,000
- ❖ CASUALTIES: 2,950 (CS); 830 (US)

Above: *Ulysses S. Grant's numerical advantage forced Robert E. Lee to stretch his lines more and more thinly. When Philip Sheridan broke the Confederate line at the Battle of Five Forks, Grant ordered an all-out attack.*

After his successful campaign in the Shenandoah Valley, Major General Philip H. Sheridan joined Lieutenant General Ulysses S. Grant in the siege of General Robert E. Lee at Petersburg, Virginia. Grant gave Sheridan an infantry corps and told him to break Lee's western flank. Lee anticipated this move and dispatched Major General George E. Pickett with 19,000 infantry and cavalry toward Five Forks, a location critical to Lee's effort to maintain the Southside Railroad as a link to General Joseph E. Johnston in North Carolina.

When Sheridan struck on April 1, 1865, Pickett and Major General Fitzhugh Lee were away at a shad bake north of Hatcher's Run. Pickett raced back to Five Forks and joined the battle in progress, but there was little he could do. Once Grant learned of Sheridan's success, he ordered a general attack all along Lee's front, which forced Lee to abandon Petersburg.

FLAGS OF THE CONFEDERACY

The first Confederate flag was the "Stars and Bars," designed by Nicola Marschall, a Prussian-born artist who had opened a portrait studio and taught art at the Marion Female Institute in Marion, Alabama. When the Civil War began, Fannie Lockett Moore, the daughter-in-law of Alabama governor Andrew B. Moore, asked Marschall to design a flag for the Confederacy.

The result was a flag consisting of two horizontal red stripes, separated by a white stripe and seven white stars, one for each of the seceded states, in a circle on a blue shield. Marschall's design was adopted as the Confederate standard on March 4, 1861. That same day it was raised over the Confederate capitol in

Right: *A selection of Confederate cavalry pennants, much sought after by memorabilia collectors today.*

Left: *The flag most associated with the Confederacy in the popular imagination is the Battle Flag. In recent years, it has become a controversial symbol for those who consider it an endorsement of slavery.*

Montgomery by Letitia Christian Tyler, granddaughter of President John Tyler.

The flag most associated in the popular imagination with the Confederacy is the "Confederate Battle Flag," which is sometimes mistakenly called the Stars and Bars. General Pierre Gustave Toutant Beauregard designed this flag after there was some confusion at the Battle of First Manassas between Marschall's flag and the

U.S. flag. The new design was red with a blue St. Andrew's cross containing thirteen white stars.

On May 1, 1863, the "National Flag" replaced the Stars and Bars. It was white with the Battle Flag in the upper right quarter. On March 4, 1865, a broad vertical red bar was added to the National Flag so that when furled it would not show only white and appear to be a flag of surrender.

FLORIDA

On the eve of the Civil War, Florida was a far cry from the powerful state it is today. In 1860 it was for all practical purposes an extension of Alabama and Georgia. It had a small population of just 78,000 whites and 63,000 African Americans. The population of New Orleans outstripped the entire population of Florida.

On December 22, 1860, Florida elected a slate of forty-two secessionist and twenty-seven cooperationist delegates. The latter by and large came from Florida's northern counties and wanted to follow Alabama and Georgia's lead. If these two seceded, the cooperationists would follow. However, the secessionist majority put down attempts to delay and called the matter to a vote on January 10. The delegates passed a secession ordinance by a margin of sixty-two to seven. Alabama did not secede until a day later and Georgia not until January 19.

The Confederate government never really gave much serious attention to the defense of Florida. In addition to the state's sparse population, its three coastal towns—Fernandina, Jacksonville, and St. Augustine—were all relatively unimportant. After the losses of Forts Henry and Donelson in February 1862, Florida received even less priority. One of Florida's greatest contributions to the Confederacy was supplying salt from its works at Apalachee Bay and St. Andrews.

Probably Florida's greatest Civil War drama was the Federal retention of Fort Pickens upon Florida's secession and the subsequent abandonment of Pensacola on May 10, 1862. Noted Floridians who served the Confederacy include General Edmund Kirby Smith, who was born in St. Augustine, Secretary of the Navy Stephen R. Mallory, and Major General William W. Loring, both adopted sons.

FLOYD, JOHN (1806–63)

John B. Floyd served as secretary of war during the administration of President James Buchanan. Floyd's tenure was controversial, involving accusations of the misuse of funds earmarked for Native Americans as well as positioning equipment in Federal properties in the South, thereby ensuring its capture upon secession. He resigned his position on December 29, 1860, in the midst of the Fort Sumter crisis.

Floyd was appointed as a brigadier general in the Confederate army on May 23, 1861, and displayed an inability to cooperate with others during the Kanawha Campaign in western Virginia. He was sent west and

Above: *John Floyd served as the controversial secretary of war for President James Buchanan before the Civil War and as an inept political general during it.*

was in command at Fort Donelson, Tennessee, when forces commanded by Brigadier General Ulysses S. Grant surrounded that position. Floyd relinquished command to his subordinate, Brigadier General Gideon J. Pillow, and then fled with his own division, leaving the rest of the command to be captured. He was relieved on March 11, 1862. He returned to Virginia and held a state military position until his health failed and he died.

FOOD IN THE CONFEDERATE ARMY

Soldiers in all armies in all eras complain about the food, but the Confederate soldier had genuine concerns. Shortages, a

lack of variety, and substandard quality of food plagued the Confederate army. Commissary General Lucius B. Northrop certainly must shoulder a good portion of the blame, but Northrop also faced serious challenges posed by inadequate transportation, disruption of agricultural production in battle areas, labor shortages, and the blockade.

At the initiation of hostilities, the Confederate soldier fared relatively well, with authorities optimistically patterning the Confederate ration standard to that prescribed for the U.S. Army.

However, shortages quickly emerged, and by the spring of 1862, the ration was officially reduced. Thereafter, regular reductions occurred. Toward the end of 1862, soldiers in the Army of Northern Virginia were receiving a daily ration of eighteen ounces of flour, four ounces of bacon, and an occasional supplement of rice, sugar, or molasses. By 1864 the flour ration was cut to one pound.

LIVING OFF THE LAND

Conditions varied depending on the soldier's exact location, with those in the west generally faring better than their eastern comrades. Soldiers operating in war-ravaged areas or conducting campaigns that necessitated nearly continuous movement suffered. Many times the tempo of the action required consuming rations uncooked.

Of course, areas under siege were especially hard hit. By July 3, 1863, the ration for the Confederate defenders of Vicksburg was announced as half a pound of mule meat. It is likely that the hungry soldiers had unofficially resorted to such measures even earlier.

In addition to the suffering incurred at Vicksburg itself, the city's loss cut the Confederacy in two and greatly reduced the food supplies previously being sent east

The soldiers sharing rations   Description on back

Above: *A Northern journalist's sketch showing Union soldiers sharing their rations with Confederate prisoners of war. The illustration was originally captioned: "The rebel soldiers were entirely without food and our men shared coffee and rations with them."*

from the Trans-Mississippi. By the time of Appomattox, General Robert E. Lee's army was subsisting only on parched corn, and Lieutenant General Ulysses S. Grant was moved to send 25,000 sets of rations to the famished Confederates when they surrendered.

Cornbread was the most consistent item in the Confederate soldier's diet. Occasionally baked loaves were issued, but usually soldiers were given dry, ground meal and left to their own devices to prepare it. A common practice was to make a corn disk called an ashcake or hoecake by mixing the cornmeal with water and salt to form a paste and then cooking it in a frying pan. Cornmeal mixed with water was also eaten as a mush.

HARDTACK

Another common staple was hardtack, although this item was more prevalent in the Federal army and often was obtained by the Confederates by capture. It was a hard, dry, square biscuit that was valued for its durability rather than its taste. However, improper storage often led to hardtack becoming infested by worms. Resourceful soldiers began to soak their hardtack in coffee, a measure that both softened the meal and caused most of the worms to float to the surface, where they could be skimmed and discarded.

One of the most highly valued items in the Confederate camp was coffee, but the tightening blockade made this commodity scarce. As a substitute, soldiers made coffee from acorns or wild chicory roots.

When circumstances allowed, Confederates were keen to trade Southern tobacco for coffee with Federal soldiers. Beans were issued green, roasted in a camp kettle, and ground with a rifle butt. Individual soldiers usually boiled the ground beans right in a cup of water without the use of a filter.

Salt was critical as a preservative, and one of Northrop's greatest challenges was maintaining control of the South's limited salt resources. Federal occupation of the salt-rich areas along the Florida coast and elsewhere made the defense of Saltville, Virginia, essential to the Confederacy, and in spite of repeated Federal efforts, the works there continued to operate throughout the war.

Capable of producing 3,000 bushels of salt a day, Saltville's utility was hindered by the South's weak transportation system. Noticeably absent from

THE FOOD QUESTION DOWN SOUTH.

JEFF DAVIS. "See! see! the beautiful Boots just come to me from the dear 1
altimore!"
BEAUREGARD. "Ha! Boots? Boots? When shall we eat them? Now?"

Above: *This* Harper's Weekly *cartoon shows President Jefferson Davis offering a new pair of boots to Pierre Gustave Toutant Beauregard who, though barefoot, would rather have food for his troops.*

the Confederate soldier's diet were fresh vegetables and sweets, and these items were best obtained in packages sent from home. Indeed, families did the best they could to send all types of food to soldiers at the front, but shortages at home made this practice difficult.

A more common means of supplementing the meager issued rations was for soldiers to purchase items from sutlers in camp. These entrepreneurs of course charged excessive prices and consumed much of the soldier's limited pay. In some cases, soldiers were able to cut out the middleman and purchase food directly from the farmer. Even more cost-effective was the practice of foraging—combing the countryside for food.

Obtaining food was one thing, cooking it was another. During sieges such as at Vicksburg and

Petersburg, cooks prepared rations that were then delivered to soldiers in the trenches. More commonly, however, soldiers prepared their own food individually or in small messes. Because both utensils and rations were scarce, pooling resources was a necessary expedient.

The messes usually consisted of between four and eight men who would each take turns cooking, cleaning, procuring rations, and all the other tasks associated with eating. They shared a common skillet or borrowed one from another mess. Messes were usually formed by groups of friends and served as a social outlet as well as a means of preparing food.

Soldiers generally ate when circumstances permitted rather than according to a set schedule, but food was almost always on their minds. One Virginia private probably spoke for the entire Confederate army when he wrote, "Next to the Yankeys Comes Rations which most interest a Soldier."

FOREIGN ENLISTMENT ACT OF 1819

The British Foreign Enlistment Act of 1819 forbade the equipping and arming of ships in British ports for use by belligerents with whom Britain was at peace. This act was a serious impediment to the Confederacy's efforts to overcome its lack of domestic shipbuilding capability by turning to England, where there were both shipyards and Confederate sympathy.

The Confederacy appointed James D. Bulloch as its representative in Liverpool to try to find ingenious ways of sidestepping the Foreign Enlistment Act and procuring ships for the fledgling Confederate navy. As a counter, President Abraham Lincoln appointed Thomas Haines Dudley as political consul in Liverpool to represent U.S. interests.

British sympathies and complicated legal process seemed to give Bulloch an advantage, but Dudley was not deterred in aggressively pleading his case. While Dudley experienced less than complete success during the war, his vigilant collection of evidence ultimately tipped the scales of justice in the Federals' favor. On September 14, 1872, some seven years after Appomattox, an international tribunal awarded the United States $15 million in reparations for the British government's failure to enforce its own neutrality laws as required by the Foreign Enlistment Act.

FOREIGN OBSERVERS

Officers from several European countries traveled to the Confederacy to witness the Civil War personally and report back to their governments. Some were mere observers, and others took more active roles. Sir Arthur James Lyon Fremantle of England is perhaps the most famous. He traveled with General Robert E. Lee and Lieutenant General James Longstreet and wrote *Three Months in the Southern States*. If Fremantle is the most famous, Heros von Borcke may have been the most active. This Prussian officer requested a leave of absence in 1861, ran the blockade, and became the chief of staff for Major General Jeb Stuart in May 1862. Borcke

Above: *The Prussian Heros von Borcke was one of several foreign officers who served with and observed the Confederate army. The practice was not unusual, as the United States had previously sent observers to the Crimean War.*

was seriously wounded at Middleburg, Virginia, in June 1863 and forced to retire. He returned to Europe in December 1864 and assisted with diplomatic efforts on behalf of the Confederacy. In 1866 he published *Memoirs of the Confederate War for Independence.* Captain Justus Scheibert was another Prussian who visited the Army of Northern Virginia. An expert on engineering, Scheibert's greatest interest was in the effects artillery had on fortifications. He published *Seven Months in the Rebel States* in which he betrays his allegiance by calling the Confederates "us." European civilians also visited the Confederacy to experience the proceedings. Charles Girard of France was one such observer who left a highly sentimental recollection of his experience in his memoirs.

FORREST, NATHAN BEDFORD
(1821–77)

❖ RANK: Lieutenant general

❖ PLACE OF BIRTH: Chapel Hill, Tennessee

❖ MILITARY CAREER:
  1861: Raised own cavalry unit; promoted to colonel
  1862: Escaped capture at Fort Donelson; wounded at Shiloh; promoted to brigadier general; raided Holy Springs
  1863: Battle of Chickamauga; promoted to major general

Nathan Bedford Forrest was a self-made man with just six months of formal education. He had helped support his widowed mother and numerous brothers and sisters from the age of fifteen. Rising from these humble beginnings, Forrest became a successful dealer of cotton, real estate, livestock, and slaves, and was also an alderman in Memphis, Tennessee. At the outbreak of the war, he enlisted in the Confederate

Left: *Although he had no formal military education, Nathan Bedford Forrest, "the Wizard of the Saddle," combined firepower and mobility to threaten Federal operations in the western theater.*

army as a private and then raised and mounted a battalion at his own expense. In October 1861 he was commissioned as a lieutenant colonel. Rather than surrender at Fort Donelson in February 1862, Forrest escaped with his command in a daring breakout through Federal lines. He covered the Confederate retreat from Shiloh and was seriously wounded on April 8. On July 6, Forrest left Chattanooga with about 1,000 men and conducted raids throughout Tennessee that caused alarm in Nashville and disrupted the operations of Major General Don Carlos Buell. On July 21, Forrest was made a brigadier general.

In December, Forrest embarked on more raids, including a December 20 attack on the important rail junction at Jackson, Tennessee. This action, combined with Major General Earl Van Dorn's raid on Holly Springs, Mississippi, forced Major General Ulysses S. Grant to withdraw back to La Grange, Tennessee, and abandon his effort to support Major General William T. Sherman's Chickasaw Bluffs operation. After quarreling with General Braxton Bragg during the Chattanooga Campaign, Forrest asked for and received an independent command in north Mississippi and west Tennessee.

Forrest was known for his great physical strength and mastery of hand-to-hand combat. When a disgruntled subordinate shot him on June 14, 1863, at Columbia, Tennessee, Forrest held his assailant's hand, pried open a knife with his teeth, and used it to deliver a mortal wound to his attacker's abdomen. Forrest was a fearsome warrior who could always be found on the part of the battlefield where the fighting was thickest. He was wounded four times, had twenty-nine horses shot from underneath him, and is credited with killing at least thirty enemy soldiers in hand-to-hand combat. He explained his battlefield success as being a product of his ability to "get there first with the most."

FORT PILLOW

Forrest was promoted major to general on December 4, 1863. On April 12, 1864, he was involved in the controversial "Fort Pillow Massacre" in which his men were accused of slaughtering African American soldiers after they had surrendered. Historians are divided on what exactly happened at Fort Pillow and what Forrest's role was.

Forrest was such a menace to Federal communications that Major General William T. Sherman said during the Atlanta Campaign, "That devil Forrest . . . must be hunted down and killed if it costs ten thousand lives and bankrupts the Federal treasury." Sherman dispatched Brigadier General Samuel D. Sturgis to occupy Forrest, and Forrest soundly defeated him at Brice's Cross Roads, Mississippi, on June 10.

Forrest also attacked Federals under Brigadier General Andrew Jackson Smith at Tupelo, but was repulsed on July 15. Forrest conducted additional operations against Sherman's communications at Athens, Alabama, on September 23–24 and then raided into west Tennessee from October 6 to November 10. While he created alarm and disruption, Forrest was unable to seriously deter Sherman from his steady approach to Atlanta.

After the fall of Atlanta, Forrest fought alongside Lieutenant General John Bell Hood during the Franklin and Nashville Campaign. On February 28, he was promoted to lieutenant general, joining Wade Hampton III and Richard Taylor as the only Confederates without formal military training to reach that rank. Forrest unsuccessfully attempted to thwart Brigadier General James H. Wilson's raid to Selma, Alabama, in March and April 1865. He surrendered in May with Lieutenant General Richard Taylor.

Forrest said he "went into the army worth a million and a half dollars and came out a beggar." He once again turned to planting and also was president of the Selma, Marion, and Memphis Railroad. He was associated with the formation of the Ku Klux Klan and was likely its first Grand Wizard.

FORT FISHER, BATTLES OF

❖ DATE: December 23–25, 1864, and January 12–15, 1865

❖ LOCATION: New Hanover County, North Carolina

❖ FORT FISHER GARRISON (C): 1,500

❖ ARMY OF THE JAMES (U.S.): 8,000

❖ CASUALTIES: 1,900 (C); 1,442 (U.S.)

With the loss of Mobile Bay, the entire Gulf Coast east of the Mississippi River was closed to Confederate shipping and blockade-runners. Wilmington, North Carolina, was the only seaport still open, and General Robert E. Lee warned that if Wilmington was not held, he could not maintain his army. Defending this key port was Fort Fisher. Located eighteen miles south of Wilmington, the fort straddled Confederate Point, a long, tapering peninsula between the Cape Fear River and the Atlantic Ocean. The Federals would launch two massive assaults, one in December 1864 and the second in January 1865, to try to capture Fort Fisher. While the first attempt failed, the second one succeeded, leaving the Confederacy completely isolated from the outside world.

FISHER TRANSFORMED

Colonel William Lamb was assigned to command Fort Fisher on July 4, 1862, and he worked tirelessly to transform a humble collection of earthworks into the largest seacoast fortification in the Confederacy. Fort Fisher's strengths were its thick earthen walls, which could absorb the impact of the largest artillery rounds of its day, and its bombproof mounds, which offered more than 14,500 square feet of protection and storage. Its weaknesses were a severe lack of personnel and the fact that it had been built to withstand a naval bombardment more so than a land assault.

The first Federal effort against Fort Fisher was an almost farcical display involving Admiral David D. Porter and Major General Benjamin F. Butler. Butler developed a scheme to fill the *Louisiana* with 215 tons of gunpowder and explode it against Fort Fisher. Butler's men would then attack the decimated fort. The Federals executed this plan on December 23, and it failed miserably. Although the powder ship had no effect on Fort Fisher, Porter proceeded to unleash a massive and indiscriminate bombardment that also achieved little. By this time, relations between Porter and Butler had deteriorated to the point that they were not even meeting face to face. Porter boasted that his bombardment had been so effective that all the army would have to do was walk inside the fort and claim possession. Although Butler had

Above: *Fort Fisher was a Confederate bastion that withstood repeated Federal attacks. As long as Fort Fisher remained in Confederate hands, the critical port at Wilmington was open to blockade-runners.*

clear misgivings, he acquiesced to landing his troops on December 25. What ensued was a halfhearted and uncoordinated effort that the Confederates easily repulsed.

The failure led to Butler's removal, and on January 6, 1865, Major General Alfred H. Terry replaced him. Terry was the perfect man for the job, and he and Porter quickly established a cooperative relationship. On January 8, 1865, Terry and more than 8,000 troops, many of them veterans of Butler's abortive attempt, embarked from Bermuda Hundred on the James River for a second attack on Fort Fisher. Opposing them, Lamb had just 1,500 men.

Terry began landing his force at 8:00 a.m. on January 12, and by

3:00 p.m., all 8,000 of his men were ashore. Each man carried three days' rations on his person, and the command had a six-day reserve of hard bread and a 300,000-round bulk supply of ammunition. Terry had come to stay, and he emphasized the point by digging a stout defensive line across the peninsula.

HEAVY BOMBARDMENT

Porter supported Terry with a merciless naval bombardment, but instead of the indiscriminate fire of the first attack, this time Porter's gunners were deliberate and effective. In the midst of this shelling, Terry led a probe of the Confederate defenses on the morning of January 14 and advanced to within 700 yards of the parapet. He decided to launch a full-scale assault the next day. That evening, he returned to Porter's flagship, where the two planned the joint attack.

The main Federal attack was made by a 3,300-man division commanded by Brigadier General Adelbert Ames and directed against Fort Fisher's western salient. Ames's three brigades attacked one after another in the type of mass close-in assault that Lamb knew was one of Fort Fisher's vulnerabilities. As waves of Federals threw themselves against the fort, the assault became a desperate hand-to-hand fight from one traverse to the next. The attackers were aided by accurate fire from Porter's ships that cleared the Confederates out of each successive gun platform just ahead of the advancing Federal soldiers.

Still, Fort Fisher held and Ames asked Terry for reinforcements. Terry committed both Colonel Joseph C. Abbott's reserve brigade and Brigadier General Charles J. Paine's division. Abbott's troops were fresh, and they were organized into 100-man teams that assaulted each traverse in turn. Losses in one team were immediately reinforced by another. Still, the Confederates refused to surrender, but after six hours of fierce fighting, Federal soldiers gained control of Fort Fisher from the river to the ocean.

SURRENDER

Once the surrounding land was in Federal control, the rest of Fort Fisher was doomed to fall, and at 10:00 p.m., the Confederates surrendered. The fighting had been horrific. Federal casualties were 955 for the army and 383 for the navy. Even after the fighting ended, casualties continued to come. In an unfortunate tragedy, two celebrating sailors accidentally ignited the fort's main powder magazine. In the explosion, 104 Federals were killed or wounded. Although the losses were heavy, the victory was significant. With the loss of Fort Fisher, the last Southern port was closed, completing the Confederacy's isolation and ending the coastal war.

FORTS HENRY AND DONELSON, BATTLES OF

- ❖ DATE: February 6 and 15, 1862
- ❖ LOCATION: Stewart County, Tennessee
- ❖ FORT DONELSON GARRISON (C): 16,171
- ❖ DISTRICT OF CAIRO (U.S.): 23,000
- ❖ CASUALTIES: 13,846 (C); 2,691 (U.S.)

Both Fort Henry and Fort Donelson blocked river approaches into the heart of Tennessee and northern Alabama: Henry from the low ground along the Tennessee River and Donelson from a more substantial position along the Cumberland. When Brigadier General Ulysses S. Grant combined with Flag Officer Andrew H. Foote to capture the two forts in February 1862, the Confederacy was dealt a severe

blow and General Albert Sidney Johnston was forced to withdraw into Mississippi.

Fort Henry was manned by about 100 artillerymen under the command of Brigadier General Lloyd Tilghman, who had sent the bulk of his force to Fort Donelson. On February 6, 1862, Grant loaded 15,000 troops onto Foote's transports and headed up the Tennessee River. Grant landed a few miles below Fort Henry, while Foote steamed ahead to shell the position. After a brief bombardment, Tilghman surrendered.

The fall of Fort Henry alarmed Johnston, who withdrew from Bowling Green, Kentucky, and sent reinforcements to Fort Donelson. Grant also received reinforcements, bringing his strength to about 23,000. On February 13, Grant

Below: *With both a superior land and naval force, Federal commander Brigadier General Ulysses S. Grant demanded the "unconditional and immediate surrender" of Fort Donelson.*

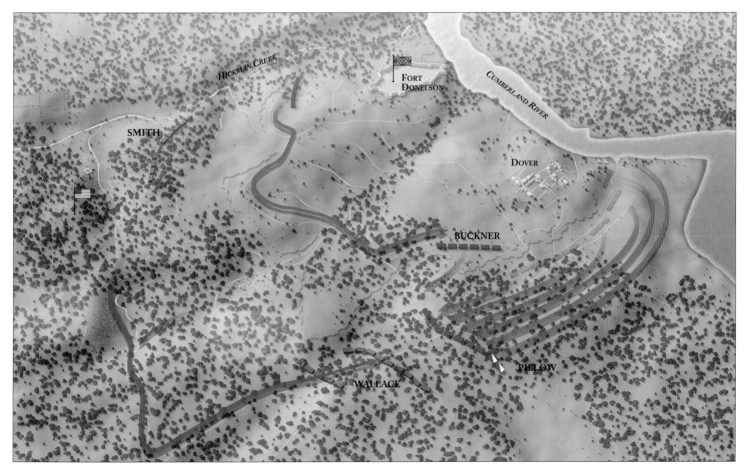

Above: *After Brigadier Generals Gideon Pillow and John Floyd ignobly fled to avoid capture, Brigadier General Simon Bolivar Buckner was left to surrender the Confederate forces at Fort Donelson.*

invested Fort Donelson, and the next day Foote began shelling it. The Confederates repulsed Foote, but Brigadier General John B. Floyd then called a council of war that initiated a bizarre chain of events. Fearing Grant would soon completely surround the fort, the Confederates executed a successful breakout to the south and then, remarkably, returned to Fort Donelson. Floyd then passed command to Brigadier General Gideon J. Pillow, who in turn passed it to Brigadier General Simon Bolivar Buckner. While Floyd and Pillow fled, Buckner was left to deal with Grant's demand for "unconditional and immediate surrender." Rather than surrender, Colonel Nathan Bedford Forrest broke through the Federal lines and escaped with some 500 men. On February 16, Bolivar surrendered his 12,500 men, giving the Federals their first major victory and winning Grant considerable fame.

FORT PICKENS, FEDERAL RETENTION OF

On January 10, 1861, the day Florida seceded from the Union, Lieutenant Adam J. Slemmer took action to ensure the Federals maintained a presence in Pensacola Bay. He spiked the guns at Fort Barrancas, blew up the ammunition at Fort McRae, and

occupied Fort Pickens. In contrast to Slemmer's defiance, the aged Commodore James Armstrong surrendered the U.S. Navy Yard intact on April 12 to a force of about 350 militia from Florida and Alabama. Not a shot was fired, and Armstrong made no attempt to evacuate property to Fort Pickens. However, Seaman William Conway led a force of thirty fellow sailors to Slemmer's position, giving the Federals a strength of 81 men at Fort Pickens.

Within two weeks of the surrender of the navy yard, U.S. secretary of the navy Isaac Toucey ordered the *Brooklyn* to deliver reinforcements to Fort Pickens. He also ordered two warships to Pensacola, but before they could arrive, Florida senator Stephen R. Mallory, the future Confederate secretary of the navy, arranged a truce with President

Below: *Fort Pickens, remnants of which are shown here, was one of a small handful of forts in the Confederate states that remained in Federal hands after secession.*

James Buchanan, that promised the Confederates would not attack Fort Pickens if the troops en route were not landed.

An uneasy freeze in the situation ensued, just one of the many unresolved issues Buchanan left for Abraham Lincoln to handle upon assuming the presidency.

Once Lincoln took office, the new secretary of the navy, Gideon Welles, gave the order in the middle of March for the troops to be landed. After much confusion over the order's exact execution, a U.S. Navy squadron arrived to reinforce Fort Pickens on April 17. This was four days after the fall of Fort Sumter, and Fort Pickens was now one of the last Federal bastions in the South.

On April 12, 15, and 18, the Confederates issued surrender demands, but each time the Federals refused. The two sides exchanged shellings and small raids until early May, when Captain David D. Porter lobbed a few mortar shells into the forts guarding the entrance to Mobile Bay. This small show of force nearby was enough to inspire the Confederates to evacuate and relinquish control of Pensacola to the Federals.

FORT PILLOW, BATTLE OF

- ❖ DATE: April 12, 1864
- ❖ LOCATION: Lauderdale County, Tennessee
- ❖ FORREST'S CAVALRY CORPS (C): 2,500
- ❖ FORT PILLOW GARRISON (U.S.): 560
- ❖ CASUALTIES: 80 (C); 574 (U.S.)

In 1861 the Confederates built a small fort on the Chickasaw Bluffs overlooking the Mississippi River in Lauderdale County, Tennessee. The position was named Fort Pillow after Major General

Gideon J. Pillow. After the Confederates abandoned the fort, the Federals, including 262 African American soldiers from the Eleventh U.S. Colored Troops, occupied it.

On April 12, 1864, Major General Nathan Bedford Forrest raided into west Tennessee and surrounded Fort Pillow. The garrison's total strength was about 560 men, and Forrest had three times that number. At 3:30 p.m., Forrest sent the Federal commander, Major William Bradford, a surrender demand. Bradford asked for one hour to make his decision and then proceeded to reposition his troops during the truce. Observing this violation, Forrest then told Bradford he had twenty minutes to make up his mind, and Bradford responded, "I will not surrender."

The exact details of what happened next are subject to debate, but Forrest's men stormed the fort and slaughtered the defenders. Many observers accuse Forrest of orchestrating a systematic massacre of the Federal soldiers, especially the African American ones, after they had surrendered. They accused the Confederates of charging amid cries of "No quarter! No quarter!

Above: *An alleged massacre of African American soldiers after they had surrendered made the Confederate victory at Fort Pillow a controversial one.*

Kill the damned niggers; shoot them down!" Indeed, the African Americans comprised 60 percent of the Federals' casualties. Forrest's defenders attribute these allegations to wartime propaganda and insist Fort Pillow was merely an overwhelming Confederate victory and that the high Federal losses were due to Bradford's refusal to surrender. Whatever the reality, "Remember Fort Pillow" became a rallying cry for African American soldiers for the duration of the war.

FORT PULASKI, BATTLE OF

- ❖ DATE: April 10–11, 1862
- ❖ LOCATION: Chatham County, Georgia
- ❖ FORT PULASKI GARRISON (C): 385
- ❖ PORT ROYAL EXPEDITIONARY FORCE (U.S.): 12,000
- ❖ CASUALTIES: 364 (C); 1 (U.S.)

Island. The critical weapons at his disposal were nine rifled cannons, a mix of thirty-pounder Parrott guns and James guns, converted from smoothbores, at Batteries Sigel and McClellan, about a mile from the Confederate position.

Gillmore initiated his bombardment on April 10, 1862, at 8:15 a.m. At first the defenders responded with respectable fires, but the accurate Federal shelling quickly dismounted or rendered unserviceable gun after Confederate gun. Fort Pulaski's once-imposing walls were reduced to rubble, and the 40,000 pounds of powder in the northwest magazine were left vulnerable to ignition. At 2:30 p.m. on April 11, the fort's commander, Colonel Charles H. Olmstead, raised a white sheet signifying his surrender.

This display of the power of rifled artillery had dangerous repercussions for the Confederacy's coastal defense system. First, Hatteras Inlet and Roanoke Island had demonstrated that

Above: *This interior view of the rear parapet of Fort Pulaski gives some idea of the fury of the Federal bombardment.*

The Federal victory at Port Royal, South Carolina, led to a Confederate withdrawal from the entire coastal area south of Charleston stretching down to Savannah, Georgia, one of the South's largest and most important cities. Fort Pulaski, on Cockspur Island at the mouth of the Savannah River, protected this vibrant commercial center.

As a young engineer officer, Robert E. Lee had worked on the construction of Fort Pulaski in 1829 and 1830, and it was a position in which he had great confidence. The fort's brick walls were seven and a half feet thick and thirty-five feet high. At the time of the Civil War, there had not been a single instance in which cannon and mortar had breached heavy masonry

walls at ranges beyond 1,000 yards, but on April 10–11, 1862, Captain Quincy A. Gillmore used rifled artillery to shell Fort Pulaski into submission.

Gillmore located his batteries on the northwestern tip of Tybee

Below: *The thick masonry walls of Fort Pulaski proved no match for the advances in rifled artillery. The loss of Fort Pulaski was one of several factors that pointed to the vulnerability of the Confederate coast.*

steam power had reversed the historic balance between ship and fort. Now, Fort Pulaski had shown the vulnerability of masonry to rifled artillery.

As a consequence of these developments, the entire coastal defense system upon which the Confederacy had come to rely was rendered obsolete.

FORT SUMTER, BATTLE OF

- ❖ DATE: April 12–14, 1861
- ❖ LOCATION: Charleston County, South Carolina
- ❖ FORCE UNDER BEAUREGARD (C): 500
- ❖ FORT SUMTER GARRISON (U.S.): 84
- ❖ CASUALTIES: 0 (C); 4 (U.S.)

Fort Sumter was a brick fort built on an artificial island in the middle of Charleston's main ship channel. It was garrisoned by eighty-four soldiers under the command of

Major Robert Anderson, who had relocated his force there from Fort Moultrie on the night of December 26, 1860. Although South Carolina had seceded on December 20, Anderson had no intention of surrendering his position.

Amid Anderson's defiance, the Confederates built a series of batteries that ringed Fort Sumter. A weak Federal attempt to resupply and reinforce the

Above: *Fort Sumter withstood repeated Federal attacks and remained a stubborn guardian of Charleston Harbor until Charleston was abandoned on February 17, 1865.*

Below: *Shells fired from guns manned by cadets from the Citadel turned back the* Star of the West *in its attempt to resupply Major Robert Anderson's garrison at Fort Sumter.*

beleaguered garrison by the unarmed *Star of the West* was turned back on January 9, 1861. In early March, Brigadier General Pierre Gustave Toutant Beauregard arrived to assume command of the Confederate forces, and on April 10 he issued a demand that Anderson surrender or face bombardment. On April 12, Beauregard commenced his attack.

There was little Anderson could do to resist. On April 13 he surrendered. In the thirty-four-hour attack, the Confederates hit Fort Sumter with 4,000 shells. Anderson evacuated the position by a steamer to New York on April 14.

In an accidental explosion while the Federals were halfway through a planned 100-gun salute, Private Daniel Hough became the first casualty of the war.

The Confederates occupied Fort Sumter and used it to repel Federal attempts to seize Charleston throughout the war. By the time the Confederates abandoned Charleston on February 17, 1865, Fort Sumter was largely just a pile of rubble. On April 14, Anderson was on hand to see the original U.S. flag reraised over the fort.

FORT WAGNER, BATTLE OF

❖ DATE: July 10 and 18, 1863

❖ LOCATION: Charleston, South Carolina

❖ FORT WAGNER GARRISON (C): 1,800

❖ TWO UNION BRIGADES (U.S.): 5,000

❖ CASUALTIES: 174 (C); 1,515 (U.S.)

Fort Wagner was a Confederate position that guarded the land approach to Charleston from Morris Island. On July 10, 1863, Major General George C. Strong led an assault on the fort that resulted in 339 casualties compared to just twelve for the Confederates. After this repulse, the Federals brought forward siege artillery and on July 18 attempted a more deliberate assault. Colonel Robert G. Shaw's Fifty-fourth Massachusetts Regiment, one of the first units made up of African American soldiers, spearheaded this attempt. Their attack is the basis of the 1989 film *Glory*. Shaw was killed in the attack, along with 25 percent of his command. The Federals briefly secured a foothold in the fort, but were driven off before reinforcements could arrive, suffering 1,515 casualties compared to 174 for the Confederates. The Confederates finally abandoned Morris Island on September 6.

FRANCE, RELATIONS WITH

France had traditional ties to the South based on previous ownership of lands ceded to the United States in the Louisiana Purchase. Also on the eve of the Civil War, France was importing 90 percent of its cotton and 75 percent of its tobacco from the Southern states. Thus the Confederacy was hopeful of obtaining French support when John Slidell arrived in Paris in early February 1862 as the Confederate commissioner.

Slidell, however, received a cool reception from Edouard Thouvenel, French minister of foreign affairs. Not only did Thouvenel disingenuously deny France had been in consultation with Great Britain about the blockade, it became obvious in this and other encounters that France was completely unwilling to act on the Confederacy's behalf before Britain did. In fact, Slidell concluded that the main Confederate diplomatic effort should be in London, not Paris.

DIVIDED OPINION

In addition to this lack of governmental support, French public opinion was divided. Republican and Orleans newspapers tended to support the Federals, largely because they associated slavery with the Confederacy and liberal institutions with the North. On the other hand, the Imperialist press and many Legitimist journals found fault with the North's political institutions. Furthermore, the average French citizen was largely concerned with the economic impact of the war in America, and because of the diminished access to cotton, many favored mediation.

France's ruler, Napoléon III, weighed these varied points of view. At first he favored a Federal victory that would result in a more powerful counterweight to the British. However, the effects of the cotton famine and sympathy for the principle of self-determination increasingly led him to consider intervention. Still, Napoléon felt he could not act alone. In 1862 and 1863, he repeatedly pressed the British to consider mediation, but was refused.

FRANCE IN MEXICO

Napoléon did attempt to influence affairs in North America via Mexico. France, Spain, and Britain dispatched a combined force there in late 1861 and early 1862 to secure a collection of debts owed to them after the Juarez government announced a two-year suspension of payments to foreign creditors. By May 1862 Britain and Spain withdrew their forces, having been satisfied Juarez would make good his debts.

Napoléon, however, left his forces in place and sent reinforcements that brought his strength there to 35,000. In June, French forces occupied Mexico City and installed Maximilian, archduke of Austria, as a puppet emperor.

Confederate diplomats tried to exploit this situation by arguing to Napoléon that his new acquisition could not possibly succeed without a Confederate victory. Seeing an opportunity for mutual gain, the Confederacy offered to extend its support to Maximilian in exchange for French recognition of the Confederacy. While Napoléon may have had some sympathy for the Confederate cause, by 1863 he realized he was overextended in Mexico, especially in light of increasing Federal battlefield victories. He proceeded to withdraw the French presence under cover of Maximilian's enthronement, leaving the hapless Maximilian to be overthrown and executed.

FRANKLIN AND NASHVILLE, BATTLES OF

❖ DATE: November 30 and December 15, 1864

❖ LOCATION: Williamson County, Tennessee

❖ ARMY OF TENNESSEE (C): 39,000

❖ ARMY OF THE OHIO (U.S.): 27,000

❖ CASUALTIES: 6,261 (C); 2,326 (U.S.)

When Lieutenant General John Bell Hood abandoned Atlanta, he headed north, hoping to recover middle Tennessee and threaten Major General William T. Sherman's communications. Rather than following Hood in force, Sherman dispatched only Major General George H. Thomas's corps. Contrary to Lieutenant General Ulysses S. Grant's desire that he attack, Thomas opted to delay Hood, who succeeded in turning Major General John M. Schofield's position near Columbia, Tennessee. By November 30, 1864, Schofield had taken up a position at Franklin, about thirty miles south of Nashville. The wisest course would have been to execute another turning movement, but the impetuous Hood attacked in a disastrous frontal assault. Hood lost over 6,000 men, as well as whatever

Above: *At the Battle of Franklin, the notoriously aggressive John Bell Hood launched a disastrous frontal assault against a strong Federal position.*

Below: *The Battle of Franklin was one of many Civil War battles that showed the power of defending with rifles from prepared positions.*

offensive capability he once had. He withdrew his 30,000 men to the outskirts of Nashville, a place occupied by 70,000 entrenched Federals.

In spite of his great advantage, Thomas continued to delay under mounting pressure from Grant. Finally, on December 15, Thomas launched a massive flank attack that had overwhelmed the Confederates by nightfall. The next day, Hood retreated after suffering some 7,000 casualties.

He eventually reached Tupelo, Mississippi, on January 10, 1865. By then, the Army of Tennessee had virtually ceased to exist as a fighting force, and Hood asked to be relieved of command.

FRATERNIZATION

In spite of being enemies in the Civil War, Northerners and Southerners shared many common bonds that made fraternization widespread during lulls between battles. Although the practice was against regulations, Confederates and Federals, especially those on picket duty, would often sally forth to enemy lines in search of companionship, conversation, news, and trade. The soldiers often shared their love of music, and during the winter of 1862 the notes of a Federal band drifted across the Rappahannock River to

Confederates at Fredericksburg. When the performance ended, a Confederate called out, "Now give us some of ours," and the Federal band treated the Confederates to a rendition of "Dixie." At the end of the song, soldiers from both sides broke into a chorus of "Home, Sweet Home."

More practical fraternizations involved trade for prized commodities such as Southern tobacco and Northern coffee. Some trades were made face-to-face. In other cases they were floated across the Rappahannock in small, homemade boats dubbed "fairy fleets." Other fraternizations were based on survival and a desire to somehow reduce the war's rising death toll. Major General John Brown Gordon wrote that as a result of the proximity of the Confederate and Federal lines at Petersburg, the pickets reached "an understanding between them,

either expressed or implied, that they would not shoot each other down except when necessary." Another item of exchange was lighthearted critiques of enemy soldiering skills or generalship. A Confederate safe behind the formidable defenses at Vicksburg teased his Federal counterpart, "When is Grant going to march into Vicksburg?" to which the quick-thinking Federal rejoined, "When you get your last mule and dog ate up."

Fraternization incidents such as these provided some relief from the horrors and drudgery of war and were an indication that, whatever their differences, Johnny Reb and Billy Yank were still Americans. After one typical friendly encounter, a Confederate soldier wrote home, "We talked the matter over and could have settled the war in thirty minutes had it been left to us."

FREEDMAN'S BUREAU

On March 3, 1865, Congress created the Bureau of Freedmen, Refugees, and Abandoned Land, popularly known as the Freedman's Bureau, as a part of the War Department designed to protect the interests of former slaves. On May 12, Major General Oliver O. Howard was placed in charge of the bureau, but President Andrew Johnson resisted the idea of such an organization. In July 1866, Congress overrode his veto and passed legislation granting the Bureau sweeping authority to become one

Below: *This 1868 illustration from* Harper's Weekly *shows the precarious position occupied by agents of the Freedman's Bureau between freed slaves demanding their rights and ex-Confederates bent on preserving the status quo.*

of the most important factors in the Reconstruction of the South.

The administrators and field agents of the Freedman's Bureau were commissioned officers from the army. The South was divided into military districts, each commanded by a major general who wielded considerable power, dealing with such matters as law and order, negotiating African American wages and labor conditions, civil court proceedings, public education and medical care, removing public officials, registering voters, holding elections, and approving new state constitutions.

His authority was supreme. The Third Reconstruction Act of July 1867 declared, "No district commander . . . shall be bound in his action by any opinion of any civil officer of the United States." For many, the sweeping powers of the Freedman's Bureau represented a dangerous challenge to civil authority. Although the work of the Freedman's Bureau is most associated with former slaves, the organization was chartered to assist whites as well. Of the 150,000 rations it issued daily in the summer of 1865, one-third went to whites. Still, white Southerners largely resented the bureau, and its agents and associates became increasingly targeted for vigilante violence.

FREE STATE OF JONES

By 1864 war-weariness and dissent had taken a toll on many Southern communities. Hardship on the home front and a lack of commitment to the Confederate cause had led to desertion from the army and evasion of the draft. In Jones County, Mississippi, a group of between fifty and a hundred like-minded individuals, all linked by

family relations and community association and united by dissatisfaction with the status quo, banded together to resist the Confederacy. The result was the "Free State of Jones."

Newton "Newt" Knight was the leader of this group. A Unionist at heart, Knight had been allowed to serve locally as a hospital orderly. He abandoned his regiment when Confederate authorities confiscated his mother's horse. He was joined by Jasper Collins, whose discontent was exacerbated by the Twenty Slave Law.

The resulting "Knight Company" was powerful enough that Confederate authorities launched two raids against it. One in April 1864 severely weakened the organization, but about twenty members, including Knight, escaped capture and continued their resistance to the Confederacy. Knight and his men were greatly assisted by women supporters who helped shelter and feed them.

FREEMAN, DOUGLAS SOUTHALL (1886–1953)

Douglas Southall Freeman was the author of the definitive four-volume *Lee's Lieutenants: A Study in Command* and the Pulitzer Prize–winning three-volume *R. E. Lee*. Freeman earned his doctorate in history from Johns Hopkins University and served as editor of the *Richmond News Leader*. His analysis of the Civil War is supportive of the "Lost Cause" ideology, and many revisionist historians considered his treatment of Lee to be hagiography.

Below: *Douglas Southall Freeman championed Robert E. Lee and the "Lost Cause" in his histories of the Civil War.*

FRENCH, SAMUEL G. (1818–1910)

Samuel G. French graduated from West Point in 1843 and served honorably in Mexico. He resigned from the U.S. Army in 1856 and began a life as a plantation manager in Mississippi. Although a native of New Jersey, he seceded with his adopted state and became Mississippi's chief of ordnance. On October 23, 1861, he was appointed as a brigadier general in the Confederate army. In the early stages of the war, he held a variety of unremarkable commands in Virginia and North Carolina.

French was appointed as a major general on October 22, 1862, and sent to Mississippi, where he took part in fighting around Vicksburg, Jackson, and Meridian. He commanded a division during the Atlanta Campaign and then went with Lieutenant General John Bell Hood to Tennessee and commanded at the Battle of Franklin. An eye infection forced French to relinquish command shortly before the Battle of Nashville. After the war he returned to his plantation in Mississippi.

FRONT ROYAL, BATTLE OF

- ❖ Date: May 23, 1862
- ❖ Location: Warren County, Virginia
- ❖ Army of the Valley (C): 16,000
- ❖ Force under Kenly (U.S.): 1,000
- ❖ Casualties: 50 (C); 904 (U.S.)

During the Shenandoah Valley Campaign, Major General Stonewall Jackson used hard marching and deception to

concentrate 16,000 men against about 1,000 Federals at Front Royal, Virginia. Aided by intelligence from Belle Boyd, Jackson attacked on May 23, 1862, and inflicted 904 Federal casualties while losing fewer than fifty of his own men. The Confederates also captured some $300,000 worth of supplies.

Jackson left Colonel Z. T. Connor and the Twelfth Georgia Regiment to guard the captured supplies. When the Federals attacked on May 30, Connor panicked, set fire to the supplies, and withdrew toward Winchester. Boyd was captured when the Federals entered Front Royal. Jackson placed Connor under arrest for his poor performance.

FUGITIVE SLAVE LAW (1850)

The Fugitive Slave Law of 1850 was a strong piece of legislation that included heavy penalties for helping fugitive slaves or assisting their escape, and placed strict responsibilities on Federal officials to recover fugitive slaves and return them to their masters. James Mason, future Confederate diplomat, drafted it.

In many ways the Fugitive Slave Law was a tactical error for the South. In exchange for recovering a small number of slaves, the antislavery ranks grew enormously.

Left: *Front Royal and other towns of Virginia's Shenandoah Valley played host to numerous battles and occupations by both armies.*

Many Northerners refused to obey the law, even breaking into jails to release captured runaways. Perhaps more ominous were the repercussions felt in the election of 1850 when many antislavery zealots, like Charles Sumner and Benjamin F. Wade, were swept into office.

FURLOUGH SYSTEM

Furloughs give a soldier authorization for a temporary absence from his unit. They are usually long enough in duration to allow the soldier to return home. Although manpower shortages made furloughs infrequent for the Confederate soldier, commanders recognized the importance of furloughs to morale and attempted to authorize them when the military situation allowed.

Furloughs were often used to ease the difficulty of another hardship or to provide an incentive or reward. For example, the Second Conscription Act required those already in service to remain, but authorized the twelve-month volunteers to receive a sixty-day furlough. Similarly, in 1864, regiments that reenlisted in the Army of Tennessee were authorized furloughs for one in every ten men. On occasion, soldiers were granted furloughs to get married or for some other special purpose. In some cases, soldiers bought furloughs from other soldiers for prices ranging from $40 to a horse.

Although obtaining a furlough was difficult in and of itself, getting home was another problem. As soldiers were stationed farther away from their homes, inadequate transportation could exhaust the better part of even a forty-day furlough. For this reason, once soldiers arrived home, they were often reluctant to leave. Some extended their stay without authorization, while others deserted.

GALLAGHER, GARY

Gary Gallagher is a noted professor specializing in Civil War history at the University of Virginia. He has written extensively on battles and generalship in the eastern theater and is well known for his studies of the Civil War in historical memory through works such as *Causes Won, Lost, and Forgotten: How Hollywood and Popular Art Shape What We Know About the Civil War* and *Lee and His Army in Confederate History*. Gallagher is representative of a generation of Civil War historians who have endeavored to bring more political, social, and cultural context to the Civil War, rather than just focusing on operational military history.

GALVANIZED SOLDIERS

Galvanized Yankees were Confederate prisoners who took an oath of allegiance to the Union and enlisted in the Federal army. The converse were the Galvanized Confederates. It should be noted that some sources reverse these definitions. "Galvanized" refers to a process by which a metal is coated with zinc to protect it from corrosion. The metal changes color, but remain the same underneath its properties. Many galvanized soldiers made the switch superficially to avoid the hardships of prison life, especially after the prisoner exchange system broke down, but inside maintained their original loyalty. One such regiment of 250 Galvanized Confederates threw down their weapons at Egypt Station, Mississippi, on December 28, 1864, and surrendered to Federal troops. Jailed as deserters, they were spared when Brigadier General Greenville M. Dodge recruited them along with other Confederate prisoners as volunteers for duty on the frontier that did not involve fighting against the Confederacy. By almost all accounts, these Galvanized Yankees

Above: *Union officer Greenville Dodge "galvanized" deserters from the Confederate army and used them to good effect in fighting outside the Civil War's main area of operations.*

performed well. Galvanized Confederates were also used at Savannah, Georgia, to oppose Major General William T. Sherman's March to the Sea, but Major General Gustavus W. Smith reported that their loyalty to the Confederate cause was extremely dubious. Those galvanized soldiers who returned to the South after the war were largely shunned.

GALVESTON, BATTLE OF

- ❖ DATE: January 1, 1863
- ❖ LOCATION: Galveston County, Texas
- ❖ FORCE UNDER MAGRUDER (C): Not known
- ❖ FORCE UNDER RENSHAW (U.S.): 260
- ❖ CASUALTIES: 50 (C); 600 (U.S.)

On October 4, 1862, the Confederates surrendered Galveston, Texas, after only token resistance to a fleet commanded by Commander William Renshaw. The peaceful reception, as well as a limited number of troops, resulted in the Federals maintaining an occupation that involved miminal security against a Confederate attack. On January 1, 1863, Major General John B. Magruder exploited this situation with a daring operation that retook Galveston for the Confederacy, making it the only major port to be recaptured during the war.

HURT PRIDE
The loss of Galveston was a serious blow to Federal pride, and Admiral David G. Farragut sent Captain Henry Bell with the *Brooklyn* and six gunboats to retake the position. Bell's force was not completely in place on January 11 when Commander Raphael Semmes arrived with the CSS *Alabama*. Semmes had learned from

Northern newspapers that Major General Nathaniel P. Banks was about to set sail with a force of 20,000 men for the Gulf of Mexico, and Semmes deduced Galveston was a likely destination for Banks's expedition. Semmes decided to try to wreak some havoc among Banks's transports as they lay at anchor outside the bar.

Semmes did not know that the Confederates had retaken Galveston ten days earlier, and was surprised when, instead of a fleet of Federal ships, he saw just five blockade ships lobbing shells at the city. Semmes stopped his ship some twelve miles offshore, and Bell dispatched the *Hatteras* to investigate the unidentified vessel.

The *Hatteras* was a former Delaware River excursion side-wheeler with only four thirty-two-pounders and a twenty-pounder rifle. It was no match for the

formidable *Alabama*, which boasted two 300-horsepower engines, six thirty-two-pounders, a 100-pound rifled Blakely, and a smoothbore eight-incher. The battle lasted just thirteen minutes. After sinking the *Hatteras*, Semmes departed for the West Indies, but Bell thought the *Alabama* might still be lurking nearby and paused to reevaluate his plan of attack, giving the Confederates time to build up their fortifications. By the end of the month, Farragut was forced to give up any plans to recapture Galveston, and it remained in Confederate hands until it surrendered on June 2, 1865.

GARNETT, ROBERT S.
(1819–61)

Robert S. Garnett graduated from West Point in 1841 and served in the Mexican War. He resigned from the U.S. Army on April 30, 1861, and became adjutant general of the Virginia state troops. He was appointed as a brigadier general in the

Confederate army on June 6, 1861, and conducted operations in western Virginia. He was killed in fighting at Carrick's (often called Corrick's) Ford on July 13, 1861, becoming the first general to die in the Civil War.

GEORGIA

Georgia was the largest and most heavily populated of the Southern states and had important coastal and inland geography. It was therefore critical to the Confederacy. It also had a long tradition of moderation. In 1850 the Georgia Platform advocated a course of giving the Compromise of 1850 a chance rather than pressing for immediate secession. By 1860, however, many Georgians were ready to act. In November, Governor Joseph E. Brown requested the legislature appropriate $1 million to arm the state and call for a convention to consider secession. On December 6, Secretary of the Treasury Howell Cobb resigned his position in the Buchanan administration and publicly announced his support for secession. His brother T. R. R. Cobb and even longtime Unionist senator Robert A. Toombs also began advocating secession. On the other hand, influential Georgians Alexander H. Stephens, Hershel Johnson, and Benjamin Hill continued to favor moderation. In consideration of voices such as these, the legislature debated for two weeks before agreeing to honor Brown's request for a convention.

Howell Cobb and other radicals launched an aggressive campaign to secure secessionist delegates, resulting in a close but definitive secessionist majority. Brown then manipulated the figures to make them appear decidedly in favor of secessionists when cooperationists were actually well represented. The delegates met in the capital of Milledgeville on January 16, 1861,

Below: *In addition to being an industrial center, Atlanta was important for its railroads. These factors made it a lucrative target for William Sherman on his destructive March to the Sea.*

and listened as representatives from South Carolina, Alabama, and Mississippi presented passionate arguments in favor of secession. Brown continued to influence the proceedings by publicizing a New York resolution to put down the "insurgent" South Carolinians. A last-gasp effort by the moderates to delay secession failed, and on January 19 the delegates voted 208 to 89 in favor of secession.

GEORGIA AT WAR

Georgians made a considerable contribution to the Confederacy. Howell Cobb was president of the Montgomery Convention, and his brother helped draft the permanent constitution. Stephens became vice president of the Confederate States and Toombs served briefly as secretary of state before resigning to serve in the army.

Lieutenant General John Brown Gordon was one of General Robert E. Lee's most competent commanders, but Governor Brown was one of President Jefferson

Davis's harshest wartime critics. Georgia was the scene of much fighting during the war, beginning with operations along the coast such as at Fort Pulaski and culminating with Major General William T. Sherman's Atlanta Campaign and devastating March to the Sea. This exposure of Georgia to "hard war" was captured for posterity in Margaret Mitchell's *Gone With the Wind*. Columbus was the site of one of the war's final land battles, and President Davis was finally captured near Irwinville.

In addition to providing some 100,000 soldiers, Georgia was critical to the logistical support of the Confederacy. It was an agricultural powerhouse with over 900 plantations of more than 1,000 acres each, and produced both cotton and rice in large quantities.

Along its coast lay Savannah, one of the South's largest and most important cities with a prewar population of about 14,000 and access to not just an excellent

Above: *This fort outside Atlanta, Georgia, shows how adept Civil War soldiers had become in constructing breastworks to protect both men and equipment.*

harbor, but also the Charleston and Savannah Railroad. Before the war, nearly $20 million worth of cotton and lumber had been exported from Savannah. Atlanta was also an important railroad hub, and Augusta, Macon, and Columbus all contributed significantly to the Confederacy's fledgling effort to industrialize. It was the presence of these logistical capabilities in a heretofore relatively protected location that made Georgia such a tempting target for Sherman in his effort to break the will of the Southern people and destroy the Confederacy's ability to sustain its armies in the field.

GETTYSBURG, BATTLE OF

- ❖ DATE: July 1–3, 1863
- ❖ LOCATION: Adams County, Pennsylvania
- ❖ ARMY OF NORTHERN VIRGINIA (C): 89,000
- ❖ ARMY OF THE POTOMAC (U.S.): 95,000
- ❖ CASUALTIES: 28,063 (C); 23,049 (U.S.)

Gettysburg is one of the Civil War's most famous battles, and was a devastating Confederate defeat. In a three-day struggle, Major General George G. Meade turned General Robert E. Lee's second invasion of the North. In the process, Lee lost a third of his force, as well as his ability to sustain future offensives.

With the loss of Lieutenant General Stonewall Jackson, Lee felt compelled to reorganize the Army of Northern Virginia into three corps. Lieutenant General James Longstreet would command one, Lieutenant General Richard S. Ewell would take Jackson's old Second Corps, and Lieutenant General A. P. Hill would command the new Third Corps. Ewell and Hill had both served ably as division commanders, but it remained to be seen if they were up to the challenge of corps command.

Building on the momentum of his victory at Chancellorsville, Lee proposed a second invasion of Northern territory, reflecting his belief in the primacy of Virginia in Confederate strategy. However, there were others who looked to the west as being the more important theater and instead favored reinforcing Lieutenant General John C. Pemberton's hard-pressed army at Vicksburg. Lee's arguments prevailed, and on June 3, 1863, he started moving his 89,000 men north from Fredericksburg, Virginia.

MEADE TAKES OVER

Major General Joseph Hooker, commander of the Army of the Potomac, was still stinging from his defeat at Chancellorsville, and he timidly shadowed Lee on a parallel route. Frustrated with Hooker's caution, President Abraham Lincoln replaced him with Meade on June 28.

In the meantime, Major General Jeb Stuart had departed on a raid on June 24, expecting to be out of contact with Lee for just thirty-six hours. Instead, Stuart would not rejoin Lee for a full week. In the interim, Lee would be painfully unaware of Federal troop dispositions. Lee advanced north into Pennsylvania virtually

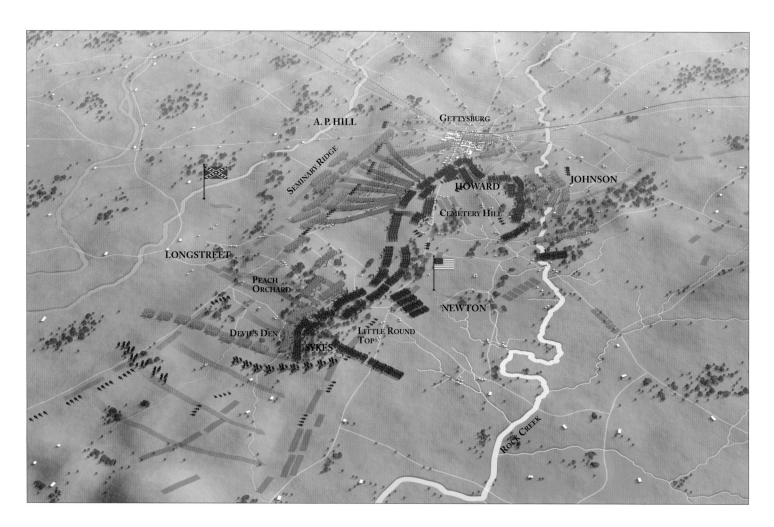

Above: *The Federal defensive position at Gettysburg assumed the shape of a fishhook, with the key terrain of Little Round Top securing what would be the hook's eye.*

unopposed, but ignorant of the Federal deployments. He finally learned from a shadowy spy named Henry Harrison that Meade had replaced Hooker and that the Army of the Potomac was in Maryland. This information was a great surprise to Lee, who now had to concentrate his forces to meet the approaching Federal threat.

By June 30, Lee had gathered most of his army in the area of Chambersburg, Cashtown, and Heidelersburg. Meade had been pushing his army north, staying to

Right: *A photograph of the Gettysburg battlefield, taken shortly after the battle. The terrain was hilly and offered plenty of cover for the defending Union army and lots of obstacles for the attacking Confederates.*

the east of Lee's army in order to protect Washington and Baltimore. On June 30, Meade advised Major General John F. Reynolds that it seemed Lee would concentrate his forces near the small town of Gettysburg. Reynolds thus sent Brigadier General John Buford Jr. and two cavalry brigades toward

Gettysburg to find Lee.

On July 1, Buford encountered a Confederate brigade that had marched to Gettysburg that morning to secure some shoes reported to be in the town. A meeting engagement ensued in which both Lee and Meade competed to rush forces to the

location. Because the Confederates were closer, Lee was able to gain the upper hand. However, Major General Oliver O. Howard wisely occupied Cemetery Hill for the Federals. This hill on the north end of Cemetery Ridge dominated the approaches to Gettysburg and would be the key to any defensive effort.

When Lee arrived on the scene, he sent word to Ewell "to carry the hill occupied by the enemy [Cemetery Hill], if he found it practicable, but to avoid a general engagement until the arrival of the other divisions of the army." It was the type of discretionary order that Jackson would have executed energetically, but Ewell, new to corps command, hesitated. As Ewell waited for the arrival of reinforcements, the Federals strengthened their defense. The opportunity to attack was lost, and Ewell ordered his corps to rest for the night.

The first day of the Battle of Gettysburg was a Confederate victory, but it also led to a serious difference of opinion between Lee and Longstreet. Longstreet was largely a defensive-minded general, and he had long-held concerns about Lee's invasion of the North. Now Longstreet tried to convince Lee to assume a strong defensive position that the Federals would be compelled to attack. Lee disagreed and told Longstreet that if Meade were still on the field the next day, the Confederates were going to attack.

Thus on July 2, Lee ordered Longstreet to make the main attack against the left of the Federal line in the vicinity of the Little and Big Round Tops. Longstreet repeated his arguments against an attack, but Lee was not persuaded. In spite of his objections, Longstreet prepared to carry out his orders.

Meade had formed his defense into the shape of a fishhook, with the tip being at Culp's Hill, the hook curving around Cemetery

Ridge, and the eye at the two Round Tops. Although Big Round Top was the taller of the two hills, Little Round Top had been recently cleared of timber, and therefore it had better observation and fields of fire. It would prove to be the key to the second day's fighting.

LITTLE ROUND TOP RETAINED

After the war, supporters of Lee and Longstreet would argue about whether or not Lee had ordered the second day's attack to begin at daylight. This argument notwithstanding, the fact remains that the attack did not occur until 4:30 p.m., and by then the Federals had belatedly rushed defenders to Little Round Top. After hard fighting, the Federals retained the key hill. Had the Confederates been able to take it, they could have

Above: *Today, cannons and monuments stand as silent reminders to the fury and bravery displayed during the Battle of Gettysburg.*

rolled up the Federal flank along Cemetery Ridge. Instead, the second day's fighting ended in a stalemate.

Earlier in the afternoon, as Longstreet had been slowly moving his men into position to attack, the long-lost Stuart returned from his pointless ride. Lee was initially furious, telling Stuart, "I have not heard a word from you for days, and you are the eyes and ears of my army." Then Lee softened, telling Stuart, "We will not discuss this matter further. Help me fight these people." By then, however, it was too late for Stuart's strung-out column to join the fight. The second day of Gettysburg was one marked by frustration on many fronts for Lee, as he could not influence his subordinates to behave as he wished.

PICKETT'S CHARGE

In spite of the disappointment Lee must have felt over the second day's failure, he remained confident in his overall success. Having struck the Federal right the first day and the left the second, Lee now resolved to attack the Federal center. Major General George E. Pickett's still-fresh division was available for this purpose. Other units would also be involved, but Pickett would be the commander most associated with the famous charge. The attack

Below: *In the popular imagination, Pickett's Charge at the Battle of Gettysburg is one of the Civil War's most enduring images.*

began on July 3 at 1:00 p.m. with a 172-gun bombardment, but most of the rounds sailed over the heads of the Federal defenders on Cemetery Ridge. With the Federal line still largely intact, Pickett began his charge at about 1:45 p.m. His men met a devastating fire from the Federal artillery, and gaps soon appeared in the Confederate line. Eventually their right and left flanks were broken, with only the center remaining.

This attack, led by Brigadier General Lewis A. Armistead, reached the "high water mark of the Confederacy," only to be repulsed by Major General Winfield Scott Hancock's defensive line.

Pickett's Charge had failed, and the remnants of his command staggered back across the field. The attack had caused 54 percent

losses to the Confederates. As Pickett's beaten men fell back, Lee said, "It's all my fault."

Although Meade had defeated Lee, it had been a close call, and Meade was in no mood to press his victory. Both sides had been badly hurt—Lee suffered 28,063 losses, Meade 23,049. In spite of urgings by President Abraham Lincoln, Meade allowed Lee to withdraw back into Virginia, ending his second invasion of the North.

GONE WITH THE WIND

Gone With the Wind, the 1936 book by Margaret Mitchell produced as a film by David O. Selznick in 1939, is perhaps the Civil War's best known literary and

In new screen splendor...
The most magnificent picture ever!

DAVID O. SELZNICK'S PRODUCTION OF MARGARET MITCHELL'S

"GONE WITH THE WIND"

STARRING

CLARK GABLE
VIVIEN LEIGH
LESLIE HOWARD OLIVIA de HAVILLAND

Left: *Both the book and film versions of* Gone With the Wind *are classics, replete with much "Lost Cause" imagery.*

of benevolent masters. Northerners are demonized as ruthless and predatory. Plantation life is glamorous and idyllic.

The film version, starring Clark Gable, Vivien Leigh, Leslie Howard, and Olivia de Havilland, largely defined the popular conception of the Civil War and Reconstruction for generations of Americans, especially in the South. Rhett Butler, Scarlett O'Hara, and Mammy are among cinema's most enduring characters.

Gordon distinguished himself during the Wilderness Campaign and Major General Jubal A. Early's operations in the Shenandoah Valley. He was promoted to major general on May 14, 1864. Returning to Petersburg, he led the assault on Fort Stedman, and during the retreat from Petersburg commanded half of General Robert E. Lee's organized infantry. Gordon surrendered with Lee at Appomattox.

After the war, Gordon lived in Atlanta and became a tireless champion of the restoration of home rule in Georgia. He was elected to the U.S. Senate three times and served as governor from 1886 to 1890. He was also instrumental in the affairs of the United Confederate Veterans and served as the organization's first commander in chief from 1890 until his death in 1904.

screen production. Mitchell, a former newspaper reporter, wrote the manuscript in 1926, showing it only to her husband before sending it to the publisher. Within three weeks of its publication ten years later, *Gone With the Wind* had attracted 176,000 readers. It was heralded as the "Great American Novel," and in 1937 it netted Mitchell the Pulitzer Prize. By the time the book was turned into a movie in 1939, over 2,153,000 copies had been sold, and the book had been translated into sixteen foreign languages.

TALES OF HEROISM

Mitchell was born and raised in Atlanta, Georgia. Brought up on stories of Southern heroism, she claimed to have been ten years old before she realized the South had lost the Civil War. Her book and the subsequent movie portray the South in a way entirely consistent with "Lost Cause" imagery. Slaves are depicted as loyal, ignorant servants

GORDON, JOHN BROWN (1832–1904)

John Brown Gordon left the University of Georgia to become a lawyer and later worked as a superintendent of a coal mine. Although he had no previous military training at the time of the Civil War, he was elected as the captain of a volunteer company known as the "Raccoon Roughs." He was later sent to Virginia. As colonel of the Sixth Alabama Regiment, he fought during the Peninsula Campaign and temporarily advanced to brigade command when Brigadier General Robert E. Rodes was wounded at the Battle of Seven Pines. Gordon was seriously wounded in the head at Antietam. Only a bullet hole in his hat prevented him from drowning in his own blood. He recovered and was promoted to brigadier general on November 1, 1862.

Above: *John Brown Gordon was an able commander during the Civil War, and active as a politician and veteran after it. Fort Gordon, Georgia, bears his name today.*

GORGAS, JOSIAH
(1818–83)

Josiah Gorgas graduated from West Point in 1841. He was commissioned as an ordnance officer and served at various arsenals and in the Mexican War. He also spent some time abroad studying European armies. Although born in Pennsylvania, Gorgas married into a prominent Alabama family. He resigned from the U.S. Army on April 3, 1861, and was commissioned as a major in the Confederate army to fill the post of chief of ordnance and quickly gained a reputation as an organizational genius.

Faced with overwhelming odds, Gorgas worked tirelessly to build the industrial and manufacturing base necessary to supply the Confederate army. He directed the Bureau of Foreign Supplies and organized the Nitre and Mining Bureau. General Joseph E. Johnston correctly proclaimed that Gorgas "created the ordnance department

Above: *Josiah Gorgas was the Confederacy's extremely capable chief of ordnance. Tirelessly working to overcome the South's limited industrial base, Gorgas achieved impressive results.*

out of nothing." His efforts were recognized with promotion to brigadier general on November 10, 1864.

After the war Gorgas operated Brierfield Iron Works in Alabama and then entered the field of education. He served as professor and chancellor at the University of the South at Sewanee, Tennessee, and as president and librarian of the University of Alabama.

GOVERNMENT, CONFEDERATE STATES

The government of the Confederate States of America had the familiar executive, legislative, and judicial branches of the United States government. A president who was limited to one six-year term of office led the executive branch. He was assisted by a vice president and six cabinet officials: the secretary of state, the secretary of the treasury, the secretary of war, the secretary of the navy, the attorney general, and the postmaster general. The legislative branch consisted of a Senate and House of Representatives. Each state had two senators who were chosen by the state legislature. Voters in the state popularly elected representatives. Although the Confederate Constitution provided the theoretical basis for the creation of a Supreme Court, the congress never passed the required enabling legislation. As a result, ultimate judicial authority remained in the state courts rather than with the central government.

GOVERNORS, CONFEDERATE

Some Civil War historians, such as Frank Lawrence Owsley, have been highly critical of the

Above: *The South's emphasis on states' rights led several of its governors to place state interests above those of the Confederacy as a whole. Zebulon Vance of North Carolina was one such governor.*

Confederacy's governors, arguing that they interfered with the war's prosecution by insisting on the pursuit of local interests and resisting centralization. Owsley points to instances like North Carolina governor Zebulon B. Vance's refusal to draw on his abundant warehouses of supplies to assist General Robert E. Lee's Army of Northern Virginia. Other observers, such as Richard McMurry, have been more charitable in their assessment of the state governors' contributions to the Confederate cause, but in the balance, the Southern emphasis on states' rights did create a tendency for governors to subordinate Confederate needs to state needs.

The following is a list of the Confederacy's wartime governors:
Alabama: Andrew B. Moore (1857–61), John G. Shorter (1861–63), Thomas H. Watts (1863–65)
Arkansas: Henry M. Rector (1860–62), Thomas Fletcher (1862), Harris Flanagin

(1862–64), Isaac Murphy
(1864–68)
Florida: Madison S. Perry
(1857–61), John Milton
(1861–65)
Georgia: Joseph E. Brown
(1857–65)
Louisiana: Thomas O. Moore
(1860–64), Henry W. Allen
(1864–65)
Mississippi: John J. Pettus
(1860–62), Charles Clark
(1863–65)
North Carolina: John W. Ellis
(1858–61), Henry T. Clark
(1861–63), Zebulon B. Vance
(1863–65)
South Carolina: Francis W.
Pickens (1860–62), Milledge L.
Bonham (1862–64), Andrew G.
Magrath (1864–65)
Tennessee: Isham G. Harris
(1857–63), Robert L. Carouthers
(elected 1863 but never
inaugurated)
Texas: Edward Clark (1861),
Francis R. Lubbock (1861–63),
Pendleton Murrah (1863–65)
Virginia: John Letcher (1860–64),
William Smith (1864–65)

In addition to the seceded states,
Confederate sympathizers elected
the following governors in
Kentucky, Missouri, and the
Arizona Territory:
Kentucky: George W. Johnson
(1861–62), Richard Hawes
(1862–65)
Missouri: Claiborne F. Jackson
(1861), Thomas Reynolds
(1862–65)
Arizona Territory: John R. Baylor
(1864–65)

As Louisiana and Tennessee
succumbed to Federal occupation,
the following Union governors were
appointed:
Louisiana: George F. Shepley
(1862–64), Michael Hahn
(1864–65)
Tennessee: Andrew Johnson
(1862–65)

GRAND GULF, BATTLE OF

- **DATE:** April 28, 1863
- **LOCATION:** Claiborne County, Mississippi
- **BOWEN'S DIVISION (C):** Not known
- **MISSISSIPPI SQUADRON (U.S.):** 7 ironclads
- **CASUALTIES:** 18 (C); 74 (U.S.)

On March 31, 1863, Major General Ulysses S. Grant began an overland march south from Milliken's Bend in an attempt to capture Vicksburg, Mississippi. On the night of April 16–17, Admiral David D. Porter ran the batteries at Vicksburg with eight of his gunboats and three transports. More steamers made the dash five days later. With Porter's vessels south of Vicksburg, Grant now had the means to cross to the east bank of the Mississippi without facing the stiffest Confederate defenses. On April 29, Grant attempted to cross the river at Grand Gulf, but he was repulsed by the strong Confederate position there.

Grand Gulf lay some thirty miles south of Vicksburg; it was the first place below the city where the river met the bluffs. There the Confederates had built two forts that boasted sixteen artillery pieces. Fifty feet above the Mississippi, Grand Gulf was a formidable defensive position.

Grant's plan was for Porter's ships to shell the Confederates into submission and then ferry Major General John A. McClernand's men across the river. To help draw Confederate attention away from Grand Gulf, Major General William T. Sherman conducted a demonstration at Snyder's Bluff north of Vicksburg.

On April 28 the Federal gunboats began a fierce bombardment of Grand Gulf that lasted five hours. Porter fired over 2,500 rounds, but was only able to inflict eighteen Confederate casualties. On the other hand, he lost eighteen men killed and fifty-six more wounded. His ships also suffered badly, and it seemed as if the attack was going nowhere. After

Below: *The Confederacy placed great stock in its artillery positions along the Mississippi River's bluffs, but David Porter was able to "run the gauntlet," making it possible for Ulysses S. Grant to attack Vicksburg without facing its toughest defenses.*

the initial failed bombardment, Grant went aboard Porter's flagship, the *Benton*, to discuss options. In Porter's mind, Grand Gulf was "the strongest place on the Mississippi." Further effort against it seemed futile. Grant agreed and withdrew his troops back to the Louisiana side of the river.

The setback was only a momentary one for the Federals. Grant soon received intelligence from a runaway slave that just twelve miles south of Grand Gulf there was an undefended crossing at Bruinsburg. Grant moved his men there and began crossing the Mississippi on April 30. Grant's capture of Port Gibson on May 1 effectively turned Grand Gulf and rendered the Confederate position there useless.

On May 7, the Confederates abandoned the once-mighty fortress, and Porter promptly occupied it and began turning it into a logistical base that helped support the remainder of the Vicksburg Campaign.

GREAT BRITAIN, RELATIONS WITH

From the very beginning of the Civil War, the Confederacy placed high hopes on European intervention. The principal object of Confederate desire was Britain, the country to which several other European powers looked for example in formulating their own response to the Civil War. Indeed, had Britain intervened, it is likely the South would have emerged as an independent nation. As it turned out, British neutrality left the Confederacy at the mercy of more powerful Federal forces and ultimate defeat.

There were certainly well-founded reasons that made the Confederacy believe Britain would intervene on its behalf. Britain, especially with its North American interest in Canada, would in many ways benefit geopolitically from a divided United States, which would redistribute power on the continent. There was also an ideological support for a Confederacy some Britons saw as being built on an aristocratic social constitution they admired. British foreign secretary Lord John Russell spoke for many when he argued that the North fought for "empire," while the South fought for "independence."

But what the Confederacy most hoped to leverage was Britain's appetite for the Southern raw cotton that the Federal blockade threatened. Boldly declaring, "Cotton is king," and with almost a quarter of Britain's population engaged in the textile business, the South reasoned Britain would not tolerate a suspension of trade.

MIXED FORTUNES

Hoping to exploit British sympathies, the Confederates dispatched James Mason to London, but Charles Francis Adams, Lincoln's much more accomplished representative, decidedly outmatched him. Nonetheless, the Confederates enjoyed some successes with Britain, particularly the ability of James D. Bulloch to organize a shipbuilding program that produced the CSS *Alabama*, *Florida*, and *Shenandoah* while carefully skirting the restrictions of the British Foreign Enlistment Act. For a time, it even appeared that early Confederate victories might persuade the British to recognize the Confederacy.

In October 1862, Chancellor of the Exchequer William Gladstone declared, "There is no doubt that Jefferson F. Davis and the leaders of the South have made an army; they are making, it appears, a navy; and they have made what is more than either—they have made a nation."

In spite of these encouragements, what the Confederates did not understand was the profound impact of slavery on their hopes for British support. Britain had abolished slavery in 1833 and had in many ways led the international movement against it. Sentiment against slavery was especially high among the British working class, and even the Lancashire textile workers who were suffering as a result of the blockade were willing to endure the hardship with the belief that the blockade was also helping to end slavery.

Although the aristocracy's penchant for order and discipline caused it to initially regard the Emancipation Proclamation as an attempt to stir up servile insurrection, even this segment of British society was generally hostile toward slavery.

Under such circumstances, the British government could not violate its own stance against slavery and the consensus of its people by supporting the Confederacy once emancipation became a war issue. With the issuance of the Emancipation Proclamation, the hopes of British intervention on behalf of the Confederacy all but died.

GREENHOW, ROSE O'NEAL (1817–64)

Rose O'Neal Greenhow was the wife of doctor and author Robert Greenhow. She became a well-connected Washington socialite whose house served as a popular meeting spot for many of the country's leading political figures, including Senator Henry Wilson, chairman of the Committee on Military Affairs. A Southern sympathizer, Greenhow was recruited by Captain Thomas

Above: *Washington socialite Rose Greenhow was a famous and highly romanticized source of intelligence for the Confederacy, but historians differ on the true value of her services.*

Jordan to use her position to gather intelligence for the Confederacy. Greenhow was given a special cipher that she used to provide Brigadier General Pierre Gustave Toutant Beauregard's staff with information concerning the Federal plans prior to the Battle of First Manassas. Beauregard credited Greenhow's information with being critical to his plans for the battle, but historians disagree as to the actual significance of her report. Indeed, Greenhow's exploits are so surrounded in romance and lore that it is difficult to separate fact from fiction.

Although Greenhow was a valuable source of intelligence, she was also indiscreet and was soon rounded up by detective Allan Pinkerton. On August 23, 1861, she was placed under house arrest at her Sixteenth Street home, a location that became a woman's

prison dubbed Fort Greenhow. After a series of security breaches at this site, Greenhow, along with her small daughter Rose, was relocated to Old Capitol Prison in January 1862. In May, she was released and sent south, where she was welcomed as a heroine and met with several high-ranking Confederate officials, including Beauregard.

In August 1863, Greenhow ran the blockade to France, where she had a private audience with Napoléon III. She placed her daughter in a convent and continued on her European tour to England, where she met with Queen Victoria. Greenhow wrote her memoir, *My Imprisonment and the First Year of Abolition Rule at Washington*, and then returned to the South with her daughter. On September 30, 1864, her ship ran aground off Wilmington, North Carolina. While she was trying to make it to shore, her small boat capsized and she drowned, an event that only added to her romanticized legend.

GREGG, MAXCY (1814–62)

Maxcy Gregg was a Mexican War veteran and ardent supporter of states' rights and secession. He was initially commissioned as a colonel in the Confederate army and was promoted to brigadier general on December 14, 1861. He commanded a brigade during the Peninsula Campaign, at Second Manassas, and at Antietam. Gregg was a brave fighter, often in the thick of the action. He was killed at Fredericksburg on December 14, 1862, and became a symbol of Confederate heroism.

HAMMOND, JAMES H. (1807–64)

James H. Hammond was the uncle of Wade Hampton III and a congressman, governor, and senator from South Carolina. He also maintained a prototypical Southern plantation called Redcliffe and was a successful cotton planter. Hammond was a staunch supporter of nullification and states' rights. As a senator he did much to popularize the notion that "Cotton is King," coining the phrase in an 1858 speech. He resigned from the U.S. Senate on November 11, 1860.

HAMPTON III, WADE (1818–1902)

Wade Hampton III was one of not just South Carolina's but also the entire South's wealthiest planters, and a bastion of the Southern aristocracy. In spite of his social position, he doubted the economy of the slave labor system

Above: *Wade Hampton was a South Carolina planter and aristocrat who, without formal military training, became one of the Confederacy's best cavalry commanders.*

and did not favor secession. He was one of the Confederacy's most dashing and bold cavalrymen, being wounded three times during the Battle of Gettysburg alone. He joined Richard Taylor and Nathan Bedford Forrest as one of only three Confederates to reach the rank of lieutenant general without formal military training.

When South Carolina seceded, Hampton raised a legion of six infantry companies, four cavalry companies, and a battery of artillery, providing much of the necessary equipment at his own expense. He was commissioned as a colonel and fought at First Manassas and during the Peninsula Campaign. He was promoted to brigadier general on May 23, 1862. On September 2, he became second in command to Major General Jeb Stuart in the Army of Northern Virginia's cavalry corps. Hampton fought at Antietam and Gettysburg and was promoted to major general on September 3, 1863. After Stuart's death, he became commander of the Army of Northern Virginia's cavalry corps and fought at Trevilian Station and throughout the Petersburg Campaign.

As horses became increasingly scarce, Hampton trained his cavalrymen to fight dismounted and returned to South Carolina to look for horses. While there, he was promoted to lieutenant general on February 15, 1865, and ordered to cover General Joseph E. Johnston's retreat through South Carolina. Because he was not technically part of Johnston's command, Hampton was considered exempt from surrendering with Johnston. He supported President Jefferson Davis's proposal to wage guerrilla war after the surrender of the eastern armies and considered heading to Texas to continue resistance. When this plan failed to materialize, he returned to South Carolina.

Immediately after the war, Hampton tried to remain out of politics for fear of impeding President Andrew Johnson's Reconstruction plan, but he was nearly elected governor of South Carolina anyway. When Radical Reconstruction began, he protested vigorously and helped restore home rule in South Carolina. He was elected governor in 1876 and 1878 and then U.S. senator in 1880. He served in the Senate until 1891 when the rising Populist movement ascended to power, replacing the Old South aristocracy as the dominant political force in South Carolina. He then served as commissioner of Pacific Railways from 1893 to 1899.

HAMPTON ROADS, BATTLE OF

❖ DATE: March 8–9, 1861

❖ LOCATION: Hampton Roads, Virginia

❖ CSS *VIRGINIA* AND JAMES RIVER SQUADRON

❖ USS *MONITOR* AND NORTH ATLANTIC BLOCKADING SQUADRON

❖ CASUALTIES: 24 (C); 409 (U.S.)

Above: *A view from the shore of the Battle of Hampton Roads, which featured the USS* Monitor *and the CSS* Virginia *(formerly the USS* Merrimack*) in history's first duel between ironclads.*

On March 8, 1861, the Confederate ironclad *Virginia* sailed into Hampton Roads off of Norfolk, Virginia, and began destroying Federal ships anchored there. Overcoming a three-month Confederate head start, the Federals had built their own ironclad, the *Monitor*, in less than 100 days and rushed it to Hampton Roads to check the *Virginia*'s rampage. On March 9, the two vessels fought history's first battle between ironclads. Although the contest was a tactical draw, the fact that the *Virginia* could no longer singlehandedly destroy the Federal fleet made it a strategic victory for the Union.

The most significant advantage the *Monitor* had over the *Virginia* was its twelve-foot draft and high maneuverability. The *Monitor*'s commander, Lieutenant John Worden, used this capability to score several hits on the *Virginia*. The pounding cracked the *Virginia*'s armor of railroad iron, but failed to penetrate the two-foot pitch pine and oak backing. The two ships dueled indecisively for two hours, then withdrew for what amounted to a half-hour intermission.

In the second two-hour engagement, the *Virginia* made an attempt to ram the *Monitor*, but, having lost its ram-beak in the previous day's fighting, this proved ineffective. Then Lieutenant Catesby ap Roger Jones, who had assumed command of the *Virginia* after Commodore Franklin Buchanan was wounded, tried to take advantage of his larger crew size and made several attempts to board the *Monitor*. The *Monitor* repulsed all efforts. Finally, Jones brought the *Virginia* to within thirty feet of the *Monitor* and struck its pilothouse at point-blank range with a nine-inch shell. Stationed immediately behind the point of impact, Worden personally felt the full effect of this concussion and commanded his helmsman to sheer off. The *Virginia* had also taken a beating, and with the ebb tide running, it withdrew across Hampton Roads to Norfolk. After the battle, the *Virginia* was still a threat, but thanks to the presence of the *Monitor*, it was no longer able to singlehandedly thwart Major General George B. McClellan's developing Peninsula Campaign.

HARDEE, WILLIAM J. (1815–73)

William Joseph Hardee graduated from West Point in 1838 and fought in the Seminole and Mexican wars. In 1855 he published *Rifle and Light Infantry Tactics*, which was the standard tactical manual in use on the eve of the Civil War. He also served as commandant of cadets at West Point and instructed tactics. He resigned from the U.S. Army on

Above: *Before the Civil War, William Hardee published* Rifle and Light Infantry Tactics, *which, in spite of its name, failed to offer significant tactical changes based on the new rifle technology.*

January 31, 1861, and was commissioned as a colonel in the Confederate army.

Hardee was made a brigadier general on June 17 and given a territorial command in Arkansas. On October 7, he was promoted to major general and fought at Shiloh and Perryville. He was promoted to lieutenant general on October 10, 1862, and commanded at Murfreesboro, Missionary Ridge, and during the Atlanta Campaign. He was a solid corps commander, earning the nickname "Old Reliable." In September 1864 he was named commander of the Department of South Carolina, Georgia, and Florida, but could do little to slow Major General William T. Sherman's advance. Hardee evacuated Savannah on December 18, 1864, and left Charleston in January 1865, ending the war fighting alongside General Joseph E. Johnston in North Carolina. After the war, Hardee served as president of the Selma and Meridian Railroad.

HARPERS FERRY, BATTLE OF

❖ DATE: September 12–15, 1862

❖ LOCATION: Jefferson County, Virginia

❖ ARMY OF NORTHERN VIRGINIA (C): 19,900

❖ HARPERS FERRY GARRISON (U.S.): 13,000

❖ CASUALTIES: 286 (C); 12,636 (U.S.)

The Battle of Harpers Ferry was a preliminary action in the Antietam Campaign. Major General Stonewall Jackson surrounded the Federal garrison there, taking 11,000 prisoners and capturing significant arms and equipment. Then the hard-marching Jackson joined General Robert E. Lee at Antietam before the indecisive Major General George B. McClellan could take advantage of Lee's divided condition.

On September 4, 1862, Lee began his Antietam Campaign. As he marched into Maryland, he had expected the Federals to abandon their 13,000-man garrison at Harpers Ferry. This strategic location blocked the lower Shenandoah Valley and with it,

Above: *Robert E. Lee could ill afford to leave the Federal garrison at Harpers Ferry in his rear as he advanced into Maryland, and he dispatched Stonewall Jackson to eliminate this threat.*

Above: *Harpers Ferry lay at the junction of the Shenandoah and Potomac rivers. Thomas Jefferson wrote that it was "perhaps one of the most stupendous scenes in nature" and "worth a voyage across the Atlantic."*

Lee's communications to the South. Although the ground vastly favored the attackers, the Federals stubbornly stayed in place, forcing Lee to deal with this unexpected threat to his rear.

As a result, Lee divided his army into four parts. Three of them under Jackson headed toward Harpers Ferry to reduce the fort, and a fourth under Major General James Longstreet headed for Boonsboro to wait for Jackson to complete his mission. Lee divided his army still again in response to unfounded reports of Federal activity around Chambersburg, Pennsylvania.

To meet this threat, Lee left a division commanded by Major General D. H. Hill in Boonsboro and shifted Longstreet northwest to Hagerstown, Maryland. To make matters worse for Lee, Jackson did not reach Harpers Ferry until September 13, a full day behind schedule. Upon arrival, Jackson encircled the Federal position, but the Federal commander did not

surrender until September 15, robbing Lee of the quick operation he needed.

While Jackson was occupied at Harpers Ferry, McClellan had an opportunity to strike Lee's divided force, but he acted indecisively. After "a severe night's march" on September 15, Jackson arrived at Sharpsburg with three divisions, allowing Lee to fight at Antietam with less of a disadvantage.

HARPERS FERRY, RAID OF
(APRIL 18, 1861)

When Virginia seceded from the Union on April 17, 1861, Lieutenant Roger Jones of the U.S. Army continued to defend the Harpers Ferry Arsenal and Armory with fifty regular soldiers and fifteen volunteers. With 360 Virginia militia marching in his direction from nearby Charles Town, Jones set fire to the facility on April 18. Some 17,000 muskets were destroyed in the blaze, but the Confederates salvaged the machinery, tools, and many musket and pistol parts. These materials were dispersed throughout the South to become the core of the Confederate ordnance

manufacturing effort. For example, the machinery for making the Model 1851 Mississippi rifle was sent to Fayetteville, North Carolina, and the equipment used to manufacture the Model 1855 rifle was sent to Richmond, Virginia.

HATTERAS INLET, BATTLE OF

- ❖ DATE: August 28–29, 1861
- ❖ LOCATION: Dare County, North Carolina
- ❖ HATTERAS ISLAND GARRISON (C): 900
- ❖ U.S. ARMY/NAVY FORCE (U.S.): 900 plus crews
- ❖ CASUALTIES: 770 (C); 1 (U.S.)

Hatteras Inlet, off the North Carolina coast, was an ideal anchorage for raiders and blockade-runners, and Confederate privateers and ships of the North Carolina navy used it as a base from which to attack Northern shipping. To defend it, the Confederates had begun work on two forts, Fort Hatteras and Fort Clark. These were hastily built earthworks equipped with cannons from the Gosport Navy Yard in Norfolk, but otherwise still under construction.

To eliminate this Confederate safe haven, the Federals launched the first joint army–navy operation of the Civil War. It would be a predominantly naval affair with Flag Officer Silas Stringham commanding a squadron of seven warships with 158 guns, four transports, and a steam tug. In the transports were nearly 900 troops under the tactical command of Colonel Rush C. Hawkins.

This Federal force left Hampton Roads on August 26, 1861, and arrived off Hatteras on the 28th. That morning, the Federals landed some 300 men and two twelve-pounder guns well north of the Confederate forts, but the army would play little part in the actual battle. Instead, Stringham used his superior naval ordnance to shell the Confederate forts while remaining out of range of hostile fire.

The Confederates abandoned Fort Clark and withdrew to Fort Hatteras, which Stringham began bombarding the next day. Demonstrating the capabilities of steam power, Stringham's ships ran past the fort, firing as they went, and then came around again on a different course, making it hard for the Confederate gunners to get their range.

Against such odds, Fort Hatteras never stood a chance, and at about noon the Confederates surrendered. The Federals captured 670 prisoners and thirty-five cannons. The only Federal casualty was a member of the landing party wounded at Fort Clark by friendly naval gunfire. Most of the Federal troops and three of the ships were left to hold the forts, and the

remainder returned to Fort Monroe with the Confederate prisoners.

It had long been a military dictum that coastal forts were superior to ships; so much so that one gun on land was considered to be equal to four on water. The entire coastal defense of the United States had been planned according to this precept. Hatteras Inlet suggested that advances in ships and their weaponry might have now negated the fort's inherent advantage. This was an unwelcome development for the Confederacy's coastal defense system.

HIGH WATER MARK OF THE CONFEDERACY (ZIEGLER'S GROVE)

Because many consider Gettysburg the turning point of the war, the "high water mark of the Confederacy" is a romantic term for the farthest point reached by

Pickett's Charge on the third day of the battle. Brigadier General Lewis A. Armistead led his brigade forward, orienting on a clump of trees on Cemetery Ridge called Ziegler's Grove and cheering his men on with his hat on his sword. Armistead briefly reached the Federal lines commanded by his old army friend, Major General Winfield Scott Hancock.

There Armistead encountered the guns of Battery A, Fourth U.S. Artillery, commanded by Lieutenant Alonzo Cushing, defending from behind a stone wall. Severely wounded, Cushing fired one of his two remaining guns, and Armistead fell mortally wounded across its muzzle. A small monument bearing the inscription "High Water Mark of the Rebellion" was placed there and dedicated in 1892.

Below: *This monument commemorates the "high water mark of the rebellion" where the Confederate forces reached their greatest point of advance at the Battle of Gettysburg in July 1863.*

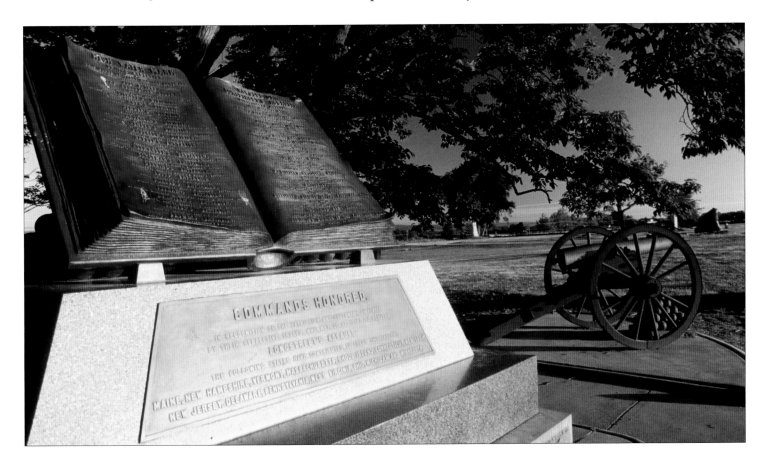

HILL, A. P.
(1825–65)

❖ RANK: Lieutenant general

❖ PLACE OF BIRTH: Culpeper, Virginia

❖ EDUCATED: West Point

❖ MILITARY CAREER:
1847-1861: Served in U.S. Army; fought in Mexican War and Seminole Wars, rising to rank of first lieutenant
1861: Colonel of the 13th Virginia Infantry Regiment at First Manassas
1862: Promoted to brigadier general, commanding a brigade; promoted to major general; commanded Hill's Light Division at Cedar Mountain, Second Manassas, Antietam, and Fredericksburg
1863: Promoted to lieutenant general after death of Jackson; corps commander at Gettysburg
1864–65: Siege of Petersburg

Ambrose Powell Hill graduated from West Point in 1847. Prior to the Civil War, he served in the Mexican War, the Seminole Wars, on the frontier, and for almost five years in the Office of the Superintendent of the United States Coast Survey. In 1856 he proposed to Ellen Marcy, who

Above: *A. P. Hill performed better as a division commander than at corps level. He had an irascible personality, which often led to disagreements with fellow commanders.*

accepted, but whose father thought she could do better than Hill and forbade the marriage. In an ironic twist, Marcy ended up marrying future Federal army general George B. McClellan.

Hill resigned from the U.S. Army on March 1, 1861, and served in western Virginia and with the reserve at First Manassas. He was appointed as a brigadier general in the Confederate army on February 26, 1862, and commanded a brigade at Williamsburg. He was promoted to major general on May 26 and fought during the Seven Days Battles. Leading his division at Mechanicsville, Hill grew restless waiting for Major General Stonewall Jackson and conducted a series of unsupported frontal attacks against the formidable Federal position. In five hours of tough fighting at Gaines' Mill, Hill helped pave the way for Brigadier General John Bell Hood's ultimately successful assault. Hill emerged from these and other episodes in the Seven Days Battles with a reputation as a combative, if not reckless, fighter, but when the *Richmond Examiner* gave Hill much of the credit that Major General James Longstreet thought was due to him, a quarrel developed between the two. Longstreet placed Hill under arrest, and there was talk of a duel. General Robert E. Lee tactfully defused the situation by transferring Hill to Jackson's command, but Hill continued to have personality clashes even in his new environment.

Hill served ably under Jackson at Cedar Mountain, Second Manassas, Harpers Ferry, and Antietam, where he marched his "Light Division" to arrive just in time to deliver a counterattack that saved Lee's right flank. Nonetheless, Hill and Jackson had several quarrels, and Jackson placed Hill under arrest on two occasions. Their ill relations required continual mediation and the attention of Lee.

At Chancellorsville, Hill was wounded by the same friendly fire that killed Jackson. When Lee reorganized the Army of Northern Virginia after Jackson's death, Hill was given command of the newly created Third Corps, which he led at Gettysburg, the Wilderness, North Anna, Cold Harbor, and Petersburg. Other than at Petersburg, Hill seemed largely overmatched by the responsibilities of corps command, a situation compounded by his ever-frail health. He was killed on April 2, 1865, in the waning days of the war.

HILL, D. H.
(1821–89)

❖ RANK: Lieutenant general

❖ PLACE OF BIRTH: Hill's Iron Works, York District, South Carolina

❖ EDUCATED: West Point

❖ MILITARY CAREER:
1847–61: Served in U.S. Army; fought in Mexican War, rising to rank of major
1861: Colonel of infantry regiment at Battle of Big Bethel
1862: Promoted to major general, commanded a division at Antietam
1863: Temporarily promoted to lieutenant general after death of Jackson; corps commander at Chickamauga

Daniel Harvey Hill graduated from West Point in 1842 and fought in the Mexican War. Afterward, he resigned his commission and taught at several colleges, including Davidson, before receiving an appointment as superintendent of the North Carolina Military Institute in 1859. Hill developed a vehement hatred of Northerners, as illustrated by a "Southern Series" of mathematical works he developed while in North Carolina. Problems in Hill's text included such scenarios as "the field of Battle of Buena Vista is six and a half miles from Saltillo. Two Indiana volunteers ran away from the battle at the same time." In 1861 Hill was commissioned as a colonel of the First North Carolina Infantry and fought in the Battle of Big Bethel. He advanced to brigadier general on June 10, 1861, and to major general on March 26, 1862.

Hill commanded a division on the Peninsula, fighting at Seven Pines and throughout the Seven Days Battles. He continued to serve at South Mountain and Antietam, and was then sent to North Carolina. He was recalled to Richmond to help defend the capital during the Gettysburg Campaign and was promoted to lieutenant general on July 11, 1863.

Hill was extremely critical of his fellow generals, including Robert A. Toombs, Theophilus H. Holmes, Stonewall Jackson, William H. C. Whiting, and even Robert E. Lee. When Hill was sent to aid General Braxton Bragg at Chickamauga, Hill wrote President Jefferson Davis that Bragg was incompetent, and recommended his removal. A staunch defender of Bragg, Davis relieved Hill instead. Because of the quarrel, the Confederate Congress

Above: *As a mathematics teacher before the Civil War, D. H. Hill wrote a textbook that used inept Northerners as the actors in many of his problems.*

never confirmed Hill's promotion, and he reverted to his previous rank of major general in the fall. After the war, Hill continued his prewar career as an educator, serving as president of the University of Arkansas and what became the Georgia Military Academy, as well as authoring an algebra textbook.

HOLMES, THEOPHILUS H. (1804–80)

Theophilus H. Holmes graduated from West Point in 1829 and served in the Seminole and Mexican wars. He resigned from the U.S. Army on April 22, 1861, and, although he was fifty-seven years old and deaf, he was appointed brigadier general in the Confederate army on June 5 by his West Point classmate Jefferson Davis.

Holmes commanded the reserve brigade at the Battle of First Manassas and was then promoted to major general and sent to command the Department of North Carolina. At the outset of the Peninsula Campaign, Holmes was ordered to send a division to Virginia, but his subsequent performance was almost comical in its ineptitude. At Malvern Hill, his troops were subjected to a murderous fire from the Federal gunboats with explosions that Major General D. H. Hill likened to "that of a small volcano." As his men scattered like quail in the bombardment, Holmes emerged from a small hut he had occupied and, cupping his hand behind his right ear, innocently remarked, "I thought I heard firing."

POSTED WEST

Like many generals who did not meet General Robert E. Lee's standards for the Army of Northern Virginia, Holmes was sent west,

where he reluctantly assumed command of the Trans-Mississippi Department. He was promoted to lieutenant general on October 10, 1862, but did nothing to warrant or justify this rank. He eventually asked to be relieved, and he was sent to North Carolina in 1864 to take charge of the state's reserves.

HOME FRONT

Life on the Southern home front defies monolithic characterization. Instead it comprised a complex series of interactions between and among such groups as civilians and soldiers, governmental authorities and citizens, slaves and whites, and Unionists and devoted Confederates.

Of course the term "home front" immediately conjures up images of women, and Southern women filled a variety of roles as nurses, heads of households, spies, and diarists. Nearly all found their traditional sphere of domesticity and motherhood under stress. Not only were they forced to assume new roles, the women were faced with new hardships. Food shortages, marauders, invasion, unsupervised slaves, and inflation all threatened Confederate women's ability to maintain life on the home front. In some cases, their letters describing the war's harsh reality motivated their soldiers to leave the army in order to return home and alleviate some of the suffering.

HOME GUARD

Many Southern communities were protected by "Home Guard" units that not only defended against Federal attack, but also helped track down deserters. Home Guard units were a desperate bunch that provided mixed results. The scarcity of men on the Confederate home front as well as governmental attention directed elsewhere

Above: *The Confederate Home Guard had broad authority to establish order in communities throughout the South. The Home Guard's performance was mixed, and many members abused their powers.*

allowed these units to operate with great discretion.

Much of the activity on the Confederate home front was devoted to providing the material needed to wage war. The South's limited prewar industrial base caused established manufacturing centers like Richmond to become even more important while new activities were established at places like Columbus, Georgia. All these sites suffered from a shortage of skilled labor.

Border states and coastal areas found themselves frequently caught up in raging battles. Winchester, Virginia, for example, changed hands over seventy times during the war. Battles not only brought destruction to the Confederate home front, they also created hordes of refugees, the lucky ones of which could find shelter at the home of a relative away from the fighting. Many Southerners were

forced to choose between life under Federal occupation or abandoning their homes to an uncertain future. When Major General William T. Sherman embarked on a campaign to break the will of the Confederate people through the tactics of "hard war," suffering on the home front reached new heights. A few Southerners who had always had Unionist sympathies welcomed Federal occupation. In some cases, varied individuals with assorted grievances against the Confederacy banded together to form their own resistance. Newton Knight's "Free State of Jones" in Mississippi is the most well-known example.

The institution of slavery also experienced changes on the Confederate home front. With less supervision, slave productivity decreased. Upon Federal occupation, some slaves joined the Federal army. Others took advantage of the changing conditions to run away.

A TIME OF CHANGE

While the Confederate home front experience was varied, it certainly represented change as social,

economic, and political mores tried to adjust to the pressures of war. Traditionally, histories of the home front experience have focused on white women, but more recent scholarship has broadened the subject to include a host of previously underrepresented groups.

HONOR, SOUTHERN

A distinctive sense of Southern honor helped shape culture, motivate secession, and direct wartime conduct and postwar attitudes in the South. Following the lead of the planter class, Southerners developed a strong code that valued manliness, feminine virtue, decorum, and personal reputation. Affronts to the Southerner's sense of honor were often met by a challenge to a duel.

Because it had come to dominate all aspects of life in the South, Southerners on the eve of the Civil War considered slavery to be honorable. If the South was honorable, then its foundational institution must also be honorable.

Northern interference with slavery and threats against Southerners' private property were challenges to Southern honor and had to be resisted. Southern secessionist rhetoric was laced with appeals to defend the region's honor. The doctrine of states' rights was predicated on this concept of maintaining the honor of one's state against attacks by outside forces.

The Southern notion of honor certainly affected wartime conduct. For example, many Southerners were motivated to volunteer for military service rather than suffer the stigma of being drafted. After the war, honor helped the region cope with its defeat. States' rights and their associated principles were worth fighting for and had to be defended. Defeat on behalf of a just cause was far more honorable than passive acquiescence. Also, as some Southerners came to consider slavery to be evil, the "Lost Cause" interpretation of the Civil War reduced slavery's importance as a cause of the war and instead focused on the more honorable idea of states' rights.

HOOD, JOHN BELL (1831–79)

- ❖ RANK: Lieutenant general

- ❖ PLACE OF BIRTH: Owingsville, Kentucky

- ❖ EDUCATED: West Point

- ❖ MILITARY CAREER:
  1853–61: Served in U.S. Army, rising to rank of second lieutenant
  1862: Commanded Hood's Texas Brigade; promoted to brigadier general; success at Battle of Gaines' Mill; commanded a division in Northern Virginia Campaign, at Second Manassas and Antietam
  1863: Led assault on Little Round Top at Gettysburg, where he was badly wounded
  1864: Commanded Army of the Tennessee in Atlanta Campaign, Tennessee Campaign, and Battle of Franklin; defeated at Battle of Nashville

John Bell Hood graduated from West Point in 1853. He was wounded in fighting against Native Americans near the Mexican border in 1857. He resigned from the U.S. Army in April 1861. He was commissioned as a lieutenant in the Confederate army and initially commanded Major General John B. Magruder's cavalry at Yorktown. On March 6, 1862, Hood was appointed as a brigadier general and given command of the Texas Brigade. During the Peninsula Campaign, he launched a desperate final charge that broke the Federal line at Gaines' Mill. On the strength of that performance, Hood's Texans became General Robert E. Lee's favorite shock troops. The bold attack also showed Hood's temperament as an aggressive, offensive-minded officer.

Hood continued to command the brigade at Second Manassas and Antietam until he was promoted to major general on October 10 and given a division in Lieutenant General James Longstreet's corps. Hood fought at Fredericksburg, and a bad wound at Gettysburg left his left arm crippled. He was sent west with Longstreet's corps to reinforce General Braxton Bragg at Chickamauga. During the fighting, Hood lost his right leg, and thereafter had to be strapped into his saddle in order to maintain his balance on his horse.

Hood was promoted to lieutenant general on February 1, 1863, and

Above: *President Jefferson Davis grew frustrated with Joseph Johnston's defensive strategy during the Atlanta Campaign and replaced Johnston with the aggressive John Bell Hood. The results were disappointing.*

commanded a corps during the Atlanta Campaign where, in spite of his usual combative nature, he forfeited an opportunity to strike Major General William T. Sherman at Cassville. When President Jefferson Davis finally had enough of General Joseph E. Johnston's defensive approach to the campaign, Davis replaced Johnston with Hood. It was a controversial decision. Even General Robert E. Lee advised Davis, "Hood is a bold fighter. I am doubtful as to other qualities necessary."

Indeed, Hood was a much better tactician than strategist. His decision to go on the offensive around Atlanta proved disastrous.

On September 1, 1864, Hood desperately withdrew north, hoping Sherman would follow him. Instead, Sherman dispatched only Major General George H. Thomas, who decisively defeated Hood at the Battles of Franklin and Nashville in Tennessee.

HOTCHKISS, JEDEDIAH (1828–99)

A native New Yorker, Jedediah Hotchkiss moved to Virginia, where he founded Mossy Creek Academy and Loch Willow School for Boys. As a sideline, he made maps, and it was this skill that would ultimately make him a valuable member of the staff of Lieutenant General Stonewall Jackson and others.

MAPPING THE VALLEY

Hotchkiss did some informal work for Brigadier General Robert S. Garnett in western Virginia before joining the Virginia militia on March 23, 1862. After just three days as acting adjutant, Hotchkiss was summoned to Jackson's headquarters and ordered to map the Shenandoah Valley from Harpers Ferry to Lexington. Throughout the Shenandoah Valley Campaign, Hotchkiss's accurate maps gave Jackson a tremendous intelligence advantage over the Federals. He also helped map the route Jackson used for his flank march at Chancellorsville.

After Jackson's death, Hotchkiss continued to make maps for General Robert E. Lee and Lieutenant General Richard S. Ewell. After the war, Hotchkiss returned to Staunton, Virginia, where he ran a school for boys, worked as a surveyor, and recorded much of the history of Jackson and the Second Corps.

IMBODEN, JOHN D. (1823–95)

John D. Imboden was a lawyer and legislator in Virginia. Before the war, he organized the Staunton Artillery, which he commanded at First Manassas. He then organized the First Partisan Rangers and fought at Cross Keys and Port Republic. Imboden was promoted to brigadier general on January 28, 1863.

In April and May 1863, Imboden conducted a raid into northwestern Virginia that cut the Baltimore and Ohio Railroad and captured several thousand horses and cattle. He conducted screening operations during the Gettysburg Campaign and was critical to the saving of the Confederate forces' wagon trains at Williamsport during the retreat. He captured Charleston, West Virginia, and fought during Major General Jubal A. Early's Shenandoah Valley Campaign in 1864. That autumn, Imboden contracted typhoid fever

Above: *John Imboden is best known for his raid in the spring of 1863 that cut the Baltimore and Ohio Railroad.*

and served the remainder of the war on prison duty in Aiken, South Carolina.

INDIAN TERRITORY

At the outbreak of the Civil War, the Indian Territory, an area that roughly corresponds to the present state of Oklahoma, had a population of at least 60,000, mostly made up of members of the Five Civilized Tribes of the Cherokee, Chickasaw, Choctaw, Creek, and Seminole. Its 7,000 slaves and proximity to Texas, Arkansas, and Missouri made the territory promising to the Confederacy. Brigadier General Albert Pike succeeded in obtaining treaties with many Native American groups who then contributed soldiers to the Confederate army. Battles fought in the Indian Territory include Fort Gibson and Honey Springs.

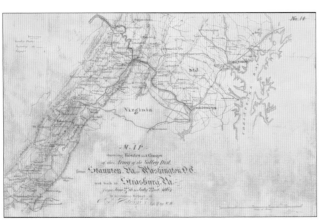

Left: *Jedediah Hotchkiss's detailed maps of the Shenandoah Valley were critical to the formulation of Confederate plans and strategy throughout Stonewall Jackson's campaign in the area.*

On May 13, 1861, Colonel Benjamin McCulloch was assigned command of the Indian Territory. On November 22, the area was designated a department and placed under the command of Pike, and then absorbed by the Trans-Mississippi Department on May 26, 1862. Subsequently, the Indian Territory went through an ambiguous command history. The *Official Records* state that on December 11, 1863, Brigadier General Samuel B. Maxey was "assigned to command of the Indian Territory" and, on May 9, 1864, he "resumed command," but there is no explanation of who commanded in the interim. On February 21, 1865, Brigadier General Douglas H. Cooper was assigned command of the "District of the Indian Territory," and on March 1, "superintendency of Indian Affairs" was added to his responsibilities.

INDIANS SERVING IN THE CONFEDERATE ARMY

As a result of the efforts of Brigadier General Albert Pike, the Confederacy secured the services of 5,145 men of the Cherokee, Chickasaw, Choctaw, Creek, and Seminole nations, who were organized into five regiments and five battalions in the Trans-Mississippi Department.

Pike's original intention was to use Native American soldiers primarily to defend their own home areas, but subsequent developments led to the Native Americans fighting not just in the Indian Territory, but in Arkansas and Missouri as well.

In the latter part of 1864, the Native American troops were organized into three brigades: Cherokee Stand Watie commanded

the First Brigade of Cherokees, Chickasaws, and Osages; Tandy Walker, a mixed-blood Choctaw, commanded the Second Brigade of Choctaws; and Daniel McIntosch, a mixed-blood Creek, commanded the Third Brigade of Seminoles and Creeks.

SOUTHERN RECRUITS

Fewer Native Americans were recruited east of the Mississippi, but two companies, consisting mainly of Cherokees, served with the Sixty-ninth North Carolina Regiment, and Catawbas served in the Fifth, Twelfth, and Seventeenth South Carolina Volunteer Infantry in the Army of Northern Virginia. White officers commanded most of these Native Americans, with the notable exception of Lieutenant John Astoo-ga Sto-ga.

Above: *Stand Watie was the most famous of the Native Americans who served with the Confederacy, advancing to the rank of brigadier general.*

While the Native Americans were skilled horsemen and scouts, and often effective raiders, they were generally poorly equipped and ill-disciplined. Their inferior government-issued weapons were sometimes supplemented by bows, arrows, and hatchets, all of which were no match for the demoralizing effect of Federal artillery. The Cherokees and Seminoles were never wholeheartedly supportive of the Confederate cause, and desertions, especially among the Cherokees, were high.

However, other Cherokees—such as those led by Watie—remained loyal, and the Choctaws and

Chickasaws were overwhelmingly faithful to the Confederacy. In many cases, the Native Americans suffered from poor treatment by white commanders who were more concerned with defending the Confederate states than Native American territories. Pay, food, and clothing intended for Native Americans were often diverted to white troops, and the supply system in the Indian Territory was plagued by corruption and fraud.

A general reorganization in late 1864 offered some improvement, but by then the Federal victory at Honey Springs on July 17, 1863, had marked the end of massed Confederate resistance in the Indian Territory.

INDUSTRY, CONFEDERATE

Industrial capitalism made few inroads in the antebellum South, where economic activity centered on raw agricultural products. For manufactured items, the South relied on the protected industries of the northern United States and Europe. This low level of industrialization served to seriously undermine the Confederate war effort, especially when considered in light of the North's industrial might. Before the war, the North had produced 94 percent of the country's iron, 97 percent of its coal, and 97 percent of its firearms. Thus when the Civil War broke out, the Confederacy faced monumental shortages of war material. All told, the South boasted a mere 18,000 manufacturing establishments compared to over 110,000 in the North.

An inventory of small arms in the new Confederacy revealed just 159,010 weapons of differing models and qualities. About 1,000 cannons, again of varying qualities and often obsolete, had been captured from Federal arsenals and facilities. The only major rolling mill in the South was Tredegar Iron Works in Richmond, Virginia, and the only gunpowder factory was near Nashville, Tennessee. The enterprising Colonel Josiah Gorgas was designated the Confederacy's chief of ordnance, and he set out to make the most of the South's limited manufacturing base.

Some of the Confederacy's enormous manufacturing deficit could be made up by blockade-running, but Gorgas also did what he could to develop domestic capability. Although a shortage of skilled labor and machinery hamstrung his efforts, Gorgas was able to organize cannon foundries in Macon, Columbus, and Augusta, Georgia, a new iron-manufacturing center in Selma, Alabama, and artillery munitions plants in Salisbury, North Carolina, and Montgomery, Alabama. The mainstay of Confederate production remained Tredegar, which stayed in operation throughout the war.

OCCUPATION PROBLEMS
Elsewhere, the Confederate industrial effort suffered severely from Federal occupation of what little manufacturing base the prewar South had. Critical iron,

Below: *Much of what little domestic industry the Confederacy had was located in Virginia, such as this shipyard on the James River near Richmond.*

gunpowder, percussion cap, rifle, artillery, and locomotive capabilities were lost in Tennessee. Shipbuilding facilities fell into Federal hands at Norfolk and New Orleans. The Confederacy's efforts to build industrial capacity experienced continual disruption when its activities had to be relocated to areas less threatened by the Federal army's advance.

Although the Confederacy was never able to match the North's industrial capability, the ingenious efforts of Gorgas made it so that the Confederate forces never lost a major battle due to a want of arms or ammunition. Moreover, the industrialization of the South during the Civil War had a marked effect on the shape of the region in the postwar period. For example, new iron mines and coalfields that were developed out of military necessity in Birmingham, Alabama, after losses in Tennessee led to the growth of Birmingham's steel industry after the war.

INFANTRY

The workhorse of the Confederate army was its infantry. More than any other branch of the service, the infantry most felt the war's physical demands and its dangers. Infantrymen usually arrived at the battlefield after a long foot march. Lieutenant General Stonewall Jackson's men became so skilled at these movements they became known as "foot cavalry." After arriving at the battlefield, if the situation permitted, infantrymen would prepare defensive breastworks for protection. Breastworks combined with the greater accuracy and range of the rifle to render infantry attacks extremely costly. As the war progressed, infantry learned to make better use of skirmishers to create some battlefield dispersion,

but the general reliance on mass still made the attacking infantry regiment a vulnerable target.

INTELLIGENCE SERVICE

Commanders rely on military intelligence to provide them with actionable information concerning the enemy and the terrain. This information must be timely and accurate, and must be processed to facilitate decision making. While the Confederates had access to numerous sources of information, the ability to interpret and use this knowledge to gain a military advantage was largely dependent on the capabilities of the individual commander.

The nature of the Civil War allowed both Confederates and Federals to make extensive use of spies in gathering military intelligence. Spies lived and operated among the enemy and obtained information by eavesdropping and keeping their eyes open. Confederate women were useful spies because their gender did not arouse suspicion and often gave them assets that men could not obtain. Spies were certainly patriotic, but usually were devoid of military training and in many cases lacked discretion. The Confederacy in particular benefited from these sources because of the number of Confederate sympathizers who remained in Washington after the war began. Included in this number was Rose O'Neal Greenhow,

who used her connections in Washington social circles to provide valuable information to the Confederacy until her arrest in August 1861. Because most of the war was fought on Southern soil, the Confederacy was also able to use spies from among its local population. Belle Boyd is probably the most famous of these types of spies, although her exploits are usually considered to be exaggerated.

Scouts differed from spies in that they operated from a base away from the enemy and then moved to the enemy to gather information of a fairly specific nature. Scouts often had more military training than spies. Sam Davis was a heroic scout for General Braxton Bragg in Tennessee until Davis was captured and executed in 1863. The

Below: *Scouts such as this one usually had more military training than spies and often produced more reliable and actionable intelligence.*

mysterious Henry Harrison scouted for Lieutenant General James Longstreet and provided critical information during the Gettysburg Campaign. Sometimes scouts were organized into military units such as "Coleman's Scouts" in Tennessee and Major John Richardson's scouts in Virginia.

The most efficient and reliable intelligence source, however, was the cavalry. Cavalrymen could use their horses' mobility to not just gather information about the enemy, but to then return to friendly lines and render a timely report that allowed commanders to take immediate action. Major General Jeb Stuart excelled at this activity and gave General Robert E. Lee a marked intelligence advantage over his Federal counterparts.

The Confederates also enjoyed a significant advantage based on their local knowledge of the terrain. Many Confederate soldiers and officers were fighting in areas with which they were very familiar. Some were even fighting in areas they had grown up in. The Confederates could exploit this knowledge by using the terrain to their advantage. Mapmaker Jedediah Hotchkiss, for example, was critical to Lieutenant General Stonewall Jackson's success in the Shenandoah Valley and at Chancellorsville.

What the Confederacy lacked was a centralized organization to collect, analyze, and distribute intelligence. In addition to spies, scouts, and cavalry units, Confederate commanders were inundated with information gleaned from newspapers, deserters, prisoners, balloons, and locals. Without an all-source intelligence center to process this raw information, it was difficult for commanders to act decisively. Lee had an innate ability to analyze his own

intelligence, but other Confederate commanders were less adept. The Confederate belief that the Federal attack on New Orleans would come from up the Mississippi River and Lieutenant General John C. Pemberton's inability to anticipate Major General Ulysses S. Grant's intentions at Vicksburg are examples.

INTERIOR LINES

Interior lines is the concept advanced by Swiss military theorist Antoine Henri Jomini of ordering one's lines of communications relative to the enemy's in order to create a maneuver advantage. The condition of interior lines is achieved when the friendly force commander can move parts of his army more rapidly than an enemy operating on exterior lines. In this way the force operating on interior lines can defeat an enemy operating on exterior lines in detail. Interior lines can be obtained either by a central position, such as Major General Stonewall Jackson used during the Shenandoah Valley Campaign, or by superior transportation systems, such as General Joseph E. Johnston exploited by sending reinforcements by rail at the Battle of First Manassas. In practical application, the superior Federal railroads often negated the Confederate geographic central position.

IRISH SOLDIERS

The largest immigrant populations in America at the time of the Civil War were in the North, but the Irish made up the most numerous group of foreigners in the Confederate army. One of the most solidly Irish units was Company I of the Eighth Alabama Regiment, known as the "Emerald Guards." Of the 109 men in the company, 104 listed Ireland as their

place of birth. The Emerald Guards went to war in dark green uniforms, carrying a banner with the Confederate colors and George Washington on one side and a harp and shamrock with the inscription "Erin-go-Bragh" on the other. Major General Patrick R. Cleburne was the Confederacy's most notable general of Irish origin. Generally speaking, the Confederate Irishmen were considered to have good senses of humor, to be well adapted to the rigors of camp life, and to be good fighters. However, many also had reputations for being quarrelsome and resistant to discipline.

Above: *Patrick Cleburne, who gained the rank of major general and a reputation as the "Stonewall of the West," was the Confederacy's most famous Irishman.*

IRONCLADS

As early as 1822, naval theorists had begun proposing that wooden ships be replaced with iron ones. The French had employed ironclads during the Crimean War (1853–56), but the new technology attracted little attention in America. Thus, on the eve of the Civil War, the United States still relied on wooden ships. Confederate secretary of the navy Stephen R. Mallory saw an opportunity for the Confederacy to offset the huge Federal naval advantage by building ironclads. However, the superior Federal industrial might quickly outstripped the Confederate effort to field this revolutionary naval technology.

While the war was still in its infancy, Mallory argued, "I regard the possession of an iron-armored ship as a matter of the first necessity . . . If we . . . follow their [the United States Navy's] . . . example and build wooden ships, we shall have to construct several at one time; for one or two ships would fall easy prey to her comparatively numerous steam frigates. But inequality of numbers may be compensated by invulnerability; and thus not only does economy but naval success dictate the wisdom and expediency of fighting with iron against wood."

RECHRISTENED IRONCLAD

With Mallory's urging, the USS *Merrimack* was converted into an ironclad that was rechristened the CSS *Virginia*, and after the *Virginia*'s initial success at

Hampton Roads, the Confederacy embarked on a rather haphazard effort to build additional ironclads.

The Confederate Congress appropriated $2 million for the purchase or construction of ironclads in Europe, but initial efforts to obtain armored vessels from this source failed. Mallory then turned his attention to domestic production. In addition to the *Virginia*, he authorized construction of two ironclads at Memphis, Tennessee, and two more at New Orleans. Only three of these contracted vessels became operational, and none were capable of operating beyond inland waters.

Throughout the war, the Confederacy initiated production of fifty-two ironclads and completed almost thirty of them. A lack of sufficient iron plate or an engine plagued many construction efforts, and other partially completed ironclads had to be destroyed to prevent Federal capture. Of all the Confederate ironclads, only the *Albemarle* obtained any of the success—albeit temporary—of the *Virginia*.

ISLAND NO. 10, BATTLE OF

❖ DATE: April 7, 1862

❖ LOCATION: Lake County, Tennessee

❖ ISLAND NO. 10 GARRISON (C): 4,000

❖ ARMY OF THE MISSISSIPPI (U.S.): 25,000, plus gunboats

❖ CASUALTIES: 3,500 (C); 78 (U.S.)

The Confederates built positions at Island No. 10 and New Madrid, Missouri, to block Federal navigation of the Mississippi River. On March 13, 1862, as Brigadier General John Pope prepared to begin siege operations against New Madrid, the Confederate force there withdrew. Pope then turned his attention to Island No. 10,

Below: *Victory at Island No. 10 catapulted John Pope to command in the east, but he was unable to repeat his earlier success when he faced Robert E. Lee at Second Manassas.*

digging a canal through the swamps to allow his boats to bypass the Confederate defenses.

CUTTING THE RETREAT

On April 7, he ferried four regiments across the Mississippi to cut off the Confederate line of retreat, forcing Brigadier General William W. Mackall to surrender 3,500 Confederates while another 500 escaped through the swamps.

The victory opened the Mississippi River to Fort Pillow, Tennessee, and enhanced Pope's reputation enough that he became commander of the Army of Virginia two months later.

IUKA, BATTLE OF

❖ DATE: September 19, 1862

❖ LOCATION: Tishomingo County, Mississippi

❖ ARMY OF THE WEST (C): 3,200

❖ ARMY OF THE MISSISSIPPI (U.S.): 4,000–4,500

❖ CASUALTIES: 700 (C); 782 (U.S.)

Confederate forces in Mississippi under Major Generals Earl Van Dorn and Sterling Price presented a twofold challenge to Major General Ulysses S. Grant. Not only did they threaten Grant's communications with Federal forces in Tennessee, they also represented possible reinforcements to the Confederate forces under General Braxton Bragg that were concentrating there in preparation for an invasion of Kentucky.

Grant resolved to act, attacking Price at Iuka on September 19, 1862. Grant had planned to trap Price in a pincer between Major Generals William S. Rosecrans and Edward O. C. Ord, but the two Federal generals failed to coordinate

their efforts and Price escaped. Price and Van Dorn then joined forces near Ripley, southwest of Corinth, on September 28. For his part, Grant ordered most of his army back to Corinth, but still was thought scattered enough by Van Dorn that the Confederates attacked Corinth on October 3.

JACKSON, THOMAS "STONEWALL" (1824–63)

❖ RANK: Lieutenant general

❖ PLACE OF BIRTH: Clarksburg, Virginia

❖ EDUCATED: West Point

❖ MILITARY CAREER:
1846–51: Served in U.S. Army, fighting in Mexican War, rising to rank of major
1862: Commanded Stonewall Brigade at First Manassas; success in Valley Campaign and Seven Days Battles under Lee; corps comander at Second Manassas, Harper's Ferry, and Antietam
1863: Success at Chancelorsville; died of wounds after accidental shooting

Thomas J. Jackson graduated from West Point in 1846. He was commissioned in the artillery and served with many of his classmates in the Mexican War. Assigned to Captain John B. Magruder's battery, Lieutenant Jackson fought with distinction at Chapultepec and was brevetted to major. He resigned his commission in 1851 and joined the faculty at the Virginia Military Institute. Professor Jackson taught natural philosophy (similar to today's physics) and artillery. Although revered at VMI today, at the time Jackson was unpopular with many of the cadets, who considered him to be a rigid taskmaster with odd personal habits. He commanded the VMI Cadet Corps that provided security at John Brown's hanging on December 2, 1859.

Jackson received a colonel's commission on April 21, 1861, and after first leading a battalion of cadets to Richmond to serve as drillmasters, he took command at Harpers Ferry. He was soon promoted to brigadier general and served with General Joseph E. Johnston in the Shenandoah Valley and at First Manassas. At Manassas, Jackson's brigade held the line at the Henry House Hill, and he was given the sobriquet "Stonewall" by Brigadier General Barnard E. Bee. Jackson advanced to major general on October 7, 1861, and became commander of the Shenandoah Valley district.

IN THE VALLEY

Jackson conducted a brilliant campaign in the Shenandoah Valley that took advantage of interior lines and hard marching to rout a total of

Left: *Stonewall Jackson was second only to Robert E. Lee in the hearts of most Confederates. Secretive, devout, hard-marching, and aggressive, Jackson scored great victories, including his masterpiece in the Shenandoah Valley.*

Above: *The loss of Stonewall Jackson at Chancellorsville was devastating to Robert E. Lee, who now lacked a trusted subordinate who could act with little supervision.*

12,500 Federals and occupy the attention of some 60,000 more. In the process, Jackson posed such a threat to Washington that President Abraham Lincoln felt compelled to withhold troops from Major General George B. McClellan's ongoing Peninsula Campaign.

Jackson then marched south to join General Robert E. Lee in the defense of Richmond. Perhaps exhausted from the Shenandoah Valley Campaign, Jackson's performance during the Seven Days Battles was uncharacteristically lethargic. Nonetheless, a partnership was forged between Lee and Jackson that would make them the Confederacy's greatest command team.

The two showed the power of this combination at the Battle of Second Manassas, where Jackson again used his incredible mobility to envelop Major General John Pope. During the Antietam Campaign, Jackson captured the Federal garrison at Harpers Ferry that threatened Lee's rear and then rapidly marched to Antietam to help Lee hold off McClellan.

In spite of his close relationship with Lee, Jackson often quarreled with his subordinates. His rigid discipline and obsession with secrecy clashed with the likes of Major General William W. Loring and Lieutenant General A. P. Hill. Nonetheless, Jackson was idolized by his troops and the Southern population.

Jackson was made lieutenant general on October 10, 1862, and given command of Lee's Second Corps. He led the corps at Fredericksburg, but his most brilliant action was at Chancellorsville, where another of his famous marches resulted in a surprise attack that destroyed the Federal flank. Unfortunately, as Jackson reconnoitered forward of his lines, he was mortally wounded by his own men.

The loss of Jackson severely impacted Lee, who had become accustomed to issuing broad, discretionary orders that suited Jackson's capabilities and temperament but were inappropriate for other of Lee's lieutenants. Lee sorely missed Jackson's initiative and offensive flair during the Gettysburg Campaign.

Jackson was an extremely religious man who contributed greatly to revivals in the Confederate army. Many saw religious connotations in his untimely death, as if he were being made a sacrifice for the sins of the Confederacy, including idol worship of Jackson. His reputation quickly reached legendary proportions in the South, and he became a prominent figure in the romance of the "Lost Cause."

JENKINS, MICAH
(1835–64)

Micah Jenkins was an aristocratic planter and an 1855 graduate of the South Carolina Military Academy (the Citadel). He founded the King's Mountain Military School and taught there until the beginning of the Civil War. Jenkins was a strong secessionist. He was commissioned as a colonel and fought at First Manassas and

Above: *Micah Jenkins, a graduate of the Citadel, was an outstanding brigade commander who was tragically killed at the Battle of the Wilderness by fire from his own men.*

during the Peninsula Campaign. He was promoted to brigadier general on July 22, 1862. He was severely wounded at Second Manassas but recovered to fight at Fredericksburg, Gettysburg, and Chickamauga. His own men accidentally killed him during the Battle of the Wilderness in an incident resembling that involving Lieutenant General Stonewall Jackson near the same place a year earlier.

JENKINS' FERRY, BATTLE OF

- ❖ DATE: April 30, 1864
- ❖ LOCATION: Grant County, Arkansas
- ❖ ARMY OF ARKANSAS (C): 10,000
- ❖ DEPARTMENT OF ARKANSAS (U.S.): 12,000
- ❖ CASUALTIES: 443 (C); 428 (U.S.)

In support of Major General Nathaniel P. Banks's Red River Campaign, Major General Frederick Steele was supposed to fix Confederate forces in southwest Arkansas. Steele's late start negated any assistance he might have provided Banks, and when Banks was forced to abandon his campaign, General Edmund Kirby Smith was able to concentrate on Steele and cut his communications. On April 25, 1864, Smith defeated Steele at Marks' Mills, causing Steele to withdraw. Smith attacked Steele again at Jenkins' Ferry on April 30, forcing him to abandon his pontoon train. The Federals suffered 428 casualties compared to 443 for the Confederates. During the fighting, African American soldiers were accused of avenging an alleged Confederate massacre of the First Kansas Colored Troops at the April 18 Battle of Poison Spring.

JOHN BROWN'S RAID
(OCTOBER 16, 1859)

John Brown was an abolitionist zealot who originally ran a station on the Underground Railroad in Richmond, Ohio. In 1855 the struggle to determine Kansas's status as a free or slave state drew Brown west, where clashes between antislavery Kansans and proslavery Missouri "Border Ruffians" were becoming routine. In May 1856, a group of 800 Border Ruffians, supported by five cannons, ransacked Lawrence, Kansas, the center of antislavery activity in the area. In response, Brown led a raid that murdered five Missourians at Pottawatomie Creek. Convinced he was an instrument of God, Brown led several more raids and greatly contributed to the violence that permeated "Bleeding Kansas."

WEAPONS FOR REVOLT
Late in 1857, Brown began making plans to lead a large-scale revolt to free the slaves across the South and "purge this land with blood." To do so, he would need weapons, and on October 16, 1859, he led a group of twenty men to seize the Federal armory at Harpers Ferry in western Virginia. Local militia blocked Brown's escape, and the next morning a company of marines commanded by Colonel Robert E. Lee stormed the fire engine house where Brown was holed up, killing ten of Brown's men and capturing Brown. Unrepentant and defiant, Brown declared, "Let them hang me." He was convicted of treason and hanged at Charles Town on December 2, 1859.

Some in the North considered Brown a martyr, and he was immortalized in the song "John Brown's Body." In the South, however, Brown exacerbated longstanding fears of slave revolts. The residual tension of John Brown's raid was one of many factors that pushed the United States closer to sectional war.

Below: *Although a failure, John Brown's raid on Harpers Ferry incited the worst fears of slave insurrection held by many Southerners.*

JOHNSTON, ALBERT SIDNEY
(1803–62)

- ❖ RANK: Lieutenant general

- ❖ PLACE OF BIRTH: Washington, Kentucky

- ❖ EDUCATED: West Point

- ❖ MILITARY CAREER:
1826–61: Served in U.S. Army and Texas army, fighting in Black Hawk War, Texan War of Independence, and Mexican War; rose to rank of brigadier general
1861: Appointed full general and commander of Western Department
1862: Killed at Battle of Shiloh

Above: *Many considered Albert Sidney Johnston to be the most promising officer to join the Confederacy, but his Civil War performance never justified such an assessment.*

Albert Sidney Johnston graduated from West Point in 1826. He served in the Black Hawk War before resigning from the army in 1834 because of his wife's poor health. After she died, he enlisted as a private in the Texas army in 1836 and was made brigadier general and commander of the army in 1837. He served as secretary of war for the Republic of Texas and saw limited action during the Mexican War.

Back in the U.S. Army, Johnston performed tedious duty as paymaster until 1855, when Secretary of War Jefferson F. Davis tapped him to command the newly formed Second Cavalry, a regiment that included such future Confederate luminaries as Robert E. Lee, Earl Van Dorn, and John Bell Hood. Johnston commanded the Department of Texas and led the Utah Expedition, designed to quiet tensions between Mormons and Federal authorities, from 1858 to 1860.

When the Civil War broke out, Johnston was commanding the Department of the Pacific in San Francisco. He resigned his post on April 10, 1861, but remained in command until his successor arrived. In the meantime, he was offered a commission in the U.S. Army as second in command to Lieutenant General Winfield Scott. Instead, Johnston led a party of over thirty other Southern sympathizers on a well-publicized journey across the Arizona desert and Apache country to offer his services to the Confederacy.

PROMOTED TO GENERAL

Johnston's arrival was heralded with great anticipation. On August 30, he was appointed as a full general in the Confederate army and given command of the Western Department. At the time, many considered Johnston to be the Confederacy's best general. President Jefferson Davis was particularly supportive of Johnston, writing, "I hoped and expected that I had others who would prove generals; but I knew I had one, and that was Sidney Johnston." Such sentiments were not confined to the South alone. William T. Sherman described Johnston as "a real general" and Ulysses S. Grant said that officers who knew Johnston "expected him to prove the most formidable man that the Confederacy would produce."

Johnston's actual wartime performance did not live up to these high expectations. The loss of Fort Donelson on February 15, 1862, compelled Johnston to withdraw his Army of the Mississippi out of Tennessee, abandoning the industrial and logistical base of Nashville, and concentrate his force at the rail junction at Corinth. This retreat damaged Johnston's credibility.

SHILOH

During the April 6 Battle of Shiloh, Johnston, perhaps still dazed by his withdrawal from Tennessee, ceded much authority to his second in command, General Pierre Gustave Toutant Beauregard. Although Johnston laid out the concept for a turning movement, he left the details of the plan to Beauregard, who instead devised and executed a frontal attack. During the actual battle, Johnston was too far forward to affect anything other than events in his immediate vicinity, and he did little to contribute as the army commander or to impose his will on Beauregard.

Johnston personally led an afternoon attack that swept the Federal defenders from their position in the peach orchard, but in the process he was struck several times. One bullet had hit him behind his right knee and cut an artery, but the injury was masked by Johnston's high-top boot. Even Johnston failed to notice the wound, telling an aide, "They came very near putting me hors de combat in that charge," but making no further complaint. In fact, Johnston was unknowingly bleeding to death. A simple tourniquet could have saved his life, but the boot continued to hide the wound, and by 2:30 Johnston was dead.

Johnston's champions argue that had he lived, he could have changed the course of the war in the western theater. An objective view of Johnston's performance, however, suggests nothing to justify such confidence.

JOHNSTON, JOSEPH E. (1807–91)

❖ RANK: Lieutenant general

❖ PLACE OF BIRTH: New York City, New York

❖ EDUCATED: West Point

❖ MILITARY CAREER:
1826–61: Served in U.S. Army in Mexican War and Seminole Wars, rising to rank of brigadier general
1861: Appointed brigadier general in Confederate army; First Manassas
1862: Made full general; commanded Army of Northern Virginia in Peninsula Campaign; wounded at Battle of Seven Pines; given command of Department of the West
1863: Vicksburg Campaign
1864: Atlanta Campaign

Joseph E. Johnston graduated from West Point in 1829. He earned a reputation for reckless bravery while fighting in the Black Hawk War, the Second Seminole War, and the Mexican War. Indeed, he was wounded five times and earned three brevets while in Mexico.

In the 1850s, Johnston held various assignments, including the chief of topographical engineers in Texas, lieutenant colonel of the First U.S. Cavalry, and acting

Right: *Joseph Johnston had a troubled relationship with Jefferson Davis and found himself in an awkward and frustrating position as commander of the Department of the West.*

inspector general for Brigadier General Albert Sidney Johnston's Utah Expedition. On June 28, 1860, Johnston was made brigadier general and assigned as the quartermaster general of the U.S. Army. He resigned from the U.S. Army on April 22, 1861.

On May 14, 1861, Johnston was appointed as a brigadier general in the Confederate army. He was the senior commander at the Battle of First Manassas, although he ceded operational control to Brigadier General Pierre Gustave Toutant Beauregard and instead concentrated on the important task of delivering reinforcements to the battle. He was appointed to the rank of full general on August 31, but the letter President Jefferson Davis sent to the Senate requesting confirmation of the nominations listed Johnston fourth, following Samuel Cooper, Albert Sidney Johnston, and Robert E. Lee. This order infuriated Johnston, who felt that his seniority in the U.S. Army should have carried over to the Confederacy. This incident was the beginning of a quarrelsome and difficult relationship between Johnston and Davis.

ACTION IN VIRGINIA
As commander of the Department of the Potomac, Johnston received Major General George B. McClellan's attack on the Virginia Peninsula in March 1862. A defensive fighter by nature, Johnston delayed up the Peninsula until the Battle of Seven Pines on May 31–June 1. Johnston was wounded in the battle and replaced in command by General Robert E. Lee, who previously was serving as Davis's military advisor. Johnston seemed to recognize that Lee was better suited for the command, confessing, "The shot that struck me down is the very best that has been fired in the Southern cause yet."

Johnston returned to duty in November 1862 and began a difficult assignment as commander of the Department of the West. Johnston was the nominal theater commander of both General Braxton Bragg in Tennessee and Lieutenant General John C. Pemberton in Mississippi. However, both of Johnston's subordinates were allowed to communicate directly with President Davis, often leaving Johnston uninformed and irrelevant. The great expanse of his territory, unclear priorities from Richmond, and other complicating factors made the experience a difficult one for Johnston, who felt he had great responsibility but little real authority.

ATLANTA
On December 27, 1863, Johnston assumed command of the Army of Tennessee and opposed Major General William T. Sherman in the Atlanta Campaign. As was his nature, Johnston used a defensive strategy to offset Sherman's numerical advantage. Although many contemporary observers,

including Lieutenant General Ulysses S. Grant, as well as later scholars considered Johnston's approach to be correct, Davis replaced Johnston on July 17, 1864, with the more offensively oriented Lieutenant General John Bell Hood.

After Hood's defeat, Johnston again assumed command of the Army of Tennessee on February 23, 1865, and offered fruitless resistance to Sherman's Carolinas Campaign. After the Battle of Bentonville, Johnston surrendered on April 26.

After the war, Johnston wrote *Narrative of Military Operations*, in which he defended his actions in the Atlanta Campaign. He and Sherman shared a mutual respect, and Johnston died of pneumonia, which he contracted by standing hatless in the rain at Sherman's funeral.

JOMINI, INFLUENCE OF

At the time of the Civil War, the United States relied on Europe for its understanding of the art of war. The most influential strategist of the European military theorists was Antoine Henri, Baron de Jomini, who became the principal interpreter of Napoleonic strategy for the American military.

Jomini was intellectually rooted in the eighteenth-century Enlightenment and thus sought to bring order to those elements of Napoleonic warfare he found chaotic and indiscriminate. In their place, he hoped to develop logical principles of war that formed a neatly organized system. In the process, Jomini brought an almost geometric approach to warfare that was designed to bring the maximum possible force to bear against an inferior enemy force at the decisive point in the theater of operations. This condition was best achieved by operating on interior lines. Jomini's Civil War influence was so great

that Brigadier General J. D. Hittle, editor of one version of Jomini's book, asserted, "Many a Civil War general went into battle with a sword in one hand and Jomini's *Summary of the Art of War* in the other."

Among those Confederates most influenced by Jomini was General Robert E. Lee. Indeed, Lee has been criticized for inappropriately applying the Jominian principles of concentration and offensive to seek a decisive victory in a way that the limited Confederate resources, particularly troop strength, could not support.

JONES, CATESBY AP ROGER (1821–77)

Catesby ap Roger Jones was appointed as a midshipman in the navy in 1836 and was promoted to lieutenant in 1849. He worked on developing naval weapons and served as ordnance officer on the *Merrimack* when he began active service in 1856. Jones resigned from the U.S. Navy when his native Virginia seceded.

Jones assisted in efforts to convert the *Merrimack* into an ironclad and became the vessel's executive officer when it was rechristened the *Virginia*. He took command of the *Virginia* after Captain Franklin Buchanan was wounded in fighting on March 8, 1862, and was the ship's captain during its famous duel with the *Monitor*. Later that year, he commanded a shore battery at Drewry's Bluff, Virginia, and the gunboat *Chattahoochee* while it was under construction at Columbus, Georgia.

He was promoted to commander in April 1863 and went to Selma, Alabama, to work on naval ordnance. He continued in this line of work for the remainder of the war.

JONES, SAMUEL (1820–87)

Samuel Jones graduated from West Point in 1841 and served on the frontier and at West Point. He resigned from the U.S. Army on April 27, 1861, and was appointed to brigadier general on July 21. He fought at First Manassas and in western Virginia until going to Pensacola in January 1862. He was promoted to major general on March 10, 1862, and served with the Army of Mississippi. In December 1862 he took command of the Department of Western Virginia with duties that included defending saltworks. He was relieved in March 1864 and sent to command the Department of South Carolina, Georgia, and Florida. By the end of the war, he was in failing health.

Above: *Salt was critical to the Confederacy as a preservative. Among Samuel Jones's most important duties was defending the saltworks in southwestern Virginia.*

JONES, WILLIAM "GRUMBLE" (1824–64)

Above: *William Jones's argumentative personality landed him the nickname "Grumble." As a case in point, a dispute with Jeb Stuart led to Jones's transfer to another unit.*

William Jones graduated from West Point in 1848 and served on the frontier until resigning in 1857 to farm. In May 1861 he was commissioned as a major in the Virginia cavalry. He served at Cedar Mountain, Groveton, Second Manassas, and in northern North Carolina, and was made brigadier general in the Confederate army on September 19, 1862. He conducted screening operations during the Gettysburg Campaign, but a disagreement with Major General Jeb Stuart led to Jones's reassignment to command of the Department of Southwest Virginia and East Tennessee. He participated in the Knoxville Campaign with Lieutenant General James Longstreet in February 1864. Jones was killed in fighting at Piedmont, Virginia, on June 5, 1864, while opposing Major General David Hunter's Shenandoah Valley Campaign.

KANSAS–NEBRASKA ACT (1854)

In 1854 Illinois senator Stephen A. Douglas proposed organizing the Kansas–Nebraska area into two territories. While Douglas's motivation was largely part of a grander design to secure Chicago as the eastern terminus for the proposed transcontinental railroad, his suggestion also had a profound impact on the politics of slavery. Douglas proposed repealing the Missouri Compromise, which had prohibited slavery north of the thirty-six-degree, thirty-minute latitude, and instead allow the status of Kansas and Nebraska to be determined based on popular sovereignty. Under this concept, the people would vote to decide if the state should be slave or free.

This measure was popular in the South because it opened the possibility of the expansion of slavery. These hopes were especially buoyed by the idea that, because Kansas was adjacent to Missouri, a slave state, the first settlers in Kansas would likely come from Missouri and be proslavery. With strong Southern support, Douglas's measure became law.

REPERCUSSIONS
The Kansas–Nebraska Act had repercussions both in the territories and nationally. Zealots from both camps flocked to Kansas trying to influence the final outcome, and the violence reached the point of civil war. The press labeled the area "Bleeding Kansas," and abolitionists like John Brown who had emigrated from the east and proslavery Border Ruffians from

Below: *Proslavery Missourians like the ones shown here flooded Kansas after the 1854 Kansas–Nebraska Act left the status of Kansas up to popular sovereignty.*

Missouri brutally attacked each other. Nationally, Douglas's proposal won him favor with Southern Whigs, who migrated to the Democratic Party, giving it an even more pronounced Southern character. On the other hand, in July 1854, Northern Whigs, Free Soilers, and Democrats met at Ripon, Wisconsin, and formed the new Republican Party. With the Kansas–Nebraska Act, American politics continued to divide along sectional lines.

KENNESAW MOUNTAIN, BATTLE OF

❖ DATE: June 27, 1864

❖ LOCATION: Cobb County, Georgia

❖ ARMY OF TENNESSEE (C): 74,000

❖ MILITARY DIVISION OF THE MISSISSIPPI (U.S.): 100,000

❖ CASUALTIES: 1,000 (C); 3,000 (U.S.)

The Battle of Kennesaw Mountain was fought between Major General William T. Sherman's Military Division of the Mississippi and General Joseph E.

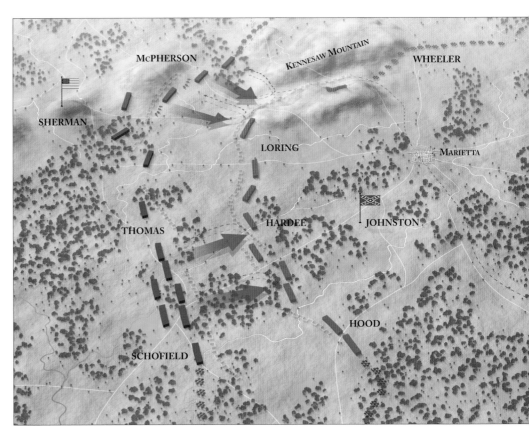

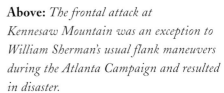

Johnston's Army of Tennessee. It was part of the larger Atlanta Campaign that stretched from Dalton, Georgia, to the outskirts of Atlanta. Along the way, Sherman and Johnston engaged in a duel in which Sherman repeatedly tried to maneuver around Johnston's flank while Johnston skillfully thwarted Sherman's attempts by withdrawing to one entrenched position after another. The only

Above: *The frontal attack at Kennesaw Mountain was an exception to William Sherman's usual flank maneuvers during the Atlanta Campaign and resulted in disaster.*

time throughout the campaign that Sherman departed from his usual flank maneuver and launched a frontal attack was at Kennesaw Mountain on June 27, 1864.

The results were catastrophic. Of the 12,000 men Sherman committed to battle, he lost about 3,000. The Confederates lost less than 1,000.

While Kennesaw Mountain proved once again the superiority of the entrenched defense, the power of the rifle, and the high cost of frontal attacks, it did not dissuade Sherman from his ultimate goal. He continued his steady advance to Atlanta and took possession of the key city on September 2.

Left: *Defending from behind stout breastworks, Johnston's well-protected Confederates inflicted 3,000 casualties on Sherman's Federal force at the Battle of Kennesaw Mountain.*

KENTUCKY

Kentucky was extremely divided as it weighed the decision of secession. Both Jefferson Davis and Abraham Lincoln had been born there, and it was a state with a strong tradition of compromise based on the efforts of Henry Clay and John J. Crittenden. Governor Beriah Magoffin, however, was a proponent of states' rights, and in late December 1860, he called the legislature into special session to call a state convention. The legislature refused Magoffin's request and adjourned until late March. On May 20, 1861, Kentucky declared its neutrality. The Confederates mismanaged this delicate situation, and Federal forces under Brigadier General Ulysses S. Grant ultimately moved into the state and secured it for the Union.

Still, Kentucky remained the state where, more than any other, the Civil War was a "war between brothers." Sixty percent of the white Kentuckians who fought during the Civil War sided with the North, while the remainder served with the Confederacy. George W. Johnson became the governor of a Confederate "shadow government" in the state. Johnson was succeeded by Richard Hawes, who was inaugurated in Frankfort on October 4, 1862, during General Braxton Bragg's Kentucky Campaign. Bragg's operation failed to result in the hoped-for rallying of Kentuckians to the Confederate cause. Other Confederate military operations in the state included a number of raids by Brigadier General John Hunt Morgan.

Famous Kentuckians who served the Confederacy include Lieutenant General Simon Bolivar Buckner, Major General John C. Breckinridge, and Major General George B. Crittenden. As a testimony to the divided nature of Kentucky, Crittenden's brother Thomas was a Federal major general.

KERNSTOWN, BATTLE OF

- ❖ DATE: March 23, 1862

- ❖ LOCATION: Frederick County and Winchester, Virginia

- ❖ VALLEY DISTRICT (C): 3,800

- ❖ FIRST DIVISION, FIFTH CORPS (U.S.): 8,500

- ❖ CASUALTIES: 718 (C); 568 (U.S.)

The Battle of Kernstown was a critical part of Major General Stonewall Jackson's Shenandoah Valley Campaign. Even though the battle was a tactical defeat for Jackson, the unexpectedly strong Confederate presence in the valley caused President Abraham Lincoln to withhold troops from Major

Below: *At the Battle of Kernstown, Stonewall Jackson mistakenly thought a large part of the Federal force had retreated, and he launched a hasty and ill-advised attack.*

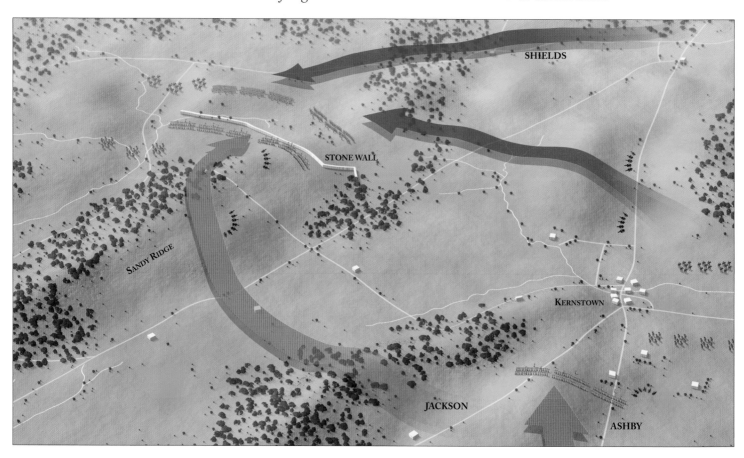

General George B. McClellan's Peninsula Campaign and use them instead to protect Washington.

Jackson was at Mount Jackson, thirty-five miles south of Winchester, Virginia, when he learned from Colonel Turner Ashby's cavalry that part of Major General Nathaniel P. Banks's army was preparing to head east to reinforce McClellan. Desiring to hold Banks in place, Jackson began hurrying his forces north. In the meantime, Ashby's troopers clashed with Brigadier General James Shields's pickets just south of Winchester on March 22.

Mistakenly thinking Shields had withdrawn all but a rear guard, Jackson attacked in force on March 23. In reality, Shields had set a trap to lure Jackson forward and then counterattack. Jackson suffered 718 casualties compared to 568 Federal losses, and was forced to withdraw four and a half miles south to Newtown.

In spite of this tactical setback, Jackson's aggressive action caused

Federal authorities to halt plans to shift forces to McClellan. Banks was held in place, Brigadier General Louis Blenker's division was withdrawn from McClellan and sent to oppose Jackson, and Major General Irvin McDowell's First Corps was withheld from McClellan. This development helped the Confederates on the Virginia Peninsula reverse McClellan's initial advantage.

KING COTTON

The South's principal cash crop was cotton, and many Confederates placed great confidence in being able to manipulate foreign reliance on Southern cotton to gain recognition and support for the Confederacy. The most likely target for this strategy was Great Britain, which was consuming three-fifths of the entire Southern cotton crop by 1860. Additionally, an estimated 5 million Britons were making their livelihood from the

textile industry. The Federal blockade posed a clear danger to Great Britain's commercial and manufacturing interests by restricting access to Southern cotton.

WIGFALL DECLARES

This was the very situation on which the South had pinned its hopes. Senator Louis T. Wigfall of Texas had defiantly proclaimed, "I say that cotton is king and that he waves his scepter not only over these thirty-three states but over the island of Great Britain and over continental Europe, and that there is no crowned head upon that island or upon the continent that does not bend the knee in fealty and acknowledge allegiance to that monarch."

To accelerate the effects of "King Cotton," the Confederacy burned some 2.5 million bales of cotton to create a shortage. The number of cotton bales exported to Europe from the South dropped from 3 million bales in 1860 to mere thousands. Unfortunately, Wigfall and his adherents had overestimated the power of cotton. For all the inconvenience of the blockade, Lord Palmerston, the British prime minister, declared that, to recognize the Confederacy "because they [the North] keep cotton from us would be ignominious beyond measure" and "no English Parliament could do so base a thing." Palmerston's defiance was encouraged by the fact that the bumper crop of 1860 had provided British mills with enough raw material to last into the fall of 1862.

BRITAIN BUYS ELSEWHERE

In fact, Britain had accumulated an inventory of over a million bales of cotton prior to the Civil War. Additionally, Great Britain had energetically pushed to open alternative cotton markets, particularly in Egypt and India, to supplement those lost to the blockade. The blockade and its threat to the supply of Confederate cotton were unpleasant to Great Britain, but they did not present the crisis that Wigfall had predicted.

KNIGHTS OF THE GOLDEN CIRCLE

The Knights of the Golden Circle was a secret society made up of Southern sympathizers in the North. It was originally founded to advocate for the extension of slavery in the 1850s,

Right: *The Knights of the Golden Circle was one of several shadowy organizations of Confederate sympathizers in the North.*

and during the Civil War it became allied with the copperheads and Peace Democrats. The organization experienced several name changes, becoming the Order of American Knights in 1863 and the Sons of Liberty in 1864. Clement L. Vallandigham was active in the original organization and became Supreme Commander of the Sons of Liberty.

KU KLUX KLAN

Many white Southerners were threatened by the political, social, and economic changes ushered in by the outcome of the Civil War. The presence and activities of free African Americans, carpetbaggers, scalawags, and Federal troops disrupted the

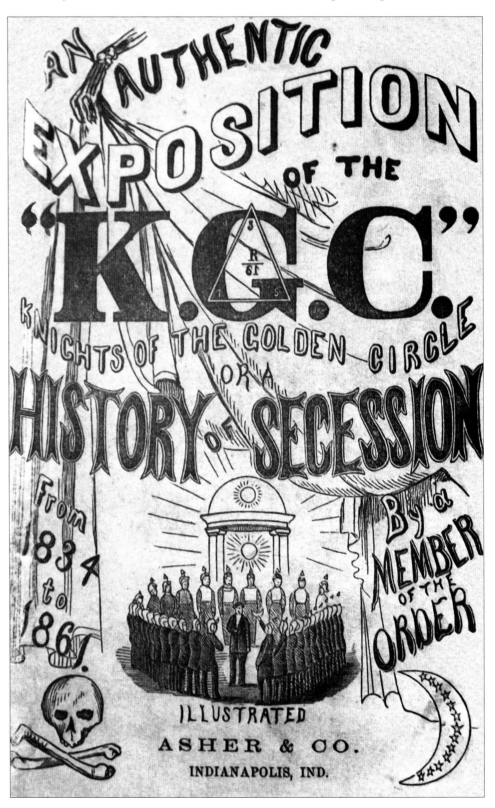

traditional Southern way of life in a way that many whites could not tolerate. This resentment took a sudden and vicious turn with the rise of the Ku Klux Klan.

The Ku Klux Klan first appeared in 1866 as a social organization in Tennessee and by later standards was almost innocuous. In these early days, night riders dressed in white hoods and played pranks on freedmen to frighten them into compliant behavior. The Klansmen's disguises were intended to portray themselves as the ghosts of the Confederate dead. Soon, however, these mild tactics gave way to unmitigated violence. The Klan became increasingly organized with its own hierarchy, rituals, and codes—all shrouded in secrecy to thwart Federal authorities. The

Klan used terrorist acts of kidnapping, torture, and murder to intimidate carpetbaggers and Republicans, keep African Americans "in their place," and attack the political and economic gains African Americans had made.

By 1869 some of the more moderate Klansmen had come to realize the organization had gotten out of hand, and it was officially disbanded. However, resurgent groups quickly surfaced with even greater vigor. Amid the growing violence, Congress launched a detailed investigation that resulted in the Ku Klux Klan Act of 1871. This legislation empowered the president to suspend the writ of habeas corpus in order to quell the violence that had come to accompany elections. The

Above: *This* Visit of the Ku-Klux *appeared in* Harper's Weekly *in 1872 and shows the terror tactics used to intimidate African Americans in the South.*

legislation met stiff resistance from many Americans, including some Northerners and even President Ulysses S. Grant's administration, as a dangerous expansion of Federal power. The Klan remained a powerful force throughout the former Confederate States, and did much to doom the Republican Reconstruction governments.

Lieutenant General Nathan Bedford Forrest is usually credited as being the Klan's first leader. Its rise was depicted as being the salvation of the post–Civil War South in the 1915 movie *The Birth of a Nation*.

LAMB, WILLIAM
(1835–1909)

William Lamb was a native Virginian who studied law at the College of William and Mary. After graduation, he served as a newspaper editor and followed politics closely. In 1858 he helped organize a militia company with which he saw limited combat early in the Civil War. In 1861 Lamb was promoted to major and ordered to Wilmington, North Carolina, as chief quartermaster for the District of Cape Fear. In that capacity, he set about building Fort Anderson on the west bank of Cape Fear. He proved himself to be very capable as an engineer.

Lamb was promoted to colonel, and on July 4, 1862, he was ordered across the river to command Fort Fisher. Against great odds, he superintended the creation of a massive defense system there that helped Wilmington remain the Confederacy's last open port.

LEE, ROBERT E.
(1807–70)

❖ RANK: General

❖ PLACE OF BIRTH: Stratford Hall, Virginia

❖ EDUCATED: West Point

❖ MILITARY CAREER:
1829–61: Served in U.S. Army; fought in Mexican War, rising to rank of colonel
1861: Military adviser to President Jefferson Davis; appointed commander of Army of Northern Virginia
1862: Success at Second Manassas and Antietam
1863: Success at Chancellorsville; stalemate at Gettysburg
1864: Battle of the Wilderness, Spotsylvania Court House, and Cold Harbor
1865: Appointed general in chief of Confederate forces

Robert Edward Lee graduated second in the West Point class of 1829, without a demerit, and served in the Corps of Engineers. He was promoted to captain in 1838 and participated in several civil and military engineering projects until serving on Winfield Scott's staff in the Mexican War, where he earned three brevets for gallantry and the admiration of Scott. Before the Civil War, Lee served as the superintendent of West Point and the lieutenant colonel of the Second U.S. Cavalry. In addition, he quelled John Brown's raid. After Virginia seceded from the Union, Lee resigned his commission and took command of the Virginia land and naval forces until they were incorporated into the Confederate states. He was subsequently appointed brigadier general in the Confederate army and attained the rank of full general on August 7, 1861. After an unsuccessful campaign in western Virginia and supervising coastal defenses in Georgia and the Carolinas, Lee was named the military adviser to President Jefferson Davis.

In this capacity, Lee attempted to defuse the volatile relationship between Davis and General Joseph E. Johnston, and had some limited success in improving communications between the two. It was also in this capacity that Lee effected his reconcentration of Confederate troops that would counter Major General George B. McClellan's initial overwhelming numerical superiority on the Peninsula and began intimating to Major General Stonewall Jackson the role he could

Above: *Taken in 1863 by Julian Vannerson, this is one of the best-known portraits of Robert E. Lee. It shows the great man in his army uniform, wearing the three stars of a lieutenant general on his collar lapels.*

play in the Shenandoah Valley to relieve Federal pressure on the Peninsula.

Lee replaced Johnston as field commander on May 31, 1862, after Johnston was wounded at Seven Pines. This event changed the course of the war. In contrast to the strained relationship between Johnston and Davis, Lee and Davis enjoyed a smooth-working collaboration. Even more significantly, Lee exchanged Johnston's largely defensive strategy for an audacious offensive–defensive strategy that would seize the initiative and dictate the timing and tempo of operations. After bringing Jackson to the Peninsula, Lee successfully repulsed McClellan and then seized the initiative by decimating Major General John Pope at Second Manassas. During the Peninsula Campaign and Second Manassas, Lee and Jackson developed a synergistic relationship that brought out the best in both men. Lee preferred to give the broad, discretionary orders on which Jackson thrived, and Jackson was able to efficiently put Lee's intent into action.

ANTIETAM

Building on the victory at Second Manassas, Lee launched the Antietam Campaign, his first invasion of Northern territory. Lee hoped to provoke Confederate-sympathizing Maryland into secession and win European recognition with a decisive victory. His decision was probably an unwise one given the exhausted condition of his men after the fighting on the Peninsula and at Second Manassas, and his lack of the necessary numbers required to wage an offensive. After the battle ended in a tactical draw, Lee was forced to return to Virginia. The campaign did indicate Lee's overwhelming confidence in his army and his firm belief in the offensive, characteristics that perhaps did not serve him in good stead given the Confederacy's scant resources.

The disparity between Lee's army and his Federal opponents made defense a better option for the Army of Northern Virginia, and Lee proved this at the Battle of Fredericksburg on December 13, 1862. More to Lee's liking, however, was his brilliant offensive victory at Chancellorsville on May 4, 1863, in which he teamed with Jackson for what has been called Lee's masterpiece. However, Lee was frustrated with his inability to completely destroy his enemy, and the battle showed his fixation with the offensive.

Chancellorsville was a costly victory for Lee because he lost Jackson. Lee was then forced to reorganize his army into three corps, because he did not have a subordinate strong enough to replace Jackson. Lee missed Jackson sorely during the July 1–3, 1863, Battle of Gettysburg, lamenting afterward, "If I [would have] had Stonewall Jackson at Gettysburg, I would have won that fight." Instead, Lee lost 28,000 men at Gettysburg, which, along with the earlier loss of Jackson, forever blunted Lee's offensive capability. The campaign also showed Lee's primary focus on Virginia and his sway with President Davis. While a strong contingent of Confederate officials favored reinforcing the threatened defenders of Vicksburg, Lee argued against weakening the eastern theater and in part justified his offensive as relieving pressure on Virginia. Although Lee was not responsible for developing a grand Confederate strategy, his powerful position and reputation certainly influenced it.

Once Lieutenant General Ulysses S. Grant assumed command of the Federal army, Lee was subjected to relentless pressure that he had not previously seen. Grant resolved to use his superior numbers to bludgeon Lee, knowing that Federal losses could be replaced while Confederate ones could not. Beginning in May 1864, Grant launched an eleven-month campaign of attrition that resulted in numerous tactical victories for Lee, such as at the Wilderness, but over the long term served to bleed Lee dry. Finally, on April 9, 1865, Lee was forced to surrender.

Assessments of Lee's generalship have swayed like a pendulum. Early biographers such as Douglas Southall Freeman idolized Lee, while later revisionists have blamed Lee for the Confederacy's defeat. Lee was at heart an offensive-minded general who sought victory through a decisive battle in the Napoleonic tradition. In this regard, Lee was brilliant, but the Confederacy simply did not have the resources to fight the way he wanted to. Still, Lee came closer than any other Southern general to bringing victory to the Confederate cause, and under the circumstances it is hard to imagine anyone else doing any better.

After the war, Lee continued to use his revered status to help the South. He became the president of Washington College (now Washington and Lee University) in an effort to help the South rebuild itself through improved education. He held the position until he died in 1870. Considered by many to be the personification of the "Lost Cause," Lee's last words were "Strike the tent."

Left: *Robert E. Lee's stately presence is well captured in this famous postwar photograph taken by Federal photographer Matthew Brady.*

LEE, STEPHEN D. (1833–1908)

Stephen D. Lee graduated from West Point in 1854 as an artilleryman and served on the frontier and in the Seminole Wars. He resigned from the U.S. Army on February 20, 1861, and as a captain served as Brigadier General Pierre Gustave Toutant Beauregard's aide during the bombardment of Fort Sumter. Lee fought during the Peninsula Campaign, Second Manassas, and Antietam before being promoted to brigadier general on November 6, 1862. He was then sent west and commanded the Confederate artillery at Vicksburg, where he was captured and paroled.

Lee was promoted to major general on August 3, 1863, and put in command of all cavalry in Mississippi. These responsibilities were extended to all cavalry west of Alabama in February 1864, and Lee became the Confederacy's youngest lieutenant general on June 23. When Lieutenant General John Bell Hood assumed command of the Army of Tennessee, Lee took Hood's old corps and led it in battles around Atlanta and at Nashville, where he was wounded. He fought in North Carolina, where he finally surrendered with General Joseph E. Johnston on April 26, 1865. Throughout his career, Lee had gained experience with the artillery, infantry, and cavalry, making him an effective corps commander.

After the war, Lee was active in Mississippi life as a farmer, politician, and veteran. He was the first president of what is now Mississippi State University, serving from 1880 to 1899. He was a founding organizer of Vicksburg National Military Park and was the commander in chief of the United Confederate Veterans from 1904 until his death in 1908.

LONGSTREET, JAMES (1821–1904)

❖ RANK: Lieutenant general

❖ PLACE OF BIRTH: Edgefield District, South Carolina

❖ EDUCATED: West Point

❖ MILITARY CAREER:
1829–61: Served in U.S. Army; fought in Mexican War, rising to rank of major
1861: Appointed brigadier general, commanded a brigade at First Manassas
1862: Commanded 15 brigades in Seven Days Battles; commanded a corps at Second Manassas and Antietam
1863: Corps commander at Gettysburg; success at Chickamauga
1864: Success at Battle of the Wilderness

James Longstreet graduated from West Point in 1842 and then served in Florida and Mexico, where he was often in the thick of serious combat. At Chapultepec, he was in front of the Eighth U.S. Infantry, carrying its colors and leading the way. He was hit with a musket ball in the thigh, fell wounded, and passed the colors to George E. Pickett. Longstreet's wound was painful and his recovery slow. During the Civil War, Longstreet showed a marked penchant for the defense, and some observers have explained this characteristic as a reaction to his personal experience with the high cost of frontal attacks in Mexico.

Longstreet resigned his commission in the U.S. Army on June 1, 1861, and was appointed as a brigadier general in the Confederate army sixteen days later. He commanded a brigade at First Manassas and was promoted to major general on October 7, 1861. He commanded a division under General Joseph E. Johnston during the Peninsula Campaign, and his excellent rearguard action at Williamsburg allowed the Confederate artillery and supply train to escape toward Richmond. Longstreet was less effective in offensive situations such as at the Battle of Seven Pines, where he took the wrong road,

Left: *Lee called James Longstreet his "Old War Horse" in spite of Longstreet's preference for the defense and his strategic differences with Lee.*

arrived late on the battlefield, and was excessively passive in command. He showed improvement during the Seven Days Battles and won the confidence of General Robert E. Lee.

SECOND MANASSAS

Longstreet combined with Major General Stonewall Jackson to trap the Federal forces at Second Manassas and then served in the Antietam Campaign. He was promoted to lieutenant general on October 9, 1862.

At Fredericksburg, Longstreet performed well in the type of defensive situation he favored. Long desiring an independent command, Longstreet was sent to Suffolk where he commanded the Department of North Carolina and Southern Virginia. During this unremarkable posting, Longstreet missed the great offensive Battle of Chancellorsville.

After Longstreet rejoined the Army of Northern Virginia, he voiced passionate arguments against General Robert E. Lee's Gettysburg Campaign. Longstreet first attempted to persuade Lee to stay on the defensive in Virginia and reinforce General Braxton Bragg around Chattanooga. When Lee remained adamant about invading Northern territory, Longstreet urged him to assume a tactical defensive position on ground that threatened Baltimore or Washington. Unable to convince Lee of his point of view, Longstreet was uninspired at Gettysburg, especially on the second day of the battle.

CHICKAMAUGA

In September 1863, Longstreet was sent with a force of over two divisions to reinforce Bragg in Tennessee. His timely arrival helped Bragg win a tactical victory at Chickamauga. In early November, Longstreet began advancing on Knoxville, where he again showed little propensity for independent command.

Longstreet returned to the Army of Northern Virginia and was wounded by his own men in the Battle of the Wilderness. He returned to action on October 19 and was put in charge of Confederate forces at Bermuda Hundred and north of the James River.

After the war, Longstreet fell out of favor with many Southerners because he joined the Republican Party. His criticism of Lee's strategy at Gettysburg also alienated him from many of Lee's supporters, even though Lee affectionately called Longstreet his "Old War Horse."

LOST CAUSE

In the two decades after the Civil War, the South struggled to make sense of its defeat. The "Lost Cause" explanation, in which the Confederacy was portrayed in a decidedly heroic and virtuous way, soon gained ascendancy. Edward Pollard, a Richmond newspaper editor, is given credit for coining the phrase in a book he wrote in 1866.

The Lost Cause ideology minimizes the role of slavery as a cause of the Civil War. Instead, secession was motivated by the South's desire to preserve the political notion of states' rights. This interpretation made the Confederate cause a noble one committed to principle rather than material interests. Lost Cause

Below: *Commitment to the ideology of the "Lost Cause" encouraged Southerners to save their Confederate money because "the South shall rise again."*

theorists describe slavery as a benevolent institution in which generous masters helped improve the inferior black race, and slaves responded to this kind treatment with loyalty and acceptance. When this representation of a peaceful antebellum environment was contrasted with the chaotic state of race relations after the war, the Lost Cause mentality helped justify the rise of the Ku Klux Klan.

CHRISTIAN VALUES

The Lost Cause also depicted the South as a Christian society, especially in contrast with the economically motivated and industrialized North. The Christian examples of General Robert E. Lee, Lieutenant General Stonewall Jackson, and others fueled this assertion, as did the piety, virtue, and sacrifice of Southern women. The Lost Cause became a form of public religion that lent a solemnity to the dedication of Confederate monuments and reverence for Confederate veterans and widows.

Perhaps most tellingly, the Lost Cause explained the Confederate defeat as the result of overwhelming Federal resources. The Confederate cause was noble and its people and way of life superior, but it could not stand against the manpower, money, and industry of the North. In this way, Southern pride was preserved and responsibility for defeat was transferred.

Although born in the South, the Lost Cause interpretation of the Civil War was accepted in many Northern circles as well, and much of the early historiography of the war is predicated on this assumption. Only in the latter half of the twentieth century did revisionist histories gain widespread ground against the Lost Cause interpretation.

LOUGHBOROUGH, MARY (1837–87)

Mary Loughborough was a Missourian who fled the state's violence with her husband James, a Confederate soldier.

Loughborough eventually found refuge in Oxford, Mississippi, where she spent much of her time caring for the wounded in hospitals. She relocated to Jackson to avoid Federal soldiers and then went to Vicksburg, where she became trapped during the siege. In 1864 she published *My Cave Life in Vicksburg*, an interesting and informative memoir of the siege from the perspective of a civilian.

LOUISIANA

Because its principal city, New Orleans, had so much of a national character as a trading and transportation center—and because its principal crop, sugar, was protected by the national tariff—secessionist fever was slow to develop in Louisiana. The Breckinridge Democrats carried

Below: *The Battle of New Orleans was a devastating blow to the Confederacy that cost it its largest city and an important economic and shipbuilding center.*

the state by a slim majority in the 1860 presidential election, but the looming inauguration of Abraham Lincoln served to alarm many moderates. This was the shift Governor Thomas O. Moore, an ardent secessionist, was waiting for, and he called for a convention to consider secession. On January 7, 1861, Louisianans elected eighty secessionists, forty-four cooperationists, and six undecided delegates. The secessionists mostly came from the wealthy class of planters in the cotton-producing parishes. The cooperationists came from either the farming regions of the northern parishes or the sugar regions of the south. Still, even the Louisiana cooperationists tended to be more inclined toward secession than their counterparts elsewhere.

By the time Louisiana's convention met, five other states had already seceded, and on January 25, 1861, Louisiana voted to follow suit by a 113 to 17 majority. One of Louisiana's most important contributions to the Confederacy was New Orleans, by far the South's biggest city with a population of 168,000, as well a key port and shipbuilding center. However, the importance of New Orleans in particular and the Mississippi River in general would ensure that Louisiana was the site of considerable fighting, to include New Orleans, Baton Rouge, Port Hudson, and the Red River Campaign.

UNDER OCCUPATION
Federal interest in New Orleans brought the war to Louisiana long before it hit most of the rest of the Deep South, and much of the state was under Federal occupation as early as the spring of 1862. Thus Louisiana became somewhat of a proving ground for President Abraham Lincoln's early attempts at Reconstruction. After Lincoln issued his "Ten Percent Plan" proclamation

on December 8, 1863, Louisianans formed a convention that met in April 1864 and created a constitution that prohibited slavery. When 6,836 voters approved the constitution compared to 1,566 opposing it, Lincoln recognized the new state government, but U.S. Congress refused to seat the state's representatives. The issue was far from settled at the time of Lincoln's assassination, and Louisiana was later submitted to Congressional Reconstruction.

Famous Confederates associated with Louisiana include diplomat John Slidell, cabinet member Judah P. Benjamin, Major Chatham Roberdeau "Rob" Wheat, Lieutenant General Richard Taylor, and General Pierre Gustave Toutant Beauregard.

LOVELL, MANSFIELD
(1822–84)

Mansfield Lovell was born in Washington, D.C., and graduated ninth in the West Point class of 1842. He served in the Mexican War as an artillery lieutenant, was wounded, and was brevetted to captain. He resigned from the army in 1854, and, with his close friend and West Point classmate Gustavus W. Smith, he established a business in New York City that promptly failed. Smith went on to become the city's commissioner of streets and offered Lovell the post of deputy.

Lovell was slow in joining the Confederacy, waiting until after the Battle of First Manassas. He overcame this late start in part thanks to Smith's lobbying on his behalf,

and on September 25, 1861, Lovell was sent to New Orleans to help Major General David Twiggs with the defense of New Orleans. While Lovell was on his way, Twiggs asked to be relieved. When Lovell reached New Orleans on October 17, he learned he had been promoted to major general and named Twiggs's successor as commander of Department No. 1.

Lovell faced many challenges in defending New Orleans, including a misunderstanding of the Federal threat, a low priority for scarce resources, and a lack of unity of effort. Nonetheless, many blamed him for the loss of the important city and port, although a court of inquiry vindicated him on July 9, 1863. However, Lovell later showed the same lack of initiative he was accused of at New Orleans in his poor performance at Corinth, Mississippi.

Below: *Mansfield Lovell faced grave challenges as the defender of New Orleans. He was unable to overcome them and was roundly criticized.*

MAGRUDER, JOHN B. (1810–71)

John Bankhead Magruder was born in Port Royal, Virginia, graduated from West Point in 1830, and served in the Seminole and Mexican wars. His victory at Big Bethel on June 10, 1861, catapulted him to immediate fame, and he was promoted to brigadier general on June 17 and major general on October 7. His brilliant deception helped buy time for the Confederacy to respond to Major General George B. McClellan's Peninsula Campaign, but later he was cautious and bumbling during the Seven Days Battles, and he was sent from Virginia to the Department of Texas in November 1862. There he somewhat redeemed himself by the daring and surprising recapture of Galveston on January 1, 1863.

After the Civil War, Magruder initially fled to Mexico, but he soon returned to Houston, where he died in 1871. He was considered by many to be a humbug for his lackluster performance on the Virginia Peninsula, but the people of Galveston remembered him as a hero and savior of the city. They removed Magruder from his modest burial site in Houston to Galveston's Trinity Episcopal Cemetery, where an impressive obelisk marks his grave.

MAHONE, WILLIAM (1826–95)

William Mahone graduated from the Virginia Military Institute in 1847. He taught at the Rappahannock Military Academy, and was chief engineer and president for the Norfolk and Petersburg Railroad. When Virginia seceded, Mahone was appointed as a quartermaster general. As a colonel in the Sixth Virginia Infantry, he helped capture the Norfolk Navy Yard and supervised the construction of the defenses at Drewry's Bluff. He was made a brigadier general on November 16, 1861. He fought in all the major battles with the Army of Northern Virginia and was promoted to major general on July 30, 1864, as a result of his exemplary action at the Battle of the Crater. After the war, Mahone returned to the railroad business and was elected to the U.S. Senate in 1880.

Above: *William Mahone's thin frame led one soldier to liken him to "a bantam rooster or gamecock." The nickname "Bantam Billy" also fit Mahone's reputation as an aggressive fighter.*

MAIL SERVICE

Postmaster General John H. Reagan faced many challenges, including the fact that the Confederate Constitution required the postal service to become self-sufficient within two years. Reagan jumped into his difficult task with both prudence and foresight. Shortly after assuming office, he announced that the Confederate postal service would not begin operating until June 1, 1861. Until then, Confederate postmasters continued selling U.S. stamps and sending their proceeds to Washington. This grace period, however awkward, allowed Reagan time to organize his affairs. Mail operations between belligerents eventually were officially prohibited, but both Northern and Southern mail carriers occasionally evaded these orders. In another important early decision, Reagan called a meeting of leading Southern railroad officials and advised them of his plan for coordinated mail routes and schedules. Although much Confederate mail, especially in the contested border areas, traveled by horseback, Reagan's appeal resulted in a large measure of cooperation from the railroad men.

AN INCREASING STRUGGLE

As Confederate resources succumbed to increased demands and Federal-occupied areas expanded, mail service obviously declined, but letters between the home front and the war front remained a cherished commodity. In many cases, furloughed soldiers going home or returning to their unit carried letters and packages. Like other aspects of the fledgling Confederacy, its postal service was remarkable for what it achieved against difficult odds. Much of the credit for the success it had is owed to Reagan's energies.

MALLORY, STEPHEN R. (1813–73)

Stephen R. Mallory was the Confederate secretary of the navy and one of only two cabinet members to serve in the same post

Above: *There was little in his past to suggest Stephen Mallory would be a capable secretary of the navy, but he showed innovation and foresight in building a Confederate navy from scratch.*

throughout the life of the Confederacy (Postmaster General John H. Reagan was the other). Mallory was born in Trinidad, but he grew up in Florida and was a Florida senator at the outbreak of the Civil War. In that capacity, he negotiated the "armistice" surrounding Fort Pickens.

As a senator, Mallory had been chairman of the Senate Committee on Naval Affairs, but Jefferson Davis likely selected Mallory to be his secretary of the navy primarily out of a desire to have a Floridian in the cabinet. Indeed, Mallory came with some baggage. He was not an ardent secessionist, and he had a reputation for associating with women of questionable virtue. Because of these considerations, Mallory was the only one of Davis's cabinet appointees whose confirmation was delayed in Congress.

In spite of this slow start, Mallory became a good secretary of the navy, using imagination and innovation to tackle the daunting task of creating a Confederate navy from scratch. He inherited just five vessels from the seceded states, and Davis had little interest in naval matters. Among Mallory's most significant contributions was his realization that ironclads offered the Confederacy a chance to offset its disadvantage in wooden ships. He was instrumental in the conversion of the *Merrimack* and the construction of other ironclads.

MANASSAS, BATTLE OF FIRST

❖ DATE: July 16–21, 1861

❖ LOCATION: Fairfax and Prince William counties, Virginia

❖ ARMIES OF THE POTOMAC AND THE SHENANDOAH (C): 34,000

❖ ARMY OF NORTHEASTERN VIRGINIA AND DEPARTMENT OF PENNSYLVANIA (U.S.): 35,000

❖ CASUALTIES: 1,750 (C); 2,950 (U.S.)

The rapid mobilizations that the Federals and Confederates pursued after Fort Sumter left both armies equally untrained. Under such circumstances, the Battle of First Manassas could have gone either way. As it turned out, the Confederates dealt the Federals a humiliating defeat that showed the nation the war would not be settled quickly.

Commanding the Federal Army of Northeastern Virginia was Brigadier General Irvin McDowell. Opposing him was Brigadier General Pierre Gustave Toutant Beauregard and the Confederate Army of the Potomac. Two other armies, Major General Robert Patterson's Department of Pennsylvania and General Joseph E. Johnston's Army of the Shenandoah, would also play key roles.

Under pressure from President Abraham Lincoln to act, McDowell developed a plan to conduct a diversionary attack of two columns against what he figured would be the center of the Confederate line at Bull Run, a small creek flowing into the Occoquan River. With the center thus held in check, the third column would move around the Confederate right flank and strike southward to cut the railroad to Richmond.

PATTERSON'S MISSION

Of key importance to McDowell's plan was the ability of Patterson to keep Johnston from reinforcing Beauregard. If Johnston got loose from the Shenandoah Valley, he could descend upon McDowell's right flank and disrupt the entire attack. In the ensuing battle, Patterson would fail this mission miserably, and Johnston would demonstrate the importance that railroads would play in the Civil War as he came to Beauregard's aid.

On July 16, 1861, McDowell got his army moving toward Manassas Junction. Excited shouts of "On to Richmond" soon gave way to straggling as the unseasoned soldiers began to feel the effects of hard marching. To make matters worse, one of McDowell's division commanders violated orders and clashed with Confederates at Blackburn's Ford. The skirmish not only compromised McDowell's plan, it also caused the Confederate War Department to order Johnston to come to Beauregard's aid. Using Colonel Jeb Stuart's cavalry to screen his movement, Johnston began extracting his force from the Shenandoah Valley, and, unbeknownst to Patterson, moving it by rail to Manassas Junction. Johnston personally reached

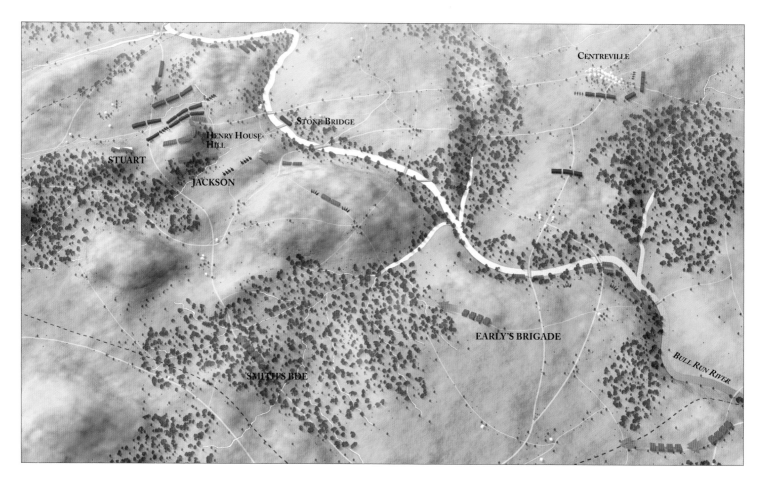

Above: *Some of the most important fighting at the Battle of First Manassas took place on Henry House Hill, where "Stonewall" Jackson earned his nickname.*

Below: *Its proximity to Washington, D.C., and its being the site of two important Civil War battles ensure a steady flow of visitors to the Manassas National Battlefield Park.*

Manassas Junction around noon on July 20, and although he was the senior officer, he deferred to Beauregard's greater familiarity with the terrain and relinquished operational command. Johnston then devoted himself to the critical role of forwarding reinforcements to the scene of the fighting throughout the battle.

On July 21, McDowell launched a diversionary attack on the Confederate line at the Stone Bridge. This attack was designed to cover the movements of two other divisions around the Confederate left via Sudley Ford and Popular Ford. However, a Confederate signal station spotted the flanking movement and warned Colonel Nathan Evans, commander of the Confederate forces at the Stone Bridge. Evans quickly moved his forces to meet this new threat and took up a position on the southern slope of Matthews Hill to cover the Manassas–Sudley Road. This adjustment spoiled the Federal opportunity to surprise the Confederate flank.

As Evans struggled to hold on, Confederate brigades commanded by Brigadier General Barnard E. Bee. and Colonel Francis Barlow arrived near the Henry House, just across Young's Branch from Matthews Hill. Evans rode to Bee and requested reinforcements, and Bee ordered the two brigades forward. Nonetheless, the

Matthews Hill position soon proved untenable, and the Confederates broke into a disorderly retreat back toward Henry House. It was now shortly before noon, and the Federal forces seemed on the verge of a great victory. One of McDowell's staff officers even rode around the field shouting, "Victory, victory! We have done it!" and late-arriving soldiers genuinely worried they had missed out on the entire war.

The tide, however, was about to turn. Around noon, Brigadier General Thomas J. Jackson's brigade, part of Johnston's Army of the Shenandoah, had marched to the sound of the firing and taken up a position on Henry House Hill. There, Jackson met an excited Bee, who told him the Federals had driven the Confederates back. Jackson calmly deployed his men, and the remnants of the commands of Evans, Bee, and Barlow regrouped behind him. Sometime during the afternoon, Bee pointed to Jackson and said he was standing there "like a stone wall," giving Jackson the nickname he carried ever after.

As the Confederates rallied,

McDowell was slow to renew his attack after his victory at Matthews Hill. To make matters worse, when he finally did get moving, McDowell frittered away his numerical advantage by piecemealed attacks. By about 4:00 p.m., the Federal attack on Henry House Hill had run out of steam, and the Confederates were free to concentrate on Chinn Ridge, where Colonel Oliver O. Howard had earlier attacked in one of McDowell's disjointed efforts. As more Confederate reinforcements arrived, Howard was forced to withdraw.

CHAOS ENSUES

By now McDowell's attack was in shambles. Units were disintegrating everywhere, and thousands of soldiers were fleeing in a mass exodus. Civilians who had ridden out from Washington to watch the battle were caught up in the chaos, and panic took control. Unable to restore order, McDowell directed a retreat to Fairfax and then to Washington. Hoping for news of a great victory, President Lincoln instead received a telegraph stating,

"General McDowell's army in full retreat through Centreville. The day is lost. Save Washington and the remnants of this army." By now, however, the victorious Confederates were almost as confused and disorganized as the Federals. There was no operational pursuit.

The Battle of First Manassas showed that neither of the two relatively large armies of new recruits nor their commanders were sufficiently trained for modern combat. It also showed that the war would not be settled in a single contest. Civil War limitations of command and control as well as the new power of the defense made possible by rifled muskets and breastworks would conspire to make it difficult to destroy an army. Realizing this, Presidents Lincoln and Davis began to call for additional volunteers in preparation for a long war.

Below: *Federal troops advance against Confederate positions at First Manassas. At this early stage of the war, both Federals and Confederates lacked the training to fight effectively at the large unit level.*

MANASSAS, BATTLE OF SECOND

❖ DATE: August 29–30, 1862

❖ LOCATION: Prince William County, Virginia

❖ ARMY OF NORTHERN VIRGINIA (C): 55,000

❖ ARMY OF VIRGINIA (U.S.): 63,000

❖ CASUALTIES: 9,500 (C); 14,500 (U.S.)

After being repulsed in his meticulously planned but poorly executed Peninsula Campaign, Major General George B. McClellan received orders on August 3, 1862, to return his army to a position south of Washington. In the meantime, a new command called the Army of Virginia had been activated in mid-July under the leadership of Major General John Pope. Ultimately, most of the Army of the Potomac would fall under Pope's command. Pope would not prove to be the commander President Abraham Lincoln hoped he would be when General Robert E. Lee defeated him at the Battle of Second Manassas on August 29–30, 1862.

When Lee knew that McClellan was abandoning the Peninsula, Lee went after Pope. On August 24, Lee ordered Major General Stonewall Jackson to cut Pope's communications line along the Orange and Alexandria Railroad, threatening Washington in the

Above: *At the Battle of Second Manassas, John Pope thought he had the Confederates on the run, but instead found himself soundly defeated.*

Below: *At the Battle of Second Manassas, Stonewall Jackson held the line against John Pope while James Longstreet delivered a decisive attack from the Confederate right flank.*

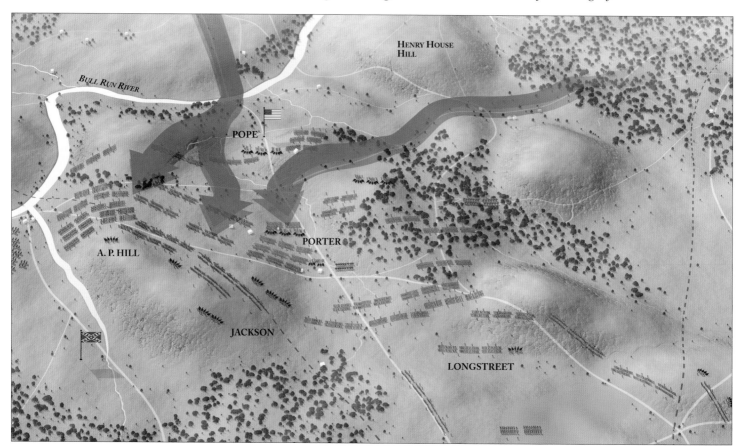

Above: *Stonewall Jackson holds a service with his officers after Second Manassas. Jackson was known for his devotion and piety. Revivals, services, and prayer meetings were regular events in his camps.*

process. Marching fifty-seven miles in two days, Jackson descended upon the railroad, destroyed the Federal supply depot at Manassas Junction, and occupied a strong defensive position a few miles west of Manassas.

Pope mistakenly thought Jackson was weakened, and, on August 29 and 30, the Federals attacked. In actuality, Pope was falling into a well-laid trap. As Jackson absorbed Pope's assault, Major General James Longstreet arrived on the scene and crashed into the Federal left with five divisions. Pope was sandwiched between Jackson's anvil and Longstreet's hammer, and the Federal forces fled in panic. Pope withdrew his demoralized force

northeast toward Washington, having suffered 14,500 casualties compared to 9,500 for Lee. The Battle of Second Manassas cleared northern Virginia of any major Federal presence and shifted the momentum in the eastern theater to the Confederates.

With Pope defeated and McClellan's army withdrawn behind the defenses of Washington, Lee saw an opportunity to carry the war into Northern territory and began planning his Antietam Campaign.

MARCH TO THE SEA (NOVEMBER 15– DECEMBER 21, 1864)

On November 15, 1864, Major General William T. Sherman destroyed the military resources of Atlanta and started marching east with some 62,000 men. Sherman

carried with him twenty days' rations, but otherwise he cut his communications and vowed to live off the land. "Where a million people live," Sherman argued, "my army won't starve."

In addition to using the countryside to supply his own army, Sherman intended to "make Georgia howl." By executing his "hard war" policy, Sherman destroyed everything in his path, resolving "to leave a trail that [would] be recognized fifty years hence."

The Confederates were able to muster little resistance to Sherman's advance, but he exacerbated their difficulties by keeping them on "the horns of a dilemma," disguising whether his true objective would be Macon or Augusta, and then Augusta or Savannah. Sherman himself even appeared content to keep the situation fluid. He wrote Major General Henry W. Halleck,

Above: *During the March to the Sea, Sherman's men destroyed Confederate railroads, often bending the ties into unusable shapes called "Sherman's neckties."*

"I must have alternatives, else, being confined to one route, the enemy might so oppose that delay and want to trouble me, but having alternatives, I can take so eccentric a course that no general can guess my objective. Therefore, have lookouts at Morris Island, South Carolina; Ossabaw Sound, Georgia; Pensacola and Mobile bays. I will turn up somewhere."

As he advanced, Sherman's target was not the Confederate armies but the Confederate will. He intended to bring the war home to a part of the South that had thus far been spared its ravages. "This movement is not purely military or strategic, but will illustrate the vulnerability of the South," Sherman explained. "They don't know what war means, but when the rich planters of the Oconee and Savannah see their fences and corn and hogs and sheep vanish before their eyes they will have something more than a mean opinion of the 'Yanks.'"

Advancing in two columns, Sherman's men destroyed railroads, houses, and crops. On November 17, Lieutenant General William J. Hardee was given the mission of opposing Sherman, but other than a few cavalry raids by Major General Joseph Wheeler, there was little the Confederates could do.

After taking less than 2,200 casualties, Sherman arrived at Savannah in December, offering the city as a "Christmas present" to President Abraham Lincoln. Sherman then took on resupplies and turned north for his Carolinas Campaign.

MARKS' MILLS, BATTLE OF

- ❖ DATE: April 25, 1864
- ❖ LOCATION: Cleveland County, Arkansas
- ❖ FORCE UNDER FAGAN (C): 4,000
- ❖ FORCE UNDER DRAKE (U.S.): 1,800
- ❖ CASUALTIES: 293 (C); 450 (U.S.)

As part of the Red River Campaign, on March 23, 1864, Major General Frederick Steele moved against Confederates in southwest Arkansas to shield Major General Nathaniel P. Banks's advance on Shreveport, Louisiana. Steele was slow in moving, which disrupted the Federal plans. When General Edmund Kirby Smith learned Banks had failed to take Shreveport and withdrawn, he dispatched his main infantry force against Steele in Arkansas. On April 25 at Marks' Mills, Brigadier General James F. Fagan attacked a Federal wagon train that was moving from Camden to Pine Bluff. After a three-hour fight, Fagan captured 211 wagons and inflicted 450 Federal casualties. The Confederates lost 293.

MARTIAL LAW

On February 27, 1862, the Confederate Congress authorized President Jefferson Davis to suspend the writ of habeas corpus and to declare martial law in "such cities, towns, and military districts as shall, in his judgment, be in . . . danger of attack by the enemy." This greatly enhanced central authority stood in stark contrast to the tradition of decentralization and individualism in the South. Martial law was declared in numerous cities including Richmond, Virginia, and New Orleans, Louisiana.

MARYLAND

Of all the border states, Maryland, a slaveholding state with strong Confederate sympathies, was the most crucial. If Maryland seceded, the Federal capital of Washington would be surrounded by Confederate territory, with Maryland on one side and Virginia on the other.

After Fort Sumter, it seemed as if this disaster for the Union might come true. A secessionist mob had jeered and thrown objects as a group of Massachusetts soldiers marched through Baltimore headed to Washington, and there were rumors that the Maryland legislature would soon vote for secession. Realizing the gravity of the situation and its potential catastrophic consequences for the Federal cause, President Abraham Lincoln intervened, suspending the writ of habeas corpus, imprisoning suspected Confederate activists, and imposing military law. These extraconstitutional measures succeeded in keeping Maryland in the Union, but did not remove the Confederate sympathies from many of the state's citizens.

Below: *President Abraham Lincoln authorized extraordinary measures to quash Confederate sentiment in the key border state of Maryland, including the arrests of secession advocates.*

In large part, it was the desire to capitalize on this situation that led General Robert E. Lee to launch his Antietam Campaign, an offensive into Maryland, in September 1862. Other battles in Maryland include Monocacy and numerous raids. Although Maryland did not secede, native sons Franklin Buchanan, George H. Steuart, Raphael Semmes, and John H. Winder fought with the Confederacy.

MASON, JAMES (1798–1871)

James Mason was a congressman and senator from Virginia and an ardent secessionist. He was noted before the Civil War as the drafter of the Fugitive Slave Law of 1850. During the Civil War, Mason was most famous as being, along with

fellow diplomat John Slidell, the focus of the *Trent* affair that brought Britain to the brink of intervening in the war.

After the *Trent* affair was resolved, Mason continued his transatlantic voyage and served as the Confederate commissioner to Britain, hoping to leverage his prior experience on the Senate Foreign Relations Committee. He was not successful in winning British recognition of the Confederacy, and on August 4, 1863, was told to end his mission in London. On September 30 he departed for Paris. After the war he fled to Canada, but returned to Virginia in 1868.

Above: *James Mason was one of the Confederate diplomats who tried to garner European support. He is most famous for his association with the* Trent *affair.*

MAURY, MATTHEW F. (1806–73)

Matthew F. Maury joined the navy as a midshipman when he was nineteen years old, and by 1834 he had published his first book, *Maury's Navigation*. An accident left him lamed for life in 1839, and he devoted his energies

Above: *Matthew Maury, the "Pathfinder of the Seas," was a world-renowned authority on oceanography and was instrumental in developing ingenious harbor and river defenses for the Confederacy.*

to study and writing. His prewar accomplishments were amazing and earned him the title "Pathfinder of the Seas."

Maury developed proposals to improve the navy, establish a naval academy, and expand the inland canal system. He also worked on compiling information about the Mississippi River. In 1842 he was named head of the Navy's Office of Hydrography and took over the Naval Observatory. He continued to produce a steady stream of writings, including *A Scheme for Rebuilding Southern Commerce* and *The Physical Geography of the Sea*. In 1856 he was named head of the National Meteorological Institute. He held a general maritime conference that standardized captains' logs, and he was the first man to describe the Gulf Stream. He instituted the system of deep-sea sounding and proposed the laying of a transoceanic cable.

When his native Virginia seceded, Maury resigned as a commander in the U.S. Navy and

was commissioned in the Confederate navy at the same rank. He served on court-martial boards, established the Submarine Battery Service, and was chief of harbor and river defenses. He invented the electric torpedo and mined the James River. In 1862 he was sent to Europe to continue his experiments with torpedoes and work on purchasing and outfitting European cruisers for service in the Confederacy. He invented a method of arranging and testing torpedoes which he was about to put into operation when the war ended. He then went to Mexico and served under Maximilian. Maury was in Europe instructing military students in the use of torpedoes, when Maximilian's government collapsed. He declined a number of positions in Europe, instead opting to become a physics professor at the Virginia Military Institute.

McLAWS, LAFAYETTE (1821–97)

Lafayette McLaws graduated from West Point in 1842 and served in Mexico, on the frontier, and on the Utah Expedition. He resigned from the U.S. Army on May 10, 1861, and was appointed as a brigadier general in the Confederate army on September 25, 1861. He fought at Yorktown on the Virginia Peninsula and was promoted to major general on May 23, 1862. He served as a division commander at Harpers Ferry, Antietam, Fredericksburg, Chancellorsville, and Gettysburg. He went to Tennessee with Lieutenant General James Longstreet but was relieved for a general lack of cooperation at Knoxville. McLaws was court-martialed, but then exonerated by President Jefferson Davis.

Vindicated, McLaws commanded the District of Georgia against Major General William T. Sherman's advance and ultimately surrendered at Greensboro, North Carolina. After the war, he worked in the insurance business and as a tax collector.

Above: *Court-martialed then exonerated, Lafayette McLaws was assigned outside the Army of Northern Virginia and ended the war defending against William Sherman's Carolinas Campaign.*

MEDICAL SERVICE AND DISEASE

The resourceful Samuel Moore was the surgeon general of the Confederacy. Moore faced numerous challenges, such as a lack of trained surgeons and shortages of medicine, supplies, and equipment caused by the blockade, but he quickly moved to address these problems. He introduced a new type of large, one-story pavilion hospital, established an effective army hospital and field ambulance corps, created laboratories to prepare medications from indigenous Southern plants, and set up an examination system that weeded out untrained doctors.

The pinnacle of the Confederate medical system was the network of general hospitals located in large cities, such as the Chimborazo Hospital in Richmond. These facilities handled the most seriously wounded and ill soldiers. Confederate brigades also established field hospitals at the rear of the battlefields. These locations were often convenient farmhouses or, if no existing structures were available, large tents. Small groups of soldiers were designated before the battle to bring seriously wounded soldiers to the rear, and regimental surgeons worked together in the field hospitals. Minié balls created ghastly wounds, and battlefield

Below: *Wounded Civil War soldiers, such as these Confederate casualties at Antietam, could expect only the most rudimentary care, and many would remain crippled for life or die of their wounds.*

surgery was rudimentary. In many cases, the best that overwhelmed surgeons could do was to amputate the wounded limb. Chloroform was often a reliable anesthetic when available, but often it was in short supply.

In addition to battlefield wounds, the Confederate soldier had to cope with the diseases that resulted from living at close quarters, poor sanitation, and limited knowledge of germs. Soldiers often drank from and urinated in the same water sources. Typhoid, smallpox, measles, tuberculosis, dysentery, and pneumonia were common. Some 162,000 Confederate soldiers died from disease compared to just 94,000 who died from wounds.

MEMMINGER, CHRISTOPHER G. (1803–88)

Christopher Gustavus Memminger came to the United States from Germany and was left as an orphan when his widowed mother died when he was four years old. He was eventually adopted by future South Carolina governor Thomas Bennett. Memminger studied law, entered politics, and helped establish the public education system in South Carolina.

Memminger opposed South Carolina's doctrine of nullification and became a cooperationist. He was a member of South Carolina's secessionist convention and wrote the state's declaration of secession. At the Montgomery Convention, Memminger chaired the committee that drafted the provisional constitution and was a member of the Commercial Affairs Committee. He served in the Provisional Confederate Congress until he was appointed secretary of the treasury on February 21, 1861.

Memminger was probably not the best selection for this demanding position. Although conscientious and methodical, he lacked the moral courage to fight for his convictions. As a result, he meticulously pursued a financial policy of paper money that he knew was destined to failure. When his plan to withdraw some of the paper money in circulation failed to stabilize the economy, he resigned on June 15, 1864. A Richmond newspaper described his tenure as secretary of the treasury: "He has done his best, but he has been overtaken—that is all." Perhaps his most memorable achievement while in office was obtaining the Erlanger loan that generated income for the Confederacy to purchase the European war materials that were essential to its survival in 1863 and 1864. After the war, he practiced law in Charleston and founded a company that manufactured sulfuric acid.

MEXICAN WAR, INFLUENCE OF

The Mexican War has been called the "rehearsal for the Civil War," because so many Civil War generals, both Federal and Confederate, served as junior officers in Mexico. At least 142 Confederate generals served in Mexico, including Robert E. Lee, Pierre Gustave Toutant Beauregard, Joseph E. Johnston, Stonewall Jackson, James Longstreet, and John C. Pemberton. President Jefferson Davis even served as a regimental commander, winning distinction at the Battle of Buena Vista. Additionally, because the Mexican War was more popular in the South than in the North (many Northerners saw it as an attempt to expand slavery), many Southerners served as enlisted men in Mexico and gained experience that would serve them well in the Civil War.

LEADERSHIP LESSONS

Although technological developments such as the minié ball and the rifle would change tactics by strengthening the defense, and railroads would bring a new mobility to the Civil War, many future Confederates learned valuable leadership skills in Mexico. Lee, for example, learned the

Below: *His Mexican War performance at the Battle of Buena Vista elevated Jefferson Davis to national prominence and may have given him excessive confidence in his military expertise.*

importance of reconnaissance and the turning movement. Other Confederate generals perhaps learned negative lessons. Many believe Pemberton learned his inflexible command style and Beauregard developed a penchant for the frontal attack in Mexico.

MEXICO, RELATIONS WITH

Geography made Mexico of great interest to the South. Indeed, support in the South for the Mexican War had been significant, in part because of the possibility of expanding slavery into any territory that might be acquired. During the Civil War, the Confederacy sent John Pickett to Mexico as commissioner in 1861–62 and as special envoy extraordinary in 1865.

The Confederate argument to its southern neighbor was that the two countries shared economic interests based on their agricultural economies. There was even a common bond to be found in the Southern slave system and the Mexican peonage system as compatible means of solving the labor problem. When Napoléon III seized control in Mexico, the Confederacy tried to exploit geographic proximity, offering itself as a buffer between a French presence in Mexico and a hostile United States. Although such logic must have appealed to Napoléon, he was still unwilling to act unilaterally in recognizing the Confederacy.

After the war, many Confederates initially fled to Mexico to escape capture. Many returned to the United States, but a significant population of exiles remained. Among those Confederates who originally went to Mexico are General Edmund Kirby Smith and Major General John B. Magruder.

MILITIAS

Militias had played an important role in America's defense since its founding. Most states required every able-bodied male between the ages of eighteen and forty-five to enroll in the

Above: *Before the Civil War, militia units in the South were important social as well as military organizations. This picture depicts elements of South Carolina's militia in 1861.*

militia and muster for drill once or twice a year. By the 1840s, however, many citizens began to resent the practice, and some states even abolished their militias.

In the South, however, the martial spirit served to keep the tradition alive. Southern men relished hunting, riding horses, fighting, and dueling, and these preferences naturally led to an enthusiasm for participation in the militia. Militias became important social as well as military organizations. When the Confederate government issued its call to arms, militia units responded en masse. The standard procedure was for the unit to first offer its services to the state, which then organized the volunteers into regiments before transferring command to the central government. This initial influx of volunteers provided an excellent foundation for the huge army the Confederacy would need to build.

MINES AND TORPEDOES

Brigadier General Gabriel J. Rains pioneered the use of land mines by burying artillery shells along the roads and beach when the Confederates evacuated Yorktown, Virginia, in May 1862. Both Federal and Confederate commanders criticized this "barbaric" method of warfare, and Rains was reassigned to the river defenses. The use of naval mines, "torpedoes" in the lexicon of the day, was considered more acceptable than mines on land. Torpedoes were detonated either by contact with a ship or by an electric current initiated by an operator on shore. Matthew F. Maury was also instrumental in experimenting with torpedoes and invented the electric version. Maury helped develop torpedo defenses for the James River, and Rains was instrumental in planning the torpedo defenses of

Above: Gabriel Rains's true calling was in ordnance development rather than battlefield command, and he spent most of the Civil War experimenting with torpedoes.

Mobile Bay and Charleston Harbor. It was at Mobile that Admiral David G. Farragut uttered his famous "Damn the torpedoes! Full speed ahead!" and successfully negotiated the mined waters. The torpedoes at Charleston were more successful, causing Federal commanders to abort plans to attack Charleston from the sea.

Other Confederates imitated these more formal efforts with torpedoes of their own. One of the most famous examples is the torpedo used to sink the USS *Cairo* on December 12, 1862, as it patrolled the Yazoo River during the Vicksburg Campaign. This incident is often cited as being the first example in history of a ship being sunk by an electrically detonated torpedo, but contemporary sources suggest that the torpedo may in fact have been detonated by a trip-wire device using a friction primer.

The use of torpedoes is an example of the Confederates' resorting to asymmetric warfare to counter the Federal resource advantage. Asymmetric warfare occurs when the weaker of two

Above: Unable to match the Federal naval power in a conventional way, the Confederates turned to asymmetric warfare, using torpedoes to protect bays, rivers, and harbors.

dissimilar opponents adopts new techniques to exploit the dissimilarity. The Confederate conventional naval threat was nearly nonexistent, but torpedoes helped make up the difference. They were a critical part of Confederate coastal and river defenses.

MISSISSIPPI

Mississippi was perhaps second only to South Carolina in terms of the presence of radicals eager to leave the Union. Efforts to provoke secession there failed in 1850 and 1851, but the gubernatorial election of fire-eater John J. Pettus by a large majority in 1859 indicated secession was still popular among many Mississippians. In his inaugural address, Pettus predicted that the growing sectional crisis would eventually lead to the abolition of slavery, with serious economic repercussions throughout the South. He argued that the establishment of a Southern confederacy would be the South's only way of maintaining slavery, and he called on other slave states to prepare for the possibility of secession. Shortly after Abraham Lincoln's election in 1860, Pettus called a special session of the legislature to consider the issue of Mississippi's secession.

The legislators responded by calling for a convention, and Mississippians elected a strong majority of secessionist delegates. The secessionists were largely young lawyers and planters who were on the rise and had a vested interest in the continuation of the slave labor system. The cooperationists and Unionists tended to be older and more politically conservative, but they never really stood a chance in the debate. On January 9, 1861, the convention voted for secession by an eighty-four to fifteen majority.

Eventually, ninety-eight of the convention's 100 members signed the ordinance.

As the nation's leading cotton-producing state, Mississippi was critical to the Confederacy's plans for "King Cotton" diplomacy. In 1859 it had produced 535 million pounds of cotton with its nearest competitor, Alabama, producing 440 million pounds. To keep up with the demand for cotton, slavery had also greatly expanded in Mississippi, which in 1860 had a population of 436,631 slaves compared to just 353,901 whites.

In addition to cotton, the Mississippi River made Mississippi important. The river was the nation's most critical economic transportation artery and would ensure Mississippi was the scene of much fighting, most notably the Vicksburg Campaign. Other noted battles in Mississippi occurred at Brice's Cross Roads and Tupelo.

Important railroads also ran through Mississippi and could be used to bring resources from the

Trans-Mississippi to the rest of the Confederacy. Corinth was known as "the crossroads of the Confederacy!" because it was there that the Memphis and Charleston Railroad met with the Mobile and Ohio line. Control of Corinth meant control of railroads from Columbus and Memphis as well as those running south into Mississippi and eastward to connect with Nashville and Chattanooga. Many Federal military and political leaders believed that if the Union could occupy two points in the South, the rebellion would collapse. Obviously, one point was Richmond. The other was Corinth, which Ulysses S. Grant called "the great strategic position at the West between the Tennessee and Mississippi rivers and between Nashville and Vicksburg." Confederate President Jefferson Davis agreed, considering the Memphis and Charleston Railroad the "vertebrae of the Confederacy." Meridian was another important railroad town, and both Corinth and Meridian were the sites of significant fighting.

In addition to President Davis, Mississippi produced Brigadier Generals Wirt Adams and William Barksdale and Major General Earl Van Dorn. In hardscrabble Jones County, where many yeoman farmers opposed slavery, Newton Knight led a motley band of guerrilla fighters who resisted Confederate authority enough to create what became known as the "Free State of Jones."

Left: *Corinth's location at the junction of two railroads made it strategically important to the Confederacy.*

MISSOURI

Missouri had long been party to the sectional crisis in the United States, beginning with the Missouri Compromise, which brought it into the Union as a slave state, to its role in fanning the violence of the "Bleeding Kansas." Governor Claiborne F. Jackson was a secessionist, but when he called for a state convention, voters responded by selecting a slate of delegates on February 18, 1861, that did not include a single announced proponent of immediate secession. The convention adopted a seven-point program that affirmed Missouri's desire to remain in the Union but also asked for a constitutional amendment that would protect slave property.

After President Abraham Lincoln's call for volunteers, U.S. soldiers under the impetuous Captain Nathaniel Lyon attacked pro-Confederate forces that had established a camp near St. Louis, and Missouri was plunged into its own internal civil war. The state convention reassembled in July and elected to remain in the Union, but Jackson called a rump legislature into session at Neosho in the southwestern corner of the state in October that decided to secede. On November 29, the Confederacy admitted Missouri and recognized Jackson's as the legitimate government. For all practical purposes, however, Missouri remained in the Union, and the Federal victory at Pea Ridge, Arkansas, on March 6–7, 1862, ensured things would stay that way.

Missouri was the site of early pitched battles such as Wilson's Creek, as well as abundant bushwhacking activity and guerrilla war by the likes of William C. Quantrill. Adopted son of the state Major General Sterling Price began a raid into Missouri on September 19, 1864. In addition to Price, other Missourians who fought with the Confederacy include Major General John S. Marmaduke and Brigadier General Francis M. Cockrell.

MISSOURI COMPROMISE OF 1820

The Missouri Compromise was part of a longstanding struggle to maintain a workable balance between slave and free states. In 1819 the United States consisted of twenty-two states, equally divided

Below: *Maintaining the delicate balance between slave and free states was critical to national politics in the prewar United States. This map shows the situation in 1821.*

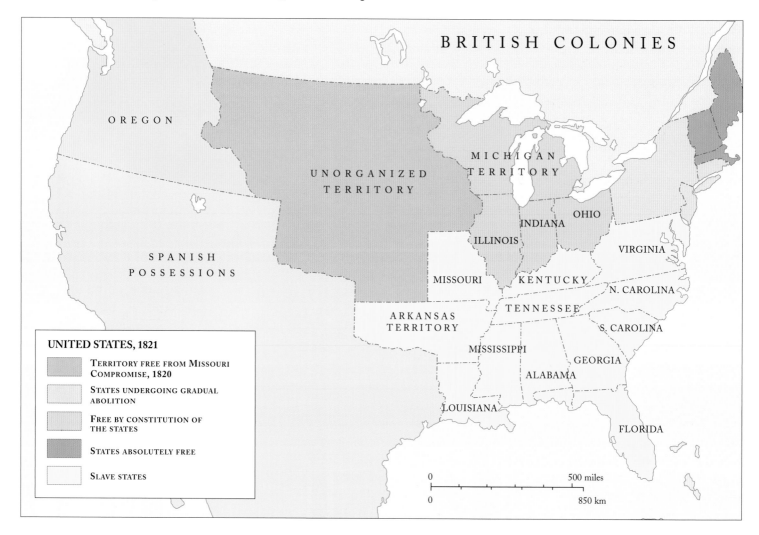

UNITED STATES, 1821

- TERRITORY FREE FROM MISSOURI COMPROMISE, 1820
- STATES UNDERGOING GRADUAL ABOLITION
- FREE BY CONSTITUTION OF THE STATES
- STATES ABSOLUTELY FREE
- SLAVE STATES

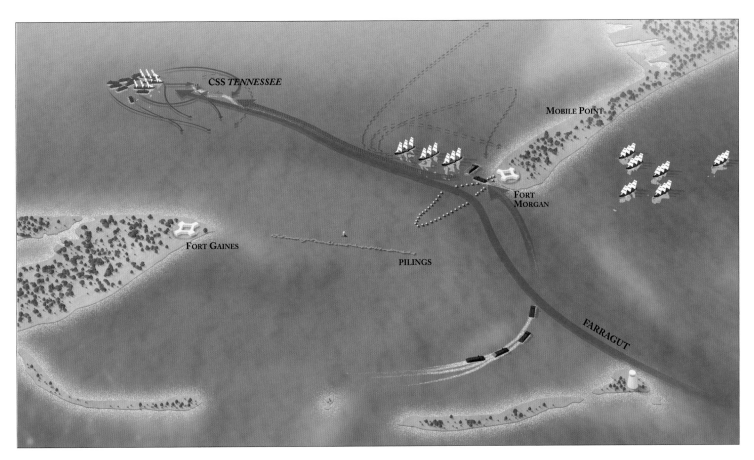

CSS TENNESSEE

MOBILE POINT

FORT GAINES

FORT MORGAN

PILINGS

FARRAGUT

between slave and free states. However, the free states had greater populations, so the North enjoyed a 105 to 81 advantage in seats in the House of Representatives. The South was adamant in its insistence that it maintain its parity in the Senate. Otherwise, it felt, the North would likely enact legislation hostile to the South's slave-based economy and way of life.

The issue reached a climax in 1819 when Missouri applied for admission to the Union as a slave state. After vigorous debate that consumed congressional business for the entire year, Illinois senator Jesse Thomas proposed a compromise in February 1820. The result was that Missouri would be admitted as a slave state and Maine, which had just separated from Massachusetts, would enter the Union as a free state. This arrangement would preserve the balance of the two types of states. However, in the future, no state from the area of the Louisiana Purchase north of the 36°30' latitude could be admitted as a slave state. The Missouri Compromise solved the

immediate crisis, but also awakened a powerful abolitionist movement in the North and did much to increase sectional tensions. The Kansas–Nebraska Act of 1854 overturned it.

MOBILE BAY, BATTLE OF

❖ DATE: August 3–23, 1864

❖ LOCATION: Mobile and Baldwin counties, Alabama

❖ BUCHANAN'S FLOTILLA AND MOBILE BAY FORT GARRISONS (C): 1,600

❖ WEST GULF BLOCKADING SQUADRON AND U.S. ARMY FORCE (U.S.): 8,500

❖ CASUALTIES: 476 (C); 319 (U.S.)

Mobile, Alabama, was extremely important to the Confederacy for a variety of reasons. With the loss of New Orleans, it became the most important Gulf of Mexico port used by the Confederate blockade-

Above: *At the Battle of Mobile Bay, David Farragut daringly passed a minefield of torpedoes and the guns of Fort Morgan, and then defeated the ironclad CSS* Tennessee.

runners. Its excellent access to the Confederate interior via nearby rivers and railroads allowed for the quick distribution of these goods, as well as for other transportation requirements. Furthermore, Mobile was critical to Alabama's industrial output. About 130 miles to its north, three ironclads were under construction at Selma. In spite of Mobile's importance, competing priorities had distracted Federal attention elsewhere until January 1864, when Admiral David G. Farragut arrived off Mobile Bay to begin gathering the ships and men he would need to attack.

Mobile would prove to be a difficult target because, although the bay stretched some thirty miles inland, its entrance was only three miles wide. Fort Gaines, Fort Powell, and the massive Fort Morgan all guarded various

Above: *Remarkably spry for a sixty-three-year-old, David Farragut climbed the rigging of the* Hartford *to get a better view of the engagement at Mobile Bay.*

approaches that had been narrowed by an extensive array of torpedoes or naval mines. A thin opening was left on the eastern edge of the minefield, providing a passageway for blockade-runners, but Fort Morgan's forty-seven guns covered this route. Behind the forts were the ironclad *Tennessee* and three wooden gunboats under Admiral Franklin Buchanan.

Because of these formidable defenses, the Navy Department sent Farragut four ironclads to augment the fourteen wooden ships he already had. He also had an initial army contingent of 2,000 troops.

Right: *Underpowered and hard to maneuver, the CSS* Tennessee *was ultimately swarmed by several Federal ships and compelled to surrender.*

The battle began on August 3 with an army attack on Fort Gaines. Farragut had hoped to simultaneously begin the naval engagement, but was delayed until August 5 by the late arrival of one of his ironclads. By the time Farragut did attack, he had the operation planned in the minutest detail. To protect his force, he led with his ironclads, followed by the wooden ships. He had originally planned to lead with his own flagship, but his officers had convinced him that the admiral should not be so exposed. Reluctantly—and later to his regret—Farragut acquiesced and assigned the *Brooklyn* to lead.

Confederates at Fort Morgan opened fire at 7:10 a.m., with Farragut's fleet a half-mile away. The *Brooklyn*, at the head of the Federal wooden ships, returned fire. Buchanan brought the ironclad *Tennessee* and the three small ships out from behind Mobile Point and lined them up behind the minefield, executing the classic naval maneuver of crossing Farragut's T and sending a raking fire down the long axis of the Federal line. By this time the *Brooklyn*, with its superior speed, had drawn even with the rear of the monitors. At this rate, Farragut would be faced with the dangerous situation of a wooden ship leading the attack.

Just then the *Brooklyn* spotted "a row of suspicious looking buoys . . . directly under our bows." Unsure of what to do, Captain James Alden ordered the ship to back engines to clear the hazard, a maneuver that compressed Farragut's entire fleet and exposed it to a murderous fire from Fort Morgan. To make matters worse, the ironclad *Tecumseh*, at the head of the formation, struck a torpedo and went down swiftly. It was at this critical moment that Farragut famously declared, "Damn the torpedoes! Full speed ahead!"

PASSING FORT MORGAN

As the Federal fleet pressed forward, its starboard batteries unloaded on Fort Morgan. The Confederates hit some of the ships, but Farragut was able to complete his run past the fort. His main

threat now was the *Tennessee*. The Federals delivered repeated broadsides, but these efforts barely dented the ironclad. Still, Buchanan knew he had to do more than just withstand the pounding. With only six hours of coal left, he had to act, and he headed straight for the Federal fleet. Farragut ordered his fleet to descend on the *Tennessee*, and, after a spirited fight, Buchanan was forced to surrender.

The one-sided naval battle had lasted but a couple of hours. Of the 3,000 Federals engaged, there were 319 casualties, including ninety-three who drowned when the *Tecumseh* sank. The percentage of Confederate naval personnel lost was much higher. Of 470 Confederates engaged, 312 were lost.

The forts did not hold out much longer. The Confederates abandoned tiny Fort Powell that night, blowing it up as they departed. Fort Gaines mustered a fainthearted show of resistance and then surrendered the next day, August 8.

On August 17, the Federals received a siege train from New Orleans, and on August 22, they began a heavy land and naval bombardment of Fort Morgan. The Confederate defenders there raised a white flag the next morning and formally surrendered at 2:30 p.m. Losses on both sides were negligible. From all three forts, the Federals captured 164 prisoners and 104 pieces of artillery.

MOBILIZATION, CONFEDERATE

The initial source of soldiers for the Confederacy came from the existing state militias, but their limited numbers could in no way meet the demands of building an entire army. In keeping with the traditional political philosophy in America that the chief responsibility for raising volunteers rested with the states rather than the central government, the Confederate government levied each state with the requirement to raise a certain number of regiments. The state governors were responsible for finding, organizing, and equipping these units before forwarding them to a camp designated by the central government.

State governors were assisted by local community leaders to recruit the necessary manpower. A prominent citizen would often announce he was organizing a company, and those community members who respected him would join his unit. Inevitably, the man who had formed the company would be elected its captain. When enough companies were recruited to form a regiment, the governor would either appoint a colonel or sometimes one would be elected. The result of this decentralized mobilization process was an army that had strong local identities, a profound sense of individualism, and a lack of standardization.

MONEY

The Confederate government began issuing its first paper money in April 1861, after the congress authorized an initial printing of $100 million in notes. The paper money policy eventually led to rampant inflation. It also led to much counterfeiting, some of which was instigated in the North in an effort to destabilize the Confederate economy. As a countermeasure, women in Richmond were paid $500 a year to sign their names to bills as they came off the presses in hopes that the multitude of signatures would somehow discourage counterfeiting.

Because the Confederacy lacked die cutters, the Treasury Department decided to accept a variety of coins, including U.S. silver, English sovereigns, French Napoleons, and Spanish and Mexican doubloons, as legal tender. The Confederacy also issued paper notes in denominations from five to fifty cents to help make change. These notes became known as "shinplasters."

Faith in Confederate currency was always thin, and by 1863, U.S. greenbacks were routinely commanding a four-to-one ratio in exchange for Confederate dollars. Confederate currency was further weakened by the states issuing their own money and allowing cities, railroads, and insurance companies to do the same. All told, an estimated $2.2 billion in paper money entered circulation in the Confederacy.

MONOCACY, BATTLE OF

❖ DATE: July 9, 1864

❖ LOCATION: Frederick County, Maryland

❖ CORPS UNDER EARLY (C): 15,000

❖ FORCE UNDER WALLACE (U.S.): 6,550

❖ CASUALTIES: 700 (C); 1,880 (U.S.)

The Confederate victory at Lynchburg, Virginia, on June 17–18, 1864, left the Shenandoah Valley open as an avenue of approach toward Washington, D.C. With General Robert E. Lee under siege at Petersburg, Lieutenant General Jubal A. Early was sent to threaten Washington to relieve pressure on Lee. In mid-June, Early headed north with a corps of roughly 15,000 men, and by July 8 he had reached the outskirts of Frederick, Maryland. Agents of the Baltimore and Ohio Railroad learned of Early's advance and alerted railroad president John Garrett. Garrett notified Major General Lew Wallace, who hastily organized a force of 6,550 men at

South Carolina voted to secede on December 20, 1860. On December 31, the state's secession convention adopted a set of resolutions written by fire-eater Robert Barnwell Rhett that proposed a convention of seceded states be held at Montgomery,

Below: *The February 18, 1861, inauguration of Jefferson Davis as president of the Confederate States of America was a cause of great celebration in Montgomery, Alabama.*

Above: *The Battle of Monocacy caused a momentary panic in the Federal capital of Washington, but Jubal Early's raid ultimately proved unsustainable.*

Monocacy Junction, Maryland, to block Early's route. On the morning of July 9, 1864, the two forces met along the banks of the Monocacy River.

The Confederate attack was uncoordinated and subordinates acted individually, but Wallace's men were nonetheless forced from their positions and fell back to Baltimore. Early did not pursue vigorously, because he felt that he could not be burdened by taking additional prisoners. The Federals suffered 1,880 casualties compared to just 700 for the Confederates.

While it was a tactical victory for the Confederates—their only one on Northern soil—the battle also afforded the Federals time to send reinforcements to Washington, which thwarted Early's designs against the capital. For this reason, Wallace is sometimes grandiosely credited for fighting "the battle that saved Washington, D.C."

Alabama, in February 1861. The purpose of this convention was to establish a Southern confederacy and draw up a constitution for it.

At the time of Rhett's proposal for a convention in Montgomery, Alabama had not yet seceded, although it did so in January 1861. Indeed, rapid action was a large part of Rhett's strategy. His hope was to allay the fears of the cooperationists who had a more conciliatory approach to the sectional crisis and generally favored unified rather than individual action. To achieve this unity, the "South Carolina Program" promised Southern union before the inauguration of Abraham Lincoln as president, and continuous communication throughout the Southern states through the dispatch of commissioners.

The resulting Montgomery Convention brought together fifty delegates from the seven seceded states of South Carolina, Georgia, Alabama, Mississippi, Florida, Louisiana, and late arrival Texas, which missed many of the early deliberations. The delegates assembled on February 4 and chose Howell Cobb of Georgia to serve as convention president. The next day, a committee of twelve chaired by Christopher G. Memminger began work on a provisional constitution; they presented their results on February 7. The document was remarkably similar to the United States Constitution and reflected the fact that although the fire-eaters had been instrumental in calling the convention, more moderate voices would dominate its actual proceedings. A permanent constitution was adopted on March 11, but delays in its ratification caused the provisional version to remain in effect until February 1862.

After adopting the provisional constitution, the delegates turned their attention to electing a

president and vice president. On February 9, Jefferson Davis and Alexander H. Stephens emerged as the men selected to fill these two offices. Davis arrived in Montgomery on February 16 and was inaugurated two days later. The convention sat in Montgomery until May 21, when Richmond, Virginia, was selected as the new Confederate capital.

MOORE, ANDREW B. (1806–73)

Andrew B. Moore practiced law and served several terms in the Alabama House of Representatives before running for governor in 1857. He was elected without opposition. Moore was a moderate on the subject of slavery, and in 1859 he was reelected governor, defeating the extremist William Sandford. Moore became more concerned with states' rights after John Brown's raid on the U.S. arsenal at Harpers Ferry.

Between the November 1860 presidential election of Abraham Lincoln and the meeting of the Alabama Convention on January 7, 1861, Moore took several decisive steps to safeguard Alabama's assets. To provide financial security, he urged banks to suspend specie payments and to exchange large amounts of capital for state bonds. Militarily, he ordered the state militia to seize the arsenal at Mount Vernon and Forts Morgan and Gaines on Mobile Bay, and he contributed more than 500 troops to assist Florida governor Madison Perry in capturing the Federal forts at Pensacola.

When Moore left the governor's office, he was appointed special aide-de-camp by his successor, John G. Shorter, and Moore helped coordinate logistical issues for troops in Alabama. After the

war, he was arrested and imprisoned at Fort Pulaski, Georgia, until August 1865. He returned to Marion, Alabama, and resumed his law practice.

MORGAN, JOHN HUNT (1825–64)

❖ RANK: Brigadier general

❖ PLACE OF BIRTH: Huntsville, Alabama

❖ EDUCATED: West Point

❖ MILITARY CAREER:
1846–47: Served in U.S. Army; fought in Mexican-American War, rising to rank of first lieutenant
1861: Raised Second Kentucky Cavalry Regiment; fought at Shiloh
1862: Promoted to brigadier general; raided Union supply lines; Battle of Hartsville
1863: "Morgan's Raid"; captured near Salineville, Ohio

John Hunt Morgan was one of the Confederacy's more dashing and romanticized figures. He was a natural leader, having served in

Above: *John Hunt Morgan, who conducted well-publicized raids into Kentucky and Ohio, was one of the Confederacy's most romanticized heroes.*

Mexico, built a successful business in Lexington, Kentucky, and raised his own militia unit, the Lexington Rifles. He was commissioned as a captain in the Confederate army in September 1861 and placed in command of a cavalry squadron. He was promoted to colonel on April 4, 1862, and fought at Shiloh. In June, he was given a brigade.

On July 4, 1862, Morgan embarked on his first raid into Kentucky. He left Knoxville, Tennessee, with two regiments and caused alarm with Federals at Tomkinsville, Glasgow, Lebanon, Cynthiana, and Crab Orchard, Kentucky, before returning to Tennessee on August 1. During the twenty-four-day raid, he had covered over 1,000 miles and captured and paroled 1,200 Federals, while losing fewer than 100 of his own men.

Morgan launched his second raid in October, capturing Lexington on October 18. He was promoted to brigadier general on December 11 and placed in command of a cavalry division. That winter, he married Mattie Ready. When Federal troops occupied Murfreesboro, a soldier asked Ready her name. She replied, "It's Mattie Ready now, but by the grace of God one day I hope to call myself the wife of John Morgan." Morgan later located her, and after a whirlwind courtship, Major General Leonidas Polk married the pair, with Lieutenant General Braxton Bragg and his staff in attendance.

Morgan then conducted a third raid into Kentucky between December 21, 1862, and January 1, 1863, destroying $2 million worth of property and taking 1,887 prisoners. On May 1, 1863, he received the thanks of the Confederate Congress for his various activities in Kentucky and Tennessee.

On July 2, 1863, Morgan began another raid to slow the Federal advance against Chattanooga. Bragg had specifically prohibited Morgan from extending his operations north into Ohio, but after initial successes in Kentucky, Morgan crossed into Ohio on July 6. Attrition of men and exhaustion of horses weakened Morgan's effort, but he passed through the suburbs of Cincinnati on the night of July 13–14. He suffered a severe defeat on July 19 as he attempted to cross the Ohio River to reenter Kentucky. He was finally captured on July 26 near New Lisbon. By then, his initial force of some 2,460 had been reduced to just 364. Throughout the raid, Morgan's men had covered an average of twenty-one miles a day, but yielded inconsequential results.

Morgan escaped from the Ohio State Penitentiary on November 26, 1863. He then commanded the Department of Southwest Virginia and was killed on September 4, 1864, in fighting at Greenville, Tennessee.

MOSBY, JOHN S.
(1833–1916)

John Singleton Mosby was one of the Confederacy's most effective partisan rangers. He commanded the Forty-third Battalion of Virginia Cavalry, a unit more commonly referred to as "Mosby's Rangers," with remarkable success in northern Virginia and Maryland. His unit began with about 100 members and grew to 200 by the end of the war, but on his operations, Mosby rarely employed more than a dozen men. As the Federal presence in Virginia increased, the area in which Mosby remained active was known as "Mosby's Confederacy."

Mosby's adult life began inauspiciously when he was released from the University of Virginia after shooting another student. He began studying law while he was in jail for the incident and then practiced law in Bristol, Virginia.

A PRIVATE AT MANASSAS

Mosby fought as a private in the First Virginia Cavalry at the Battle of First Manassas before being commissioned as a first lieutenant in February 1862. Shortly afterward, he began scouting for Major General Jeb Stuart and helped guide him on his ride around Major General George B. McClellan's army during the Peninsula Campaign.

In January 1863, Mosby was given permission to organize a group of partisans to conduct guerrilla warfare in the Loudoun Valley of northern Virginia. In March, he led a daring raid on Fairfax Courthouse in which he captured Brigadier General Edwin H. Stoughton. Mosby subsequently received a steady string of promotions, becoming a major in April, a lieutenant colonel in February 1864, and a colonel in December. Nicknamed the "Gray Ghost," he remained a continual irritant to the Army of the Potomac, causing Lieutenant General Ulysses S. Grant to devote considerable energy to Mosby

Above: *Although partisan operations were of overall mixed effect for the Confederacy, John Mosby was a constant menace to the Federals in the Shenandoah Valley.*

during the 1864 Overland Campaign. As the war drew to a close, Mosby refused to surrender, instead disbanding his force on April 20, 1865.

After the war, Mosby again practiced law. His reputation suffered among Southerners when he supported Grant for president and became a Republican. However, Mosby's political connections allowed him to serve as consul in Hong Kong, in the General Land Office, and as an assistant attorney in the Department of Justice.

MUDD, SAMUEL A. (1833–83)

Samuel A. Mudd was a country doctor with a practice on a farm five miles from Bryantown, Maryland. He was a proslavery Confederate sympathizer who often expressed disapproval of President Abraham Lincoln. At 4:00 a.m. on the day after Lincoln's assassination, John Wilkes Booth arrived at Mudd's house. Mudd treated Booth's fractured leg and then provided Booth directions to the next destination on his escape route. Booth departed Mudd's house on April 15, 1865.

On April 18, Lieutenant Alexander Lovett questioned Mudd, who said he had recently treated a stranger. A military commission tried Mudd and others associated with the assassination, and evidence was presented that suggested Mudd had a previous relationship with Booth as well as emphasizing Mudd's Confederate sympathies. However, Mudd's attorney argued it was no crime to provide medical treatment to an injured man. The commission convicted Mudd of conspiracy and sentenced him to life imprisonment, although President Andrew Johnson pardoned Mudd in one of his last acts in office.

MURFREESBORO, BATTLE OF

❖ DATE: December 31–January 2, 1863

❖ LOCATION: Rutherford County, Tennessee

❖ ARMY OF TENNESSEE (C): 37,000

❖ ARMY OF THE CUMBERLAND (U.S.): 44,000

❖ CASUALTIES: 10,266 (C); 13,249 (U.S.)

After withdrawing from Kentucky, General Braxton Bragg established a position along the Nashville–Chattanooga railroad line at Murfreesboro, Tennessee. Federal forces under Major General Don Carlos Buell came south and occupied Nashville. Buell was then replaced by Major General William S. Rosecrans.

Rosecrans slowly built up his readiness, amassing a huge logistical base at Nashville. He finally began advancing on December 26, 1862, but before Rosecrans could attack, Bragg struck the Federal right flank in a surprise attack on December 31 that collapsed that part of Rosecrans's line.

Both armies were silent on January 1, and then Bragg renewed the attack, hitting the Federal left on January 2. The Confederate attack was slow in developing and was defeated by well-placed Federal artillery. Although Bragg had scored a tactical victory, his army was exhausted, and he fell back to Tullahoma. Rosecrans also was spent and did not resume operations until June.

Below: *Well-placed artillery was critical to the Federals at the Battle of Murfreesboro. Although Braxton Bragg scored a tactical victory, the fighting left both sides exhausted.*

MUSIC, IMPORTANCE OF

Music was a critical component of maintaining Confederate morale, both on the home front and in camp. The war gave rise to some 600 pieces of sheet music that celebrated the Confederate cause, including the "Bonnie Blue Flag," "Stonewall Jackson's Way," and "The Manassas Quickstep." Of course, "Dixie" is the anthem most associated with the Confederacy. Audiences in search of diversions from the war's hardships flocked to the stage to hear professional performances. A popular performer was "Blind Tom" Bethune, a self-taught Georgia slave who reportedly knew 7,000 tunes, including his own "Battle of Manassas."

Soldiers in camp also prized the release music offered, and some regiments formed musical clubs that gave performances. One of the more famous was found in the Fourteenth

Above: *Because of its underdeveloped lithography industry, few illustrated music sheets were issued in the South either before or during the war, making this version of "Our National Confederate Anthem" a rare artifact.*

Right: *Music such as "Beauregard's March" captured the martial spirit of the Confederacy both in camp and on the home front.*

Tennessee Regiment. Company and regimental bands also provided martial music to accompany drilling and marching, as well as giving the occasional concert. Even General Robert E. Lee said, "I don't believe we can have an army without music."

However, the most popular expression of music was not these organized performances, but rather an individual fiddler or banjo player who entertained his messmates around the evening campfire. Occasionally these musicians would serenade their officers or, if the situation allowed, the ladies in the surrounding area.

NAVAL ACADEMY

The Confederate Naval Academy was established in 1863 on the James River when the *Patrick Henry* was made into a school ship manned by thirteen faculty and staff. The first class had about fifty midshipmen, but was later increased to sixty. Confederate law limited the number of acting midshipmen to 106, but a more practical size restriction was the fact that the *Patrick Henry* could only accommodate about thirty of the midshipmen. The remainder were housed on other ships in active service that gave the midshipmen

valuable experience, but also disrupted the course of instruction. In 1864 plans were made to rectify the situation by building cabins at Drewry's Bluff. Naval Academy midshipmen were among the first to resist the 30,000-man Army of the James as Major General Benjamin F. Butler advanced up the Appomattox–James River Peninsula from Bermuda Hundred in May 1864.

NAVY

Secretary of the Navy Stephen R. Mallory faced an almost impossible task in building a Confederate navy. At the beginning of the Civil War, the U.S. Navy numbered some ninety ships of all types. By 1864 that number had grown to 670. The Confederate navy started out with no ships, inherited five from the seceded states, and grew to about 130. Still, the Confederacy simply lacked the industrial shipbuilding capacity to keep up with the North. The Federal navy's superior strength allowed it to not just control the coastline but to use steam power to penetrate into the heart of the Confederacy via large rivers like the Mississippi. There was little the Confederate navy could do to counter this threat.

The navy Mallory envisioned was designed almost entirely for the purpose of defeating the Federal blockade. To this end, Mallory developed a two-pronged approach. First he would confront the blockade directly by building domestically or buying abroad a few powerful ships that by quality would outmatch the Federal advantage in quantity. As he explained to his wife, "Knowing that the enemy could build one hundred ships to one of our own, my policy has been to make ships so strong and invulnerable as would compensate for the inequality of numbers."

OVERSEAS PRODUCTION

Because of the South's limited industrial capacity, Mallory relied on James D. Bulloch to leverage British sympathies and shipyards. These efforts succeeded in obtaining four vessels for the Confederacy, the CSS *Shenandoah*, *Florida*, and *Alabama*, all built in Britain, and the CSS *Stonewall*, which was built in France. Overseas ship production, however, was a lengthy and uncertain process, so Mallory also did what he could to build domestically. His principal hope lay in ironclads, which offered the promise of wreaking havoc against the Federal wooden fleet. Throughout the war, the Confederacy initiated construction of fifty-two ironclads and

completed almost thirty of them. Although this was an impressive achievement given the Confederacy's limited resources, the fact remained that the ironclads produced in Southern shipyards were little more than armored, floating artillery batteries, capable of little more than harbor defense.

Institutionally, Mallory modeled the Confederate navy on the customs and regulations of the

Above: *Although the Confederate navy experienced a shortage of enlisted men, it had more experienced officers than it had ships for them to command.*

U.S. Navy. This included the creation of "offices" such as the Office of Provisions and Clothing or the Office of Orders and Detail. Pay tables also followed Federal patterns. The Confederate navy even continued the Federal practice of allocating each enlisted man a ration of a half-pint of spirits or wine a day.

Mallory found himself short of almost everything but officers. There he had the opposite problem—too many experienced officers for the few available command positions. Men like Josiah Tattnall Jr. and Franklin Buchanan had commanded squadrons at sea in the U.S. Navy and now were competing for a handful of converted tugs and river steamers. While promotion was rapid in the Confederate army, Confederate navy officers usually ended the war at the rank they had entered it or at best received one promotion.

PROVISIONAL NAVY

In May 1863, Mallory ingeniously created an entirely new naval service called the Provisional Navy of the Confederate States. All enlisted men were automatically transferred to this new organization, but commissioned officer billets would be filled only by presidential appointment. This technique allowed Mallory to select those younger officers who showed promise and advance men based on talent rather than strictly by seniority.

Mallory had no such embarrassment of riches in the enlisted ranks. The Confederate navy's enlisted strength peaked at

4,500, at least 25 percent below requirements, and its average enlisted strength was probably around 3,000.

Without an indigenous seafaring population, the South simply had a small natural pool of personnel. Free African Americans could enlist with the approval of the local squadron commander or the Navy Department, and slaves could serve with their master's permission.

Although accurate figures are not known, a fair number of African Americans served in the Confederate navy as coal heavers, stewards, and, in some select cases, highly skilled tidewater pilots.

In the final analysis, the creation of a Confederate navy was a remarkable achievement against overwhelming odds, but still a woeful counter to its powerful Federal opponent.

With the Confederacy's lengthy coast and numerous rivers, the Federal navy could strike anywhere it liked, and the small Confederate navy could defend only a few important isolated locations. In spite of Herculean efforts, the Confederate navy showed little in the way of tangible results.

Below: *The Battle of New Bern illustrated the threat the Federals could pose to Southern logistics by attacking along the vulnerable Confederate coast.*

NEW BERN, BATTLE OF

- ❖ DATE: March 14, 1862
- ❖ LOCATION: Craven County, North Carolina
- ❖ FORCE UNDER BRANCH (C): 4,500
- ❖ COAST DIVISION (U.S.): 11,000
- ❖ CASUALTIES: 578 (C); 470 (U.S.)

After its victory at Roanoke Island on February 8, 1862, the Burnside Expedition prepared to attack New Bern, a location of strategic importance not only as North Carolina's second largest port, but also as the site of an important railroad. From New Bern, the Atlantic and North Carolina Railroad ran to a vital junction at Goldsboro. Major General Ambrose E. Burnside's March 14 victory at New Bern represented a significant expansion of the Federal logistical strategy to defeat the Confederacy.

With the fall of Roanoke Island, Confederate forces at New Bern bolstered their defenses and prepared for a Federal attack. As was common all along the Confederate coast, the defenders were outmatched. On February 10, thirteen Federal gunboats under Commander Stephen Rowan

routed Captain William F. Lynch's little "Mosquito Fleet." This defeat left the Confederates with no armed warships that could challenge the attackers.

By the second week of March 1862, however, a line of log and earth breastworks had been established downriver from New Bern. These positions were manned by some 4,500 green North Carolina troops, all under the command of Brigadier General Lawrence O'Bryan Branch. The key to the Confederate defense was Fort Thompson, which mounted thirteen heavy guns.

On March 11, Burnside set sail with 11,000 men to a rendezvous with Rowan's warships. On March 13, Burnside's men landed at New Bern without opposition, advanced to within two miles of the Confederate defensive line, and camped for the night. When the Federals attacked the next day, they were able to exploit a gap in the Confederate line and slice through the defense. The Confederates lost 64 killed, 101 wounded, and 413 missing, compared to 90 killed and 380 wounded for the Federals.

INTO THE INTERIOR

In the wake of a string of successful Federal coastal operations at places like Hatteras Inlet, Port Royal, and Roanoke Island, the Confederates had by and large withdrawn to the interior. Given their limited resources, they may have had no choice, but the loss of New Bern seems to have shown the dangers of this strategy. With possession of New Bern, the Federals were poised to project power from the coast into the interior of the Confederacy. Fortunately for the Confederates, Burnside's romp was cut short when he was ordered to reinforce Major General George B. McClellan's failing campaign on the Virginia Peninsula.

NEW MARKET, BATTLE OF

❖ DATE: May 15, 1864

❖ LOCATION: Shenandoah County, Virginia

❖ ARMY OF NORTHERN VIRGINIA (C): 4,090

❖ DEPARTMENT OF WEST VIRGINIA (U.S.): 6,500

❖ CASUALTIES: 540 (C); 840 (U.S.)

As part of Lieutenant General Ulysses S. Grant's coordinated spring offensive in 1864, Major General Franz Sigel advanced up the Shenandoah Valley with some 6,500 men. He was resisted by Confederate cavalry led by Brigadier General John Imboden, who was later reinforced by Major General John C. Breckinridge. Included in Breckinridge's force was a battalion of cadets from the Virginia Military Institute.

When it became apparent on May 15, 1864, that Sigel was not going to attack, Breckinridge decided to go on the offensive. After maneuvering his force to create an illusion of having greater strength, Breckinridge pressed

Below: *This reenactment of the Battle of New Market commemorates a Confederate victory over a serious Federal threat to the Shenandoah Valley.*

forward. As the battle seesawed back and forth, Breckinridge reluctantly committed the young VMI cadets. Sigel responded with a poorly executed counterattack and then began withdrawing. He ultimately ordered a general retreat to Strasburg.

THREAT UNHINGED

Although a secondary battle, New Market had important consequences. The Confederate victory unhinged the Federal threat to the Shenandoah Valley, thereby preserving the valley's agricultural output and safeguarding the western flank of the Army of Northern Virginia. It was also the end of Sigel's rather inglorious military career. He was relieved of command on May 19.

Below: *Preparations for the defense of New Orleans were complicated by Confederate debate over whether the attack would come from upriver or downriver. In the end, Farragut attacked from the sea.*

NEW ORLEANS, BATTLE OF

❖ DATE: April 25, 1862

❖ LOCATION: Orleans and St. Bernard Parishes, Louisiana

❖ DEPARTMENT NO. 1 (C): 4,000

❖ DEPARTMENT OF THE GULF (U.S.): 15,000

❖ CASUALTIES: None

New Orleans was identified as a key Federal objective from the Civil War's very outset. It was by far the South's biggest city with a population of 168,000, as well as being a key port and shipbuilding center. After the Federals captured it on April 25, 1862, Charlestonian diarist Mary Chesnut lamented, "New Orleans gone—and with it the Confederacy. Are we not cut in two?" Although not as decisive as Chesnut imagined, the Federal victory at New

Orleans was a huge step toward splitting the Confederacy in two and reopening the Mississippi River. It was the pivotal battle of the Gulf Campaign.

New Orleans's defenses were built around forts Jackson and St. Philip, which guarded the Mississippi approaches seventy-five miles south of the city. Major General David Twiggs initially was in charge of the Confederate forces there, but his infirmity and advanced age made him ill-suited to the important task. On October 17, 1861, Major General Mansfield Lovell replaced him.

Lovell found the New Orleans defenses woefully deficient, but in addition to the lack of men and equipment, the Confederate effort suffered from disagreement over the direction from which the inevitable Federal attack would come. Throughout the preparation of New Orleans's defenses, many felt the true threat would come from upriver. Even if the attack came

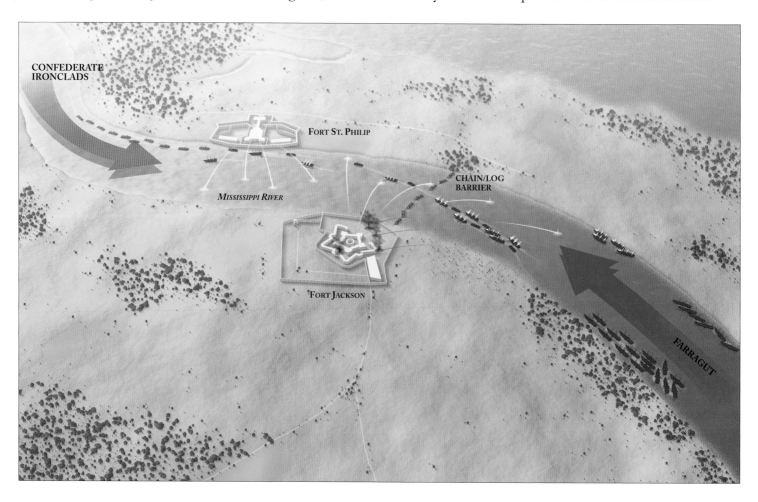

CONFEDERATE IRONCLADS

FORT ST. PHILIP

MISSISSIPPI RIVER

CHAIN/LOG BARRIER

FORT JACKSON

FARRAGUT

toward New Orleans and anchored for the night fifteen miles below the city.

Before dawn on April 25, Farragut was up and moving toward New Orleans. The city was in panic, and Lovell had torched the levee and retreated. As Farragut pulled alongside the city, he hammered it with broadsides. He then dispatched his marines to take possession of the Federal mint, post office, and customshouse, and replace the Confederate flag with the Stars and Stripes on all public buildings. Captain Theodorus Bailey, commander of Farragut's Red Division, worked his way through an angry mob and demanded the city's surrender, but the mayor claimed to be under martial law and without authority. When Farragut threatened a bombardment, the mayor and common council declared New Orleans an open city.

In the meantime, the forts had refused Porter's demand to surrender, so Porter resumed his bombardment. He made a second offer two days later, but still the forts refused. Finally, as word drifted downriver of New Orleans's fate, Confederate morale broke and the defenders surrendered. On May 1, Butler and the army began a controversial occupation of New Orleans.

from the Gulf of Mexico, these planners argued that the powerful Forts Jackson and St. Philip could handily repulse a Federal attack, especially one consisting of wooden ships. This misunderstanding of the Federal intentions plagued New Orleans's defensive preparations.

However, in the first encounter between the Federals and Confederates at New Orleans, Commodore George N. Hollins routed the inexcusably complacent Federal flotilla commanded by Captain John Pope. This Confederate triumph on October 12, 1861, embarrassed the Federals and boosted Confederate morale, but it really did nothing to further the security of New Orleans or stem the growing Federal buildup of naval forces that would eventually fall under the command of Admiral David G. Farragut and army forces led by Major General Benjamin F. Butler. Both officers used the recently captured Ship Island as a staging area for their growing commands.

The initial Federal assault on New Orleans was a mortar bombardment engineered by Captain David D. Porter. Porter believed that his twenty-one mortar schooners could shell the Confederate forts into submission, which would then allow Butler's soldiers to easily occupy New Orleans. From April 18 to 23, Porter furiously pounded the forts, but his hoped-for results failed to materialize.

PASSING THE FORTS

With this failure behind him, Farragut launched a well-planned naval attack shortly after midnight on April 24. His fleet took fire from both the forts and the Confederate ram *Manassas*, but the passage never really was in doubt.

After successfully steaming past the Confederate defenses, Farragut ordered Porter to demand the surrender of the forts and told Butler to bring up his army troops. Farragut then pushed on

NEWSPAPERS

Strong sentiment in favor of freedom of the press and other civil liberties allowed Southern newspapers to publish at will during the Civil War. This freedom prevailed even when the newspapers' unrestrained reports became a major source of intelligence for the Federals or when newspaper editors used their platforms to be highly critical of President Jefferson Davis and his administration. Nonetheless, Secretary of War George W. Randolph represented the dominant government view when he said he hoped "this revolution . . . may be closed without suppression of one single newspaper in the Confederate States."

Many Southern newspapers helped stoke the flames of secession, most notably Robert

Below: *Among the more influential of the Southern newspapers was the* Charleston Mercury. *This announcement of South Carolina's secession is one of the Civil War's iconic images.*

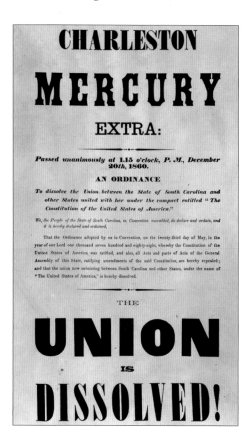

Barnwell Rhett's *Charleston Mercury.* However, throughout the war, Rhett became a vehement opponent of the Davis administration. Edward Pollard of the *Richmond Examiner* was another of the president's greatest critics. Southern editors were also lavish in their criticism of Confederate military leadership, causing General Robert E. Lee to lament that it appeared the Confederacy had "put all our worst generals to commanding our armies, and all our best generals to editing newspapers."

Newspapers were highly prized by soldiers on the front, and Confederates and Federals occasionally exchanged them when the opportunity presented itself. However, in the latter years of the war, shortages of ink and paper, as well as uncertain mail delivery, made newspapers an increasingly scarce commodity throughout the Confederacy.

NORTH CAROLINA

North Carolina's interest in Southern nationalism was vested more in the yeoman class's support for democracy rather than any influence of a slaveholding aristocracy. In 1851 both the legislature and the citizens had rejected secession, and this attitude continued to dominate in contrast to the growing radicalism in South Carolina. North Carolina's mountainous Appalachian and Piedmont regions were particularly soft on secession, which found its greatest support in the eastern part of the state. Although Governor John W. Ellis favored secession, in a referendum held on February 26, 1861, North Carolinians narrowly rejected a convention.

In spite of this initial tepid response, North Carolina was reenergized by President Abraham Lincoln's call for volunteers after Fort Sumter. Ellis called a special session of the legislature, and the body responded by unanimously voting North Carolina out of the Union on May 20, the principal debate being whether to base secession on the right of revolution or on the traditional state-sovereignty compact theory.

Throughout the war, North Carolinians remained resistant to centralized efforts by President Jefferson Davis. Governor Zebulon B. Vance, a staunch advocate of states' rights, often resisted Davis, including opposing a railroad being built to connect Danville, Virginia, and Goldsboro, North Carolina, a project both Davis and General Robert E. Lee argued was necessary to supply the Army of Northern Virginia. Such pleas notwithstanding, Vance protested that the line would divert commerce from the western counties of his state to Virginia.

North Carolina also was especially opposed to government efforts to levy a 10 percent "tax in kind" on agricultural produce in 1863. By that year, noticeable agitation for peace without realization of Confederate war objectives had surfaced in the state legislature.

In spite of these objections, 125,000 North Carolinians fought for the Confederacy, a contribution greater than that of any other state. With just one-ninth of the Confederate population, North Carolina supplied one-sixth of its soldiers and absorbed about a quarter of its casualties. Among North Carolinians serving in the war were Lieutenant General D. H. Hill, Major General Robert F. Hoke, and Brigadier General James J. Pettigrew.

North Carolina also played an important role in the logistical support of the Confederacy,

Above: *Joseph Johnston surrendered his army to William T. Sherman in April 1865. Ironically, Johnston and Sherman developed a relationship of mutual respect after the war.*

especially by its transportation assets. Wilmington was the Confederacy's last port to remain open, and throughout the course of the war, about 100 blockade-runners sailed in and out of its harbor. New Bern was the state's second largest port, and the terminus of the Atlantic and North Carolina Railroad, which ran to a vital junction at Goldsboro. At Goldsboro, the line intersected with the Wilmington and Weldon Railroad, which carried supplies to Richmond and points north.

SHERMAN ARRIVES

In addition to coastal war sites like New Bern, Fort Macon, and Fort Fisher, North Carolina saw fighting toward the end of the war during Major General William T. Sherman's Carolinas Campaign. Still, North Carolinians showed little of the open disdain for Sherman's men that the Federals encountered in South Carolina, and the state was spared much of the destruction experienced to its south. General Joseph E. Johnston was

able to offer little resistance as Sherman marched through North Carolina, surrendering at Bentonville on May 3, 1865.

NORTHROP, LUCIUS B. (1811–94)

Lucius Bellinger Northrop graduated from West Point in 1831 and served on the frontier and in fighting against Native Americans. As a lieutenant he developed a friendship with Jefferson Davis and testified on Davis's behalf at a court-martial.

Northrop was severely wounded in the Second Seminole War when he accidentally shot himself in the knee, and he was placed "on permanent sick furlough" in 1839. He then began studying medicine, which resulted in his being dropped from the army rolls for practicing on charity patients in Charleston, South Carolina. Secretary of War Davis reinstated him eight months later.

Northrop resigned from the U.S. Army on January 8, 1861, and was commissioned as a colonel in the Confederate army and made commissary general. He was given a special appointment as a brigadier

general on November 24, 1864. Northrop had briefly served in the Subsistence Department in Washington after his prewar wound, but he was woefully unprepared to tackle the manifold logistical problems faced by the Confederacy. At the beginning of the war, he delegated responsibility to various agents to purchase goods throughout the Confederacy, but speculators drove up prices and caused rampant inflation. The Impressment Act of March 1863 began regulating such procurements, but met stiff resistance from farmers. When Northrop was able to obtain the necessary supplies, the South's inadequate transportation system made it difficult to get them to the troops.

These legitimate difficulties were exacerbated by Northrop's peevish personality, and he became one of the Confederacy's most unpopular officials. In January 1865 the Confederate Senate acquitted him of the charge of inadequately feeding Federal prisoners. Perhaps based on their longtime friendship, Davis stood by Northrop until February 1865, when the Confederate House demanded his relief, an action that was also supported by General Robert E. Lee. Northrop held no other position in the Confederacy and farmed near Charlottesville, Virginia, after the war.

NULLIFICATION CRISIS (1832–33)

The Tariff of 1828, often called the Tariff of Abominations, placed duties as high as 50 percent on raw wool, pig and bar iron, hemp, and whiskey. The measure was unpopular in the South, and when Andrew Jackson was elected president, many Southerners, especially in South Carolina, were hopeful he would adjust the tariff schedule. Jackson, however, showed little interest in taking any action that would reduce customs dues and therefore reduce Federal income. Senator Henry Clay introduced a new schedule in 1832 that provided some relief, but still retained high duties on textiles and iron.

In the midst of this debate, John C. Calhoun helped lead a group known as the "nullifiers" to victory in the October state elections in South Carolina. In November the nullifiers held a convention and issued the Ordinance of Nullification that declared the tariffs of 1828 and 1832 null and void within South Carolina. The ordinance was a direct challenge to Federal authority, forbidding the collection of customs within the borders of South Carolina after

Below: *Southern women played an important role in shaping attitudes toward the war. Here a South Carolina woman sews a defiant palmetto cockade at the time of the 1832 Ordinance of Nullification.*

February 1, 1833, and prohibiting the state's citizens from aiding Federal authorities in customs collections. If the Federal government responded with force to collect the tariff, the ordinance claimed South Carolina would be justified in seceding from the Union.

President Jackson responded decisively to this challenge by issuing a "Proclamation to the People of South Carolina" on December 10, 1832. Jackson argued that no state could unilaterally nullify a Federal law or secede from the Union. He warned that nullification was disunion and that disunion effected by armed force was treason. Jackson hoped that the people of South Carolina would follow Federal law, but if they did not, he also expressed a willingness to use force.

South Carolina found itself awkwardly isolated. Its radical stance found little support, even in the South. A showdown was avoided when Clay proposed the Compromise Tariff of 1833, which diffused tensions. On January 21, 1833, South Carolina suspended its implementation of its Ordinance of Nullification and on March 2, Jackson signed the compromise tariff. Later in the month, South Carolina repealed the Ordinance of Nullification.

Still, South Carolina nullified the Force Bill Jackson had requested to give him the authority to use Federal troops to enforce Federal law in the state. South Carolina had still defied a Federal law, and the overall issue of authority remained

unresolved. South Carolina had also firmly established itself as the most defiant of the Southern states.

OATH OF ALLEGIANCE

On July 2, 1862, the U.S. Congress passed legislation requiring that every civilian or military officeholder take an "Ironclad Oath," swearing his allegiance to the Constitution and affirming that he had never voluntarily borne arms against the United States or aided rebellion in any way. President Andrew Johnson ignored the requirement in making such politically important appointments as revenue assessor, tax collector, and postmaster, but during Radical Reconstruction, the oath was used effectively to bar ex-Confederates from office.

OCCUPIED CONFEDERATE TERRITORY

As Federal armies advanced into large sections of Virginia, Arkansas, South Carolina, Louisiana, Mississippi, Tennessee, and the rest of the South, Southern citizens had to decide to either become refugees or live under occupation.

Among those Southerners to first taste the hard hand of occupation were the citizens of New Orleans, which Major General Benjamin F. Butler occupied on May 1, 1862. Butler enacted numerous draconian measures. Virginia too felt the hardships of occupation when Major General John Pope issued General Order No. 11 on July 23, 1862, requiring the arrest of all disloyal males and forcing them to either take a loyalty oath or be exiled further south.

Left: As the Federal army advanced, it occupied Southern territory and established encampments such as this one on Decatur Street in Atlanta, Georgia, in the fall of 1864.

Many of these occupied areas became test cases for Reconstruction. Tennessee had always had strong Unionist sentiment in the east, and after the Federal victories at Forts Henry and Donelson in February 1862, President Abraham Lincoln saw an opportunity to try to reclaim the state for the Union.

In March, Lincoln appointed Andrew Johnson military governor of Tennessee, granting him sweeping powers to suspend habeas corpus, appoint and remove

Below: *Confederate prisoners of war stand beside a railroad waiting to be transported to a prison camp in Tennessee.*

officials, and call and supervise elections. Tennessee became the first state to undergo "wartime Reconstruction," with Johnson calling for a state convention in 1864. Eventually, Tennessee, Louisiana, and Arkansas were reorganized according to procedures specified by Lincoln, but not accepted by Congress.

There was some resistance to Federal occupation in the form of raiders and guerrillas, causing commanders to devote resources to security. By the time Lieutenant General Ulysses S. Grant became general in chief in 1864, the Federal army had captured over 100,000 square miles of the Confederacy and was using one-third of its soldiers to garrison territory and guard communications. Among the most well-known resisters to Federal occupation was Colonel John S. Mosby in northern Virginia.

OFFENSIVE–DEFENSIVE STRATEGY

While the concept of states' rights and the desire to maintain the territorial integrity of the nation suggested the Confederacy defend at its borders, the reality of the military situation rendered this course impossible. After the stunning defeat at Port Royal Sound, South Carolina, on November 7, 1861, General Robert E. Lee concluded that the enemy "can be thrown with great celerity against any point, and far outnumbers any force we can bring against it in the field." He responded by assembling the scattered Confederate coastal forces at the most probable points of Federal attack. The abandonment of Pensacola, Florida, on May 9, 1862, taught President Jefferson Davis a similar lesson. He conceded, "I acknowledge the error of my attempt to defend all the frontier, seaboard and inland." Instead, he planned on "abandoning the seaboard in order to defend the Tennessee line which is vital to our safety." Lee's and Davis's decisions reflect the realization that priorities would have to be established.

The result was an offensive–defensive strategy by which the Confederates would accept Federal penetrations into the interior of the South and then counterattack at an advantageous time to cut them off. Lee described the concept in 1863, writing, "It is [as] impossible for [the enemy] to have a large operating army at every assailable point in our territory as it is for us to keep one to defend it. We must move our troops from point to point as required, and by close observation and accurate information the true point of attack can generally be ascertained . . ."

Partial encroachments of the enemy we must expect, but they can always be recovered, and any defeat of their large army will reinstitute everything." This strategy allowed the Confederacy to husband its limited offensive capability and prioritize its resources, although it also accepted the necessity of allowing some of its territory to be subjected to Federal occupation, hopefully only on a temporary basis. It also took advantage of the fact that as the Federals entered Confederate territory, they lengthened their lines of supply and found themselves in hostile and unfamiliar territory.

The scheme worked well so long as the Federals maintained an uncoordinated strategy that allowed the Confederates to shift forces from one threatened area to another, and that the Confederates had sufficient resources to conduct offensive operations.

When Lieutenant General Ulysses S. Grant became general in chief, he established a comprehensive strategy for the spring of 1864 that pressured the Confederates on all fronts. These simultaneous advances as well as Confederate personnel shortages caused the offensive–defensive strategy to become overwhelmed.

OFFICERS, ELECTION OF

To ease the infringement on individualism posed by conscription, the Confederate government gave soldiers the privilege of electing officers at the company level. Since units were often formed locally, relatives, neighbors, and friends commonly served in the same company, making the elections very personal affairs. Campaigns were conducted with all the promises and machinations of any political process. The result was that in many cases, popular rather than competent officers were placed in command.

OWSLEY, FRANK LAWRENCE (1890–1955)

Frank Lawrence Owsley was a noted Southern historian at Vanderbilt University and the University of Alabama. In 1932 he confided to a colleague, "The purpose of my life is to undermine . . . the entire Northern myth from 1820 to 1876."

Owsley's writing focused on issues such as "King Cotton" diplomacy, defense of the Southern way of life, and the role of the small farmer. He pioneered the use of the U.S. Census as a valuable historical resource but has been criticized for being selective in the data he chose to use to prove his arguments. Throughout his career, he remained a consistent apologist for the Confederacy and the South.

PALMERSTON, LORD (1784–1865)

Lord Palmerston was Great Britain's prime minister from 1859 to 1865. He initially pursued a noninterventionist approach toward the Civil War, but the *Trent* affair of November 8, 1861,

Below: *Prime Minister Lord Palmerston's interest in recognizing the Confederacy was largely dependent on Confederate success on the battlefield.*

aroused his ire against the North. The Confederate victory at Second Manassas in August 1862 brought him closer still to recognizing the Confederacy. However, when General Robert E. Lee was repulsed at Antietam in September, Palmerston's enthusiasm cooled, and he never again seriously considered recognition.

PAROLE SYSTEM

In a practice that seems strange to modern sensibilities, captured Civil War soldiers were able to give a pledge that they would not again bear arms until being properly exchanged for an enemy soldier who had also been captured. These soldiers were considered "paroled" and were on their honor to abide by the agreement. Paroles occurred early in the war, but the first formal exchange did not take place until February 23, 1862. Until that time,

the Federal government had been reluctant to enter into negotiations for fear of giving legitimacy to the Confederacy.

Giving parole released the capturing unit of the responsibility of providing logistical support for the prisoners, and it was often done for tactical reasons. It served its purpose well until Lieutenant General Ulysses S. Grant became general in chief and virtually ended prisoner exchanges in an effort to further press the Confederate manpower shortage.

PARTISAN RANGERS

One of the potential advantages that the Confederacy had owing to the war being fought on its soil was the ability to mobilize irregular partisan forces to threaten isolated Federal detachments,

Above: *There were several units of partisans and guerrillas that operated throughout the Confederacy. Many proved to be more trouble than they were worth, but Mosby's Rangers provided valuable service in the Shenandoah Valley.*

supply lines, and guard outposts. In spite of the effectiveness of such forces, the Confederate government was reluctant to sanction them, fearing that they would be hard to control and that they would siphon manpower away from traditional units. Secretary of War Judah P. Benjamin represented this view when he declared, "Guerrilla companies are not recognized as part of the military organization of the Confederate states, and cannot be authorized by this department."

Nonetheless, these partisans captured the public imagination, leading advocates like the *Richmond Dispatch* to urge in May 1861 that the Virginia countryside be "made to swarm with our guerrillas." In response to such pressure, on March 27, 1862, Virginia authorized that at least ten companies of "rangers and scouts" be formed to conduct operations in the state's Federally occupied counties. One month later, the Confederate Congress passed a Partisan Ranger Act that called for the formal organization of partisan units at company, battalion, and regimental levels. In addition to receiving the same pay as regular soldiers, these units were also paid for the arms and ammunition they captured from the enemy and delivered to a designated Confederate quartermaster. The Confederacy's most famous partisan was Colonel John S. Mosby.

While partisans proved a useful distraction to Federal forces and inflicted damage well beyond their numbers, they also tended to a certain degree of lawlessness, caused Federal commanders to retaliate against civilian populations, and robbed manpower from regular units. General Robert E. Lee stated, "The evils resulting from their organization more than counterbalance the good they accomplish." On February 15, 1864, the Confederate Congress repealed the Partisan Ranger Act, although Mosby and fellow partisan Hanse McNeill were given special permission by Secretary of War James A. Seddon to continue raiding.

PAY

Pay in the Confederate army was low and irregular. Infantry and artillery privates were initially paid $11 a month, corporals $13, sergeants $17, first sergeants $20, and engineer sergeants $34. There was no increase for common soldiers until June 1864, when Congress voted a pay raise of $7 for all noncommissioned officers and privates. Pay was also slow in arriving, often being six months late and sometimes as much as a year behind. By the time the pay finally arrived, inflation had often taken away much of its value.

In the officer ranks, infantry colonels received $195, compared to $210 for those in the artillery, engineers, and cavalry. A brigadier general was paid $301. In the cases of both officers and enlisted men, Confederate soldiers received less than their Federal counterparts.

Soldiers usually just grumbled about the poor pay in letters home, but on rare occasions units collectively protested by acts of insubordination, and individuals sometimes deserted. More common were efforts by the men to supplement the meager pay by selling small items to their fellow soldiers. It was obvious that most Confederate soldiers joined the army for reasons other than financial gain.

PEA RIDGE, BATTLE OF

❖ DATE: March 7–8, 1861

❖ LOCATION: Benton County, Arkansas

❖ ARMY OF THE WEST (C): 16,000

❖ ARMY OF THE SOUTHWEST (U.S.): 10,500

❖ CASUALTIES: 4,600 (C); 1,349 (U.S.)

In January 1862, Major General Earl Van Dorn was appointed commander of the Trans-Mississippi Department. He developed a plan to join forces with Major General Sterling Price, who had recently been forced out of Missouri into Arkansas, and strike

Above: *Although Franz Sigel was largely incompetent, he represented an important German constituency, and his soldiers adored him. This musical score is an attempt to exaggerate Sigel's role at the Battle of Pea Ridge.*

the overextended lines of Federal forces commanded by Brigadier General Samuel R. Curtis.

On March 7, Van Dorn launched Price on his main attack against Curtis's left rear at Elkhorn Tavern while Brigadier General Benjamin McCulloch and Brigadier General Albert Pike launched diversionary and secondary attacks. Van Dorn's intention was to envelop Curtis around the south end of Pea Ridge at Leetown. It was a poorly planned attack made more difficult by the cold weather, an exhausting fifty-five-mile march, and the fact that Van Dorn himself was sick and had to direct the battle from an ambulance. Curtis had also anticipated Van Dorn's attack and repositioned his forces to deliver a devastating fire across McCulloch's flank. The armies battled fiercely at Leetown, and the day ended with Price holding Elkhorn Tavern, but

Above: *After the Confederate defeat at the Battle of Pea Ridge, initiative in Arkansas shifted to the Federals.*

with the Confederates in general disarray.

Van Dorn resolved to attack again the next day, but by then, Curtis had contracted his lines and was well prepared in the fields south of Pea Ridge. On March 8, he launched a furious counterattack and drove Van Dorn from the field. The Confederates then retreated from Arkansas, surrendering the initiative there to the Federals.

PEACE INITIATIVES

The Confederacy attempted several peace initiatives throughout the war, but they all failed because of the mutually exclusive Federal goal of restoring the Union and the Confederate objective of independence. The first attempt at a peace conference began on February 25, 1861, when President Jefferson Davis nominated A. B. Roman, Martin Crawford, and John Forsyth to go to Washington. The delegation had communicated their intentions to Secretary of State William H. Seward through intermediaries, most notably Supreme Court justice John Campbell of Alabama. Still, when the Confederates arrived in Washington, Seward ignored them, refusing to give legitimacy to their cause by any official recognition.

The most famous effort was the Hampton Roads Peace Conference, held aboard a steamer in Hampton Roads, Virginia, on February 3, 1865. President Abraham Lincoln and Seward represented the Federals while Vice President Alexander H. Stephens, Senator Robert Hunter, and Campbell were the Confederate commissioners. The conference was the result of efforts by Major General Francis P. Blair Jr., who had unofficially discussed the possibility of such a meeting with Davis, suggesting the two armies declare a truce in order to unite under the Monroe Doctrine to thwart French designs in Mexico. While Lincoln and Seward offered generous compensation for slaveholders, they insisted on the abolition of slavery and the return of the seceded states to the Union. Hunter knew that the Confederacy's days were numbered, and he recommended accepting the Federal terms, but Davis would not consider it.

PELHAM, JOHN
(1838–63)

A cadet at West Point, John Pelham resigned to join the Confederate army as an artilleryman. He was well known for his ability to select the most advantageous ground for the placement of his guns. He fought at First Manassas, during the Peninsula Campaign, at Second Manassas, Antietam, and Fredericksburg, where for nearly

Above: *John Pelham's bravery and boyish good looks earned him much admiration and the nickname "Gallant Pelham."*

two hours, he and his men held up the advance of the Federal left with primarily just one gun. Observing this performance, General Robert E. Lee described Pelham as "gallant."

Pelham's youth and attractive features made him the beau ideal of the Confederacy. He was noted for his modesty, charm, and courage, and in spite of his youthful appearance, his men followed him faithfully. He was mortally wounded at Kelly's Ford on March 17, 1863, and posthumously promoted to lieutenant colonel.

PEMBERTON, JOHN C. (1814–81)

John C. Pemberton graduated from West Point in 1837. He served in the Seminole and Mexican wars, in fighting against Native Americans, and on the Utah Expedition. Although Pemberton was from Pennsylvania, he resigned from the U.S. Army on

April 24, 1861, probably because of his Virginian wife. He was commissioned as a lieutenant colonel in the Confederate army on April 28, 1861, and then embarked on a meteoric rise to major general on January 15, 1862.

In March, Pemberton was given command of the Department of South Carolina and Georgia. His principal mission in this capacity was to ensure the defense of Charleston, and while he succeeded in this objective, he suffered from strained relations with South Carolina governor Francis W. Pickens. On September 24, General Pierre Gustave Toutant Beauregard replaced Pemberton, and on October 1, Pemberton was informed he would assume command of "the state of Mississippi and that part of Louisiana east of the Mississippi River," where he arrived on October 9. On October 13, Pemberton was promoted to lieutenant general.

Above: *John Pemberton was clearly outgeneraled by Ulysses S. Grant during the Vicksburg Campaign, and became the subject of much criticism throughout the South.*

Pemberton's elevation to such an advanced position of responsibility was puzzling to many. By all accounts, Pemberton was an honest and good man, but he certainly had demonstrated no qualifications for high-level command. He was unprepared for the demands of the Vicksburg Campaign, and he surrendered the Mississippi River strongpoint on July 4, 1863.

Pemberton's reputation suffered drastically after Vicksburg. Many accused him of being a traitor because of his Northern birth. He resigned his lieutenant general's commission on May 18, 1864, and served the rest of the war faithfully as a lieutenant colonel of artillery.

PENINSULA CAMPAIGN

❖ DATE: March–July 1862

❖ LOCATION: Virginia Peninsula

❖ ARMY OF NORTHERN VIRGINIA (C): 71,000

❖ ARMY OF THE POTOMAC (U.S.): 90,000

❖ CASUALTIES: 20,614 (C); 15,849 (U.S.)

On March 17, 1862, Major General George B. McClellan began an amphibious turning movement of 90,000 Federal soldiers designed to advance on Richmond up the Virginia Peninsula. His move was made possible by the fact that his landing site at Fort Monroe was one of a handful of garrisons still under Union control after secession and by the timely arrival of the *Monitor* at Hampton Roads on March 9 to neutralize the threat of the *Virginia*.

On April 4, McClellan began to advance up the Peninsula, but a brief encounter with Major General John B. Magruder's Warwick River defensive line led the ever-cautious

McClellan to cease maneuvers and initiate siege operations. These lasted until May 3, when the Confederates abandoned Yorktown and withdrew up the Peninsula. Major General James Longstreet covered the withdrawal with a sharp delaying action at Williamsburg.

While General Joseph E. Johnston, the overall commander of the Confederate forces, traded space for time, General Robert E. Lee, then serving as President Jefferson Davis's military adviser, effected a reconcentration of forces that would ultimately turn the tables on McClellan's offensive. For the time being, however, Johnston's withdrawal up the Peninsula forced the Confederates to abandon

Norfolk. This left the *Virginia* without a home port, and, rather than surrender it to the Federals, the Confederates blew up the ironclad on May 11.

With the *Virginia* gone, the James River was open as an avenue of attack to Richmond. On May 15, Flag Officer Louis M. Goldsborough attempted to project a Federal naval force up the river, only to be repulsed at Drewry's Bluff, less than eight miles south of Richmond.

In the midst of the Federal offensive on the Peninsula, Major

General Stonewall Jackson launched his own campaign in the Shenandoah Valley. His success there led President Abraham Lincoln to withhold Major General Irvin McDowell's corps to protect Washington rather than join McClellan. This development allowed the Confederates on the Peninsula to act more aggressively. On May 31, Johnston attacked in hopes of taking advantage of the fact that McClellan had split his force on opposite sides of the Chickahominy River. In the ensuing Battle of Seven Pines, Johnston tried to isolate and destroy the separated Federal forces, but failed. During the fighting, Johnston was wounded, and on June 1, Lee arrived on the battlefield with orders from Davis to take command.

Lee quickly took advantage of the opportunity created by Jackson's success in the valley. On June 8, he wrote Jackson, asking him if he could bring his forces to the Peninsula. Once Jackson arrived, Lee had the manpower he needed to go on the offensive. On June 26,

the Battle of Mechanicsville began a series of hard-fought battles, collectively known as the Seven Days Battles. Although Lee took high casualties in assuming the offensive against a larger foe, the cautious McClellan was unnerved by the Confederate aggression and decided to abandon his campaign.

After the loss at the Battle of Gaines' Mill, McClellan began withdrawing to Harrison's Landing, where he would be under the protection of Goldsborough's gunboats. As McClellan withdrew, there was sharp fighting at Savage's Station (June 29), White Oak Swamp (June 30), and Malvern Hill (July 1), but Lee was frustrated in his attempts to cut off McClellan's retreat. Lee had turned the Federals back from Richmond, but he was unable to decisively defeat them. Safe at Harrison's Landing, McClellan consolidated his forces until they were withdrawn to northern Virginia to support Major General John Pope and the threat he was then facing at Second Manassas.

PERRYVILLE, BATTLE OF

- ❖ DATE: October 7–8, 1862
- ❖ LOCATION: Boyle County, Kentucky
- ❖ ARMY OF TENNESSEE/ARMY OF THE MISSISSIPPI (C): 53,000
- ❖ ARMY OF THE OHIO (U.S.): 60,000
- ❖ CASUALTIES: 3,396 (C); 4,211 (U.S.)

In the summer of 1862, General Braxton Bragg developed a plan to combine his Army of Tennessee with units in eastern Tennessee commanded by Major General Edmund Kirby Smith and invade Kentucky. Bragg hoped to defeat Major General Don Carlos Buell and the Army of the Ohio, and encourage Kentucky, a slave state with Confederate sympathies, to leave the Union. At a minimum,

Below: *The Federals were unable to bring their entire force to bear during the Battle of Perryville, leaving Braxton Bragg with a tenuous Confederate victory.*

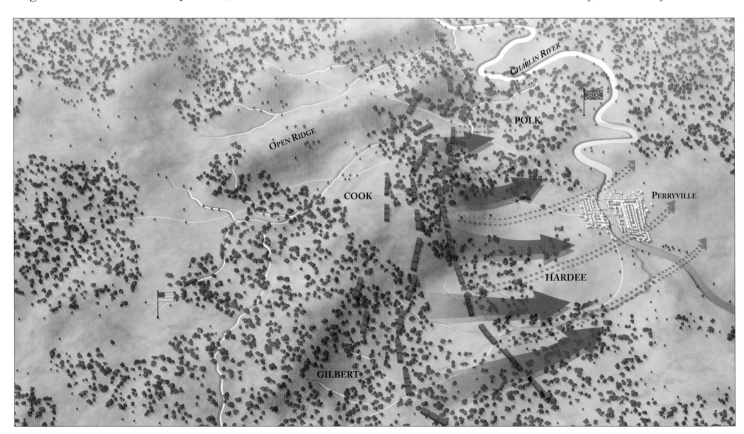

Bragg expected to draw thousands of Kentucky volunteers to his army. Leaving a 16,000-man covering force under Major General Earl Van Dorn at Tupelo, Mississippi, Bragg set out on his operation in mid-July. The climax of Bragg's invasion was the Battle of Perryville on October 8, 1862. Although Bragg bested Buell in this engagement, the Confederates could not capitalize on the victory, and Bragg was forced to withdraw from Kentucky.

BRAGG SHADOWED

Beginning on July 23, Bragg moved the bulk of his 35,000-man force some 800 miles along a circuitous route from Tupelo to Chattanooga, Tennessee. Buell shadowed Bragg's movement at an incredibly slow pace, and Bragg succeeded in beating Buell to Chattanooga. On July 31, Bragg met there with Smith to develop a strategy.

Smith had commanded the 18,000-man Department of East Tennessee since March and had established his headquarters in Knoxville, some 100 miles northeast of Chattanooga. While Smith had expressed a series of concerns about the threat Buell posed to Chattanooga, he had done little about it. Instead, Smith was secretly developing a plan to drive into Kentucky, and he was perfectly content to let Bragg do the hard job of fighting Buell. These manipulations contributed to a lack of unity of effort between Bragg and Smith.

Having put himself in the best situation possible in terms of troops and responsibilities at Bragg's expense, Smith set out on August 13 for his grand campaign. Although seemingly experiencing initial success, as Smith drove deeper into Kentucky, he overextended himself and created a perilous supply situation with Federal forces in his rear. He

requested Bragg move forward to draw off the Federals, and on August 28, Bragg began moving his army north from Chattanooga toward Kentucky.

RICHMOND, KENTUCKY

With Bragg coming to his aid, Smith fought and won a battle at Richmond, Kentucky, on August 29–30. He captured 4,000 Federals, 10,000 stands of arms, nine guns, and a complete wagon train full of supplies. Additionally, the Federals suffered 206 killed and 844 wounded, while Smith lost only 78 killed and 372 wounded. It was an impressive victory that left Smith virtually unopposed in eastern Kentucky.

But instead of pressing his advantage, Smith went on the defense and waited to see what developed as a result of Bragg's move north. On September 14, Bragg reached Glasgow, Kentucky, where he issued a proclamation that began, "Kentuckians, I have entered your State with the Confederate army of the West, and offer you an opportunity to free yourselves from the tyranny of a despotic ruler." Bragg then planned to use his strategic location to combine with Smith to threaten Louisville.

Above: *Chevaux-de-frise defenses line the side of this country road near Perryville, sometime after the battle. Such defenses would restrict the movement of infantry, and disrupt cavalry assault.*

Bragg set out to meet Smith at Bardstown, but when Bragg arrived he found that Smith was still in Lexington. In fact, Smith seemed completely uninterested in cooperating with Bragg and apparently was willing to let Bragg proceed to Louisville alone. Bragg, however, was in no position to make such a move.

On September 30, Smith did join Bragg in Frankfort, where he was preparing to ceremoniously inaugurate a secessionist government. In spite of this gesture, Bragg had thus far failed to receive the influx of volunteers he had expected.

In the meantime, Buell had accumulated a force of 60,000 troops, and on October 1, he began marching toward Bardstown. Bragg was still in Frankfort, helping install the newly proclaimed Confederate government, while his widely scattered force manned a fifty-mile front that extended from Bardstown northeast to Shelbyville.

After preliminary skirmishing that began on October 2, the two armies stumbled into each other on October 7 as they were both desperately looking for water. At first the Confederates repulsed the Federal attack, but renewed Federal efforts forced the Confederates to withdraw east toward Perryville.

Finally leaving Frankfort, Bragg rode to Perryville to assume command and after numerous delays, launched an attack at 2:00 p.m. on October 8. The Confederates experienced initial success, finding a gap between two Federal corps, but the Federals rallied to stop the penetration.

Remarkably, Buell did not know until 4:00 p.m. that a fierce battle was on. Atmospheric conditions masked the sounds of the battle, and he arrived on the scene too late to have a real impact. The end result was that only nine Federal brigades were heavily engaged while fifteen others that were within close supporting distance played little part.

The Federals lost 4,211 in the fighting compared to 3,396 on the Confederate side. Bragg had won a victory, but he then was also also still facing the entire Army of the Ohio. He wisely decided to withdraw from Kentucky to Morristown, Tennessee, having accomplished little of long-term significance by his grand campaign.

PETERSBURG, SIEGE OF

- ❖ DATE: June 19, 1864–April 3, 1864
- ❖ LOCATION: Petersburg, Virginia
- ❖ ARMY OF NORTHERN VIRGINIA (C): 52,000
- ❖ ARMY OF THE POTOMAC (U.S.): 67,000–125,000
- ❖ CASUALTIES: 3,500 (C); 8,400 (U.S.)

Throughout the spring of 1864, General Robert E. Lee had successfully thwarted Lieutenant General Ulysses S. Grant's attempts to turn the Confederate defenses and break through to Richmond. Running out of maneuver room, Grant decided to shift his Army of the Potomac south of the James River and use the river as his line of supply for an advance on Petersburg, about twenty miles south of Richmond. Petersburg was a shipping port as well as a rail center, and many of the supplies headed for both Richmond and Lee's army passed through there, making it critical to the survival of the Army of Northern Virginia. The struggle to control this strategic location resulted in the longest siege of the war, lasting until April 3, 1865, when Lee withdrew west.

Once Grant decided to shift his line of advance, he got a jump on Lee, crossing the James River and reaching Petersburg while it was still defended by only a skeleton

Below: *During the ten-month siege of Petersburg, Ulysses S. Grant was able to use his superior numbers to stretch Robert E. Lee's lines to the point of breaking.*

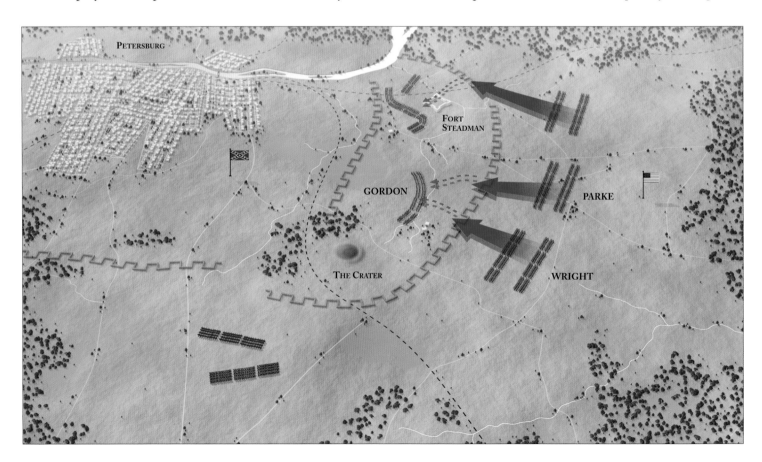

Above: The Federal army prepared a series of trench lines that subjected Petersburg to a devastating siege and threatened Robert E. Lee's rail communications.

that as Lee weakened inside Petersburg, Grant grew stronger outside.

Inevitably, Lee would be exhausted, but Grant did what he could to hurry this conclusion, including the disastrous July 30 Battle of the Crater that left about 5,300 Federal casualties compared to just 1,032 Confederates. Grant was more successful on August 18 when Major General Gouverneur K. Warren seized the Weldon Railroad, Lee's connection to Weldon and Wilmington, North Carolina.

On August 25, Lee won a victory at Reams Station, twelve miles south of Petersburg, but he was still unable to use the Weldon Railroad farther north than Stony Creek Depot, sixteen miles south of Petersburg. From there, supplies had to be moved by laborious wagonloads.

As the siege continued, Grant kept extending his lines to the

Confederate force. However, the Federals failed to press their advantage and capture the prize, and the Confederates then were able to strengthen their lines. Grant launched an uncoordinated attack with his entire army on June 18,

1864, but was repulsed. By then Lee had arrived with reinforcements. The next day, Grant began a siege.

During the siege, Grant built up a huge logistical base at City Point that benefited from outstanding rail and water communications. Grant had access to excellent supply, repair, and medical facilities to help sustain his force. The result was

Below: During the siege of Petersburg, the Federals built up an enormous supply depot and maintenance facility at City Point.

west. He was never able to get around Lee, but he forced Lee to stretch his lines to the breaking point. The scales clearly tipped in the Federals' favor in March 1865 when Major General Philip H. Sheridan and most of his cavalry joined Grant from the Shenandoah Valley. Grant gave Sheridan an infantry corps and told him to break Lee's western flank.

In the ensuing Battle of Five Forks on April 1, Sheridan succeeded in doing just what Grant had hoped. Grant then ordered a general attack all along the Petersburg front.

Faced with this threat, Lee was forced to abandon Petersburg, and the city fell on April 3. The siege of Petersburg had lasted almost ten months and was spread over 176 square miles. It had involved six major battles, eleven engagements, and numerous other contacts. Throughout it all, Grant's men suffered 42,000 casualties compared to 28,000 for Lee. However, as was the case throughout the Virginia Overland Campaign, Grant could replace his casualties, and Lee could not.

PICKETT, GEORGE E.
(1825–75)

❖ RANK: Major general

❖ PLACE OF BIRTH: Richmond, Virginia

❖ EDUCATED: West Point

❖ MILITARY CAREER:
1846–61: Served in U.S. Army; fought in Mexican War
1861: Commissioned as a colonel in command of the Rappahannock Line
1862: Promoted to brigadier general; led brigade at Seven Pines and Gaines' Mill, where he was wounded; promoted to major general in command of a division
1863: Led division at Gettysburg

Above: *George Pickett graduated last in his class at West Point. Having served with distinction in the Mexican War, his generalship suffered after Gettysburg.*

George E. Pickett graduated last in the West Point class of 1846. He served in Mexico, winning some distinction carrying the Eighth U.S. Infantry colors over the ramparts to victory at Chapultepec. He later served on the Texas frontier. He was a captain when he resigned from the U.S. Army on June 25, 1861, and was commissioned as a colonel in the Confederate army. He was promoted to brigadier general on February 13, 1862, and fought well during the Peninsula Campaign until he was severely wounded in the shoulder at Gaines' Mill. He was promoted to major general on October 11 and commanded the Confederate center at Fredericksburg.

Pickett is best remembered for his association with the fateful charge on the third day of the Battle of Gettysburg on July 3, 1863. Pickett's division was repulsed amid

enormous casualties. The defeat left Pickett bitter, especially toward General Robert E. Lee, and Pickett's generalship after Gettysburg was unremarkable.

On September 23, 1863, Pickett took the remnants of his division to recuperate and recruit in southern Virginia and North Carolina, with Pickett serving as department commander. He was defeated at New Bern, North Carolina, in January 1864 and fought well against Major General Benjamin F. Butler at Drewry's Bluff in May. He fought at Cold Harbor and participated in the Petersburg and Appomattox campaigns, including being defeated at Five Forks on April 1, 1865. By this stage of the war, there was little hope for the Confederacy, but Pickett had exacerbated the situation by leaving his troops poorly positioned for battle while he departed for a leisurely shad bake.

Pickett was relieved by Lee after the Battle of Sayler's Creek on April 6, but lingered with the Army of Northern Virginia and surrendered at Appomattox. After the war, he was offered a generalship by the khedive of Egypt and a position as U.S. marshal by Ulysses S. Grant, but instead chose to pursue the insurance business in Virginia. Pickett died in relative poverty, still distraught over his defeat at Gettysburg, but just as assuredly famous for it.

PICKETT'S CHARGE
(JULY 3, 1863)

On July 3, 1863, the third day of fighting at Gettysburg, General Robert E. Lee ordered Major General George E. Pickett's still-fresh division to attack the Federal center. Pickett relished in the glory of the planned attack, but his corps commander, Lieutenant General James Longstreet, shared none of Pickett's enthusiasm and renewed his objections to Lee's offensive strategy.

When Lee told Longstreet 15,000 men would make the attack, Longstreet replied, "The 15,000 men who could make [a] successful assault over that field" could not be found. Longstreet later wrote, "That day at Gettysburg was one of the saddest of my life."

Indeed, as the time to attack neared, Longstreet could barely order its initiation. As Colonel E. Porter Alexander, Longstreet's artillery chief, prepared for a 172-gun preassault bombardment, he received a note from Longstreet asking Alexander to determine whether or not the artillery had done enough damage to make the attack viable. Alexander replied that

he would not be able to assess the results to that degree of accuracy, but added that if there was an alternative to Pickett's Charge, it ought to be explored.

Alexander began his bombardment at 1:00 p.m. It was a ferocious cannonade, but most of the rounds sailed harmlessly over the heads of the Federal positions on Cemetery Ridge. To make matters worse for the Confederates, Alexander was quickly running out of ammunition. After about thirty minutes, he sent Pickett a note, telling him that now was the best time to attack.

With his command staged in the woods on Seminary Ridge, Pickett rode to Longstreet and asked, "General, shall I advance?" The reluctant Longstreet could not bring himself to do more than merely nod his head. With that unenthusiastic

gesture, Pickett was off. Orienting on a little clump of trees known as Ziegler's Grove, Pickett's men had a half-mile of open field ahead of them. Secure behind breastworks and stone walls, the Federal infantry held its fire, while the artillery tore holes in the Confederate lines. Still the Confederates advanced with their formations largely in order. At about 100 feet from the enemy, Pickett's men halted to dress their lines in preparation for the final assault.

Pickett's division had Brigadier General James L. Kemper's brigade on the right front with Brigadier General Richard B. Garnett's on the left. Brigadier General Lewis A. Armistead was in the center rear.

Below: *Pickett's Charge was the climactic moment of the Battle of Gettysburg and an important piece of "Lost Cause" imagery.*

Eventually the Confederate right and left flanks were broken, with only Armistead's brigade able to continue forward. Armistead's objective was a low stone wall on the western slope of Cemetery Ridge that was defended by the Second Corps, led by Major General Winfield Scott Hancock, a dear friend of Armistead's from the "Old Army."

At one point, 150 Confederates poured over the wall and momentarily broke the Federal line, but the defenders recovered, rushed forward fresh artillery, and opened fire less than ten yards from Armistead and his men. As Federals closed in from all sides, Armistead reached a captured Federal cannon, put his hand on it, and was fired on at point-blank range.

Armistead's isolated men could not sustain their momentum, and the spot became known as the "high water mark of the Confederacy." Federal reinforcements rushed in from adjacent parts of the line and threw back the Confederate attack.

"I HAVE NO DIVISION NOW"

Pickett's Charge had failed, and the scattered remnants of his command staggered back across the field. The attack had caused 54 percent losses to the Confederates. One survivor wrote, "It was a second Fredericksburg . . . only the wrong way." The results were a powerful testimony to the impact of modern weapons and the futility of frontal assaults across open terrain.

When Pickett reached Lee, Lee ordered him to re-form his division in case of a counterattack. Pickett reportedly replied, "General, I have no division now." Indeed, Pickett remained bitter toward Lee for the rest of his life. Years after the war, he said of Lee, "That old man had my division massacred."

Nonetheless, Pickett's Charge is one of the most enduring images of the romanticized Civil War. The thought of brave men—tragic heroes, full of devotion to the Confederacy—charging gallantly to their death against overwhelming odds is the very embodiment of the "Lost Cause." To many, that is what Pickett's Charge represents.

PIKE, ALBERT (1809–91)

Albert Pike ran out of money before completing his education at Harvard, but nonetheless built a distinguished prewar career as a teacher, poet, lawyer, and newspaperman. He also had served in the Mexican War and won a $140,000 suit on behalf of the Creek Native Americans. At the outbreak of the Civil War, he parlayed these experiences into a commission as a brigadier general on August 15, 1861, with the responsibility to negotiate treaties with the Native Americans west of the Arkansas River to ally them with the Confederacy.

Pike told the Native Americans that President Abraham Lincoln intended to open the Indian Territory to free white settlement, thus giving the Confederates and the Native Americans common cause to

resist the Federals. Pike obtained treaties with the Chickasaws, Choctaws, and Seminoles, but found the Creeks and Cherokees more difficult. He eventually worked through Stand Watie to gain Cherokee support, but was only able to obtain a treaty with the Lower Creeks. When the Upper Creeks marched toward Kansas seeking Federal protection, a Confederate force under Colonel James McIntosh annihilated them in fighting on December 26–27, 1861.

Pike led a Native American force in a lackluster performance at Pea Ridge on March 7–8, 1862, and soon became embroiled in tension with Trans-Mississippi Department commander Major General Thomas C. Hindman. Pike resigned from the Confederate army on July 12 and lived in semiretirement in Arkansas and Texas for the remainder of the war. Both Federals and Confederates grew to view him with suspicion. Confederate Brigadier General Douglas H. Cooper felt Pike was "either insane or untrue to the South." After the war, Pike was most noted for his advocacy of Freemasonry.

PILLOW, GIDEON J. (1806–78)

Gideon J. Pillow used his considerable connections with President James Polk to become a major general in the Mexican War, and established a reputation as one of that war's most conniving and incompetent political generals. When Tennessee seceded, he was appointed as a senior major general of the state troops, but was chagrined when he did not retain

Left: *Albert Pike was one of the Confederacy's more flamboyant personalities. His efforts to recruit Native Americans for the Confederacy met with mixed success.*

Above: *Gideon Pillow was one of the Confederacy's worst political generals. His behavior at Fort Donelson was shameful.*

command when those troops were transferred to the Confederate army. He eventually was appointed as a brigadier general in the Confederate army on July 9, 1861, and fought at Belmont on November 7. He was second in command at Fort Donelson where after Major General John B. Floyd ignominiously passed him command, Pillow passed it to Brigadier General Simon Bolivar Buckner and fled with Floyd to avoid capture.

Buckner surrendered to his old friend Brigadier General Ulysses S. Grant, who asked him where Pillow was. Buckner replied, "Gone. He thought you'd rather get hold of him than any other man in the Southern Confederacy." Grant replied, "Oh, if I had got him, I'd let him go again. He will do us more good commanding you fellows." Such was the extent of Pillow's reputation as a general.

After the debacle, Pillow was reprimanded and relieved of field command. He was subsequently assigned to the volunteer and conscription bureau in Tennessee and later as commissary general of

prisoners after Major General John H. Winder died in February 1865. After the war, he practiced law with wartime governor of Tennessee Isham G. Harris.

PLANTATIONS

Plantations were the sites of large-scale farming operations devoted to primarily a single money crop. The exact crop varied throughout the Southern states. In Virginia, it was tobacco. In South Carolina, it was rice or cotton. In Louisiana, it was sugar or cotton. In Mississippi and other states of the Deep South, it was almost exclusively cotton. Plantation operations gained economies of scale by a vast slave labor system.

The most efficient plantations were able to supplement the money crop with a variety of other pursuits, including other farming activities, livestock production, and a host of craftsmen and artisans. Around the mansion were a variety of other structures, including a kitchen, offices, school, dairy, stables, gin, press, utility buildings, and slave cabins. These large plantations became virtually self-

Below: *A Southern plantation by the Mississippi River. Idyllic representations of Southern plantations belied the plight of many slaves subjected to cruelty.*

sufficient domains of the plantation owner who exercised total control over all aspects of the operation. For many Southerners, the plantation became the symbol of the ideal culture and civilization that defined the region and a bastion of independence and local authority.

While there were only a small number of these large plantations, they became the example that the smaller plantation owners sought to emulate in terms of not just agriculture, but in social customs and codes as well. The large plantation owners became the Southern aristocracy, commanding an unmatched political, economic, and social influence. The plantation became the center of the Southern way of life.

A LIFE ON THE LAND
This idyllic version of plantation life became a fixture in the romance and imagination of the South. The slave system was described as paternalistic and benign, and the slaves loyal and content. In contrast to the industrialized North, Southern planters saw themselves as leisurely enjoying the bounty of the land rather than relentlessly pursuing money in the factory setting. Among the activities indicative of this enjoyment of life, leisure, and land was the fox hunt.

Indeed, hunting became a popular activity for planters who often found themselves relatively isolated from the regular company of other whites.

Many Northerners, such as Harriet Beecher Stowe and Frederick Law Olmsted, presented an entirely different view of plantation life, emphasizing the brutalities and excesses of the slave system. What developed was an increasingly emotional disparity between what many Southerners considered the epitome of culture and civilization, and what a like number of Northerners saw as pure evil. These opposing worldviews were among the many tensions that precipitated the Civil War.

POLITICAL GENERALS

The shortage of suitable professional senior officers, the need to placate valuable constituencies, and the need to build national cohesion led President Jefferson Davis (and President Abraham Lincoln as well) to appoint many political generals. While most of these men lacked military training and competence, their appointments helped solidify support for the war among whatever interest group they represented. For example, the Southern tradition of states' rights certainly encouraged the appointment of state political leaders, such as former Virginia governor Henry A. Wise, to generalships.

The political gains of such a course notwithstanding, many of these appointees proved disappointing on the Civil War battlefields. Brigadier General Gideon J. Pillow, who cowardly abandoned his command at Fort Donelson, is a notorious example of a political general. On the other hand, Brigadier General Robert A. Toombs fought well at Antietam, where he was instrumental in delaying Brigadier General Ambrose E. Burnside's crossing of the Rohrbach Bridge.

POLK, LEONIDAS (1806–64)

❖ RANK: Lieutenant general

❖ PLACE OF BIRTH: Raleigh, North Carolina

❖ EDUCATED: West Point

❖ MILITARY CAREER:
1861: Commissioned as a major general in command of Department No. 2, Kentucky
1862: Commanded First Corps at Shiloh and Perryville; promoted to lieutenant general
1863: Commanded wing at Chickamauga; given command of Department of Mississippi and East Louisiana

Leonidas Polk graduated from West Point in 1827. While a cadet, Polk became friends with future Confederate president Jefferson Davis. Polk also converted

Above: *Leonidas Polk, the "Fighting Bishop," was killed by an artillery round while reconnoitering during the Atlanta Campaign.*

to Christianity and resigned his commission just six months after graduation in order to pursue the Episcopal ministry. In 1838 he was made missionary bishop of the Southwest and in 1841 bishop of Louisiana. He played an important role in the foundation of the University of the South at Sewanee, Tennessee, even laying its cornerstone in 1860.

Once the Civil War began, Davis prevailed upon Polk to join the Confederate army, and he was appointed as a major general on June 25, 1861. Given his scant prewar army service, this commission was clearly out of proportion with Polk's military talent. While not a distinguished combat leader, Polk did prove very popular with his troops and maintained an impressive command presence.

Perhaps showing his lack of military experience, Polk impetuously occupied Columbus, Kentucky, on September 4, 1861. This action violated Kentucky's professed neutrality and allowed the Federals to manipulate the situation to their advantage. He went on to fight at Belmont and Shiloh, before being promoted to lieutenant general on October 10, 1862.

Polk served under General Braxton Bragg at Perryville and Murfreesboro, and joined many in concluding Bragg needed to be replaced. Polk forwarded this recommendation to Davis, suggesting that General Joseph E. Johnston assume command. After Chickamauga, Bragg relieved Polk for not attacking when ordered to do so, but Davis reinstated him. By now a serious anti-Bragg movement had developed, and Polk joined other high-ranking officers, including James Longstreet, Simon Bolivar Buckner, Patrick R. Cleburne, D. H. Hill, and William Preston, in signing a petition again requesting Davis remove Bragg from command, contending, "The

Army of Tennessee, stricken with complete paralysis, may deem itself fortunate if it escapes from its present position without disaster." Still Davis supported Bragg, replacing him only after Bragg asked to be relieved.

During the Atlanta Campaign, Polk, Johnston and Lieutenant General William J. Hardee rode forward on June 14, 1864, to reconnoiter Pine Mountain. The three generals presented a tempting target for Federal artillery and, while Johnston and Hardee scurried to safety, the slower-moving Polk was hit and instantly killed. Johnston pulled his troops off of Pine Mountain the next day, and the Federals occupied the abandoned position. Upon arrival they found a sign that read, "You damned Yankee sons of bitches have killed our old Gen. Polk."

POOR WHITES

Poor whites formed the bottom rung of the white Southern social hierarchy. They usually lived in the infertile backcountry or pine barrens and eked out a hand-to-mouth existence. Many lacked ambition, and upper-class whites tended to dismiss them and use their laziness as evidence that the Southern labor system had to rely on African American slaves.

Derisively called "clay-eaters" or "hill-billies," poor whites were looked down upon by everyone, including African Americans. However, since African Americans insulated them from the very base of the social ladder, poor whites were usually highly prejudiced.

POPULAR SOVEREIGNTY

Popular sovereignty was a doctrine often associated with Stephen A. Douglas that held that the people of a given territory should be able to decide for themselves if the territory should be slave or free. The Kansas–Nebraska Act of 1854 stated that the issue of slavery in those two territories would be decided on the basis of popular sovereignty.

PORT GIBSON, BATTLE OF

❖ DATE: May 1, 1863

❖ LOCATION: Claiborne County, Mississippi

❖ FORCE UNDER BOWEN (C): 5,500

❖ ARMY OF THE TENNESSEE (U.S.): 20,000

❖ CASUALTIES: 787 (C); 861 (U.S.)

After Major General Ulysses S. Grant crossed the Mississippi River at Bruinsburg on April 30, 1863, as part of his Vicksburg Campaign, he still needed to secure a foothold on the east side of the river. The nearest high ground was twelve miles away at Port Gibson. Confederate forces were out of position to successfully keep Grant from Port Gibson, and his victory there on May 1 left him safely ensconced on high, dry ground on the Mississippi side of the river. It was a painful missed opportunity for Lieutenant General John C. Pemberton to stop Grant's advance toward Vicksburg.

After crossing the river, Grant ordered Major General John A. McClernand's 20,000-man corps forward from Bruinsburg toward Port Gibson. The only Confederate forces available to oppose McClernand were the 5,500 men commanded by Brigadier General John S. Bowen. Wanting to maintain flexibility, Bowen ordered Brigadier General Martin Green to place his brigade between Bruinsburg and Port Gibson on April 30, while Bowen held most of his forces in reserve to see what developed.

Early on May 1, McClernand closed on Port Gibson. As he approached, he divided his force into two columns. The difficult terrain prevented the two forces from supporting each other, which weakened the Federal numerical advantage. Initially, Bowen was able to check McClernand's advance, but at around 11:00 a.m. the Federals achieved a breakthrough on the Confederate left flank. Bowen tried to counterattack, but when Grant committed Major General James B. McPherson's corps to the fight, Bowen realized his situation was hopeless. The Confederates began an orderly withdrawal, and the Federals advanced to within two miles of Port Gibson. When he entered the town, Grant reportedly pronounced it "too beautiful to burn." He had what he wanted anyway—a secure foothold on the east side of the Mississippi River.

PORT HUDSON, SIEGE OF (MAY 27–JULY 9, 1863)

Port Hudson was a Confederate strongpoint that protected the Mississippi River approximately twenty-five miles north of Baton Rouge, Louisiana. Beginning with a bombardment orchestrated by Admiral David G. Farragut on March 14, 1863, Port Hudson withstood repeated Federal land and naval attacks and finally was subjected to a siege that lasted from May 27 to July 9, 1863. Siege hardships were particularly acute at Port Hudson and the Confederates suffered over 7,200 losses, including 5,500 men taken prisoner.

The defense of Port Hudson was complicated by a paucity of Confederate resources and a lack of

Above: *Confederate suffering during the siege and bombardment of Port Hudson rivaled that experienced at Vicksburg.*

prioritization. President Jefferson Davis instructed Lieutenant General John C. Pemberton to "hold both Vicksburg and Port Hudson," twin tasks clearly beyond Pemberton's capabilities. Vicksburg had surrendered July 4, and Port Hudson's capitulation left the Federals in complete control of the Mississippi.

PORT ROYAL, BATTLE OF

- ❖ DATE: November 7, 1861
- ❖ LOCATION: Beaufort County, South Carolina
- ❖ PORT ROYAL GARRISONS (C): 3,000
- ❖ GREAT SOUTHERN EXPEDITION (U.S.): 12,000, with 74 vessels
- ❖ CASUALTIES: 100 (C); 31 (U.S.)

Port Royal Sound, South Carolina, was the finest natural harbor on the Southern seaboard, and its possession was critical to the Federal navy's ability to execute the blockade of the Atlantic coast. On

October 20, 1861, Captain Samuel F. Du Pont led a "Great Southern Expedition" of seventy-four vessels, including transports for a land force of 12,000 men, out of Hampton Roads. The Confederates quickly ascertained Du Pont's intentions, and, on November 6, President Jefferson Davis reorganized the coasts of South Carolina, Georgia, and north Florida into a single department, naming General Robert E. Lee as its commander.

In spite of these preparations, the Confederates remained at a huge disadvantage when Du Pont attacked on November 7. Port Royal Sound was big enough to allow maneuver, and Du Pont developed a brilliant plan to use his steam engines to keep his ships moving in an elliptical pattern that would keep the two Confederate forts, Walker and Beauregard, under continuous fire. Du Pont brushed aside a weak Confederate flotilla of three tugs, each mounting one gun, and a converted river steamer, and turned his attention to the forts. With each pass of the elliptical maneuver, Du Pont's squadron widened its course so as to bring its guns closer to the target. These constant changes in speed, range, and deflection made the Federal

fleet extremely hard for the Confederate gunners to engage.

Confederate resistance did not last long. As Du Pont began his third ellipse, he received word that Fort Walker had been abandoned. Fort Beauregard, which was merely an adjunct to Fort Walker, surrendered soon thereafter.

The Federals lost eight killed and twenty-three wounded. The Confederates lost about 100 in total. The victory gave the Federals an excellent harbor that became the home base for the South Atlantic Blockading Squadron for the remainder of the war. Moreover, it struck a blow in both the sentimental heartland of secession and in an important cotton-producing region.

The loss convinced the Confederacy that it was impossible to defend the entirety of its vast coast, and Lee instituted a new policy to focus the South's limited resources. Confederate defenses at Fort Pulaski, Georgia, and Charleston were strengthened to withstand greater bombardments, waterways that might be used by Federal ships were obstructed, and the scattered Confederate forces were assembled at the most probable points of Federal attack. In spite of these efforts, the advantage in the coastal war clearly lay with the Federals.

PORT ROYAL EXPERIMENT

With the Federal victory at Port Royal Sound, South Carolina, on November 7, 1861, many coastal and Sea Island planters withdrew farther inland to escape Federal occupation. With the sudden departure of their masters, many African Americans found themselves entirely unprepared for their new freedom. Soon many Northern social activists with a

Above: *The Battle of Port Royal showed the threat posed by the Federal navy and caused a panic on the South Carolina coast.*

strong moral commitment to abolition descended on the Sea Islands to help the former slaves transition to freedom. In what became known as the Port Royal Experiment, the region became the cradle of South Carolina's first African American schools and free labor initiatives. It also served as a fertile recruiting ground for African American Federal soldiers.

PRAIRIE GROVE, BATTLE OF

- ❖ DATE: December 7, 1862
- ❖ LOCATION: Washington County, Arkansas
- ❖ TRANS-MISSISSIPPI ARMY (C): 11,059
- ❖ ARMY OF THE FRONTIER (U.S.): 9,216
- ❖ CASUALTIES: 1,317 (C); 1,251 (U.S.)

When Major General Thomas C. Hindman took command of the Trans-Mississippi Department, he vowed to "drive out the invader [from Arkansas] or perish in the attempt." On December 3, 1862, he started advancing north from Van Buren with 11,000 men, heading for an isolated Federal force commanded by Brigadier General James G. Blunt at Cane Hill. Blunt requested reinforcements from Brigadier

Above: *Thomas Hindman, in command of the Trans-Mississippi Department, was unable to make good his vow to regain Confederate control of Arkansas.*

General J. Francis Herron some 120 miles away in Springfield, Missouri. When Hindman learned of Herron's approach, he established a position at Prairie Grove, ten miles west of Fayetteville. Hindman and Herron fought to a standstill for much of December 7, and then Blunt arrived to increase the Federals' odds. Hindman requested a truce to gather his casualties and then withdrew after midnight. The defeat at Prairie Grove ended whatever slim chance the Confederates had of regaining northern Arkansas.

PRICE, STERLING (1809–67)

Sterling Price had a distinguished prewar career as a legislator, lawyer, farmer, Mexican War brigadier general, and governor of Missouri. As Missouri divided between Unionists and secessionists, Price sided with the secessionists and recruited a force of some 5,000 soldiers. He was popular with the men, who affectionately called him "Old Pap."

Price united with Brigadier General Benjamin McCulloch and fought at Wilson's Creek on August 10, 1861, commanding the Missouri State Guard. Price then occupied Springfield and captured a Federal brigade at Lexington on September 20. However, in the face of increased Federal pressure, Price withdrew to Arkansas and formally joined the Confederacy on March 6, 1862 with an appointment as a major general.

MISSOURI RAID
Price fought at Pea Ridge, Shiloh, Iuka, Corinth, Helena, and during the Red River Campaign. Then in September 1864 he launched a raid into Missouri. At first he met only

Above: *Sterling Price was a popular Missourian who was unable to overcome the superior Federal strength in Missouri and Arkansas.*

limited resistance, but as he advanced farther into the state Federal opposition increased, and he was defeated at Westport on October 24. He then embarked on a circuitous path of retreat that took him to Kansas, back into Missouri, and through the Indian Territory before reentering Confederate lines at Laynesport, Arkansas. He was in Texas when the war ended, and escaped to Mexico. When Maximilian's government collapsed, Price returned to Missouri.

PRISONS AND PRISONERS OF WAR

B arely able to meet the logistical demands of their own soldiers, Confederate authorities were hard-pressed to secure and care for Federal prisoners. Major General John H. Winder served as commissary general of all prison camps east of the Mississippi River

from November 21, 1864, until his death on February 7, 1865. On March 30, 1865, Major General Daniel Ruggles replaced Winder. Winder, Ruggles, and others associated with the Confederate Bureau of Prison Camps labored manfully under nearly impossible conditions. While Federal prisoners suffered from overcrowding, inadequate food, and unsanitary conditions, Confederate authorities did the best they could under the circumstances, even designating the same ration allotment for Federal prisoners as received by Confederate soldiers.

Prison facilities ranged across fortifications, former jails and penitentiaries, altered buildings such as old tobacco warehouses, enclosures around barracks or

Below: *These Confederate prisoners at Belle Plain Landing, Virginia, were captured in May 1864. By then, the Federals had adopted a policy of resisting prisoner exchanges in order to further stress Confederate manpower.*

tents, and open stockades. Libby and Belle Isle in Richmond, Salisbury in North Carolina, Cahaba in Alabama, Castle Pickney in Charleston, and Andersonville in Georgia were significant Confederate prisons. Libby Prison housed only officers and Belle Isle held enlisted men. The Federals made several forays to try to free prisoners held in Richmond, most notably the Kilpatrick–Dahlgren Raid of February 28 to March 4, 1864.

The Confederates also maintained two prisons in Richmond and Petersburg that both bore the name Castle Thunder. The one in Petersburg was used to house Federal prisoners, who gave it its name because of the sound of artillery fire during the siege of the city. The one in Richmond was used to contain political prisoners, spies, and criminals charged with treason. Its guards had a reputation for unnecessary brutality. Once Richmond fell, the prison was used by the Federals to hold Confederates charged with war crimes. Confederate prisoners generally fared better than their Federal counterparts thanks to the North's more abundant resources, but prison life was still Spartan and unhealthy. Confederate prisoners were held at places like Johnson Island in Lake Erie, Camp Morton in Indianapolis, Camp Douglas south of Chicago, and Point Lookout in Maryland.

Below: *Libby Prison in Richmond, Virginia, was used to house captured Federal officers.*

PRIVATEERS

On April 17, 1861, President Jefferson Davis published an invitation to ship owners to apply for letters of marque and reprisal that would authorize them to act as privateers. Prospective privateers had to post a bond ranging from $5,000 to $10,000, depending on the size of the crew, as a guarantee they would not engage in piracy or otherwise embarrass the Confederacy. Armed with these licenses, the bearers were authorized to capture Federal commercial ships and sell them for their own profit as contraband of war. The Confederate government also promised to pay the privateers 20 percent of the value of any Federal warship they destroyed. Entrepreneurs were quick to seize this opportunity, forming syndicates to underwrite the costs of arming and manning the vessels. By May 6, the day Congress ratified Davis's announcement, more than 3,000 applications had been submitted to state and Confederate authorities.

Below: *The* Rattlesnake *served the Confederacy as a lightly armed cruiser and blockade-runner under different names before becoming a privateer.*

President Abraham Lincoln did not sit idly by in this effort to control the seas. On April 19, he declared a blockade of the Confederate shoreline. He also stated that any private party found holding a Federal merchantman would be tried for piracy. Lincoln was not alone in questioning the legality of Davis's action. Both Britain and France had signed the Declaration of Paris in 1856, which condemned privateering.

In the early days of the war, privateers enjoyed much success. The *Calhoun* began operations in May and took six prizes over a five-month period, including three in its first seventy-two hours of action in the Gulf of Mexico. However, increased Federal blockading in the Gulf soon shifted most privateers to the Atlantic. When several privateers were captured, Lincoln proceeded with his threat to try them for piracy. Davis retaliated by warning Lincoln that if any privateers were executed, a like number of Federal prisoners would be killed. Rather than escalating the situation with needless deaths, Lincoln amended his policy and treated all captured privateers as prisoners of war.

The Confederate privateers instilled panic in the northeastern coastal towns and drove up maritime insurance rates. Many American shipments were shifted to foreign vessels. In spite of pleas to devote more resources against the privateers, Secretary of the Navy Gideon Welles instead focused on strengthening the blockade. His theory was that privateering would stop once the Confederate ports were closed.

Welles's strategy proved correct. By the end of 1861, most privateers, unable to penetrate the blockade with their deep-draft prizes, began shifting to the more promising venture of blockade-running. In their place, destructive Confederate commerce raiders such as the CSS *Alabama*, commissioned on August 24, 1862, began to appear.

PRYOR, ROGER A. (1828–1919)

Roger A. Pryor was a Virginia newspaper publisher, lawyer, and ardent secessionist. He resigned his seat in the U.S. Congress on March 3, 1861, and soon went to Charleston, South Carolina, to observe the developments at Fort Sumter. Although he urged the Federal garrison be shelled, Pryor declined an offer to fire the first shot.

Pryor represented Virginia in the Confederate Congress, but resigned to become a colonel in the Third Virginia Infantry. He was made a brigadier general on April 16, 1862, and commanded a brigade during the Peninsula Campaign and a division at Antietam. He resigned his commission on August 18, 1863, because he did not have a command. He then enlisted as a private in the cavalry and was captured around Petersburg in November 1864 while acting as a special courier during an informal

Above: *Although an ardent secessionist, Roger Pryor declined an offer to fire the Civil War's opening shot.*

truce. President Abraham Lincoln intervened and arranged for Pryor's exchange. After the war, he settled in New York and served as a newspaperman, lawyer, and judge.

QUAKER GUNS

Quaker guns were military deceptions in which a log was painted black in order to look like a cannon at a distance. Their name comes from the pacifist religious group. Confederate forces often employed Quaker guns to help offset their inferior troop strength. The technique was particularly useful in helping to hold the enemy in place while the Confederates executed a withdrawal. Quaker guns were

Right: *Quaker guns, like this one at Centreville, Virginia, in March 1862, were used to deceive the enemy.*

used to cover withdrawals from Centreville after First Manassas, Yorktown during the Peninsula Campaign, and throughout General Joseph E. Johnston's retrograde from Dalton to the outskirts of Atlanta, Georgia.

QUANTRILL, WILLIAM C. (1837–65)

William Clarke Quantrill was a Confederate bushwhacker who operated in Kansas and Missouri. Before the war, he was involved in various nefarious pursuits such as gambling and petty theft. When the Kansas–Missouri border area became embroiled in guerrilla warfare, Quantrill took advantage of the situation for his own personal gain. He fought at Wilson's Creek and then conducted guerrilla operations in Missouri, capturing Independence on August 11, 1862. On August 15, he was commissioned as a captain in the Confederate army. In November, he went to Richmond, Virginia, to try to gain greater rank. He was promoted to colonel, but Quantrill thought he deserved more. Regardless of his rank, he certainly never operated under any Confederate authority. He rejoined his 150-man company in early 1863. In his absence, his men had been active in Kansas and Missouri.

EWING TAKES ACTION
In 1863 the Federals created the District of the Border and appointed Brigadier General Thomas Ewing Jr. commander of the First Division, Army of the Frontier. As one of his first acts to secure the Kansas–Missouri border, he imprisoned several

Above: *One of William Quantrill's most notorious incidents of bushwhacking took place at Lawrence, Kansas, in 1863— 150 men and boys were killed.*

Confederate sympathizers, and on August 13, five women were killed and dozens more were seriously injured when a jail collapsed. Quantrill was already infuriated by Ewing's heavy-handed policies, but this incident accelerated his desire for vengeance. In retaliation, he attacked the abolitionist seat of Lawrence, Kansas, on August 21, exhorting his men to "Kill! Kill! Lawrence must be cleansed, and the only way to cleanse it is to kill!" His bushwhackers slaughtered 150 men and boys, and destroyed about a $1.5 million worth of property. Quantrill ordered that women not be harmed, but several were robbed

of their wedding bands. He then fled back to Missouri.

Ewing responded by issuing Order No. 11, which expelled some 20,000 Missourians from the border counties. The Federals then destroyed the vacated homes and farms. Ewing's actions only escalated the violence, and on October 6, Quantrill ambushed a wagon supply train at Baxter Springs, Kansas, killing many Federals after they had surrendered.

THE GANG BREAKS UP

Quantrill's brutal tactics found disfavor among most Confederate officials. Brigadier General Henry E. McCulloch wrote, "Quantrill's mode of warfare, from all I can learn, is but little if not at all removed from that of the wildest savages." In late October, Quantrill withdrew to Texas for

the winter and quickly lost control of his men. A combination of idle time, rivalry, complaints over inequitable distribution of spoils, and, in some cases, disillusionment over the bloody excesses of past operations led to Quantrill's gang breaking into factions. His most serious challenges came from George Todd and William "Bloody Bill" Anderson.

Quantrill eventually left the border area and with a handful of men headed for Washington, D.C., intending to assassinate President Abraham Lincoln. Quantrill was fatally wounded by Federal troops in Kentucky on May 10, 1865. Before he died twenty days later, he was baptized a Roman Catholic and left his lover Kate Clarke $500 in gold, which she used to open a house of ill repute in St. Louis.

RAILROADS

The Civil War has been called "the first great railroad war." Both sides used railroads to transport men and equipment, and otherwise nondescript towns such as Corinth, Mississippi, became battlegrounds because of their status as railroad junctions. Unfortunately for the Confederacy, the advantage of controlling this important resource lay with the Federals. Of the 31,000 miles of railroad in 1860, only 9,000 miles were in the states of the Confederacy, and these lines were of decidedly inferior quality.

On the eve of the Civil War, there were generally three railroad systems in the United States. The first was an east–west system running north of the Ohio River and connecting the old Northwest and the trans-Mississippi west with the east. The North retained control of this rail system, along with the northern rivers, canals, and Great Lakes, to form a high-capacity transportation network that allowed rapid movement of troops, supplies, and produce between the eastern and western theaters. The second system was a less efficient one along the eastern seaboard that connected Chattanooga, Atlanta, and Richmond. Both sides used the prewar lines between Richmond and Washington and the east–west lines throughout Virginia during the war. The third system ran parallel to the Mississippi River and aided armies operating in the Mississippi Valley.

Based on geography and the Jominian principle of interior lines, it appeared that the Confederacy could use its railroads to concentrate and disperse forces much faster than the Federals could. In actuality, the railroads in the South were ill suited for wartime use. The antebellum transportation system in the region had been designed to move goods to such ports as New Orleans, Richmond, Norfolk, Charleston, Savannah, and Wilmington rather than to ship them across the South. Few east–west lines connected the southern system, and only one line traversed the mountain barrier connecting Richmond with Chattanooga and the Mississippi River at Memphis. Additionally, southern railroad systems featured different gauges that necessitated the unloading and reloading of cargo en route. The inefficient Confederate railroad system was placed under even greater strain because of the Federal blockade. The result of all these factors was that the superior Federal railroad system often diluted the importance of the Confederate advantage of central position.

TO CHICKAMAUGA

A prime example of this phenomenon occurred in September 1863 when Lieutenant General James Longstreet's 12,000-man corps traveled by rail, on interior lines, from Virginia to northern Georgia, where it reinforced General Braxton Bragg's Army of Tennessee at Chickamauga. Longstreet's corps traveled some 800

Left: *Railroads were vital to the Confederate war effort. Federal work parties like this one at Atlanta destroyed railroads with precision.*

miles in about twelve days. Two weeks after the Confederate victory there, the Federal Eleventh and Twelfth corps, totaling 25,000 men, traveled 1,200 miles from Virginia to the Chattanooga front, where they reinforced the defeated Army of the Cumberland. This movement on exterior lines also took about twelve days, even though the distance was greater and the number of troops larger. In this case, the more efficient Union railroads demonstrated the potential to nullify Confederate interior lines.

RAINS, GABRIEL J. (1803–81)

Gabriel J. Rains graduated from West Point in 1827 and fought in the Second Seminole War and the Mexican War. On July 31, 1861, he resigned as a lieutenant colonel in the U.S. Army. Upon joining the Confederacy, he was appointed as a brigadier general and commanded a brigade during the Peninsula Campaign, but his true passion was science, and he was ill-suited for field command. He demonstrated his natural calling by pioneering the use of land mines by burying artillery shells along the roads and beaches as the Confederates withdrew up the Peninsula.

The use of land mines was considered by many to be an uncivilized form of warfare, but naval mines, known as "torpedoes" during the Civil War, were acceptable. On June 18, Rains was assigned to the river defenses and eventually became head of the Confederate Torpedo Bureau in June 1864. He was instrumental in laying out torpedo defenses for Mobile Bay and Charleston Harbor. His brother, George Washington Rains, was also a Confederate officer who served largely in ordnance operations.

RAMS

Rams were often old riverboats that had been converted by reinforcing their hulls and filling their bows with timber so that they could survive deliberate collisions with enemy boats. A true ram carried little or no armament other than its ram, so its utility was limited to combat against other vessels. The CSS *Virginia* was a more versatile ironclad ram that included projectile weapons. Other famous Confederate rams are the *Albemarle*, *Tennessee*, *Arkansas*, and *Stonewall*.

RAMSEUR, STEPHEN D. (1837–64)

Stephen D. Ramseur graduated from West Point in 1860 and resigned from the U.S. Army on April 8, 1861. He fought throughout the Peninsula Campaign and was promoted to brigadier general on November 1, 1862. He fought at Chancellorsville, Gettysburg, the Wilderness, and Spotsylvania. He was promoted to major general on June 1, 1864, and given command of a division.

When he was mortally wounded in fighting at Cedar Creek on October 19, 1864, Ramseur was taken to Major General Philip H. Sheridan's headquarters at Belle Grove and died in the company of several West Point classmates who had remained with the Union. The night before the battle, he had learned of the birth of his daughter.

Right: *A grandson of Thomas Jefferson, Secretary of War George Randolph was critical to the development of the Confederacy's conscription and personnel policies.*

RANDOLPH, GEORGE W. (1818–67)

George Wythe Randolph, a grandson of Thomas Jefferson, served six years as a midshipman in the U.S. Navy before entering the University of Virginia. After graduation, he began practicing law and became a respected and popular member of Richmond's social and professional community.

Randolph devoted much of his leisure time to studying military affairs, and he organized an artillery company in the Virginia militia. After John Brown's raid, Randolph's interests became increasingly political, and he became a strong proponent of Virginia's secession.

Once Virginia seceded, Randolph entered active service with his howitzer company. He distinguished himself at the Battle of Big Bethel and was promoted to colonel. The promotion allowed Randolph the opportunity to devote more time to policy matters, and he developed a plan to address the personnel problem the Confederacy would face when the terms of its initial enlistments

would expire by the spring of 1862. He then received another promotion to brigadier general and was given responsibility for the defense of the coastline around the Virginia–North Carolina border. A report he prepared on the coastal defense situation made a favorable impression on President Jefferson Davis.

In spite of this meteoric rise, Randolph opted to leave the army and run for Congress. He was soundly defeated, but on March 22, 1862, he became secretary of war, replacing Judah P. Benjamin, who had been discredited by the Confederate defeat at Roanoke Island. Under these circumstances, Randolph's military background made him a wise choice for secretary of war, and he performed well in the position.

Building on his previous study of the manpower situation, Randolph became an influential advocate for the Conscription Act. He was also instrumental in formulating the command structure in the western theater. However, Randolph suddenly resigned his position on November 15, 1862, over a dispute with President Davis and once again took field command, only to resign in late 1864 because of failing health.

RANK SYSTEM

Until Ulysses S. Grant was named lieutenant general on March 9, 1864, the Federal army had only brigadier generals and major generals. On the other hand, the Confederate army had brigadier generals who commanded brigades, major generals who commanded divisions, lieutenant generals who commanded corps, and generals who commanded armies. Otherwise, the Federal and Confederate armies had similar rank structures.

RANSOM JR., ROBERT
(1828–92)

Robert Ransom Jr. graduated from West Point in 1850. He served on the frontier and taught cavalry tactics at West Point. He resigned from the U.S. Army on May 24, 1861. He was appointed as a brigadier general in the Confederate army on March 6, 1862, and commanded a brigade during the Seven Days Battles. He fought at Harpers Ferry, Antietam, and Fredericksburg. He was promoted to major general on May 26, 1863, commanding in North Carolina and Richmond.

In October Ransom took command in east Tennessee, and in April 1864 he returned to Richmond to help defend Bermuda Hundred. He then fought under Major General Jubal A. Early in the Shenandoah Valley until poor health caused him to resign in August. His health prevented him from providing additional service of any significance.

RAYMOND, BATTLE OF

- ❖ DATE: May 12, 1863
- ❖ LOCATION: Hinds County, Mississippi
- ❖ GREGG'S TASK FORCE (C): 3,000
- ❖ SEVENTH CORPS, ARMY OF THE TENNESSEE (U.S.): 10,000
- ❖ CASUALTIES: 569 (C); 442 (U.S.)

After crossing the Mississippi River on April 30, 1863, Major General Ulysses S. Grant decided to advance on Jackson rather than heading directly for Vicksburg. His intention was to isolate the Confederate forces in

Above: *John Gregg fought a spirited battle at Raymond. He was one of John Pemberton's few inspired and reliable generals.*

Vicksburg from any outside assistance. By this time, Lieutenant General John C. Pemberton was confused by seemingly contradictory instructions from President Jefferson Davis to "hold both Vicksburg and Port Hudson" and from General Joseph E. Johnston to strike Grant. Pemberton elected to play it safe and consolidate his forces west of the Big Black to protect Vicksburg. Davis ordered reinforcements to Jackson and told Johnston to take command personally in Mississippi. In the meantime, the only Confederate force in Jackson was a small brigade that Brigadier General John Gregg had recently brought there from Port Hudson.

Grant advanced northeast from Port Gibson with an objective of cutting the railroad link between Vicksburg and Jackson. To facilitate foraging, the Federals advanced on a wide front, with Major General John A. McClernand's corps on the left, Major General William T. Sherman's coming up in the center, and Major General James B. McPherson's on the right.

Above: *The Battle of Raymond was part of Ulysses S. Grant's overall effort to isolate the Confederate force at Vicksburg.*

The multiple axes kept the Confederates guessing as to Grant's true intentions.

GREGG OUTNUMBERED

As the Federals advanced, Gregg's scouts saw only the lead elements of McPherson's corps, and their report led Gregg to grossly underestimate the size of his enemy. Thinking he faced only a small detachment, Gregg marched his 3,000-man brigade out of Jackson and encountered McPherson's 10,000-man corps at Raymond on May 12. Gregg attempted to turn McPherson's right flank, but had insufficient forces to do so. Although McPherson piecemealed his forces into the attack, he still prevailed thanks to overwhelming numbers. After a series of uncoordinated attacks and counterattacks by both armies, Gregg withdrew to Jackson.

Gregg's tenacious resistance as well as reports that Johnston was assembling an army in Jackson convinced Grant to modify his plans. Rather than risk being caught in between Pemberton and Johnston, Grant decided to shift his objective from the railroad and first deal with Johnston before turning his attention to

Pemberton. The resulting Battle of Jackson on May 14 isolated Pemberton in Vicksburg.

REAGAN, JOHN H. (1818–1905)

John H. Reagan was born in Tennessee but moved to Texas, where he established a career as a lawyer and judge. He served two terms as a Democratic congressman

Above: *Tennessee-born Texan John Reagan served as the able postmaster general for the Confederacy.*

and was a delegate to the Texas secession convention. At the Montgomery Convention, he helped frame the Confederate Constitution.

President Jefferson Davis appointed Reagan to be his postmaster general, and Reagan remained in that position for the duration of the war. He faced numerous obstacles as postmaster general, including a constitutionally mandated requirement that postal expenses not exceed postal income. Nonetheless, under his capable leadership, the Confederate mail service continued to function throughout the war.

As the war drew to a close, Reagan also assumed duties as secretary of the treasury and advised Davis on surrender terms. He was extremely loyal to Davis and was the only cabinet member to remain with Davis throughout his flight from Richmond to Georgia in the ending days of the war.

After Reagan was captured, he was imprisoned until December 1865. Upon his release, he returned to Texas and served as a congressman, senator, and chairman of the Texas Railroad Commission.

REBEL YELL

The famous "rebel yell" first appeared at the Battle of First Manassas and became a mainstay of Confederate charges throughout the war. The yell served the purpose of releasing pent-up emotions in the shouter and instilling fear in the hearer. It was also used for motivation while on the march, with one unit starting the yell and other units passing it up and down the column.

The exact yell was not uniform throughout the Confederate army, with troops from different states each having their unique version. In general terms, historian Bell Irvin Wiley describes it as "an unpremeditated, unrestrained, and utterly informal hollering," but a contemporary newspaper admitted the yell "paragons description." Indeed, postwar efforts to re-create the yell have resulted in great variety. Among the common suggestions are "Yeeeeeeeeee-ahhhhhhhhhhh!" and "Woh-who-ey! Who-ey!" Regardless of the yell's exact nature, it is one of the Confederate soldier's most enduring legacies.

RECONSTRUCTION

Before his assassination, President Abraham Lincoln had given every indication that he favored a relatively mild approach to the defeated Confederacy. As Federal armies occupied Tennessee, Arkansas, and Louisiana, Lincoln installed military governors, but discouraged Northerners from flooding the South to fill political offices. Instead, he preferred for loyal locals to step forward. He also had pardoned former Confederates who took a loyalty oath to the United States and its Constitution.

In December 1863, Lincoln outlined his full plan for restoration of the Confederate states to the Union. Under this plan, when one-tenth of a state's citizens who had voted in the presidential election of 1860 had taken the loyalty oath, they could establish a government that prohibited slavery. Lincoln would recognize this new government, and in 1864, Tennessee, Louisiana, and Arkansas were reorganized according to these procedures.

Lincoln issued his plan by presidential proclamation, and many in Congress, both radicals and moderates, felt he had overstepped his bounds and encroached on a responsibility they felt lay with Congress. Congress responded with the Wade-Davis Bill, which described a much more difficult path to a state's restoration. This measure required a majority of the citizens in the state to take the loyalty oath before the state could be reorganized, and only those citizens who could affirm their past loyalty were allowed to vote for representatives to the constitutional convention. Former Confederate officials were not allowed to serve as representatives to the conventions, and the new constitution was required to prohibit them from voting or holding office.

The Wade-Davis Bill put Lincoln and Congress at loggerheads. Lincoln vetoed the bill, and Congress responded by refusing to seat representatives from the states Lincoln had allowed to reorganize. The larger issue of what shape Reconstruction would take was still unresolved at the time of Lincoln's assassination.

When Andrew Johnson succeeded Lincoln as president, he began following Lincoln's plan of a moderate path to restoration. On May 29, 1865, he issued two proclamations. One granted amnesty to former Confederates, with the exception of certain high-level individuals, who would take a loyalty oath. In the second

Left: *After the assassination of Abraham Lincoln in April 1865, Radical Republicans asserted themselves, eventually leading to the impeachment of President Andrew Johnson.*

proclamation, Johnson appointed William Woods Holden as provisional governor of North Carolina. In a program that would outline his broader plan for Reconstruction, Johnson instructed Holden to reorganize the state along Johnson's interpretation of Lincoln's original direction.

Southern states quickly exploited Johnson's lenient terms, voting into office many former Confederate leaders. Johnson exacerbated the situation by freely issuing pardons, including one to former vice president of the Confederacy Alexander H. Stephens, who was then elected senator from Georgia. Emboldened, Southern states became increasingly obstinate, and African Americans and Southerners

Below: Frank Leslie's Illustrated Newspaper *depicts the withdrawal of Federal troops from New Orleans. Without Federal troops present, white Southerners were able to regain political and economic control of the ex-Confederate states.*

loyal to the Union came under increased threat. Repressive "Black Codes" soon began to appear.

By the end of 1865, Congress had had enough. Radicals like Thaddeus Stevens and Charles Sumner found common cause with moderates, and a majority quickly coalesced to challenge Johnson. Motivations varied. Some were concerned for the safety and opportunities of the South's African Americans. Others saw a more restrictive policy as being vital to the Republican Party broadening its base. Many were suspicious of Johnson because he was from Tennessee. Some were just vindictive and thought the rebellious South had been treated too gently for too long.

JOINT COMMITTEE
In December 1865, the Joint Committee on Reconstruction was formed to develop an alternative to Johnson's plan. The Joint Committee took decisive action.

In February 1866, it extended the life and expanded the powers of the Freedman's Bureau. In April it proposed the Fourteenth Amendment, which would guarantee due process and equal protection of the law. Johnson opposed these measures and refused to execute them, but he was losing popularity with the voters. In the November elections, most of his supporters were defeated, giving Congress a mandate to make the Fourteenth Amendment the basis for Reconstruction. Flexing this muscle, Congress passed a Reconstruction Act on March 2, 1867, that returned the ex-Confederacy to military rule.

Tennessee had already been readmitted to the Union based on its earlier ratification of the Fourteenth Amendment, but the other ten ex-Confederate states were divided into five military districts commanded by a general who had complete authority and Federal troops to back him up.

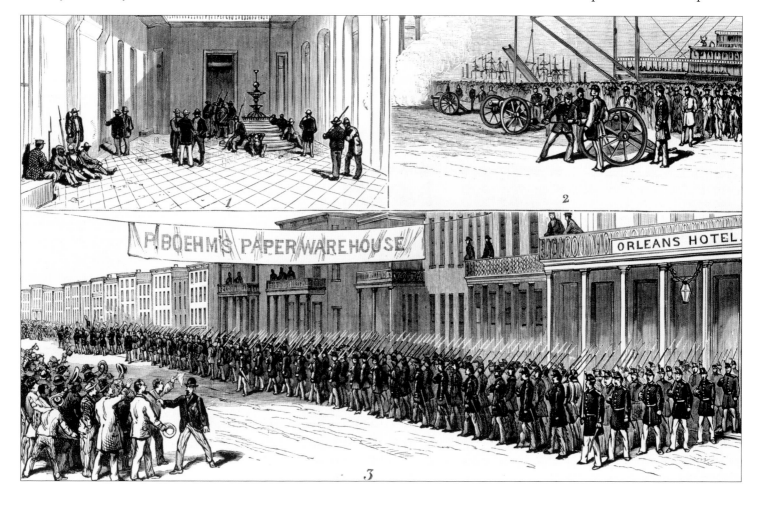

These commanders were to determine the eligible voters who would then elect a constitutional convention. Once a state had presented Congress with an acceptable constitution and ratified the Fourteenth Amendment, its delegates could be seated.

Under this Congressional or Military Reconstruction, Republicans gained control of the South. Protected by Federal troops, African Americans not only voted, but were elected to office. Johnson, however, continued to clash with Congress, removing three district commanders whom he deemed too sympathetic to the radicals and instructing commanders to not question the past behavior of those who took the oath of allegiance. When Johnson sought to replace Secretary of War Edwin M. Stanton in the summer of 1867, he did so in a way that violated the Tenure of Office Act, which required that any officeholder who had been appointed by the president with the Senate's consent was to serve until the Senate had approved his successor. Congress had earlier enacted the legislation to limit Johnson's power. Now it gave Congress an excuse to impeach Johnson, which it did on February 24, 1868. Johnson escaped conviction by one vote, but his leadership had clearly been rejected. In his stead, Ulysses S. Grant became the Republican nominee for president in 1868 and won the election.

Grant's second term was rocked by scandal and a weak economy. Grant began to see Reconstruction efforts as an unnecessary distraction, and he began to slowly lessen the Federal presence in the South. Traditional white Southerners began to reassert themselves, rolling back the gains made by African Americans. In the contested election of 1876, a deal was struck by which the electoral college votes of the three

Above: *White Southerners resisted many efforts of the Freedman's Bureau to empower African Americans, such as this burning down of a freedmen's schoolhouse in Memphis.*

Southern states still under Republican rule—South Carolina, Louisiana, and Florida—would go to the Republican candidate Rutherford B. Hayes. In exchange, the Federal troops would be withdrawn from those states, allowing them to return to home rule. Reconstruction was over, and white Southerners moved quickly to restore the status quo they fondly remembered. The result, according to many, was that the South lost the Civil War but won the Reconstruction.

RED RIVER CAMPAIGN

❖ DATE: March 10–May 22, 1864

❖ LOCATION: Louisiana

❖ ARMY OF WESTERN LOUISIANA (C): 30,000

❖ ARMY OF THE WEST (U.S.): 27,000

❖ CASUALTIES: 1,500 (C): 2,900 (U.S.)

In order to counter the French designs on Mexico, the Federals developed a joint thrust to establish a presence in at least some part of Texas. The plan was for Major General Nathaniel P. Banks to lead 17,000 troops up the Bayou Teche while Major General Andrew Jackson Smith led 10,000 more up the Red River. Major General Frederick Steele was supposed to bring another 15,000 from Little Rock, Arkansas. Opposing this force were 30,000 Confederates in General Edmund Kirby Smith's Trans-Mississippi Department.

The offensive began on March 10, 1864, but almost immediately ran into problems and delays. In fact, Steele was so late in starting, he played no part in the operation. Banks reached Alexandria on March 24, but found further progress impeded by low water and the impending loss of Smith's corps to the Atlanta Campaign. Nonetheless, Banks ordered an advance on Shreveport.

Up to this point, Lieutenant General Richard Taylor had withdrawn 200 miles in the face of Banks's advance, but as he arrived in the vicinity of other Confederate forces, he established a defensive position at Sabine Crossroads near Mansfield. In the battle there on

Above: *The Civil War displaced many Southern whites and African Americans. Refugees fled with whatever they could carry to escape the ravages of war.*

April 8, the Federals were routed, and Banks decided to abandon the campaign. Taylor attacked again on April 9 at Pleasant Hill, but was repulsed. Confederate forces harassed Banks's retreat, but by May 26, all of Banks's men had safely reached Donaldsville, Louisiana.

Taylor felt that he could have destroyed Banks if Edmund Kirby Smith had consolidated forces. A quarrel developed between the two, and Taylor was reassigned from Smith's command. Banks was highly criticized for his mismanagement of the operation and resigned.

REFUGEES

Countless numbers of Southern civilians, including the wife of Robert E. Lee, were forced to abandon their homes and become refugees in order to escape the advancing Federal army and the ravages of war. Refugees faced difficult decisions about what to take with them. Some managed to take their slaves with them when they fled, but many slaves took this

opportunity to find their freedom. Well-off Southerners hired coaches and hauled off everything they could. Others carried their most prized possessions in handmade carts piled high with baggage. The least prosperous felt lucky to escape with their clothes and what they could carry in their arms. As if these hardships were not enough, gangs of bandits preyed on the hapless refugees. Because of its isolation from the major fighting, Texas was a popular destination for refugees who could reach it. However, even the friends, family, and kind strangers who took in refugees suffered by having to share scarce food with additional hungry mouths.

REGIMENTS

Regiments were the principal fighting elements of the war. While specific organizations varied, an infantry regiment in the

Confederate army had ten companies. Sometimes, three of the companies were organized into a battalion. A colonel commanded the regiment. The Confederacy raised the equivalent of 764 regiments that served for all or most of the war. If militias and other irregular units are included, the Confederacy raised the equivalent of slightly over 1,000 regiments. Although regiments theoretically had about 950 members, casualties and replacement procedures caused strength to decline throughout the war.

REGIONAL AND CULTURAL IDENTITY

Southerners identified themselves much more regionally than did their Northern counterparts. For some, the distinction was drawn from the prevailing story that Southerners were descendants of the Cavalier stock of old England whose lineage extended from aristocratic Normans who had invaded in 1066 and conquered the lowly Saxon rabble whose descendants later immigrated to the North. Fire-eater Robert Barnwell Rhett was one of this theory's most vocal champions.

Other Southerners claimed a regional distinctiveness based on climate. James D. B. DeBow argued, "Everything in warm climates is superior to everything in cold climates." Therefore, the southern United States must be superior to the northern part. Certainly, the fact that climate supported agriculture in the South gave many Southerners a sense of contrast between their agrarian way of life and the more industrialized North.

In general, Southerners had a great loyalty to their states, a fact which gave birth to the idea of states' rights. When the interests of the state appeared challenged by the Federal government, Southerners tended to close ranks and view the matter from a local perspective.

What most set the South apart, however, was the institution of slavery, upon which its economy, politics, social structure, and way of life had come to depend. On the eve of the war, DeBow crowed, "We of the South are about to inaugurate a new civilization. We shall have new and original thought; negro slavery will be its great controlling and distinctive element."

ELEVEN SECEDE

As a result of the combination of these and other factors, many Southerners saw themselves as having developed a distinct regional identity. The election of Abraham Lincoln in 1860 threatened the survival of this identity, and eleven states elected to secede rather than to succumb to what they felt was an inevitable subordination of their interests to the growing power of the Northern states.

RELIGION

The Second Great Awakening, which lasted roughly from 1800 to 1840, made evangelical Protestantism the dominant religion in the United States, and the South was particularly homogeneous in its Protestant majority. The principal denominations were Baptist, Methodist, Presbyterian, and Episcopalian, with the latter two groups being highly represented among the richer classes. Outside Protestantism, there was a small minority of religious skeptics, Jews, and Catholics (who had larger representation in Louisiana and Maryland), and even fewer numbers of Quakers, Unitarians, and liberal sects. The occasional non-Protestant, such as the highly capable Judah P. Benjamin, a Jew who served the Confederacy as attorney general, secretary of war, and secretary of state, found himself "distrusted for his exotic qualities."

The result of this homogeneity was a strong consensus on the reality of human sinfulness and the promise of salvation. Yet, as is often the case, hedonism and fundamentalism coexisted in the Southern soul. For example, the biblical account of the curse of the "sons of Ham" was used to justify African slavery, and many churchgoing masters thought nothing of abusing their slaves.

The Southern brand of Protestantism was highly personal. Therefore, it placed strict demands on the individual, but limited the role of the church. Individuals were admonished to live upright and obedient lives, but the church was prohibited from pursuing the cause of social justice. This phenomenon explains the failure of Unitarianism and transcendentalism to gain much traction in the South. These philosophies tended to call humans to perfection. Southerners seemed to accept the frailty of the human condition to the point of celebrating it.

Most Southern Protestant denominations had divided from their Northern counterparts before the Civil War, and most Southern churches were strong supporters of the Confederate cause. Southern sermons often portrayed the Confederates as God's chosen people and the Federals as philistines with whom God would deal in his own time. They also

Below: *Churches and congregations played an active role in the war effort. Reverend John McGill was the Catholic bishop of Richmond during the Civil War.*

Above: *Religious Southerners interpreted the outcome of the Civil War in various ways as they came to grips with defeat. Shown here are the ruins of Circular Church and Secession Hall in Charleston, South Carolina, shortly after the war's end.*

sought to explain tragedies such as the death of Stonewall Jackson in a religious context. Churches served as centers of volunteer action in support of the Confederate cause, collecting both monetary and material donations. Historian Emory M. Thomas suggested, "Among all the institutions in Southern life, perhaps the church most faithfully served the Confederate army and nation."

OPENLY DEVOUT

Many prominent Confederates were highly public in professing the role of religion in their lives. President Jefferson Davis was baptized and confirmed in St. Paul's Episcopal Church in Richmond in May 1862 and proclaimed several official days of fasting, humiliation, and prayer.

Lieutenant General Stonewall Jackson was a strong supporter of observing the Sabbath and agonized over his decision to fight the Battle of Kernstown on a Sunday. Lieutenant General Leonidas Polk, a West Point graduate who was also an Episcopal bishop, served in the Confederate army as a corps commander. General Robert E. Lee and Major General Jeb Stuart were also highly visible Christians. The strong example of these leaders was certainly a factor in the revivals that swept the Confederate army in 1863 and 1864.

The strong religious beliefs prevalent in the South allowed many Confederates to place the war in broader, religious context. Some never lost their faith, such as the Confederate at the end of March 1865 who affirmed his "unshaken faith in the ultimate triumph of that cause" and declared he was "provoked and annoyed that any human being, who had faith in God, should doubt." Others, like Brigadier General Josiah Gorgas,

saw God's hand in defeat, asking, "What have we done that the Almighty should scourge us with such a war—so relentless and repugnant."

The theme of defeat as a punishment for sin was a common one. Some identified the sin as slavery and others as a failure to correct the abuses of slavery. Certainly, a growing difficulty in rationalizing religious conviction with the realities of human bondage created a sense of guilt in the South. Religion helped assuage these concerns via the "Lost Cause" ideology of the postwar era. The role of slavery was minimized, and the image of the Confederacy as a Christian nation was carefully groomed. Defeat was explained not as the result of any flaw in the Confederacy but rather as being part of God's inexplicable will— something to be accepted even if not understood.

REVIVALS IN THE CONFEDERATE ARMY

In the spring of 1863 and then again in the winters of 1863–64 and 1864–65, great revivals swept the Confederate army. The Reverend John Jones estimates that 150,000 Confederate soldiers made professions of faith during the war. In the winter of 1863–64 alone, 15,000 soldiers of the Army of Northern Virginia were converted. Reports of 200 baptisms in a single day and 2,000 soldiers attending services were not uncommon. General Robert E. Lee closely followed these developments, and his chaplains reported that as they briefed him on the revival's progress, "we saw his eyes brighten and his whole countenance glow with pleasure."

REVIVAL AT MOSS NECK

Perhaps the most famous of the Confederate revivals occurred at Lieutenant General Stonewall Jackson's camp in Moss Neck, Virginia, during the winter of 1863–64. While in camp, the pious Jackson consciously endeavored to see to "the spiritual improvement of the army." Several of his biographers attribute the revival in part to Jackson's personal efforts. Frank Vandiver writes that "the great revival later so famous in the annals of the Confederate army owed much of its origin to the diligent labors of Deacon Jackson, who overcame inertia in all quarters." James Robertson likewise notes that Jackson "planned personally to superintend . . . a new awakening. His devotion would be the catalyst."

To this end, Jackson appointed the Reverend Beverley Tucker Lacy as his "chaplain-general" and oversaw the formation of the Second Corps Chaplains' Association. With Jackson's support, his men quickly set about building log chapels throughout the camp, and attendance at services was formidable.

While Jackson did much to create conditions in which religion could flourish, the specific catalyst for this revival is often credited to the preaching of the reverends Joseph C. Stiles and A. M. Marshall. Marshall was a devout private in the Twelfth Georgia Infantry who had recently received a chaplain's commission. His fervent preaching aroused men not just in his own regiment but in the Forty-fourth Georgia Infantry as well. Stiles then joined Marshall in a series of camp meetings that generated a great revival that

spread throughout the entire Army of Northern Virginia. Jackson himself heard Stiles's preaching and described him as "a great revivalist."

RHETT SR., ROBERT BARNWELL (1800–76)

Robert Barnwell Rhett Sr. was a fire-eating South Carolina congressman, senator, and newspaper editor. In the early 1840s, he organized a radical secessionist movement called the Bluffton Movement and was a delegate to the Southern Rights Convention in 1852. Rhett used his *Charleston Mercury* as a vehicle to pronounce vehement secessionist rhetoric.

Rhett was in large part the mastermind behind the

Above: *Fire-eater Robert Barnwell Rhett used his* Charleston Mercury *to advocate secession and criticize the Davis administration.*

Montgomery Convention and served as a member of the Provisional Confederate Congress. Although his extreme fire-eating views precluded him from significant public office in the Confederacy, he did serve as chair of the committee that drafted the permanent constitution. He also served on the Foreign Affairs and Financial Independence committees.

Rhett's radical stance helped defeat him in his bid for a seat in the First Confederate Congress, and he became an outspoken opponent of President Jefferson F. Davis. Although he has been called the "Father of Secession," Rhett spent most of his energy during the war as a critic.

RICH MOUNTAIN, BATTLE OF

❖ DATE: July 11, 1861

❖ LOCATION: Randolph County, Virginia

❖ FORCE UNDER PEGRAM (C): 1,300

❖ FORCE UNDER McCLELLAN (U.S.): 5,000

❖ CASUALTIES: 553 (C); 46 (U.S.)

After retreating from Philippi, Virginia, in June 1861, Confederate troops commanded by Colonel Robert S. Garnett began preparing a position overlooking the Staunton–Parkersburg Turnpike at Rich Mountain, just west of Beverly. This position was called Camp Garnett and was manned by Lieutenant Colonel John Pegram and 1,300 men.

Major General George B. McClellan advanced with 5,000 troops and on July 11, 1861, attacked about a mile behind Pegram's position, cutting off the Confederate retreat route to Beverly. Part of Pegram's force

Above: *The Federal victory at Rich Mountain in July 1861 helped solidify Unionist sentiment in the western counties of Virginia.*

escaped, but Pegram was unable to link up with Garnett and surrendered his remaining 553 men on the night of July 12–13. The victory helped remove the Confederate presence from the northwestern counties of Virginia, which helped pave the way for West Virginia's admission to the Union as a state in 1863.

RICHMOND, VIRGINIA

Richmond, Virginia, located at the fall line of the James River, was critical to the Confederacy as both a manufacturing and political

Right: *The arsenal at Richmond, once the site of some of the Confederacy's most important industrial output, lies in ruins in April 1865.*

center. Unlike other Southern cities, it had a solid industrial base, including the Tredegar Iron Works, which made Richmond the home of the South's iron industry. Flour mills and tobacco factories processed agricultural products, and the city's railroad and port facilities made it an important transportation

and shipping site. A strong network of banks provided financial support to development and trade. The result of this balanced economy was that Richmond was the most advanced city in the South.

Still, Richmond was spared the evils of industrialization that many Southerners feared. Its population

Right: *Richmond was the Confederate capital and a key industrial center. It was the objective of several Federal campaigns.*

of 37,910 was drawn largely from its own countryside, and when planters moved to town they brought with them the genteel character of country life. Free African Americans and slaves comprised a third of Richmond's population. Most of the slaves served in domestic positions. Although still beholden to slavery, Richmond lacked many of the system's extreme cruelties that plagued other parts of the South. The city also played host to a collection of fine, largely upper-class Episcopalian churches, the nationally known *Southern Literary Messenger* magazine, the luxurious Spotswood Hotel, and the influential Democratic newspaper the *Richmond Enquirer*. Richmond's many amenities and comfortable way of life made it a good place to live.

These qualities, as well as the overall importance of Virginia to the Confederacy, resulted in Richmond being highly visible among Southern cities. On May 21, 1861, the decision was made to transfer the capital there from Montgomery, Alabama. This choice put the Confederate capital on the war's front line, and Richmond came under repeated Federal pressure, beginning with the Peninsula Campaign of 1862.

Richmond's transformation to the capital of the Confederacy was incomplete in that government properties did not belong to the nation, as they did in Washington. Instead, Richmond was a state capital whose facilities were used by the Confederate government. Even the White House of the Confederacy was leased by the Confederate government from the City of Richmond.

Richmond's wartime growth was impressive. Approximately 1,000 government employees made the trip from Montgomery to the new capital. By the end of the war, the Confederacy employed some 70,000 civil servants. As Richmond's population increased, food shortages and other pressures stressed the city. The famous Bread Riot of April 1863 was one result. Security concerns also caused President Jefferson Davis to declare martial law in the city on March 1, 1862, and Brigadier General John H. Winder was appointed provost marshal general and given the complex and controversial task of maintaining order. Winder also served as commander of Richmond's Libby and Belle Isle military prisons.

Once Petersburg fell on April 2, 1865, Richmond was left isolated. The city surrendered the following day. In the chaos associated with the city's fall, fires, looting, and lawlessness destroyed much property.

RIFLES AND MUSKETS

The smoothbore musket commonly used in the Mexican War was loaded by dropping a ball down the barrel. This procedure required that the barrel be of greater diameter than the ball. The result was that when fired, the ball would bounce along the sides of the barrel, limiting both range and accuracy.

Above: *The M1855 Springfield, along with other rifles used during the Civil War, changed the nature of warfare by greatly increasing range and accuracy.*

In 1849 a French army captain named Claude E. Minié developed a way to load a rifled musket as easily as a smoothbore. The minié ball was a cylindro-conoidal bullet that was slightly smaller in diameter than the barrel and thus could be easily dropped down it. One end, however, was hollow, and when the rifle was fired, expanding gas widened the sides of this hollow end so that the bullet would grip the rifling and create the spinning effect needed for accuracy. Just as a spiraling pass with a football is superior to a wobbly pass, the ensuing aerodynamic stability increased the range and accuracy of the rifle. When the United States adapted the Model 1855 Springfield rifle to take .58-caliber minié ammunition, the difference was significant. The smoothbore musket had a range of 100–200 yards. The new rifle was effective at 400–600 yards.

THE ENFIELD RIFLE
During the Civil War, a variety of private contractors produced Springfields for the South, and Confederate soldiers also obtained the rifle by capture. The most popular rifle in the Confederate army, however, was the Enfield, a muzzle-loader that had a bore diameter of 0.577 inch (14.66 mm) and was designed to fire a bullet similar to the minié ball called the Pritchett. The rifle's tolerances were

such that it could accommodate the .58-caliber (14.7 mm) bullet designed for Springfield rifles, but this practice inevitably led to a certain amount of clogging. The Enfield had an effective range of 400–600 yards and a theoretical rate of fire of three rounds per minute. It weighed nine pounds and three ounces, including its bayonet.

What the Enfields, Springfields, and other rifles did was make the defense tactically stronger than the offense. The increased range and accuracy of the rifle afforded defenders, especially when protected by breastworks, a great advantage, and frontal attacks against entrenched defenders were generally ripped to pieces. Confederate soldiers took advantage of this development at places like Fredericksburg, Kennesaw Mountain, and Cold Harbor, but

other Confederates suffered its effects in attacks like Pickett's Charge.

RIVERS, IMPORTANCE OF

The rivers of the Confederacy helped shape Civil War military strategy and presented the Confederacy with different situations in the east and the west. In the east, the Potomac, Rappahannock, York, and James rivers ran from the western mountains to the east. They were flanked by swampy tributaries and had limited crossings, and well-known and easily defended fords. Although access to these rivers from

Below: *Rivers were often used as obstacles to support defensive efforts. Here Union troops are repulsed in an effort to cross the Rappahannock River at Fredericksburg.*

the Chesapeake Bay gave Federal warships an avenue into the interior of Virginia, such as Major General George B. McClellan tried to exploit during the Peninsula Campaign, for the most part their east–west orientation served as obstacles to north–south movement and therefore helped the Confederate defense. General Robert E. Lee often incorporated rivers into his defensive lines, such as at Fredericksburg and Hanover Junction.

In the west, the situation was less auspicious for the defenders. The Cumberland drained northern Tennessee and southern Kentucky, flowed south to Nashville, and then turned north to join the Ohio River at Smithland, Kentucky. The Tennessee River ran from the mountains of east Tennessee through the strategic cities of Knoxville and Chattanooga, on to Huntsville and Florence, Alabama, then north to the Ohio River. The Mississippi was the most important transportation artery in the country during the Civil War. It flowed from the north through St. Louis, Missouri, to Cairo, Illinois, where it was joined by the Ohio. It then continued south to New Orleans and the Gulf of Mexico. This path literally split the South in two, making comunications with Arkansas, Texas, and Louisiana often difficult for the eastern Confederacy. The orientation of these western rivers favored Federal attacks, as campaigns such as those at Forts Henry and Donelson and Vicksburg demonstrated.

ROANOKE ISLAND, BATTLE OF

❖ DATE: February 7–8, 1862

❖ LOCATION: Dare County, North Carolina

❖ ROANOKE ISLAND GARRISON (C): 2,500

❖ BURNSIDE EXPEDITION (U.S.): 10,000

❖ CASUALTIES: 2,500 (C); 251 (U.S.)

Roanoke Island is twelve miles long by three miles wide and sits just off the eastern tip of a low-lying marshy peninsula that divides the Albemarle Sound and the Pamlico Sound on the North Carolina coast. It was the first objective of the Burnside Expedition, a campaign in which the Federals began to show the true promise of army–navy cooperation and greatly expanded the logistical impact of the coastal war.

Brigadier General Henry A. Wise was responsible for the defenses of Roanoke Island, but, in addition to his own irascible personality and limited military talent, he was hindered by a paucity of resources, antiquated equipment, and too few troops. As a result, Forts Blanchard and Huger, as well as the 2,500 soldiers manning them, were ill-prepared to receive a Federal attack. The naval component of the Confederate defenses was equally inauspicious. Captain William F. Lynch commanded a miniscule "Mosquito Fleet" of two side-wheel steamers, six tiny gunboats, and a floating artillery battery.

AMPHIBIOUS DIVISION
In contrast, the attackers consisted of a specially recruited 10,000-man "coastal" or amphibious division commanded by Brigadier General Ambrose E. Burnside and supported by a naval component led by the capable Flag Officer Louis M. Goldsborough.

On February 7, 1862, Burnside and Goldsborough attacked. Goldsborough quickly brushed aside Lynch's little fleet and Burnside, using some pioneering techniques that would be replicated in the amphibious landings of

Left: *The capture of Roanoke Island was an easy Federal victory that was the harbinger of more Confederate coastal vulnerabilities.*

World War II, disembarked his men at Ashby's Landing. By midnight, Burnside had 10,000 men landed and setting up a temporary camp in preparation for an assault the next morning.

LAND ASSAULT

The land assault was launched at 7:00 a.m. on February 8. Supported by close naval gunfire and attacking both to the front and flanks, the Federals quickly overwhelmed the meager Confederate defenses. The Federals captured nearly the entire 2,500-man garrison. Twenty-three Confederates were killed and 58 wounded. Federal losses were 37 killed and 214 wounded. Roanoke Island was the Federals' first major land victory east of the Alleghenies.

The defeat set off a wave of recrimination in the South, and the Confederate Congress investigated the situation and found Secretary of War Judah P. Benjamin to blame. Succumbing to the public outcry, President Jefferson Davis removed Benjamin as secretary of war—only to then reassign him as secretary of state.

RUFFIN, EDMUND (1794–1865)

Edmund Ruffin was a successful Virginia agriculturist and writer, as well as an ardent secessionist. Along with William L. Yancey and Robert Barnwell Rhett, he was one of the most vehement fire-eaters. He traveled to Charles Town to witness John Brown's hanging, hoping that Brown's abortive abolitionist raid would "stir the sluggish blood of the South." At sixty-five years old, he was even able to borrow a Virginia Military Institute uniform and join the cadets in securing the execution site. On March 3, 1861, the day

before President Abraham Lincoln's inauguration, Ruffin left Virginia for already-seceded South Carolina to "avoid being . . . under his [Lincoln's] government even for an hour." Determined to have a part in the historic events unfolding at Fort Sumter, Ruffin joined the Palmetto Guard, South Carolina Battery. After a signal gun was fired at 4:30 a.m. on April 12, Ruffin pulled the lanyard on a Columbiad and laid claim to having fired the first hostile shot of the Civil War. He also participated at the Battle of First Manassas.

Aside from these symbolic acts in the early days of the war, like most fire-eaters, Ruffin was replaced by more moderate voices once secession had become reality.

Above: *Fire-eater Edmund Ruffin claimed to have fired the opening shot of the Civil War. Rather than subject himself to Federal authority, Ruffin committed suicide after the end of the war.*

He became disenchanted with President Jefferson Davis, calling him "tender-conscienced and an imbecile." Ruffin could not abide the defeat of the Confederacy.

On June 17, 1865, he wrote in his diary, "I here declare my unmitigated hatred to Yankee rule." He then placed a gun in his mouth and with a forked stick he pushed the trigger, committing suicide rather than living in what he considered "the now ruined, subjugated and enslaved Southern States."

RUSSELL, LORD JOHN (1792–1878)

Lord John Russell was the British foreign secretary during the Civil War. He could see how an independent Confederacy might serve British strategic interests, and on several occasions he displayed sympathy toward the Confederacy. However, his support was cautious and his signals mixed. In the final analysis, he rejected Confederate overtures for recognition.

Russell carefully crafted the British response to the Federal blockade. While he did not want to see British ships harassed, he also wanted to preserve Britain's freedom to execute its own blockades in the future. At a time when the early Federal blockade was still forming, Russell deemed it in compliance with the 1856 Declaration of Paris that required "blockades, in order to be binding, must be effective."

Russell initially agreed to meet Confederate diplomat James Mason only unofficially, and then gave him a cool reception. When Mason later tried to present a formal request that Britain recognize the Confederacy, Russell refused to see him. However, Russell also toyed with the idea of mediation based on the early Confederate battlefield victories. In September 1862, he wrote that the time had come "for offering mediation . . . with a view to the recognition of the independence of the Confederacy." If mediation failed, Russell

Below: *British foreign secretary Lord John Russell refused to commit to support of the Confederacy.*

suggested that Britain recognize the South. On October 13, he went so far as to send a memorandum to the cabinet members proposing an armistice so that the situation could be fully considered. However, the Confederate setbacks in 1863 served to quench Russell's already mixed feelings. On June 30, 1863, he ended hopes of a parliamentary motion for Confederate recognition proposed by John Arthur Roebuck in debate in the House of Commons. In 1863, Russell also belatedly began enforcing Britain's Foreign Enlistment Act, which shut down Confederate shipbuilding efforts in Britain. Like many other Britons, Russell had some measure of sympathy for the Confederacy, but not enough to outweigh the realization that Federal victory appeared inevitable.

RUSSIA, RELATIONS WITH

The Confederacy had little hope of gaining support from Russia, which saw a strong United States as a useful counter to Russia's potential French and British enemies. A glimmer of hope surfaced in October 1862 when France circulated a letter to Britain and Russia suggesting mediation, but both parties declined. For the Russians, the reason was simply a vested interest in the continuation of the United States. Indeed, several Russian ships visited New York and San Francisco in the fall of 1863. While the primary motivation for the visits was to get the ships safely out of their home ports at a time when there was fear of a British attack, the trips nonetheless were interpreted by many as a sign of U.S.-Russian friendship. Against such slim odds of success, a Confederate mission to Russia was rejected by the Senate in December 1863.

SABINE CROSSROADS, BATTLE OF

- ❖ DATE: April 8, 1864
- ❖ LOCATION: DeSoto Parish, Louisiana
- ❖ DISTRICT OF WEST LOUISIANA (C): 7,000
- ❖ FORCE UNDER BANKS (U.S.): 12,000
- ❖ CASUALTIES: 1,500 (C): 2,900 (U.S.)

During Major General Nathaniel P. Banks's Red River Campaign, Lieutenant General Richard Taylor was forced to withdraw to defensive positions three miles southeast of Mansfield, Louisiana, at Sabine Crossroads. On April 8, 1864, Taylor attacked Banks's advancing force and attempted to turn the Federal right but was stopped. Banks then withdrew, and Taylor attacked him the next day at Pleasant Hill. The Battle of Sabine Crossroads marked the end of Banks's advance and the failure of his Red River Campaign. Although he had repulsed Banks, Taylor complained that General Edmund Kirby Smith's unwillingness to concentrate his forces prevented the annihilation of the Federal army.

SALISBURY PRISON

Shortly after North Carolina's secession, the Confederate government purchased an empty cotton factory in Salisbury, the state's fourth-largest town with a population of 2,000, and converted it into a prison. The first prisoners, a group of 120, entered the prison on December 9, 1861, and by May of 1862 there were 1,400 men held there. As time passed, disloyal Confederates, Confederate deserters, Confederate criminals, and civilians joined the Federal prisoners. The Federal decision to quit exchanging prisoners in 1864 and the transfer of prisoners to Salisbury from other prisons resulted in the population growing to 5,000 by October 1864. By November, the population had doubled to 10,000, although the facility had originally been intended to handle a quarter of that number. Conditions rapidly worsened, and the death rate skyrocketed from 2 to 28 percent.

In the waning days of the war, a new exchange program led to Salisbury's prisoners being shipped to Wilmington and Richmond. The prison then became a supply depot and held no prisoners when Major General George Stoneman Jr. arrived there on April 12, 1865.

Salisbury Prison had a total of nine commandants throughout its history, including Major John Henry Gee, who in 1866 was tried for war crimes stemming from his treatment of prisoners. He was found innocent, unlike the only other Confederate prison commandant brought to trial, Henry Wirz of Andersonville, who was convicted and hanged.

Below: *In spite of the somewhat idyllic depiction here of Salisbury in 1863, Confederate prisons quickly became overcrowded and conditions steadily declined.*

SCALAWAGS

Even more hated throughout the former Confederate states than carpetbaggers were scalawags, native Southerners who sided with the Republicans and freedmen politically. Scalawags were considered traitors by traditional white Southerners and vilified as "white negroes." Like the carpetbaggers, scalawags were a diverse lot that defied the standard stereotypical characterization. Their ranks included wartime Unionists as well as secessionists, soulless opportunists, and realists with a vision for a modernized "New South." What united them all was the conviction that their interests lay with the Republicans.

Noted scalawags include James L. Alcorn, a cotton black marketeer during the war who afterward manipulated the African American vote to become governor of Mississippi. Less sinister was Lieutenant General James Longstreet who, in spite of his wartime service, was labeled a scalawag by many when he joined the Republican Party. As with the carpetbaggers, scalawags came under increasing attack from the Ku Klux Klan and similar groups and individuals.

SECESSION

Secession, the actual withdrawing of a state from the Union, was the result of a lengthy process by which the Southern states felt increasingly at odds with the larger United States. Events like the Nullification Crisis, the Missouri Compromise, the Wilmot Proviso, the Compromise of 1850, the Fugitive

Right: *News of Lincoln's election prompted secessionist rallies throughout the South, including this one in Savannah, Georgia.*

Above: *This cartoon depicts the battle of wills between the outgoing Buchanan administration determined to preserve the Union and South Carolina's effort to foment secessionist sentiment.*

Slave Law, and the Dred Scott case all inched the United States closer and closer to crisis. The election of President Abraham Lincoln finally convinced the Deep South states that the differences were irreconcilable. The second round of states to leave the Union pondered secession longer, but ultimately made their decision based on

Lincoln's call for volunteers after Fort Sumter.

Secession occurred in the following sequence:
South Carolina—December 20, 1860
Mississippi—January 9, 1861
Florida—January 10, 1861
Alabama—January 11, 1861
Georgia—January 19, 1861
Louisiana—January 26, 1861
Texas—February 1, 1861
Virginia—April 17, 1861
Arkansas—May 6, 1861
North Carolina—May 20, 1861
Tennessee—June 8, 1861

SECESSIONVILLE, BATTLE OF

- ❖ DATE: June 16, 1862
- ❖ LOCATION: Charleston, South Carolina
- ❖ FORCE UNDER EVANS (C): 2,000
- ❖ FORCE UNDER BENHAM (U.S.): 6,600
- ❖ CASUALTIES: 204 (C); 685 (U.S.)

The defenses surrounding Charleston, South Carolina, were among the toughest the Confederacy had to offer, but the Federals thought they had discovered an opening on May 16, 1862, when Robert Smalls, a twenty-three-year-old slave employed by the Confederates as the pilot of the *Planter*, escaped with his vessel and brought news that the Confederates had abandoned their positions guarding the seaward approaches to James Island. This development left Charleston vulnerable to an attack from the rear across the island. Standing in the way was the small command of Colonel Thomas G. Lamar near Secessionville, a community whose name stemmed from a time when a group of young married planters "seceded" from the older people of the area.

Admiral Samuel F. Du Pont immediately saw the opportunity for a coup de main joint operation to seize Charleston, and on June 2 he landed two of Major General David Hunter's divisions, backed by considerable naval support, on James Island. However, instead of pushing forward against the meager Confederate resistance, Hunter convinced himself he was grossly outnumbered. He ordered Brigadier General Henry W. Benham, the commander of the force, to not attack until ordered. For two weeks the Federals idled away their advantage while the Confederates reinforced the island. When Benham finally disobeyed his orders and attacked on June 16, he was badly defeated. Fearing a Confederate counterattack, Hunter ordered the evacuation of James Island and relieved Benham for disobeying orders.

SEDDON, JAMES A. (1815–80)

James A. Seddon was a Virginia congressman until 1851, when he resigned due to ill health. During the secession crisis he was a Virginia delegate to the failed Washington peace conference. He served in the First Confederate Congress until he became secretary of war on November 21, 1862. Although President Jefferson Davis was not prone to seek counsel from his cabinet, Seddon was successful in seeing the war in the bigger picture and was able to create the Department of the West. He was less successful in administrative matters and failed to coordinate logistical operations or gain Davis's cooperation. Seddon's health continued to plague him, and he resigned on February 16, 1865.

SEMMES, RAPHAEL (1809–77)

Raphael Semmes was a Marylander who became a midshipman in 1826 and served in the navy during the Mexican War, about which he wrote in *The Campaign of General Scott* and *Service Afloat and Ashore During the Mexican War*. He resigned from the U.S. Navy as a commander on February 15, 1861, and went to Montgomery, Alabama, then the Confederate capital. President Jefferson Davis sent Semmes north to purchase war materiel before

Above: *Raphael Semmes, known as the "Wolf of the Deep," captained the* Alabama, *the Confederacy's most successful commerce raider.*

hostilities actually commenced, and Semmes went to New York and New England, returning with percussion caps and thousands of pounds of powder.

Semmes was commissioned as a commander and placed in charge of the Lighthouse Bureau until he converted a former packet steamer, the *Havana*, into a commerce raider, rechristened the *Sumter*. Semmes ran through the blockade and sailed on a six-month cruise that took eighteen prizes, and then he abandoned his ship at Gibraltar and headed for England. There he became captain of the *Alabama*, the Confederacy's most famous commerce raider.

From September 1862 until June 1864, Semmes wreaked havoc, capturing or destroying sixty-nine ships, including the *Hatteras*, which he sank off Galveston, Texas, on January 11, 1863. His streak finally ended when the *Kearsarge* sank him off of Cherbourg, France. Semmes escaped aboard an English yacht and made his way back to the

Confederacy, where he was promoted to rear admiral. He took command of the James River Squadron until the Federal advance on Richmond forced its destruction. When the Davis administration fled to Danville, Virginia, Semmes followed, arriving on April 3, 1865, with a contingent of 400 sailors. Davis made Semmes a brigadier general and ordered him to prepare to defend the new Confederate capital. Semmes surrendered with General Joseph E. Johnston in North Carolina, using his brigadier general rank on his parole papers to forestall any efforts to try him for his commerce-raiding activities. After the war, he was a professor at the Louisiana Military Institute, a lawyer, and a newspaper editor. He also wrote *The Cruise of the Alabama and Sumter* and *Memoirs of Service Afloat*.

SEVEN DAYS BATTLES (JUNE 25–JULY 1, 1862)

- ❖ DATE: June 25–July 1, 1862
- ❖ LOCATION: Virginia
- ❖ ARMY OF NORTHERN VIRGINIA (C): 92,000
- ❖ ARMY OF THE POTOMAC (U.S.): 104,100
- ❖ CASUALTIES: 20,204 (C); 15,855 (U.S.)

When General Robert E. Lee replaced General Joseph E. Johnston after the Battle of Seven Pines, Lee quickly brought Major General Stonewall Jackson to the outskirts of Richmond from the Shenandoah Valley. The additional manpower allowed Lee to go on the offensive, and, in a series of hard-fought battles collectively known as the Seven Days, Lee defeated Major General George B. McClellan and forced him to

Above: *The Battle of Gaines' Mill inflicted the most casualties of any of the Seven Days Battles. In spite of the costs, the battle was a Confederate victory because it convinced McClellan to abandon the Peninsula Campaign.*

abandon his Peninsula Campaign.

When Major General Jeb Stuart returned from his ride around McClellan's army on June 15, 1862, he informed Lee that it was possible to get around the Federal right flank and threaten McClellan's Richmond and York River Railroad supply line. Armed with this information, Lee told Jackson, "The sooner you unite with this army the better." Jackson hurried south, but he was exhausted from his Shenandoah Valley Campaign, and his performance during the Seven Days would show it.

CONFEDERATE PLAN

Lee's plan was for Jackson to march down from a point due north of Mechanicsville and attack Major General Fitz John Porter from the flank and rear. Major General A. P. Hill would lead an attack across Mechanicsville Bridge that would be joined by Major Generals D. H. Hill and James Longstreet. Before Lee could put his plan in effect, McClellan launched a small, inconsequential attack on June 25 against Oak Grove, a wood in the area of Williamsburg Road and the Richmond and York River Railroad. This would become the opening battle of the Seven Days.

Oak Grove did nothing to thwart Lee's planned attack at Mechanicsville, but Jackson's uncharacteristic slowness did. When Jackson failed to show up as planned, A. P. Hill grew impatient and initiated the attack. The result was an unsupported attack against a strong defense

rather than the turning movement Lee had hoped for. In four futile assaults, the Confederates lost more than 1,500 dead and wounded. The Federals lost fewer than 400.

In spite of the victory, the ever-cautious McClellan felt both his supply line and position were threatened. He began a retreat, ordering Porter to pull back to a defendable position covering the Chickahominy River bridges. Porter ended up at an elevation that was known locally as Turkey Hill, another excellent defensive position.

Lee continued with his plans to threaten McClellan's communications with the railroad, ordering A. P. Hill and Longstreet to occupy the Federals from the front while Jackson and D. H. Hill would envelop the rear. Again Jackson was slow in arriving and foiled Lee's plans. The ensuing Battle of Gaines' Mill degenerated into a slugfest as Lee fed reinforcements into the fight as soon as they arrived, and Porter, without much help from McClellan, used his superior position to hang on for dear life. Finally, an attack spearheaded by Brigadier General John Bell Hood broke the Federal line. With his defense cracked, Porter had no choice but to retreat.

Above: In the Seven Days Battles, Robert E. Lee was frustrated in his attempts to destroy the Federal army. One problem was Stonewall Jackson's uncharacteristic hesitancy at White Oak Swamp.

Gaines' Mill was the largest and most costly battle not just of the Seven Days, but also of the entire Peninsula Campaign. A total of 96,100 men had been on the field. In less than nine hours of fighting, Porter had suffered 6,837 total casualties and Lee 7,993. The loss caused McClellan to announce his plans to abandon the campaign and shift his base to Harrison's Landing,

Below: This contemporary sketch shows the fighting at Mechanicsville (also known as Beaver Dam Creek) between a Federal division under McCall and Confederate forces under Jackson.

where he would be under the protection of Flag Officer Louis M. Goldsborough's gunboats.

LEE DISPATCHES STUART

Unsure of McClellan's intentions, Lee sent Brigadier General Jeb Stuart on a reconnaissance. Stuart brought back word that McClellan was in full-scale retreat, and Lee set out to intercept the fleeing Federals. Major General John B. Magruder caught up with McClellan's rear guard on June 29 at Allen's Farm, two miles short of Savage's Station, but instead of attacking, Magruder originally established a defense. He eventually launched an uninspired attack, made worse by another failure of Jackson to arrive in time. To Lee's great frustration, the Federals were allowed to escape.

Lee caught up with the Federals again on June 30 at Glendale and had an excellent chance to destroy McClellan. However, the Confederates were again unable to coordinate their attacks, in part because Jackson took such a long time to cross White Oak Swamp. McClellan continued his retreat to Malvern Hill, another formidable defensive position, where on July 1 the Federal artillery defeated a Confederate attack, enabling McClellan to complete his withdrawal to Harrison's Landing and entrench.

The Seven Days Battles were over. Lee had turned back McClellan's attack and saved Richmond, but had been unable to do the greater damage he had hoped for.

SEVEN PINES, BATTLE OF

❖ DATE: May 31–June 1, 1862

❖ LOCATION: Henrico County, Virginia

❖ ARMY OF THE POTOMAC (C): 41,816

❖ ARMY OF NORTHERN VIRGINIA (U.S.): 44,944

❖ CASUALTIES: 6,134 (C); 5,031 (U.S.)

On May 28, 1862, General Joseph E. Johnston learned that Major General Stonewall Jackson's Shenandoah Valley Campaign had caused so much concern for the safety of Washington that President Abraham Lincoln had withheld Major General Irvin McDowell's corps from joining Major General George B. McClellan's Peninsula Campaign. Up to this point, Johnston had been completely on the defensive in responding to

Above: *The most significant outcome of the Battle of Seven Pines was the replacement of Joseph Johnston as commander in chief by Robert E. Lee after Johnston was wounded.*

McClellan's threat to Richmond. This news changed the strategic situation dramatically, and Johnston was now in a position to act more aggressively. The result was the Battle of Seven Pines, sometimes called the Battle of Fair Oaks, from May 31 to June 1.

Johnston learned from reconnaissance that there were two vulnerable Federal corps south of the Chickahominy River. His plan was to isolate and destroy these corps, but he mismanaged the battle, issuing unclear instructions and failing to synchronize his forces. Over two days of fighting, the Confederates lost 6,134 killed, wounded, or missing, and the Federals 5,031. Johnston accomplished none of his objectives, and after midnight on June 2, the

Confederates retreated to the west. During the fighting, Johnston was wounded, and on June 1, General Robert E. Lee arrived on the battlefield with orders from President Jefferson Davis to take command.

SHELBY, JOSEPH O. (1830–97)

Before the Civil War, Joseph O. Shelby was a wealthy landowner and businessman in Missouri. During the "Bleeding Kansas" era, he actively sided with the proslavery cause. At the start of the Civil War, he organized a cavalry company and proceeded to fight in every major campaign west of the Mississippi River. He was promoted to brigadier general on December 15, 1863, and conducted a series of operations in conjunction with Major General Sterling Price's raid into Missouri in September

Above: *The First Battle of Winchester (May 25, 1862) was one of several fought during Stonewall Jackson's masterful Shenandoah Valley Campaign.*

and October 1864. When the war ended, Shelby fled to Mexico with 600 men on a military expedition in support of Emperor Maximilian. After the death of Maximilian ensured any colonization effort would fail, Shelby returned to Missouri. In 1893 President Grover Cleveland appointed him U.S. marshal.

SHENANDOAH VALLEY CAMPAIGN

❖ DATE: March–June, 1862

❖ LOCATION: Virginia

❖ ARMY OF THE VALLEY (C): 17,000

❖ FOUR FIELD ARMIES (U.S.): 60,000

❖ CASUALTIES: 2,691 (C); 5,416 (U.S.)

On March 7, 1862, General Joseph E. Johnston ordered all of his troops east of the Blue Ridge Mountains, some 42,000 effectives, to withdraw to the Rappahannock River, nearly half the distance to Richmond. Only Major General Stonewall Jackson's 5,400 men would remain in the Shenandoah Valley to threaten the right flank of any Federal advance. With this small force, Jackson used superior generalship, interior lines, and hard marching to not only defeat portions of four Federal armies totaling 60,000 men in the Shenandoah Valley but also disrupt Major General George B. McClellan on the Virginia Peninsula.

The Shenandoah Valley was of great strategic importance both as an agricultural center and as a potential Confederate avenue of approach into Washington. Before McClellan departed on his Peninsula Campaign, President Abraham Lincoln had ordered him to leave behind an adequate force to guarantee Washington's safety. McClellan assigned this responsibility to Major General Nathaniel P. Banks, but otherwise did very little to placate Lincoln's concerns.

In fact, McClellan was much more concerned with building his force on the Peninsula than he was with anything else. As soon as he could, McClellan wanted Banks to join him, and indeed, by March 20, Brigadier General Alpheus S. Williams and his 7,000 men had started to Manassas and Brigadier General James Shields's 9,000-man division had dropped back from Strasburg and was prepared to follow. Because Jackson's main mission in the valley was to prevent Banks from joining McClellan, Jackson had to check these movements. The result was the Battle of Kernstown on March 23. Although a tactical defeat for Jackson, his aggressive action renewed Lincoln's fears for Washington's safety and caused Federal authorities to halt plans to shift forces to McClellan. Instead, Banks was held in place, Brigadier General Louis Blenker's division was withdrawn from McClellan and sent to oppose Jackson, and Major

Left: *A contemporary sketch showing the Battle of Cross Keys, June 8, 1862. After checking John Frémont at this battle, Dick Ewell moved to Port Republic to support Stonewall Jackson.*

General Irvin McDowell's First Corps was withheld from McClellan. The Federals then established three separate and independent commands: McDowell's Department of the Rappahannock, Banks's Department of the Shenandoah, and Major General John C. Frémont's Mountain Department. These three commanders reported directly to Washington, and no general on the scene was charged with synchronizing their operations. This uncoordinated command structure would ultimately contribute to Jackson's success.

In April, Major General Richard S. Ewell arrived to reinforce Jackson with 8,500 men. Jackson also received permission to use Brigadier General Edward "Allegheny" Johnson's small division, which brought Jackson's total strength to 17,000. Jackson left Ewell to hold Banks in place and then, keeping his own plans secret even from his subordinates, went on the move.

On May 8, he surprised Banks by suddenly appearing at McDowell, thirty-two miles west of Stanton. There he defeated Frémont's 6,000 men,

preventing them from combining forces with Banks.

By mid-May, part of Banks's army was again preparing to depart to join McClellan outside Richmond. Jackson used a cavalry screen to make Banks think he was headed toward Strasburg, and then turned unexpectedly across the Massanuttens, joined with Ewell at Luray, and with their combined 16,000 men struck the unsuspecting 1,000 Federals at Front Royal on May 23. Jackson tore through the town, and the Federals fled toward Strasburg. Then Banks and Jackson began a race to Winchester. On May 25, the two armies collided in what became

another victory for Jackson.

These events were occurring right as McClellan's efforts were beginning to bear fruit on the Peninsula. Indeed, on May 18, McClellan had received a telegram from Secretary of War Edwin M. Stanton announcing that McDowell's First Corps would be marching from Fredericksburg, where it had been held previously for fear of Washington's safety, and would soon join him. But Jackson's success in the valley was beginning to have a much broader impact. President Lincoln, who had never been comfortable with McClellan's provisions for Washington's safety, was now seriously worried. On May 24, Lincoln telegraphed McClellan, "In consequence of Gen. Banks' critical position I have been compelled to suspend Gen.

Below: *The Confederates dug trenches throughout the Shenandoah Valley, including these remnants of what was once Fort Edward Johnson.*

Above: *By burning the bridge at Cross Keys, Dick Ewell prevented John C. Frémont's troops from assisting James Shields at Port Republic.*

McDowell's movement to join you." In spite of protests from both McDowell and McClellan, the order stood.

Lincoln and Stanton became obsessed with the idea of trapping Jackson, and they ordered McDowell and his 40,000-man corps to join Frémont's at Strasburg. At the beginning of June, Banks, Frémont, and Shields started converging on Jackson from the west, north, and east in the hopes of bagging him at Strasburg.

"FOOT CAVALRY"

To take full advantage of his central position in the valley, Jackson had developed an excellent routine for his marches, and his command had become so mobile, it was nicknamed the "foot cavalry." Now Jackson used these techniques to march his men fifty miles in two days to escape the Federal trap closing in on Strasburg and then fell back to Harrisonburg. Frémont and Shields pursued on parallel roads that would eventually meet at Port Republic. Jackson positioned Ewell four miles to the northwest at Cross Keys and stationed his own men on the rolling hills of Port Republic.

On June 8, Ewell handily repulsed Frémont's weak attack at Cross Keys and then withdrew during the night to assist Jackson at Port Republic. There, Jackson was in a close fight with Shields, but Ewell arrived just in time to turn the tide. Frémont could hear the fighting and took up the pursuit, but Ewell's rear guard had burned the bridge Frémont needed to cross. Frémont could only watch helplessly as Jackson and Ewell defeated Shields and forced him to withdraw.

In the meantime, General Robert E. Lee, then serving as President Jefferson Davis's military adviser, had realized how Jackson's success in the valley could be used to threaten McClellan's plans for the Peninsula. After Lee replaced the wounded Johnston as army commander in Virginia, he put his ideas in action, communicating to Jackson plans to unite their two forces to go on the offensive on the Peninsula. On June 18, Jackson began moving his men toward Lee, where they fought in the Seven Days Battles.

SHILOH, BATTLE OF

❖ DATE: April 6–7, 1862

❖ LOCATION: Hardin County, Tennessee

❖ ARMY OF THE MISSISSIPPI (C): 44,000

❖ ARMIES OF THE TENNESSEE AND THE OHIO (U.S.): 62,000

❖ CASUALTIES: 11,694 (C); 13,047 (U.S.)

The Battle of Shiloh was a two-day struggle for control of western Tennessee that began on April 6, 1862, with a surprise Confederate attack by General Albert Sidney Johnston's Army of the Mississippi. In spite of this initial Confederate success, Major General Ulysses S. Grant, commander of the Army of the Tennessee, rallied his forces, and, after receiving reinforcements, routed the Confederates on the second day of the battle. The defeat dashed Confederate hopes of recovering the initiative in western and middle Tennessee, and thus of regaining control of Nashville and the state's iron-producing areas.

After Grant's victories at Forts Henry and Donelson in February

1862, Johnston withdrew from Tennessee and concentrated his forces at Corinth, Mississippi. At the same time, Grant had assembled some 45,000 men at Pittsburg Landing, Tennessee, about twenty miles northeast of Corinth, where he would wait for the arrival of Major General Don Carlos Buell's Army of the Ohio from Nashville. Perhaps a mile and a half southwest of Pittsburg Landing lay Shiloh Church, the feature that would give the battle its common name.

SURPRISE OFFENSIVE

Grant's men were camped for administrative convenience rather than defense because Grant assumed the next action would be his attacking Corinth. He never considered Johnston might launch his own offensive. However, when Johnston received word that Buell was fast approaching, he decided to strike before the two Federal armies could unite. Johnston laid out the broad concept for an attack that

envisioned turning the Federal left and threatening Grant's communications with the river, but he left his second in command, General Pierre Gustave Toutant Beauregard, to determine the exact details. Instead of the turning movement Johnston intended, Beauregard developed a plan for a frontal attack.

The Confederates executed a painfully slow march from Corinth that, by the evening of April 5, brought them within a half-mile of the Federal outposts. The armies had exchanged fire during the Confederate advance, but the Federal high command remained oblivious to any danger. Instead, the Confederate contacts were attributed to reconnaissance patrols rather than any impending attack.

To the Federals' surprise, Major General William J. Hardee's Third Army Corps brushed aside a small Federal patrol before dawn on April 6. Behind Hardee marched Major General Braxton Bragg's Second Army Corps, followed by

Major General Leonidas Polk's First Army Corps and then Brigadier General John C. Breckinridge's Reserve Corps. Hardee's and Bragg's men were deployed in line of battle while Polk's and Breckinridge's advanced in column formation.

FRONTAL ATTACK

The massed linear formations of Hardee and Bragg had little room to maneuver in the thick terrain. The result was a frontal attack in which it appeared that the Confederates hoped to use sheer numbers to simply overpower the Federals. Beauregard had made no provision for placing a large number of troops on the Confederate right, as Johnston's plan had required. In fact, Beauregard appears to have never intended anything but a frontal attack.

Below: *Albert Sidney Johnston's planned turning movement developed into an unimaginative frontal attack during the Battle of Shiloh.*

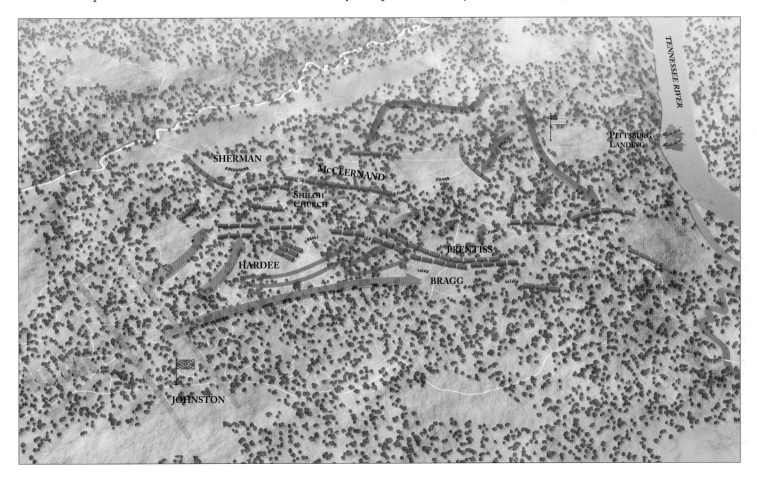

The Confederate attack hit the part of the Federal line occupied by Brigadier General Benjamin M. Prentiss's Sixth Division of some 5,400 effectives. In spite of being outnumbered, Prentiss was able to repulse as many as eleven piecemealed and uncoordinated assaults, buying the Federals valuable time to recover from their initial surprise. The fury of the fighting in this area lent it the name the "Hornet's Nest."

While his men bludgeoned themselves against Prentiss, Johnston noticed a ten-acre peach orchard just to the right of the Hornet's Nest. The rear of the peach orchard was on the Sunken Road, and Federal troops occupied

Below: One of the reasons Pierre Gustave Toutant Beauregard gave for halting action on the first day of the Battle of Shiloh was the presence of Federal gunboats, shown in the distance in this contemporary rendering of the battle.

a line to its front. Johnston personally led a 5,000-man attack that forced the Federals through the peach orchard and back to the cover in the Sunken Road, but the Confederate success was a costly one. Johnston was struck by a minié ball, but his high-top boot concealed the wound site, and he needlessly bled to death around 2:30 p.m.

Beauregard assumed command, and continued the Confederates' unimaginative attack. Instead of turning the crumbling Federal flanks and driving on to Pittsburg Landing, he remained focused on the Federal center. However, rather than the ineffective infantry charges of previous efforts, the Confederates attacked with the support of sixty-two massed guns, at the time the largest concentration of artillery in American military history. Aided by this firepower, the Confederates succeeded in forcing the regiment defending the

Federal left to withdraw back to Pittsburg Landing.

This opening of the Federal left was exactly what Johnston had envisioned in his initial attack plan, and a massive Confederate push there may have successfully turned the Federal position. Instead, the attackers moved to their left, back toward the Hornet's Nest. With attacks now coming from the front and both sides, Prentiss's gallant defense had taken all it could stand, and the Federal line began to give way. By 5:30 p.m., Prentiss was surrounded and compelled to surrender, but not before he had halted the Confederate advance for several critical hours while the Federal line elsewhere was given a chance to stabilize.

GRANT FALLS BACK
While Prentiss had been delaying the Confederate attack, much of the rest of Grant's army was falling back to Pittsburg Landing. Initially

caught off guard, Grant rallied and began organizing the stragglers into units and forming a new defensive line. Eventually he built a line three miles long that ran inland at a right angle from the Tennessee River above Pittsburg Landing, northwest toward Owl Creek. There he held on until reinforcements from Buell's army began arriving at 7:00 p.m.

Grant was now beginning to sense that the tide was turning in the Federals' favor. While the Federals were getting stronger with the arrival of every one of Buell's 35,000 troops, the Confederate attack clearly had culminated. Beauregard, some two miles from the battlefront, did not have Grant's clear picture and believed the Confederate attack had carried the day. He directed Bragg "that the pursuit be stopped; the victory is complete; it is needless to expose our men to the fire of the gunboats." Bragg protested, and many others have likewise decried

Beauregard's decision as the great "Lost Opportunity" to press on to decisive victory.

As both armies suffered through a miserable night, Grant steeled his resolve. In a famous exchange, Major General William T. Sherman began a conversation saying, "Well, Grant, we've had the devil's own day of it, haven't we?" "Yes," Grant replied and after a pause added, "Lick 'em tomorrow, though." Such was the essence of Grant's generalship and approach to modern war. It was the deciding factor at Shiloh.

Grant told Sherman he planned to attack at dawn, hoping to strike before Beauregard had a chance to. Without any formal plan of attack, the Federals crashed into the Confederate line on April 7 and enjoyed quick success. The numbers were clearly on the Federal side. Buell's reinforcements had brought Grant's strength back up to where it had been the first day, while the previous fighting had reduced

Above: *The carnage on both sides as a result of the Battle of Shiloh was devastating. Shiloh was the bloodiest battle in American history up to that time, with almost 25,000 casualties.*

Beauregard's numbers by half. The battle followed the odds, with Grant easily retaking most of the ground he had lost earlier. By 2:30 p.m., Beauregard had decided to withdraw back toward Corinth. Grant's men were too exhausted to pursue effectively.

The Battle of Shiloh took American warfare to a new level of magnitude and lethality. It was the biggest battle fought in North America to that date. Of the 62,000 Federals engaged, 13,047 were killed, wounded, or missing. The Confederates suffered 11,694 casualties from their 44,000-man army. Moreover, by not destroying Grant's army, the Confederate forces in the west were now committed to a war of attrition that the South lacked the resources to win.

SHIP ISLAND, FEDERAL OCCUPATION OF (SEPTEMBER 17, 1861)

Ship Island is a low, sandy, relatively desolate island off the shore of Biloxi, Mississippi. Its utility to the Federals was as a base to support blockade operations in the Gulf of Mexico, as well as a potential jumping-off point for an assault against either Mobile, Alabama, or New Orleans, Louisiana. In spite of the island's strategic importance, the Confederates did not seriously try to defend it. The Federals occupied it without resistance on September 17, 1861.

Federal navy forces commanded by Admiral David G. Farragut and army forces commanded by Major General Benjamin F. Butler quickly descended on Ship Island and began preparing for an attack on New Orleans that finally occurred

Below: A sketch of Ship Island. In spite of the importance of Ship Island in relation to New Orleans and Mobile, the Confederates did not put much effort into its defense.

on April 25, 1862. In addition to its role in supporting this operation and the blockade, Ship Island served as a prison and detention center. Once Butler began his heavy-handed occupation of New Orleans, many uncooperative Confederates were imprisoned at Ship Island.

SHIPBUILDING

The Confederate navy entertained no grand design of challenging the powerful Federal navy. Instead it wished merely to prevent the capture of a few strategic locations and to hold open or reopen ports to foreign commerce. However, even these modest objectives would require the Confederacy to acquire or build ships.

Because of the limited domestic shipbuilding capability, much energy went into purchasing ships overseas, and the energetic James D. Bulloch spearheaded an effort that resulted in the acquisition of the British-built cruisers *Florida*, *Alabama*, and *Shenandoah* and the French-built ram *Stonewall*. Domestic production, however, was plagued by shortages of facilities,

materials, and labor that led to very limited results.

Secretary of the Navy Stephen R. Mallory decided that the best use of the Confederacy's limited resources was to build a few powerful ironclads to wreak havoc with the Federal navy's wooden ships. The initial effort came when Confederate engineers raised the *Merrimack*, a 350-ton, forty-gun U.S. steam frigate that the Federals burned and scuttled when they abandoned Gosport Navy Yard on April 20, 1861. Naval Constructor John Luke Porter and Lieutenant John Mercer Brooke began converting the hulk into what would become the Confederacy's first ironclad, the *Virginia*. In August 1861, the Confederate Congress also appropriated $160,000 for "the construction, equipment, and armament of two ironclad gunboats for the defense of the Mississippi and the city of Memphis." As a result, construction got underway at Memphis for vessels to be named the *Alabama* and *Tennessee*. The bill also appropriated $800,000 "for defenses of New Orleans," and, as a result, Asa and Nelson Tift were awarded a contract to begin constructing the *Mississippi* at New Orleans. On September 18, work began on a fourth ironclad, the *Louisiana*, under the control of E. C. Murray at New Orleans.

As an alternative to Mallory's plans to focus on ironclads, Matthew F. Maury proposed building a fleet of small wooden gunboats designed for river and harbor defense. Maury was convinced the South lacked the resources necessary to build large ships, and his Spartan designs were intended to be built economically and quickly. In December 1861, Congress authorized $2 million to produce not more than 100 ships according to Maury's specifications. Maury took charge of construction,

and keels were laid for fifteen vessels in shipyards on the Rappahannock, Pamunkey, and York rivers, as well as in Norfolk, but only two—the *Hampton* and the *Nansemond*—were completed. The others were burned to prevent capture.

In May 1862, Mallory succeeded in diverting what remained of Maury's original $2 million to ironclad production, but he also embarked on his own program to build wooden ships, which resulted in the *Pee Dee* being built at Mars Bluff, South Carolina, the *Macon* at Savannah, Georgia, the *Chattahoochee* at Safford County, Georgia, and the *Morgan* and the *Gaines* at Mobile. Mallory also was able to get contracts for the construction of at least twelve more ironclads. In fact, although a few more wooden ships would be built from the spring of 1862 until the end of the war, the Confederate shipbuilding program would focus on ironclads. It was a disparate effort that included ships built under the direction of the navy, the War Department, several state governments, and private citizens. Early losses of Pensacola and Norfolk made New Orleans the Confederacy's most important shipbuilding center, but activity

there was also an example of the decentralized nature of the effort. By 1861, every shipyard in New Orleans was busy building, converting, or repairing some type of warlike vessel, but few were actually earmarked for the fledgling Confederate navy. While the *Louisiana* and *Mississippi* were being built under Mallory's contracts, a third ironclad, the *Manassas*, was a private enterprise built to be a profit-making privateer.

A LACK OF EFFICIENCY

The construction was in most cases a confused and competing effort that did not use efficiently the scarce Confederate resources that had been made even more limited by the Federal blockade. By sealing the mouth of the Mississippi, the Federals forced the New Orleans shipbuilders to bring the iron and machinery they needed from Virginia and the eastern Confederacy by rail. The rickety Southern railroads were inadequate to transport such loads efficiently. For example, construction of the *Mississippi* was delayed while a Richmond firm shipped the propeller shaft across the Confederacy to New Orleans.

Nonetheless, New Orleans was a hubbub of shipbuilding activity, and fears of Confederate ironclads being built there did much to accelerate Federal plans to attack the city.

With the loss of Memphis, Selma, Alabama, about 130 miles north of Mobile along the Alabama River, became a critical facility. Richard Bassett established a shipyard there, and although the equipment was rudimentary, the proximity to the iron mills at Brierfield and rolling mills at Birmingham and Atlanta made the location convenient. Another important nearby facility was the Confederate States Naval Iron Works at Columbus, Georgia.

Mallory had contracted for two ironclads, the *Huntsville* and *Tuscaloosa*, to be built in Selma, but these projects faltered in order to give priority to the *Tennessee*, which was launched from there in February 1863 and used in the defense of Mobile. Selma was also the site for the final outfitting of the *Nashville*, an ironclad that had been built at an improvised shipyard at Cypress Creek inlet, just above the city wharf at Montgomery. Other efforts at different sites along the Alabama and Tombigbee rivers also succumbed to a lack of resources, especially shortages of iron.

CORNFIELD SHIPYARD

Some Confederate shipbuilding efforts labored under seemingly impossible conditions. The *Albemarle* was built at Edwards Ferry, North Carolina, in a cornfield beside the Roanoke River. Metal was so scarce that Commander James Cooke had to scour the local countryside looking for any scraps he could find, a practice that earned him the nickname

"Ironmonger Captain." What made these hardships palatable was the fact that the waters at Edwards Ferry were too shallow to accommodate the Federal gunboats that routinely patrolled eastern North Carolina. The construction of the *Albemarle* is a testimony to the Herculean efforts of the Confederate shipbuilders, but also an example of the impact of the Federal control of the Confederate coastline and its more advanced facilities.

In the final analysis, Mallory's ironclad program was simply too ambitious for the Confederacy's meager resources. The result was that many vessels were begun but never completed, and even those that were finished had serious deficiencies. Mallory's initiative also motivated the Federal navy to embark on its own ironclad building program, an effort the more industrialized North was much better resourced to undertake. The result was a tremendous mismatch between the two navies.

SLAVERY

As the American colonists tried to meet the labor requirements of the New World, they first turned to indentured servants. When this source proved inadequate to meet demand, the colonists began importing slaves from Africa. Although the first slaves were introduced as early as 1619, significant numbers did not arrive until after 1697. By this time there was already a strong slave trade infrastructure built up in Africa based on centuries of internal African trading and the Islamic slave trade. This already established system was able to easily expand to meet the new demand in America. During the eighteenth century, some 500,000 slaves were imported to America, with a peak period in the 1780s when some 88,000 slaves

reached America annually. While opposition to the institution of slavery was slower in developing, opposition to the slave trade crystallized in 1807 when Britain, the dominant world power, abolished the slave trade. The United States voted to abolish the trade that same year, but the legislation was not scheduled to go into effect until 1808. In spite of the prohibition against the slave trade, enough male and female slaves had been imported to the United States to sustain slavery domestically by reproduction. Some illegal slave trading also continued.

The climate of the North precluded the large agricultural plantations of the South, so slavery was much less profitable and there

Above: *This idyllic depiction of contented slaves and of a homogeneous Southern way of life stood in sharp contrast to the cruelty many slaves experienced.*

were far lower numbers of slaves there. In the South, however, slavery became critical, first to the economy and then to the region's social and political fabric. Expanding cotton markets and improved textile machinery led to a dramatic increase in demand for cotton, which led to a proportionate rise in prices. Tobacco and rice production was also very profitable and as also dependent on slave labor. These developments brought wealth to the South, specifically to large landowners. The result was that Southerners came to believe slavery was essential to economic prosperity, and the institution thus had to be protected.

A variety of arguments were used to defend slavery. It was justified on biblical grounds both because the apostle Paul seemed to condone it and as a result of the curse of the "sons of Ham." Slavery was argued as being in the best interests of the "racially inferior" African Americans because it introduced them to Christianity and other blessings of Western civilization. Proponents of the "New Athens" school, such as George Fitzhugh, argued that slavery was necessary to free white men from common labors so they could devote their energies to art, philosophy, and other higher pursuits. The result was a South that was considered culturally superior to the materialistic North. Thus the South began to believe that slavery was not just critical to its economy, but to its society as well.

Because the large plantation owners controlled most of the agricultural South's wealth, this slave-owning class emerged as the elite in Southern society and came to dominate the political process as well. Defending slavery and protecting opportunities for its expansion came to be the primary concern of Southern political activity.

Issues of expansion of slavery to the west, the handling of fugitive slaves, and constitutional protections for slavery dominated Southern politics, and men like John C. Calhoun and Jefferson Davis earned their reputations as defenders of slavery—and therefore defenders of the South— against what was perceived by many as an increasingly hostile and domineering

North. The collective result of all these developments was that Southerners, whether they held slaves or not, considered slavery to be critical to maintaining the way of life they had come to value.

SYSTEMS OF LABOR

Slave labor was organized in either the timework or gang system common on Mississippi cotton plantations or the task system common to South Carolina and Georgia rice fields. Under the gang system, slaves of approximately equal ability were grouped together to form work parties that labored from sunrise to sundown, regardless of productivity. Under the task system, slaves were given daily assignments and work continued until the task was completed. A white overseer closely supervised all slave labor. The overseer was critical in executing the desires of the plantation owner and ensuring discipline, productivity, and compliance. Because overseers were

so grossly outnumbered by the slaves, a trusted African American driver would often be employed to supervise specific tasks in order to allow the overseer to focus his attention elsewhere. Both overseers and drivers made liberal use of the whip to ensure compliance.

In spite of this supervision, the fear of slave uprisings and revolts was ever present in the minds of white Southerners. In some areas of the cotton-rich Mississippi Delta, slaves comprised 75 percent of the population. Slave revolts and plots of insurrection, such as those associated with Denmark Vesey in 1822, Nat Turner in 1831, and John Murrell in 1835, led to strong measures by whites to limit the slaves' ability to assemble and possess weapons. These rules were enforced off the plantation by routine slave patrols.

Below: *A slave auction. Slaves were often separated from their families when they were sold at auctions.*

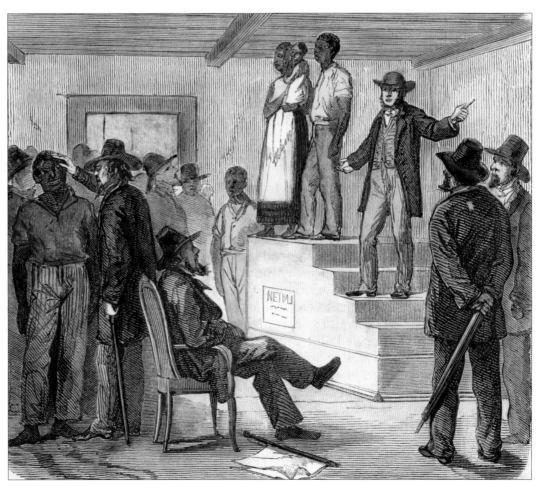

The South staved off what it considered a repeated onslaught of Northern activity to curtail slavery through measures such as the Missouri Compromise, the Kansas–Nebraska Act, and the Compromise of 1850. However, many Southerners interpreted the election of Abraham Lincoln as president in 1860 to mark the ascension to power of a party completely hostile to the Southern interests that were so inexorably intertwined with slavery. Rather than passively await the inevitable attack on their economic, social, and political institutions, many Southerners saw secession as the only option.

SLIDELL, JOHN
(1793–1871)

John Slidell was born in New York, but moved to Louisiana to practice law in New Orleans. In 1845, he acted as America's minister-delegate to Mexico in a diplomatic effort to avoid war. The mission was a disappointing failure, and Slidell returned to Washington to recommend that President James Polk "act with promptness and energy" using military means.

After Mexico, Slidell served as a senator from Louisiana, gained a national reputation as a prominent Democrat, and enjoyed personal prestige during the Buchanan administration. He cast in his lot with Louisiana when the state decided to secede, and in the late summer of 1861, President Jefferson Davis appointed him to the post of commissioner to France. During the transatlantic voyage, Slidell and fellow emissary James Mason became the center of the *Trent* affair that nearly brought Great Britain into the Civil War. That incident peacefully resolved, Slidell arrived in Paris in early February 1862.

Slidell found a cool reception in France, where officials had largely decided not to act on the Confederacy's behalf unless Britain did. Although Lincoln's issuance of the Emancipation Proclamation effectively ended Confederate hopes of European intervention, Slidell continued his diplomatic efforts. As late as March 5, 1865, he had an interview with Napoléon III and found the situation largely unchanged from 1862. "My interview with the Emperor resulted as I supposed it would," Slidell lamented. "He is willing and anxious to act with England but will not move without her." After the war, Slidell remained in exile in France and Britain, where he died in 1871.

SMITH, EDMUND KIRBY (1824–93)

❖ RANK: General

❖ PLACE OF BIRTH: St. Augustine, Florida

❖ EDUCATED: West Point

❖ MILITARY CAREER:
1845–61: Served in U.S. Army in Mexican War
1861: Promoted to lieutenant colonel, then brigadier general after Shenandoah Valley Campaign
1862: Promoted to lieutenant general after success at Battle of Richmond,
1863: Given command of Trans-Mississippi Department

Edmund Kirby Smith graduated from West Point in 1845 and served in Mexico, as a mathematics instructor at West Point, and on the frontier. On the eve of the Civil War, Smith refused to surrender Fort Colorado in Texas to state militia under Colonel Benjamin McCulloch, but he ultimately resigned from the U.S. Army on April 6, 1861, when his native Florida seceded. He was commissioned as a colonel in the Confederate army and then

Above: *Edmund Kirby Smith ended the war in command of an isolated Trans-Mississippi Confederacy with little fighting power.*

promoted to brigadier general on June 17, commanding a brigade at First Manassas. He was promoted to major general on October 11 and given command of a division. In March 1862 he went to Knoxville, Tennessee, to assume command of the Department of East Tennessee. In this capacity, he invaded Kentucky in an operation that was plagued by a lack of unity between Smith and General Braxton Bragg. Smith won a decisive victory at Richmond, Kentucky, on August 30, but the campaign began to unravel shortly afterward. He joined forces with Bragg for the Battle of Perryville on October 8. Although Smith was given the thanks of Congress and promoted to lieutenant general on October 9 as a result of this campaign, the Confederates were forced to withdraw from Kentucky, having achieved little of strategic consequence.

In February 1863 Smith was assigned to the Trans-Mississippi

Department, where he soon replaced Lieutenant General Theophilus H. Holmes as commander. After Vicksburg fell in July, Smith's district was cut off from the eastern Confederacy, and he operated with an unprecedented amount of autonomy, so much so that the area became known as "Kirby Smithdom." He was promoted to general on February 19, 1864, and thwarted Major General Nathaniel P. Banks in the Red River Campaign. As departmental commander, Smith had a quarrelsome relationship with Major General Richard Taylor, and Taylor was eventually given a separate command. Smith surrendered on June 2, 1865, making his the last Confederate army to do so.

After the war, Smith fled to Mexico and then Cuba before returning to the United States in November 1865. He served as president of the University of Nashville from 1870 to 1875 and taught mathematics at the University of the South at Sewanee for eighteen years. Although Smith's February 19, 1864, promotion was never confirmed, he is generally credited as being the last of the Confederacy's full generals to die.

SMITH, GUSTAVUS W. (1821–96)

Gustavus Woodson Smith graduated from West Point in 1842 and was commissioned in the engineers. He provided capable but limited service in the Mexican War, where he served as second in command of an engineering company. He resigned from the army in 1854 to pursue a career in civil engineering, and in this capacity he advanced to the position of commissioner of streets in New York City.

Smith was born in Kentucky, and, like his native state, he initially chose a neutral course early in the Civil War. After five months, he declared himself for the Confederacy and reported to Richmond. He received an appointment as a major general in spite of his rather limited qualifications. Only Albert Sidney Johnston and Leonidas Polk had previously received so high an initial commission, but Smith did not live up to these expectations.

Although personally courageous, Smith was ill-equipped for the responsibilities of high command. When General Joseph E. Johnston was wounded during the Battle of Seven Pines, Smith temporarily assumed command, but was indecisive. When President Jefferson Davis met with Smith to ascertain the situation, Smith was so unimpressive that Davis replaced him with General Robert E. Lee.

Smith was then sent to command the area between the Rappahannock River in Virginia

Above: *Gustavus Woodson Smith briefly assumed command when Joseph E. Johnston was wounded at the Battle of Seven Pines.*

and the Cape Fear River in North Carolina. His being headquartered in Richmond allowed him to serve as interim secretary of war from March 17 to 20, 1862. He resigned from the Confederate army on February 17, 1863, when six other officers were promoted ahead of him to lieutenant general. He served out the remainder of the war in a variety of volunteer, civilian, and state militia positions.

SOCIAL STRUCTURE IN THE SOUTH

Although only 25 percent of all Southerners owned slaves, slavery was the key ingredient in the Southern social structure. Slave ownership enabled the highest class of Southerners to not only prosper economically, but also control most aspects of Southern society. At the other end of the scale of Southern whites, slavery at least provided a buffer between the "poor whites" and the bottom of the social ladder. It was slavery that separated the South from the North, and as a result, historian Gary Gallagher argues that by the time of the Civil War "an entire generation of Southern young men . . . had come of age with a sense of Southern cultural identity, commitment to slaveholding, and a willingness to defend these values against a Northern culture."

At the top of the Southern social hierarchy were the aristocratic planters who owned at least 800 acres of land and maintained a labor force of forty or more slaves. Representing only 8,000 members of a total population of some 6 million whites, these large planters wielded power well out of proportion to their numbers. Indeed, they dominated the political, social, and economic life of the

Above: *This drawing depicts the owner and the overseer of the Buena Vista cotton plantation in Clarke County, Alabama. Overseers were the key to a plantation's success or failure.*

South. Wade Hampton III of South Carolina and Howell Cobb of Georgia are examples of this class.

Second to this elite were the smaller-scale planters who owned 200 acres of land or less and had fewer than forty slaves. Indeed, two-thirds of all Southerners who owned slaves owned fewer than ten. Although this social class totaled some 80,000 members, it still was a small portion of the total Southern population. While these planters did not enjoy the wealth and privilege of the elite, they were socially linked to the higher class and saw them as something to which to aspire.

Next in order was a small professional class of doctors, lawyers, preachers, and the like, as well as a larger group of merchants.

This class provided services to the planters and was on the outskirts of their social circles.

The overwhelming majority of Southern whites were small independent farmers who worked between fifty and a hundred acres and had one or two slaves, if they had any at all. These farmers relied on their own families for labor and were occasionally able to supplement this force with a hired hand. They lived largely at the subsistence level, with only a small cash income. On the same social level were the small merchants who inhabited towns and villages throughout the South.

At the bottom of the white social scale were the "poor whites" who eked out a living on marginal lands. This group was often considered lazy and prone to criminality by the higher classes. Although clearly without the resources to own slaves, this group was intensely prejudiced because the low status of African Americans in Southern life insulated these whites from the lowest depths of society.

AFRICAN AMERICANS

Beneath all these whites were the almost 4 million African Americans who lived in the South. Some 250,000 of these were free African Americans who lived in large towns and cities and had either been emancipated by their owners or had purchased their own freedom. They tended to be skilled barbers, carpenters, masons, blacksmiths, domestics, and tradesmen. A small handful of free African Americans even owned slaves.

The 3.5 million other African Americans in the South were chattel slaves, considered property that could be bought and sold without regard to individual rights. Some worked in domestic positions

and accumulated some privilege based on their proximity to the master and his family. These slaves often considered themselves superior to the vast majority of slaves who worked as field hands. While a select few rose to the position of driver, a trusted enforcer of the rigorous work regime, most were unable to escape the backbreaking labor of the cotton and rice plantations.

SOLDIER

The Confederate soldier defies a standard description. Throughout the war, a total of about 750,000 "Johnny Rebs" served the Confederacy, and they came in all shapes and sizes. Most were Southern-born, but thousands were born in Northern states. Others were of foreign birth, mainly Irish and German. Louisiana, whose population in 1860 was 10 percent foreign-born, contributed the most nonnatives to the Confederacy, followed by Texas. Native Americans also joined the Confederate ranks as soldiers, and in March 1865, Congress authorized the enlistment of African Americans, although the war ended before any saw active service. There were even a handful of women soldiers, including Malinda Blalock of the Twenty-sixth North Carolina Regiment, who secretly enlisted as Sam Blalock in order to be with her husband.

Confederate soldiers came from all walks of life. Most were farmers, but students, professionals, craftsmen, and laborers were also represented. As the war dragged on, however, policies such as substitution and the Fifteen Slave Law increasingly filled the ranks with the lower classes.

The Conscription Act of April 1862 drafted men aged eighteen to thirty-five. In September the upper age was raised to forty-five. In February 1864, new legislation established the ages as from seventeen to fifty. Nonetheless, the highest percentage of boys younger than eighteen and men older than forty-five was probably seen in 1861 and early 1862, when patriotism and enthusiasm for the war was at its peak. Throughout the war, most Confederate soldiers were between the ages of eighteen and thirty-five.

Vast numbers of Confederate soldiers were illiterate, leaving for historians a paucity of diaries and letters through which to study the common soldier. Especially early in the war, a number of well-educated men enlisted, but these men were usually made officers in short order. Generally speaking, the Confederate soldier brought with him a sense of individualism that characterized the South. Most were naturally resistant to discipline and tended to interpret orders broadly. The most noteworthy manifestation of this high regard for democracy was in the practice of electing company officers.

SOUTH CAROLINA

South Carolina had long been the champion of states' rights and Southern nationalism, dating back at least to the Nullification Crisis of 1832–33. It was the first state to secede from the Union, a process facilitated by its constitutional provision that legislators rather than voters select presidential electors. When these legislators convened on November 5, 1860, to choose electors, it appeared as if Abraham Lincoln was poised to win the national election for president. Thus Governor William Henry Gist kept the legislature in session to await the results, and when Lincoln's victory was certain, Gist requested a secession convention, and the

legislators called for an election of delegates. The convention met on December 17 and three days later unanimously voted to secede.

South Carolina's secession created a dilemma concerning the Federal garrison at Fort Sumter. South Carolina claimed the fort was now state property and demanded that the Federal troops there leave. Major Robert Anderson, the garrison commander, refused to abandon his post and the ensuing standoff led to the opening shots of the Civil War.

South Carolina's coastline became the site of early fighting with the capture of Port Royal in November 1861. The Federal presence sent many planters fleeing inland, leaving many of their slaves behind them. These newly freed African Americans benefited from the efforts of the Port Royal Experiment to help them make the transition from slavery to freedom.

Charleston remained the scene of much fighting throughout the war, although Federal efforts to capture it from the sea were repeatedly repulsed. The city was finally evacuated on February 17–18, 1865, as Major General William T. Sherman approached when he turned north after his March to the

Sea. Sherman's men saw South Carolina as the instigator of the Civil War, and they ensured its citizens paid a heavy price for being the birthplace of secession. The capital of Columbia was particularly hard-hit.

RICE-GROWING AREA

In addition to excellent harbors like Port Royal and Charleston, South Carolina also contributed to the Confederacy as a major rice producer. Cultivation of this crop had reached its peak in the decades just before the Civil War. By 1840 the Georgetown District was producing nearly half of the total rice crop of the United States, and the port exported more rice than any port in the world. The massive Hampton plantation produced 250,000 pounds of rice in 1850 alone. The Citadel also served as a training ground for many Confederate military leaders.

South Carolina's early fire-eaters, such as Robert Barnwell Rhett, played little role after secession, but

Below: *This cartoon lampoons both the shortsightedness of South Carolina's secessionist sentiment and the impotence of President James Buchanan's response.*

they certainly served as active critics of the Davis administration. Other notable Confederates from South Carolina include Christopher G. Memminger, Davis's first secretary of the treasury, and Wade Hampton III, Joseph Kershaw, and Micah Jenkins, who all served as generals.

SPOTSYLVANIA, BATTLE OF

❖ DATE: May 8–21, 1864

❖ LOCATION: Spotsylvania County, Virginia

❖ ARMY OF NORTHERN VIRGINIA (C): 52,000

❖ FORCE UNDER GRANT (U.S.): 100,000

❖ CASUALTIES: 12,000 (C); 18,000 (U.S.)

After failing to defeat General Robert E. Lee at the Battle of the Wilderness on May 5–7, 1864, Lieutenant General Ulysses S. Grant continued to keep the pressure on Lee by initiating a march to flank and cut him off at Spotsylvania Courthouse. Using excellent analysis of the available intelligence, Lee ascertained Grant's intentions and narrowly beat Grant

to the strategic location. Once there, Lee established a defense and defeated several attacks by Grant, including ones on May 9, 10, 12, and 18.

As the two armies arrived in the Spotsylvania area throughout May 8, they built corresponding lines of earthworks east and west of the Brock Road. The Confederate line

Below: *Emory Upton launched an innovative attack on the "Mule Shoe" salient at the Battle of Spotsylvania. He broke the Confederate line, but was eventually driven back by the Confederate Second Corps.*

Above: *As this contemporary sketch shows, the extensive forest and thick vegetation around Spotsylvania was detrimental to the employment of heavy artillery.*

ended up including a huge salient, or bulge, pointing north in the direction of the Federals. Its shape gave rise to this part of the battlefield being dubbed the "Mule Shoe." Grant probed both of Lee's flanks on May 9 and 10 without success.

One of the Federal attacks on May 10 involved twelve regiments led by Colonel Emory Upton, a twenty-four-year-old visionary less than three years out of West Point.

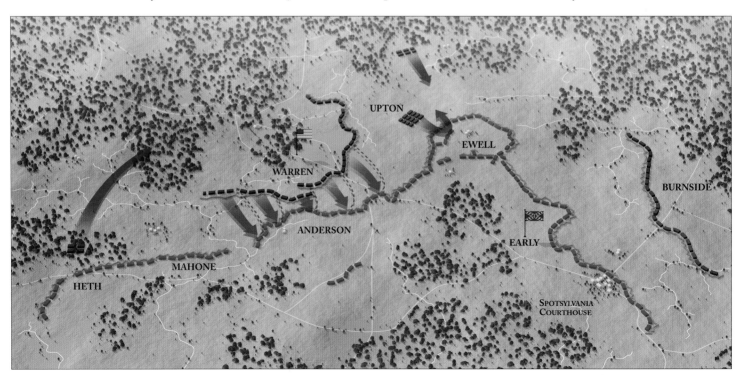

Instead of launching a broad frontal attack in line, Upton advanced in column formation. In order to maintain momentum, the Federals closed without firing en route—an eventuality Upton ensured by having all but his first rank advance with uncapped muskets. The attack enjoyed remarkable initial success, but without additional support, Upton was unable to hold his gains and was forced to withdraw.

GRANT REPEATS TACTIC

The new tactic impressed Grant, and he decided to try it again, this time by throwing Major General Winfield Scott Hancock's entire Second Corps against the Mule Shoe. On May 12 at 4:30 a.m., a massed attack of 20,000 Federals advanced, and in just fifteen minutes they were pouring through gaps in the Confederate lines. Hancock captured 4,000 Confederate prisoners. The contested area became known as the "Bloody Angle."

In a desperate attempt to restore the breach, Lee counterattacked and completed a new line of entrenchments across the base of the salient. For nearly twenty hours the fighting continued almost unabated in what may have been the most ferociously sustained combat in the entire war. There

Above: *The Federals were able to make several penetrations at Spotsylvania, but Robert E. Lee was always able to rally the Confederate line.*

Below: *Field hospitals like this one at Spotsylvania provided what comfort they could to the casualties of battle.*

was more inconclusive fighting on May 18 and 19, but the Confederate line held. Federal losses at Spotsylvania included the popular Major General John Sedgwick. In a related battle at Yellow Tavern, the famed Confederate cavalryman Major General Jeb Stuart was killed. Fighting mostly behind the protection of entrenchments, Lee suffered just 12,000 casualties compared to Grant's 18,000. Having survived this close call, Lee withdrew on May 20 to a new position at Hanover Junction, thwarting another attempted turning movement by Grant.

ST. ALBANS RAID
(OCTOBER 19, 1864)

On October 15, 1864, Lieutenant Bennett Young and twenty-five raiders casually entered St. Albans, Vermont, a small town about twenty miles south of the Canadian border. Dressed in civilian clothes, the band obtained lodging and began to scout the town. On October 19, Young announced himself as a Confederate officer, and his group proceeded to rob three banks. A Federal cavalry captain who was home on leave gathered a group of citizens that forced the Confederates to flee to Canada. As they departed, Young's men tried to fire the town, but little damage was done. The raiders were captured by Canadian authorities and underwent trials and extradition procedures that lasted past the end of the Civil War. While the United States pressed for extradition of the men as criminals, Canadian officials instead deemed them military belligerents and, to preserve Canada's neutrality, would not convict them of a crime.

STATES' RIGHTS

The importance of states' rights to the Confederacy was steeped in the tradition of John C. Calhoun and the political theory that a state could protect its own interests by declaring a federal law null and void within its borders. As Northern growth outpaced Southern, the South began more and more to view the idea of states' rights as a protection against dominance by the majority in the federal government.

During the Civil War, the notion of states' rights hamstrung President Jefferson Davis's efforts to create the type of powerful centralized government that was necessitated by modern war. Governors such as Joseph E. Brown of Georgia resisted what they considered impositions on states' rights, such as when Davis tried to control the disposition of state troops. After the war, apologists for the "Lost Cause" cited states' rights as the primary reason for secession, rather than defense of slavery.

STEPHENS, ALEXANDER H.
(1812–83)

Alexander H. Stephens was a Georgia lawyer, legislator, and congressman. He was initially opposed to secession, classifying himself as part of Georgia's "Union element," but he followed his state into the Confederacy and became President Jefferson Davis's vice president. Throughout the war, he advocated moderation and states' rights. His commitment to these principles often put him at odds with Davis's efforts to prosecute the war in a more centralized fashion. Stephens became an opponent of Davis, and he did much to fuel Georgia governor Joseph E. Brown's resistance to Davis. In 1862 Stephens actually became the leader of the Confederate Senate opposition to the Davis administration. Stephens considered Davis "weak and vacillating, timid, petulant, peevish, obstinate, but not firm."

Like many, Stephens was overly confident of the power of cotton diplomacy. He was also a consistent proponent of peace and participated in the failed Hampton Roads Peace Conference of 1864. After the war, he was arrested and held in Boston for six months. Upon his release, he returned to Georgia and was elected to the U.S. Senate in 1866, but was not allowed to take his seat. He then became a staunch opponent of Reconstruction and the broad interpretation of the Fourteenth Amendment.

Left: *Although he was the vice president, Alexander Stephens often challenged Jefferson Davis's authority.*

He bought the *Atlanta Southern Sun* in 1871 and wrote editorials criticizing any cooperation between Democrats and liberal Republicans. From 1873 to 1882 he served in the House of Representatives, and from 1882 until his death in 1883, he was governor of Georgia.

STONE MOUNTAIN

Stone Mountain is a 1,686-foot elevation in DeKalb County, Georgia, upon which have been carved likenesses of Confederate heroes Jefferson Davis, Robert E. Lee, and Stonewall Jackson.

The idea for this "Confederate Mount Rushmore" was begun as early as 1911 by Helen Plane, a charter member of the United Daughters of the Confederacy.

Below: *Honoring President Jefferson Davis, Robert E. Lee, and Stonewall Jackson, Stone Mountain is commonly known as the "Confederate Mount Rushmore."*

After several false starts, including interruptions caused by contract disputes, the death of carver Augustus Lukeman, and extended disruption during World War II, the carving was officially completed in 1972.

STUART, J. E. B. "JEB"
(1833–64)

❖ RANK: Major general

❖ PLACE OF BIRTH: Patrick County, Virginia

❖ EDUCATED: West Point

❖ MILITARY CAREER:
1861: Commissioned as a lieutenant colonel; led regiment at First Manassas; promoted to brigadier general
1862: Promoted to major general; success at Antietam and Fredericksburg
1863: Took command of corps at Chancellorsville; Gettysburg Campaign
1864: Battle of the Wilderness

Graduating from West Point in 1850, James Ewell Brown "Jeb" Stuart received a commission in the cavalry. He was stationed in Texas and Kansas before serving as a volunteer aide to Colonel Robert E. Lee during John Brown's raid. On May 10, 1861, Stuart resigned his captain's commission and two weeks later received a commission as colonel of Confederate cavalry.

Stuart organized the First Virginia Cavalry and fought at First Manassas. He was promoted to brigadier general on September 24, 1861, and he commanded a cavalry brigade during the Peninsula Campaign, where he helped cover the Confederate retreat to Williamsburg on May 4, 1862.

From June 12 to 15, Stuart rode entirely around Major General George B. McClellan's army. Returning to a hero's welcome, Stuart told General Robert E. Lee that the Federal right flank was vulnerable, information that helped set up the Battle of Mechanicsville. Stuart later brought Lee indications

that McClellan had abandoned his offensive and was beginning to withdraw. He was promoted to major general on July 25, 1862.

CHANCELLORSVILLE

Another of Stuart's intelligence triumphs occurred at Chancellorsville, where he reported that Major General Joseph Hooker's flank was "in the air," setting up Lieutenant General Stonewall Jackson's famous flank

Below: *His ride around George McClellan's army on the Virginia Peninsula in June 1862 was one of Jeb Stuart's greatest exploits.*

attack. In actions such as these, Stuart's cavalry provided the Confederates with an excellent reconnaissance capability and gave Lee a marked intelligence advantage over his opponents, who had no equivalent to Stuart. Stuart was skilled not just at obtaining information—he also had a great knack for interpreting what he saw and providing Lee with a perceptive intelligence summation.

Although Stuart's greatest utility was in gathering intelligence, he fought in the war's largest cavalry battle at Brandy Station, Virginia, on June 9, 1863. The battle revealed to the Federals that Lee

Below: *Jeb Stuart was one of the Confederacy's most dashing cavalrymen and a valuable asset to Robert E. Lee.*

was moving north for his Gettysburg Campaign, and Stuart was criticized for his performance in the Southern press. Some see Stuart's ill-advised Gettysburg raid as an effort to restore his reputation after this setback. Stuart set out on this ride on June 24 and did not return to Lee until July 2, forcing Lee to fight the Battle of Gettysburg without detailed knowledge of the Federal army's dispositions.

After this poor showing, Stuart fought at the Wilderness and Spotsylvania, before being mortally wounded on May 11, 1864, at the Battle of Yellow Tavern.

SUBMARINES

The Confederacy established the Submarine Battery Service in the fall of 1862 under the supervision of Matthew F. Maury. A branch of the Confederate navy, the service's purpose was to augment the efforts of the Torpedo Bureau by laying minefields and building torpedo boats to attack Federal blockaders.

Above: *The Confederate submarine CSS Hunley made history by sinking the USS Housatonic with a spar torpedo on February 17, 1864.*

A pioneering torpedo boat was the *David*, a steam-powered, semi-submersible vessel armed with a spar torpedo. Once the vessel was underway, only the pilot and crew cockpit and the smokestack were above water. On October 23, 1863, the *David* damaged the *Ironsides* at Charleston, causing the blockaders to adopt a series of strict measures to ward off future attacks. Confederate work with submarines ultimately resulted in the invention of the hand-propelled *Hunley*, a true submarine that sank the *Housatonic* at Charleston on February 17, 1864.

The Submarine Battery Service was a highly professional organization that operated with a great degree of secrecy and esprit de corps. Lieutenant Hunter Davidson replaced Maury as its commander when Maury went to Europe.

SUBSTITUTES

As early as the fall of 1861, the Confederacy began releasing volunteers from the army if they could furnish an able-bodied replacement to serve in their stead. This practice of substitution was codified in the First Conscription Act of April 16, 1862, in an attempt to mitigate resistance to what was the continent's first draft. Under these procedures, a conscripted man could report to the camp with a substitute, and if the substitute was found to be medically qualified and not subject to military service of his own, the originally drafted soldier could return home, while the substitute fulfilled his obligation.

Many saw substitution as unfairly favoring Southerners of means, and protests against the practice increased as the war progressed. Soldiers returning home on leave from the front lines found it demoralizing to see able-bodied men who had avoided service. Many saw it as evidence that the Confederacy was engaged in "a rich man's war and poor man's fight." Nonetheless, the practice grew and became something of a cottage

Below: *The policy of substitution allowed drafted men to pay for a replacement. Many Southerners objected to the measure as unfairly favoring the wealthy.*

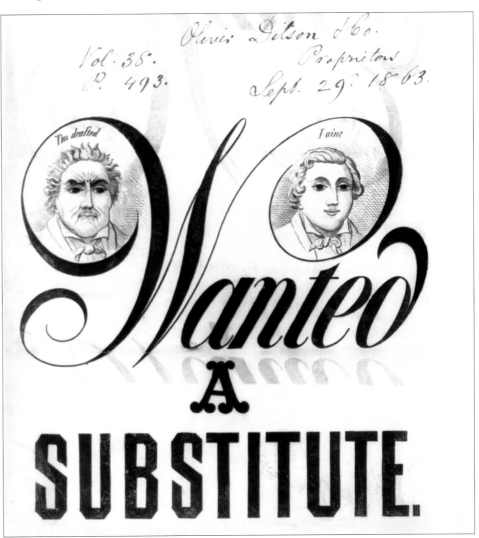

industry, complete with its own brokerages. Newspapers carried advertisements offering substitutes for prices ranging from $500 in 1862 to thousands of dollars toward the end of 1863. In November 1863, Secretary of War James A. Seddon offered the conservative estimate that some 50,000 men had obtained substitutes.

FRAUD AND CORRUPTION

Inevitably, the system became adulterated by fraud and corruption. The provision allowing only one substitute per month in each company was frequently violated. Some substitutes subsequently deserted, only to offer their services again under a different name.

Unscrupulous examiners allowed unfit substitutes to be accepted. Most substitutes were motivated solely by mercenary gain and had little devotion to the cause. Throughout the war, the system defied reform, and in early 1864, Congress decided to abolish it altogether.

SUPPLY SYSTEM

The Civil War supply system relied on the railroad, the depot, and the wagon. Matériel would flow from factories in industrial centers like Richmond and Atlanta to base depots. Ideally, these loads were moved by railroad or inland waterways, but the South's deficiencies in these transportation systems often slowed progress. From there, supplies were shipped to advanced depots, usually in a city on a major transportation artery within the rear of the department.

Nashville was an important Confederate depot, but the strategic significance of depots made them a prized target for Federal attack. The loss of depot locations such as Nashville severely hindered Confederate supply operations. While campaigning, armies would

establish temporary advanced depots that could be serviced by river or rail. Until General Joseph E. Johnston withdrew to positions along the Rappahannock River in March 1862, Manassas Junction served as a useful advanced depot for the Confederates. From these locations, mule-drawn wagons carried supplies forward to the field units.

SURRENDER, SEQUENCE OF

The major Confederate commanders surrendered in the following order:

General Robert E. Lee—
April 9, 1865
General Joseph E. Johnston—
April 26, 1865
Lieutenant General Richard Taylor:—May 4, 1865
General Edmund Kirby Smith—
May 26, 1865

The last Confederate general to surrender was Brigadier General Stand Watie, who surrendered on June 23, 1865. Captain James I. Waddell did not surrender the CSS *Shenandoah* until he turned the ship over to British authorities on November 6, 1865.

TACTICS

In the early days of the Civil War, many volunteers and state troops were drilled according to Winfield Scott's *Infantry Tactics*, a largely outmoded three-volume set published in 1835. Scott's tactics emphasized disciplined order over speed, and mass over maneuver. He stressed close-ordered lines of either two or three ranks and discouraged the use of any movement faster than the quick-time rate of 110 steps per minute.

Scott's *Infantry Tactics* served the army well in Mexico, but the advent of the rifle and the minié ball

necessitated a change in tactics even before the Civil War. In 1855 the army adopted future Confederate lieutenant general William J. Hardee's *Rifle and Light Infantry Tactics* as its standard. In spite of the manual's promising title, Hardee's modifications were rather modest. Aside from increasing Scott's rate of advance to a double-quick-time speed of 165 steps per minute, most of Hardee's changes dealt with how to handle the new rifle rather than the changes it would bring to battlefield tactics.

In fact, the army largely ignored the impact the new technology would have on tactics. For example, when the Delafield Commission was sent to Europe to observe and study the Crimean War, its lengthy report made no mention of the use of the rifled musket, instead devoting detailed discussion to the leggings used by Russian soldiers. What little reform that was accomplished in the years preceding the Civil War

Above: *Winfield Scott's* Infantry Tactics *remained a popular manual on the eve of the Civil War, but it failed to account for the changing tactical conditions caused by the rifle.*

Above: *Difficult terrain like that at Allatoona Pass (fought over on October 5, 1864) favored the defense and allowed smaller units to repel larger attacks.*

came from Secretary of War Jefferson Davis's insistence that light infantry tactics be adopted for all units. This meant reducing the line of the infantry from three to two ranks and placing increased emphasis on skirmishers.

Nonetheless, formations remained rigidly in the old Napoleonic style, with men standing shoulder to shoulder and intervals between units small. A brigade in this tight alignment would occupy a front of just 1,300 yards, with divisions commonly attacking in a "column of brigades." The lines were maintained rigidly parallel to allow for a massed or uniform volley at the halt and to maximize the shock effect. Commanders knew such a formation presented a vulnerable target, but they felt that an attack coming in successive waves would eventually bludgeon the defenders into submission.

If the army was slow to grasp the impact of the rifle, many officers did learn the value of the turning movement. Scott had executed a number of these in his march from Vera Cruz to Mexico City, and astute junior officers like Robert E. Lee quickly realized the superiority of gaining victory by maneuver rather than costly frontal attack. However, reliance on line-of-sight communications made it difficult to control large units in the more complicated maneuvers, and many Civil War generals clung stubbornly to the frontal attack.

BATTLEFIELD CHANGES

Many Civil War soldiers realized before their commanders that the greater accuracy of the rifle, especially when fired from behind protective breastworks, forced men in shoulder-to-shoulder battle lines to increase their dispersion

and lengthen their lines. As individuals spread apart, the density of soldiers on the battlefield decreased. The increased ranges also led armies to form for battle farther apart. This increased the distance over which an infantryman had to advance to close with the enemy. The dangers of this prolonged exposure to enemy fire greatly strengthened the power of the defense, and battles came to be decided much more by firepower than by shock action. All told, battles took longer to fight and the ability to achieve a decisive result became increasingly elusive. For generals steeped in the Napoleonic tradition, such as Lee, this was a frustrating development.

TALIAFERRO, WILLIAM B. (1822–98)

William B. Taliaferro fought in the Mexican War, served in the Virginia legislature, and commanded a militia company at Harpers Ferry after John Brown's raid. He was commissioned as a colonel in the Confederate army and was promoted to brigadier general on March 6, 1862. He fought in the Shenandoah Valley Campaign, at Second Manassas, and at Fredericksburg. In February 1863, he was sent to Savannah and then Charleston, where he defended Fort Wagner on July 18, 1863. He was promoted to major general on January 1, 1865, and surrendered with General Joseph E. Johnston in North Carolina.

TAX, INCOME

Taxation in the Confederacy began on August 19, 1861, when the Confederate Congress authorized a "war tax" of 0.5 percent on all property. Early that month, the United States had provided for its first income tax at a rate of 3 percent on all incomes exceeding $800 a year. Collection of the tax in the Confederacy was left to the individual states and was far from perfect. On April 23, 1863, the Confederacy established a progressive income tax. Incomes less than $500 were exempt. Beyond that, rates ranged from 5 percent for incomes between $500 and $1,500, to 15 percent for incomes above $10,000. The law also included a 10 percent tax on agricultural products. There were numerous loopholes in the tax procedures, and historian E. Merton Coulter has concluded after careful study that the Confederacy raised just 1 percent of its income from taxes.

TAYLOR, RICHARD (1826–79)

❖ RANK: Lieutenant general

❖ PLACE OF BIRTH: St. Matthews, Kentucky

❖ EDUCATED: Harvard and Yale

❖ MILITARY CAREER:
1861: Promoted to brigadier general and commanded a Louisiana brigade during the Shenandoah Valley Campaign
1862: Promoted to major general
1863: Battles of Fort Bisland and Irish Bend
1864: Successful in Red River Campaign

Richard "Dick" Taylor was the son of President Zachary Taylor and the brother of President Jefferson Davis's first wife. He was the product of education both in Europe and at Harvard and Yale. At the outbreak of the war, he was a sugar plantation owner in Louisiana and state senator. He was a member of the state's secession convention. Originally commissioned as a colonel, he was quickly promoted to brigadier general on October 21, 1861. He commanded a brigade during the Shenandoah Valley Campaign and the Seven Days Battles, during which he was ill and led his troops from an ambulance.

Taylor was promoted to major general on July 28, 1863, and

Below: *Richard Taylor was at times a troublesome subordinate, but performed better during independent operations.*

commanded the District of Western Louisiana. He proved to be a troublesome subordinate for Trans-Mississippi Department commander General Edmund Kirby Smith. Taylor was a parochial officer who protested unified action with the besieged Confederates across the Mississippi River at Vicksburg. When pressed into cooperation, he complained, "Remonstrances were to no avail. I was informed that all the Confederate authorities in the east were urgent for some effort on our part in behalf of Vicksburg, and that public opinion would condemn us if we did not try to do something."

Still he insisted, "That to go two hundred miles and more away from the proper theater of action in search of an indefinite something is hard; but orders are orders." He performed better when his own territory was threatened during the Red River Campaign of 1864, including winning the Battle of Sabine Crossroads on April 8 and earning a promotion to lieutenant general.

LATE SURRENDER

On August 15, 1864, Taylor assumed command of the Department of East Louisiana, Mississippi, and Alabama. He briefly commanded the Army of Tennessee before it moved to the Carolinas. Taylor stayed in the west and surrendered on May 4, 1865, the last commander east of the Mississippi to do so.

Taylor had lost his fortune during the war, but he used his political connections with Presidents Andrew Johnson and Ulysses S. Grant to lobby on the South's behalf during Reconstruction. His book, *Destruction and Reconstruction,* is considered to be among the best memoirs produced by a Civil War general.

TELEGRAPH

Both Confederates and Federals used the telegraph for strategic and operational communications in the Civil War. This system greatly enhanced command and control by connecting field headquarters with rear areas. However, because the South lacked the resources and factories to produce wire, the Confederacy had to rely on existing telegraph lines that limited the telegraph's operational significance. The Federals benefited from the magneto-powered Beardslee device, which allowed operators to hook

Below: *A Federal cavalryman cuts a telegraph line. Telegraph communications were critical to both armies, and cutting wires was a favorite pastime of cavalry raiders.*

insulated wire into existing trunk lines to reach into the civilian telegraph network, and extend communications from the battlefield to the rear areas. The Confederacy impressed civilian telegraphers and facilities, but a lack of resources precluded it from developing a capability as extensive and efficient as that possessed by the Federals.

TENNESSEE

Tennessee was a divided state on the eve of the Civil War. Native son John Bell, a moderate, had carried the state in the 1860 election. Yeoman farmers in the east were largely Unionist, planters in the west were more receptive to secession, and the middle of the state was split. Although Governor Isham G. Harris was a secessionist, the overriding political sentiment in the state was Unionist. Only in the aftermath of Fort Sumter did the legislature, with Harris's urging, declare a military alliance with the Confederacy on May 7. The citizenry confirmed this act with a vote to secede on June 8.

Tennessee was critical to the Confederacy both as a shield for the cotton states and for its own industrial output. In the southeastern portion of the state, Chattanooga was the juncture of the South's only railroad from the Atlantic to the Mississippi. In the southwest, Memphis was a vibrant river port that helped connect the eastern and western halves of the Confederacy. In the northern central section, Nashville was an industrial base with such activities as a field artillery plant that was established after secession. Tennessee also contributed the bulk of the Confederacy's niter that fed the key powder mill in Augusta, Georgia.

MOUNTAIN UNIONISTS

Tennessee also came with some problems for the Confederacy. Its strong Unionist sentiment in the eastern mountains formed a network with like-minded mountaineers in Virginia and North Carolina. Geography favored invasion, with the Tennessee River providing an avenue of approach into western Tennessee and northern Alabama, and the Cumberland River leading to Nashville. Federal gunboats could use these arteries to enter the agricultural and industrial centers of the South. Under such pressure, Tennessee was difficult to defend, and in February 1862, President Abraham Lincoln appointed Andrew Johnson military governor of occupied Tennessee. This head start contributed to Tennessee's early readmission to the Union in 1866.

Tennessee quickly became one of the war's principal battlegrounds, with important actions fought at Forts Henry and Donelson, Shiloh, Murfreesboro, Chattanooga, Chickamauga, and Nashville. Noteworthy Confederates who were born in Tennessee include Nathan Bedford Forrest, Alexander Peter Stewart, and Sam Davis.

TEXAS

Texas had strong regional ties to the Southern states dating back to its admission into the Union as a slave state in 1845, the result of a long and hard-fought advocacy led by elder Southern

statesman John C. Calhoun. When Texas's annexation touched off the Mexican War, many Southerners volunteered to fight for a cause that was much more popular in the South than in the North.

However, on the eve of the Civil War, Texas's governor was its longtime hero Sam Houston, a vehement opponent of secession. Houston refused to call the legislature into session or respond to demands for a convention to consider the secession issue. When a group of influential secessionists that included Williamson S. Oldham took it upon themselves to declare an extralegal convention, Houston responded by calling a special session of the legislature in hopes that it would denounce the

Above: *Even long-time Texas leader Sam Houston, hero of the Mexican War, could not stem the state's secessionist sentiment.*

proceedings. Instead, the legislators approved the convention that then met in Austin in late January 1861. On February 1, Texas voted to secede by a margin of 166–8, pending the confirmation by a popular vote. This popular vote concurred with the convention's decision at a ratio of more than three to one. Houston stood by his principles, refusing to take an oath of allegiance to the Confederacy. He was deposed as governor on March 18.

Before Texas had even ratified its ordinance of secession, Brigadier General David Twiggs, still a member of the U.S. Army, delivered nineteen Federal army posts to Colonel Benjamin McCulloch, representing the state of Texas. The action caused Twiggs to be dismissed from the U.S. Army on March 1. In spite of Twiggs's premature relinquishing of Federal property, the delay in seceding caused the Texas delegation to arrive late for the Montgomery Convention and miss the debate on the provisional constitution and the election of the president and vice president.

CENTER OF AGRICULTURE

Texas was an impressive agricultural producer. For example, in 1850, it had four times as many cattle and horses as the rest of the entire South. Because of its distance from the main Civil War battlefields, Texas was able to continue its agricultural production throughout the war. However, the marginal Confederate transportation system worked against the reliable delivery of these items. Texas also provided the Confederacy with the port of Galveston, but again its distance from the geographic center of the South limited its effectiveness. Between 50,000 and 80,000 Texan troops served in the Confederate army.

While Texas was largely isolated from the eastern Confederacy after the loss of Vicksburg, Major General Nathaniel P. Banks did launch his ill-fated Red River Campaign in the spring of 1864 in part to try to secure Texas from the French activity in Mexico. Other fighting in Texas occurred at Galveston, the only port to be recaptured by the Confederates, and Palmito Ranch, one of the war's last land battles. Notable Confederate Texans were the outspoken Senator Louis T. Wigfall, a transplanted South Carolinian, Postmaster General John H. Reagan, born in Tennessee, and Kentucky-born Lieutenant General John Bell Hood.

TILGHMAN, LLOYD (1816–63)

Lloyd Tilghman graduated from West Point in 1836 but resigned from the army shortly thereafter to pursue a career in civil and railroad engineering. He served as a volunteer aide to Major General David Twiggs in the Mexican War and then returned to the railroad business. He was appointed as a brigadier general in the Confederate army on October 18, 1861. In February 1862, he surrendered Fort Henry. He was killed on May 16, 1863, fighting a rearguard action as the Confederates withdrew from Champion Hill during the Vicksburg Campaign.

Below: *Lloyd Tilghman, commemorated by this statue at Vicksburg National Military Park, died in May 1863 while covering the Confederate retreat from Champion Hill.*

TOOMBS, ROBERT A. (1810–85)

Robert A. Toombs served as a U.S. congressman and senator from Georgia. He was a moderate, only reluctantly joining the Democratic Party after first being a Whig. At the Montgomery Convention, he and other moderates gained control from the fire-eaters.

Below: *Robert Toombs served the Confederacy both as a politician and as a battlefield general. His best military performance was at the Battle of Antietam in September 1862.*

Although he had hoped to be president, Toombs instead was appointed the Confederacy's first secretary of state. It was a position he accepted with some hesitancy, fearing President Jefferson Davis would give the office little authority. Toombs resigned the position on July 19, 1861, to become a brigadier general. He simultaneously retained his seat in the Confederate Congress.

Toombs was not a professional soldier and had little awe for those who were. He often complained that the epitaph of the Confederate army would be "Died of West Point." After being admonished by Major General D. H. Hill for his performance at Malvern Hill, Toombs challenged Hill to a duel.

The actual duel was never fought, and Toombs went on to perform exceptionally well at Antietam. When he failed to be promoted, he resigned from the army on March 4, 1863, and returned to Georgia, where he lost an election for the Senate. In 1864 he became inspector general of the Georgia militia. He was an outspoken critic of the Davis administration.

INTO EXILE

After the war, Toombs fled to Cuba and then London to avoid being arrested for treason. He returned to the United States in 1867, but never applied for a pardon and never again held public office. He resumed his law practice but suffered a series of personal tragedies, including his wife's insanity and his own blindness and alcoholism.

TRANS-MISSISSIPPI CONFEDERACY

The Trans-Mississippi Confederacy included the seceded states of Arkansas, Texas, and most of Louisiana, as well as the large number of Confederate sympathizers in Missouri. These four states covered 600,000 square miles and contained some 2.7 million people, which was 20 percent of the Confederacy's population. Texas especially was critical to the Confederacy as an agricultural producer. Also in the region were remote Confederate possibilities in New Mexico, Arizona, and even California, as well as the more promising Indian Territory, where an effective force of Cherokees commanded by Brigadier General Stand Watie fought for the Confederacy.

The fluid situation in this vast area led to friction between Major General Sterling Price, commander of the Missouri State Guard, and Brigadier General Benjamin McCulloch, commander of a group of Arkansas and Louisiana troops. On January 10, 1862, President Jefferson Davis attempted to create some unity of effort by forming the Trans-Mississippi District, consisting of northwestern Louisiana, most of Arkansas and Missouri, and the Indian Territory. Major General Earl Van Dorn assumed command of this district on January 29 and created the Army of the West, only to be defeated at Pea Ridge in northern Arkansas on March 7–8, 1862, a battle that secured Federal control of Missouri and threatened Arkansas.

On May 26, 1862, Davis created the Trans-Mississippi Department, which included Texas, the Indian Territory, Arkansas, Missouri, and western Louisiana. On May 31 Major General Thomas C. Hindman was named commander. His defeat at Prairie Grove on December 7 furthered Federal control of Arkansas. This loss served as the catalyst for another change, and Lieutenant General

Theophilus H. Holmes assumed command. Holmes was largely inept and knew he was not up to the responsibility. He eventually asked to be relieved and have his assistant, Lieutenant General Edmund Kirby Smith, replace him. Smith assumed command in February 1863.

The inefficiencies of the Confederate departmental system contributed to Smith's failure to provide meaningful assistance to the besieged forces at Vicksburg, and when the Mississippi River stronghold fell in July, the Trans-Mississippi became for all purposes a separate command. Smith enjoyed such discretion that his region was known as "Kirby Smithdom." He exercised his expanded powers by attempting to appoint a number of generals, an authority reserved under Confederate law for the president. President Jefferson Davis originally reversed Smith's appointments, but later confirmed some of them. Smith also created the excessively bureaucratic and scandal-ridden Trans-Mississippi Cotton Bureau. He even conducted his own diplomacy, meeting with

French representative Camille Polignac late in the war to propose a system of gradual emancipation in exchange for French support.

Some die-hard Confederates saw the Trans-Mississippi as a last hope for continuing the fight, even by means of guerrilla warfare, after the surrender of the eastern armies. However, on June 2, 1865, Smith's command became the last Confederate department to surrender. In the final analysis, Confederate hopes for the vast potential of the Trans-Mississippi succumbed to distance, low priority, and frequent violations of unity of effort.

TRAVELLER

Traveller was General Robert E. Lee's horse. Originally named Jeff Davis and then Greenbrier, Traveller was purchased by Lee for $200 in late 1861. Traveller weighed about 1,100 pounds and

Below: *Robert E. Lee's horse Traveller became one of many beloved symbols of the Confederacy.*

stood nearly sixteen hands high. After the war, he went with Lee to Washington College in Lexington, Virginia, where hairs from his tail became highly prized souvenirs. Traveller died in 1871, a year after Lee, and was buried next to the Lee Chapel at Washington College.

TREDEGAR IRON WORKS

Tredegar Iron Works, located in Richmond, Virginia, between the Kanawha Canal and the James River, held a unique position in the Confederacy as a prewar industrial plant ready to be converted to war production. In 1861 it had a workforce of 900 and was the only major rolling mill and the more important of the two first-class foundries and machine shops in the South. Joseph R. Anderson, a West Point–trained engineer, purchased

Below: *Tredegar Iron Works in Richmond was one of the few reliable centers of industrial output in the Confederacy.*

the works in 1843 and specialized in revolvers and gun carriages before the war. Even after Anderson was commissioned in the Confederate army and later obtained a field command, he remained active in Tredegar's business. After being wounded, he returned to full-time work there in July 1862. His industry and resourcefulness were critical to Tredegar's success, and his devotion to the cause was complete. "We will make anything you want," he told the Confederate government, "work night and day if necessary, and ship by rail."

Under Anderson's capable leadership, Tredegar became semiautonomous. Anderson built his own tannery and shoe factory, ran cloth through the blockade, and bought livestock from neighboring states to produce part of his workers' food and clothing needs to spare them from inflationary prices. During the war, Tredegar produced nearly 50 percent of the cannons in the Confederacy, and by 1863 its workforce had expanded to 2,500. Tredegar was also a technological

innovator, producing the armor for the ironclad *Virginia* and developing new armaments such as the superior Brooke rifled naval gun. In spite of Anderson's Herculean efforts, Tredegar still suffered from shortages of both skilled labor and materials throughout the war.

Tredegar suspended operations in April 1865, but a battalion of 350 plant workers successfully repulsed fire and mobs during the Confederate evacuation of Richmond. Anderson reopened Tredegar in 1867 after receiving his parole, and the plant was an important contributor to the region's industrial recovery in the postwar era.

TRENT AFFAIR

On November 7, 1861, James Mason and John Slidell, Confederate commissioners to Great Britain and France respectively, set sail for Europe from Havana aboard the *Trent*, a British contract mail packet. On the next day, a Federal warship, the

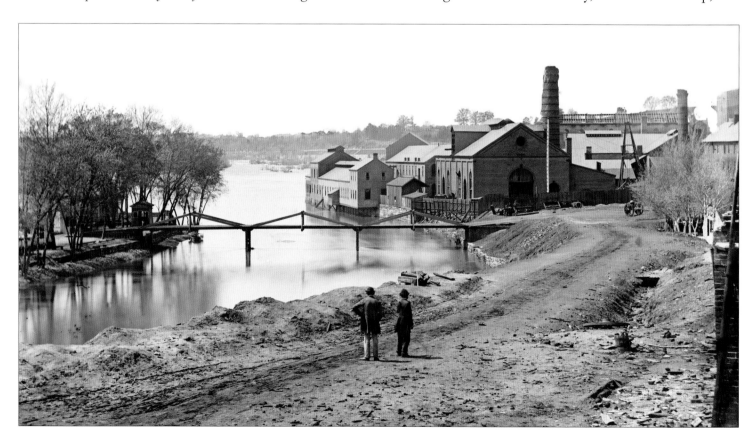

Above: *Confederate diplomat John Slidell became a center of international attention during the* Trent *affair.*

San Jacinto, intercepted the *Trent*. The *San Jacinto*'s commander, Captain Charles Wilkes, acting without orders, removed Mason and Slidell and carried them to Boston. The British considered this act to be a blatant violation of their neutrality and freedom of the seas, as well as an insult to them as a great power. The *Trent* affair created a crisis that nearly brought Europe into the war.

In response to this affront, Great Britain mobilized for war. Eight thousand British troops were ordered to Canada, arms and munitions for them were loaded onto ships, and dispatches were sent to Admiral Alexander Milne instructing him to prepare the Great Atlantic Fleet for the possibility of war.

Several factors soon worked to temper this initial belligerent response. The first was the practical issue of Canada's security. Canada was virtually indefensible from the British viewpoint, in no small part because Canada's railroad and telegraphic communications ran parallel to the border and were vulnerable at many locations. On the contrary, the Union's railroads struck the border at right angles in several places and afforded great opportunities for a concentrated attack into Canada.

This situation was compounded by Canada's reluctance to provide for its own defense. The colony seemed to feel that if war arose out of a crisis such as the *Trent* affair, defense would be a British responsibility. Consequently, little preparation for war had been attempted in the event that diplomacy failed.

GHOSTS OF 1812

The final weakness involved in Canada's defense was its very location. While Britain was an ocean away, the hostile Union was right across the border. This situation caused many Britons to fear that the Union would succumb to the temptation to compensate for any land lost to the Confederacy by seizing Canada. These onsiderations revived apprehensive memories of the American invasion of Canada during the War of 1812. That effort had involved only 2,500 men, but Lord John Russell, the British foreign secretary, feared that "we may now expect forty or fifty thousand."

This concern for Canada's defense gave Federal secretary of state William H. Seward a chance to end the crisis through smooth diplomacy. He offered to allow the British soldiers sent to Canada to cross Maine and thus avoid delay in the icebound St. Lawrence.

This display of good faith did much to pacify the British, but the ultimate end to the crisis did not come until December 27 when Seward gave Lord Lyons, the British minister in Washington, a statement guaranteeing the release of Mason and Slidell and acknowledging that reparation was due to Great Britain.

Throughout the affair, the Confederacy could only helplessly watch as its hopes for British intervention melted away. If anything, the peaceful outcome of the *Trent* affair only served to strengthen British–American ties.

Below: *Charles Wilkes's impulsive removal of James Mason and John Slidell from the* Trent *brought Britain and the United States to the brink of war.*

TULLAHOMA CAMPAIGN (JUNE 23–30, 1863)

After the Battle of Murfreesboro, General Braxton Bragg withdrew to establish defensive positions to protect Chattanooga. After delays that infuriated authorities in Washington, Major General William S. Rosecrans finally began pursuing Bragg on June 23, 1863. Rosecrans advanced in five separate columns, a maneuver that greatly deceived Bragg. When Federal troops began appearing in multiple locations, Bragg ordered a retreat to Tullahoma. On June 30, he continued his retreat to behind the Tennessee River. By surrendering so much territory, Bragg made Chattanooga extremely vulnerable. His failure to resist Rosecrans caused great criticism of Bragg.

TUPELO, BATTLE OF

- ❖ DATE: July 13–15, 1864
- ❖ LOCATION: Lee County, Mississippi
- ❖ DEPARTMENT OF ALABAMA, MISSISSIPPI, AND EAST LOUISIANA (C): 8,000
- ❖ FORCE UNDER SMITH (U.S.): 14,000
- ❖ CASUALTIES: 1,300 (C); 648 (U.S.)

In late June 1864, Major General Andrew Jackson Smith's corps returned to Major General William T. Sherman's army from the ill-fated Red River Campaign. Sherman ordered Smith to conduct

Below: *This cannon and monument commemorate the Battle of Tupelo, where Confederates led by Stephen Lee and Nathan Bedford Forrest fought Federals commanded by Andrew Jackson Smith.*

operations designed to reduce the threat Lieutenant General Nathan Bedford Forrest posed to Sherman's communications as he advanced on Atlanta. Smith's cavalry occupied Tupelo, Mississippi, on July 13, and Lieutenant General Stephen D. Lee, who commanded Confederate forces that included Forrest's, moved to attack. Smith repulsed several Confederate assaults, and withdrew on July 15. Although Smith was proud that he had held his own against Forrest, Sherman ordered him to reengage Forrest to prevent him from getting into Tennessee.

TWENTY (FIFTEEN) SLAVE LAW

The Twenty Slave Law was a controversial exemption measure passed by the Confederate

Congress on October 11, 1862, that deferred from military service any planter or overseer with more than twenty slaves. Proponents argued the act was necessary to maintain agricultural production and to prevent slave insurrection. Opponents considered the exemption to place an unfair burden for fighting the war on the lower classes. Indeed, some enterprising planters took to dividing their slaves into gangs of twenty, put them on separate tracts of land, and made their sons or other relatives overseers in order to obtain additional exemptions. The Twenty Slave Law generated such a public outcry that it directly contributed to resistance to conscription. Jasper Collins, one of the leaders of the antigovernment "Free State of Jones" in Mississippi, was among those incensed by the legislation.

In response to these criticisms, Congress amended the law on May 1, 1863, making it applicable only to overseers on plantations belonging solely to "a minor, a person of unsound mind, a femme sole [single woman], or a person absent from home in the military or naval service of the Confederacy." Furthermore, planters were required to swear an affidavit that they had been unable to secure an overseer not liable for military service and to pay $500 for the exemption. To further cut down on abuses, only men who had been overseers prior to April 16, 1862, on plantations that had not been divided since October 11, 1862, could qualify for exemptions. On February 17, 1864, Congress reduced the requirement to fifteen slaves but also required planters with exempted overseers to deliver to the government 100 pounds of bacon or its equivalent for every slave and to sell surplus produce to the government or to soldiers' families at government prices.

UNIFORMS

Confederate uniforms varied based on unit, location, and time period. The regulation uniform included a long, double-breasted tunic coat of cadet gray with two rows of buttons and was trimmed at the edges, collar, and cuffs with a special color designating the soldier's branch of service. Blue meant infantry, red artillery, and yellow cavalry. The trousers were sky blue, cut loose at the leg and long enough to cover much of the shoe. Overcoats were gray flannel, double-breasted, and fitted with capes. The regulation cap was a kepi with a cloth crown, colored to designate the wearer's branch of service.

In spite of these noble intentions, few Confederate soldiers actually wore these fine uniforms. In fact, the Confederate government required its volunteers to furnish their own clothes, and soldiers

Right: *The three chevrons on this uniform would identify its wearer as a sergeant.*

Above: *A collection of Confederate army memorabilia, including a flag, swords, belt, pistol, and kepi. Uniform items and artifacts such as these are highly prized by collectors and reenactors.*

Above: *Many uniform items signified something specific about the soldier, such as the crossed cannons of an artilleryman, the cavalryman's gloves, and the red kepi of the Zouave.*

UNION SYMPATHIZERS IN THE SOUTH

Secession was not universally popular in the South, and Unionism was particularly strong in the mountainous areas of western Virginia, eastern Tennessee, and western North Carolina. However, once the states had seceded, much of the Unionist sentiment was suppressed by the affirmative association of the Confederacy with the positive notions of patriotism and self-defense. Unionism, on the other hand, was associated with dissent and negativism, and in most parts of the Confederacy it was quickly labeled treasonous behavior.

In certain places, however, Union sentiment was strong enough to demand action. The most notable

Below: *Not all Southerners wanted separation from the Union. One challenge to Confederate nationhood were Federal sympathizers such as these shown at a secret meeting in Louisiana.*

arrived at camp wearing whatever they could to approximate the regulation uniform. Volunteer groups of patriotic women sewed many Confederate uniforms.

While most Confederate soldiers were underdressed, a few special units like the Louisiana Zouaves and the Emerald Guards adopted their own flashy uniforms, certainly at the war's outset anyway. As the war progressed, uniforms became simpler and less diverse. The Confederate government did much to improve standardization by obtaining cloth from both overseas and domestic manufacturers.

The typical Confederate soldier ended up wearing a slouch hat; a gray or butternut wool shell jacket; gray, butternut, or blue trousers; and low-heeled brogan shoes.

example is the western counties of Virginia, which left Virginia to become the new state of West Virginia in 1863. In some localized areas like the "Free State of Jones" in Mississippi, Unionism was strong enough to establish Confederate authority. More common was the case of Winston County, Alabama, where Union sympathizers were forced into the mountains from where they harassed Confederate communications between northern Alabama and western Tennessee. Likewise, Union sympathizers in eastern Tennessee repeatedly burned bridges and tore up railroad tracks.

UNITED CONFEDERATE VETERANS

The United Confederate Veterans was formed in New Orleans on June 10, 1889, in large part thanks to the efforts of Colonel J. F. Shipp. At the time there were already large state veterans' organizations in Virginia and Tennessee, but Shipp envisioned a general organization along the lines of what the Grand Army of the Republic offered for Federal veterans. The first reunion of the United Confederate Veterans was held in Chattanooga, Tennessee, on July 3–5, 1890. Major General John Brown Gordon served as the first commander in chief until his death in 1904. He was succeeded by Lieutenant General Stephen D. Lee, who served until his death in 1908. In 1896 the Sons of Confederate Veterans was formed to continue the tradition of the United Confederate Veterans.

UNITED DAUGHTERS OF THE CONFEDERACY

The United Daughters of the Confederacy is an organization open to women who are blood descendants of men and women who served honorably in the Confederate army, navy, or civil service or gave "material aid to the cause." It traces its heritage to the Daughters of the Confederacy in Missouri and the Ladies' Auxiliary of the Confederate Soldiers Home in Tennessee, which came into existence in the 1890s.

Caroline Meriwether Goodlett of Tennessee and Anna Davenport

Below: *Women of the United Daughters of the Confederacy photographed in 1912. The organization's members dedicate themselves to honoring the memory of Confederate veterans.*

Raines of Georgia were the founders of the National Association of the Daughters of the Confederacy, which was organized in Nashville, Tennessee, on September 10, 1894. At its second meeting in Atlanta, Georgia, in 1895, the organization changed its name to the United Daughters of the Confederacy. It was incorporated as such under the laws of Washington, D.C., on July 18, 1919.

Particularly in the late nineteenth and early twentieth centuries, the UDC was instrumental in raising money for the Confederate veterans' memorials that grace many Southern towns. It helped raise the funds necessary for the Confederate Memorial that was unveiled in Arlington National Cemetery in 1914.

The efforts of the UDC also resulted in stained-glass windows that honor General Robert E. Lee and Lieutenant General Stonewall Jackson being placed in the National Cathedral in Washington,

D.C., in 1957. The UDC maintains an important collection of documents related to Southern history at the Caroline Meriwether Goodlett Library, located at its headquarters in Richmond, Virginia.

Right: *The United Daughters of the Confederacy were responsible for erecting this monument to John Hunt Morgan in Lexington, Kentucky, in 1911.*

Below: *Members of the United Daughters of the Confederacy, such as the women in this 1912 photograph, must be blood descendants of those who honorably served the Confederacy.*

side. The fact that many Confederate and Federal officers knew each other from their days as cadets contributed to a unique familiarity between the two armies and, in some cases, an appreciation for the opposing commander's strategic thinking.

Among the many Confederate officers who were West Point graduates were: Robert E. Lee (class of 1829), Joseph E. Johnston

UNITED STATES MILITARY ACADEMY

In 1817 Sylvanus Thayer replaced Captain Alden Partridge as superintendent of the United States Military Academy at West Point, New York, and began correcting some of the deficiencies Partridge had caused. Thayer broadened and standardized the curriculum, established a system to measure class standing, organized classes around small sections,

improved cadet discipline, created the office of commandant of cadets, and improved military training. Cadets who were trained under Thayer's improved system provided valuable service as junior officers in the Mexican War, and by the time of the Civil War, these West Pointers had advanced to senior leadership positions. All told, 151 Confederate and 294 Federal generals were West Pointers. Of the Civil War's sixty major battles, a West Pointer commanded on both sides in fifty-five, and in the other five battles, a West Pointer commanded on one

Above: *As superintendent of the United States Military Academy, Sylvanus Thayer was responsible for the early training of many Civil War generals.*

(1829), John C. Pemberton (1837), James Longstreet (1842), and Stonewall Jackson (1846). President Jefferson Davis graduated from West Point in 1828. Both Robert E. Lee and Pierre Gustave Toutant Beauregard served as superintendents of West Point, with Beauregard serving only from January 23 to 28, 1861, before being replaced because of his Southern sympathies.

VALLANDIGHAM, CLEMENT L. (1820–71)

Clement L. Vallandigham was a lawyer and Democratic politician from Ohio. He served in the state legislature and U.S. Congress and was an outspoken critic of President Abraham Lincoln and a highly visible copperhead.

In spite of his politics, Vallandigham did not encourage disloyalty and treason. Instead, he saw himself as a counter to the Republicans and an advocate of peace. Nonetheless, on May 1, 1863, he made a political speech at Morton, Ohio, in which he asserted that the war could be concluded by negotiation and that Lincoln was needlessly shedding blood. Vallandigham's comments were interpreted as being in violation of Major General Ambrose E. Burnside's General Order No. 38, which had been issued on April 19 and announced that "the habit of declaring sympathies for the enemy [would] be no longer tolerated," and that violators would face punishment by the military. Vallandigham was placed under military arrest and found guilty of making disloyal declarations with the purpose of weakening the government. He was sentenced to confinement for the duration of the war.

Burnside's harsh treatment of Vallandigham caused Lincoln much embarrassment, and Vallandigham exploited every minute of it to enhance his stature. Lincoln removed himself from the awkward situation by changing Vallandigham's sentence from confinement to banishment to within Confederate lines. A military escort deposited him at a Confederate outpost, but his criticism of President Jefferson Davis's handling of the war soon resulted in Vallandigham being ejected from the South as well.

Vallandigham then slipped through the Federal blockade to Nassau and later settled in Canada, returning to the U.S. to deliver the keynote address at the 1864 Democratic Convention in Chicago. He then became supreme commander of the Sons of Liberty, a secret organization of Confederate sympathizers in the North. After the war, Vallandigham made several unsuccessful attempts to be elected to public office. He is considered one of several possible inspirations for Everett Hale's 1863 short story "The Man Without a Country."

VAN DORN, EARL (1820–63)

❖ RANK: Major general

❖ PLACE OF BIRTH: Claiborne County, Mississippi

❖ EDUCATED: West Point

❖ MILITARY CAREER:
1842–61: Served in U.S. Army, fighting in Mexican War, rising to rank of major
1861: Appointed to colonel commanding Confederate forces in Texas; promoted to brigadier general in command of Trans-Mississippi District
1862: Unsuccessful at Battle of Pea Ridge and Second Battle of Corinth
1863: Success at Battle of Thompson's Station

Earl Van Dorn graduated from West Point fifty-second in the fifty-six-man class of 1842. He saw a significant amount of fighting against Native Americans on the frontier as well as service in the Mexican and Seminole wars. He resigned from the U.S. Army on January 31, 1861, and soon succeeded Jefferson Davis as Mississippi's state major general. On March 16, Van Dorn was commissioned as a colonel in the Confederate army and placed in command of Forts Jackson and St. Philip below New Orleans. On April 11, he became commander of the

Left: *Earl Van Dorn's destructive raid against the supply depot at Holly Springs altered Ulysses S. Grant's approach to the Vicksburg Campaign.*

Department of Texas, and on April 20 he captured the *Star of the West* at Galveston. He was promoted to brigadier general on June 5 and major general on September 19, commanding a division in Virginia.

In January 1862, Van Dorn took command of the Trans-Mississippi Department, and on March 7–8 he was defeated in the poorly fought Battle of Pea Ridge, Arkansas. He then withdrew into Mississippi and became commander of the District of Mississippi.

There Van Dorn was strategically located, along with Major General Sterling Price, to both threaten Federal operations in Mississippi and reinforce General Braxton Bragg in Tennessee.

This opportunity, however, was thwarted by a Confederate lack of unity of effort and strategic vision. Van Dorn was defeated at Iuka on September 19 and again at Corinth on October 3–4. He was court-martialed for neglect of duty, but was later vindicated at trial.

CAVALRY COMMANDER

Van Dorn finally found his calling on December 12, 1862, when Lieutenant General John C. Pemberton ordered him to take command of all the cavalry in the vicinity of Grenada, Mississippi, and launch a raid against Major General Ulysses S. Grant's communications. On December 18, Van Dorn left Grenada with 3,500 cavalrymen, and on December 20 he descended upon the Federal depot at Holly Springs, destroying an estimated $1.5 million worth of supplies there.

From there, Van Dorn proceeded north, destroying as much of the railroad as he could before returning to Grenada on December 28. A twin raid was conducted by Van Dorn and Brigadier General Nathan Bedford Forrest against the important rail junction at Jackson, Tennessee, on December 20. The

raids left Grant in serious danger and forced him to withdraw to La Grange, Tennessee, abandoning his effort to support Major General William T. Sherman's Chickasaw Bluffs operation.

Van Dorn conducted another raid in March 1863 in which he routed a Federal brigade at Spring Hill, Tennessee. Van Dorn, however, was a notorious womanizer and may have become involved with a local married woman.

On May 8, he was shot and killed by Dr. James Peters, who accused Van Dorn of "violating the sanctity of his home." The exact circumstances surrounding the incident remain a mystery, and Van Dorn's supporters argued that Peters acted for political or financial reasons.

VETERANS' PENSIONS

Having not survived the war, the Confederate States of America provided no veterans' pensions like those the U.S. Government provided its Civil War veterans. Instead, the individual ex-Confederate states began offering pensions at various times and under various circumstances. For example, in 1867 Alabama began granting

pensions to Confederate veterans who had lost arms or legs. In 1886, it began granting pensions to veterans' widows, and in 1891 the law was amended to grant pensions to impoverished veterans or their widows. North Carolina began granting pensions in 1867 to Confederate veterans who were blinded or lost an arm or leg during their service. In 1885, it began granting pensions to all other disabled impoverished Confederate veterans or widows. The other ex-Confederate states adopted similar policies. In addition to the eleven seceded states, Oklahoma, Kentucky, and Missouri all offered some form of pension.

VETERANS' REUNIONS

Confederate veterans began gathering for reunions as early as the 1870s. These meetings accelerated when the United Confederate Veterans was formed on June 10, 1889. Perhaps the

Below: *A meeting of Confederate veterans in Gettysburg, Pennsylvania, in 1913. The "Tar Heel" banner identifies these veterans as former members of a North Carolina regiment.*

Above: *Confederate veterans of the Battle of Gettysburg gather for a reunion almost fifty years after the end of the Civil War.*

most famous reunion occurred on July 1, 1913, when Federal and Confederate veterans descended on Gettysburg for the fiftieth anniversary of the battle.

The highlight of the gathering was the July 3 reenactment of Pickett's Charge in which 120 members of Major General George E. Pickett's division charged 180 veterans of the Philadelphia Brigade defending Cemetery Ridge. In one of the era's most iconic photographs, the aged veterans are shown shaking hands across the stone wall.

The United Confederate Veterans held its final national reunion in 1951, and a U.S. postage stamp was issued to mark the occasion.

VICKSBURG CAMPAIGN AND SIEGE

❖ DATE (SIEGE): May 18–July 4, 1863

❖ LOCATION: Warren County, Mississippi

❖ ARMY OF MISSISSIPPI (C): 33,000

❖ ARMY OF THE TENNESSEE (U.S.): 77,000

❖ CASUALTIES: 32,697 (C); 4,835 (U.S.)

At the time of the Civil War, the Mississippi River was the single most important economic feature of the continent. It was also a natural boundary between the eastern and western halves of the Confederacy. If the Federals could gain control of the Mississippi

River, they would not only secure the free flow of their internal commerce, they would cut the Confederacy in two in a way that challenged its very identity as a nation. Standing in the way of this plan was the Confederate strongpoint of Vicksburg, defended by Lieutenant General John C. Pemberton. After a long campaign of maneuver and siege, Major General Ulysses S. Grant compelled Pemberton to surrender on July 4, 1863, securing a Federal victory that many consider to be more important even than Gettysburg.

STRATEGIC LOCATION
Vicksburg is located about 300 miles downstream from Memphis, Tennessee, where the Mississippi River makes a hairpin turn, and the river channel there narrows to a quarter-mile and runs 100 feet deep.

Above: *Federal artillerymen train their guns toward Vicksburg. The Federal forces commanded by Ulysses S. Grant laid siege to the city and slowly strangled Vicksburg into surrendering.*

Standing high on a bluff, Vicksburg could dominate river traffic at this strategic point.

Grant had some 44,000 effectives in his Army of the Tennessee, but he faced the problem of how to get them from Memphis to Vicksburg. He could not approach by the river because of Vicksburg's strong batteries, but the terrain surrounding Vicksburg was so wet and swampy that it made military ground movement there impractical as well.

Between December 1862 and March 1863, Grant tried at least five separate plans to break through to Vicksburg, including a disastrous repulse at Chickasaw Bluffs and several schemes to dig canals or otherwise use the tangled system of rivers, bayous, and swamps to find a

Right: *Before initiating siege operations, Ulysses S. Grant carried out two ill-fated assaults on May 19 and 22, 1863, on the strong Confederate defenses at Vicksburg, taking almost 1,000 casualties in the process.*

way to approach Vicksburg from the rear. All failed, but when the spring of 1863 began to dry out the soggy ground, Grant was ready.

NAVAL ASSISTANCE

Grant's plan was to avoid a frontal assault on the Confederate defenses by marching his army down the west side of the Mississippi to a point below Vicksburg. There the troops would meet vessels commanded by Admiral David D. Porter that would ferry the men across the river. To accomplish this, Porter

would have to "run the gauntlet" past the Vicksburg batteries.

On March 31, Grant began his overland march with Major General John A. McClernand's corps in the lead, followed by Major General James B. McPherson. Major General William T. Sherman's corps stayed behind to protect the base of operations above Vicksburg. Grant also created several highly successful diversions to distract Pemberton, the greatest being a cavalry raid led by Colonel Benjamin H. Grierson. On the night of April 16–17, Porter ran the

batteries at Vicksburg with eight of his gunboats and three transports. More steamers made the dash five days later. With Porter's vessels south of Vicksburg, Grant now had the means to cross to the east bank of the Mississippi without facing the stiffest Confederate defenses.

Pemberton had about the same size force that Grant did, but all the movements and diversions left Pemberton confused and unsure of himself. His force was widely scattered and certainly not properly positioned to oppose Grant. To make matters worse, Pemberton had no naval support that could challenge Porter.

Grant was now south of Vicksburg, but he was on the west side of the Mississippi River. On April 28, he made an attempt to force a crossing at Grand Gulf, but

was easily repulsed by the well-placed Confederate batteries there.

Undeterred, Grant soon received intelligence from a runaway slave that just twelve miles south of Grand Gulf there was an undefended crossing at Bruinsburg. Grant moved his men there and began crossing the Mississippi on April 30. By the end of the day, Grant had 22,000 Federals on the Mississippi side of the river. Brigadier General John S. Bowen attempted to halt Grant's advance inland, but Grant brushed this small force aside and established a foothold at Port Gibson.

Grant studied his options and then decided to cut loose from his line of supply, and set off in a northeastward direction with the objective of cutting the railroad link between Vicksburg and Jackson. In

part, Grant lived off the land, but he also received a steady stream of wagons from his newly established base at Grand Gulf.

PEMBERTON PLAYS SAFE

Advancing on multiple axes to facilitate foraging and keep Pemberton guessing, Grant cut a swath toward central Mississippi, with Pemberton offering little resistance. Divided by instructions from President Jefferson Davis to "hold both Vicksburg and Port Hudson" and from General Joseph E. Johnston to strike Grant, Pemberton played it safe and consolidated his forces west of the

Below: *The surrounded Confederate positions were subjected to fire from both land- and river-based Federal forces at Vicksburg.*

Above: *Ulysses S. Grant (left) negotiates with Confederate commander John Pemberton. Grant decided to parole Pemberton's men after they surrendered at Vicksburg.*

Big Black to protect Vicksburg. In the meantime, Davis ordered reinforcements to Jackson and told Johnston to take command personally in Mississippi.

A small brigade commanded by Brigadier General John Gregg marched out of Jackson and encountered an entire division of Major General James B. McPherson's corps at Raymond on May 12. Gregg fought valiantly but was simply outnumbered and had to withdraw back to Jackson. Still, the tenacious Confederate resistance as well as reports that Johnston was assembling an army in Jackson convinced Grant to modify his plans. Rather than risk being caught in between

Pemberton and Johnston, Grant decided to shift his objective from the railroad and first deal with Johnston before turning his attention to Pemberton.

On May 13, Grant sent Sherman and McPherson on two separate axes toward Jackson. That same day, Johnston arrived in Jackson and, betraying his predetermined pessimism for the entire affair, declared, "I am too late." Behind a small screen from Gregg, Johnston withdrew to the north. On May 14, the Federals began their assault on Jackson and captured it against little resistance. Grant neutralized anything of military value, and with Johnston out of the picture and Jackson under control, he had Vicksburg isolated. Grant could now turn west and deal with Pemberton.

As Pemberton marched east in an unpromising attempt to unite with Johnston at Clinton, Grant's forces

surprised him near Champion Hill. In what would prove to be the decisive battle of the campaign, Grant defeated Pemberton and forced him to retreat back to his Vicksburg defenses. Pemberton was now isolated, with no offensive options.

Grant pursued Pemberton and hoped to defeat him before he could improve his already formidable defenses. Grant hurled two impetuous assaults against the Vicksburg fortifications, one on May 19 and a second on May 22. Both failed. Grant then decided to lay siege to Vicksburg, knowing that time was on his side.

The siege phase of the campaign lasted six weeks, and the results were largely inevitable. Every day, Grant's force became stronger thanks to his solid logistical base that provided reinforcements and supplies. Pemberton, on the other hand, became steadily weaker, as both his army and the civilian population of Vicksburg consumed the finite provisions in the city.

Using formalized European siege tactics, Grant dug fortifications facing the Confederate works and battered the Confederate strongpoints with siege batteries. Porter's vessels contributed to the siege both with fire from the river and by delivering supplies. Within the siege lines, the Federal troops dug approaches and exploded mines on June 25 and July 1 but undertook no general assaults after the failed effort on May 22.

As the siege dragged on, morale within Vicksburg deteriorated. When Pemberton polled his generals to see if they thought a breakout was possible, they unanimously said no. On July 3, he opened negotiations with Grant.

Initially Grant demanded unconditional surrender, but later agreed to terms that allowed the Confederates to give up their weapons and then be paroled. On July 4, the Federals took control of Vicksburg. Often overshadowed by the twin Federal victory at Gettysburg, Vicksburg is arguably the more decisive of the two battles. With the parole of Pemberton's army, the Confederacy lost critical manpower.

The Federals could now concentrate on the only remaining Confederate army in the west, the Army of Tennessee. In addition to facilitating their own commerce, by controlling the Mississippi the Federals also bisected the Confederacy, leaving it with logistical and strategic problems as well as damaging the Confederacy's sense of nationhood.

VIRGINIA

On the eve of the Civil War, Virginia was the most important state in the South, if not in the entire United States. It had provided the nation with seven presidents, Richmond was the South's only truly industrialized city, Norfolk was one of its handful of shipbuilding centers, and the Shenandoah Valley was an agricultural breadbasket. Virginia's secession was absolutely critical to the Confederacy, but as an Upper South state, Virginia was decidedly conservative. The delegates selected on February 4, 1861, for the state convention consisted of forty-six secessionists and 106 moderates. Governor John Letcher was a moderate, ex-president and Virginian John Tyler attempted to arrange a sectional compromise, and Robert E. Lee opposed secession. Unionist sentiment was particularly strong in the far western counties, which had little stake in slavery. On the other hand, fire-eater Henry A. Wise, a former governor, organized a "Spontaneous Southern Rights Convention" to encourage secession. While the radical rhetoric increased, the moderates still retained a sufficient majority to stall action.

Like other border states, what prodded Virginia into motion was President Abraham Lincoln's call for volunteers in the aftermath of Fort Sumter. Rather than bear arms against their fellow Southerners, the Virginia convention on April 17 voted for secession by an 88–55 margin. Almost immediately, dissenters from the western counties began plans to separate from the state. Their efforts ultimately succeeded, and on April 20, 1863, Lincoln issued a proclamation declaring the new state of West Virginia be admitted to the Union.

In recognition of Virginia's importance, the Confederate capital was moved to Richmond from Montgomery, Alabama, in May. This decision, as well as Virginia's status as a border state, ensured that Virginia would be a battleground throughout the war. Key battles fought there are too numerous to list in full, but include First and Second Manassas, the Peninsula Campaign, the Shenandoah Valley Campaign, Fredericksburg, Chancellorsville, and the 1864–65 Overland Campaign.

Virginia's contributions to the Confederate leadership were also phenomenal, including General

Below: *A key strategic location, much of Virginia suffered horribly during the Civil War, as shown by these ruins of Haxall's Mills in Richmond.*

Robert E. Lee, General Joseph E. Johnston, Lieutenant General Stonewall Jackson, and many others. The Virginia Military Institute also served as a productive training ground for junior leaders, and the fledgling Confederate Naval Academy was located along the James River.

Lee's preeminence in the Confederate army and his devotion to Virginia were critical in shaping Confederate military strategy and ensuring that the eastern theater would be the priority.

Although Virginia contributed greatly to the Confederate war effort, it also suffered horribly in its defeat. By the war's end 80 percent of eligible Virginia men had served in the army. Their absence, combined with the devastation wrought by invading Federal soldiers, produced enormous hardship throughout the state, especially in places like the Shenandoah Valley that felt the "hard war" tactics of Major General Philip H. Sheridan.

VIRGINIA MILITARY INSTITUTE

In 1839 the Virginia legislature approved replacing the guard company at the Lexington Arsenal with a military school intended to provide the state with a pool of competent militia officers, engineers, and teachers. This school became the Virginia Military Institute, a critical source of Civil War leadership for both Virginia and the Confederate army. Of the sixty-four regiments Virginia raised in 1861, twenty-two were commanded by VMI graduates.

On a broader scale, of the 1,902 VMI graduates from 1839 to 1865, 1,781 served in the Confederate army. As a testimony to the VMI's contribution to the Confederate cause, on the eve of the Battle of Chancellorsville, Lieutenant General Stonewall Jackson surveyed the ranks and saw many

former cadets and VMI associates in command positions. He turned to his cavalry leader, Colonel Thomas T. Munford, VMI class of 1852, and said, "The Institute will be heard from today." Jackson himself had served at the VMI as a professor of natural philosophy (known today as physics) and an instructor of artillery from August 13, 1851, to the outbreak of the war. Today, he is honored with a prominent statue on the VMI grounds.

After abolitionist John Brown was captured at Harpers Ferry and sentenced to be hanged for treason, there was fear that there might be an attempt to help him escape. Under the order of the governor, Jackson moved a contingent of cadets to Harpers Ferry, where they helped to maintain order in the days before and following Brown's execution. As tensions in the United States continued to mount, Jackson advised the cadets in April 1861 that "the time for war has not yet come, but it will come and that soon; and when it does come, my advice is to draw the sword and throw away the scabbard." When the Civil War finally began, VMI cadets were ordered to Richmond to serve as drill instructors for Confederate recruits. Pursuant to these instructions, Jackson moved 200 cadets to Richmond on April 21, 1861, where they reported to Confederate headquarters at Camp Lee. The school resumed "normal" operations in January 1862 with 269 cadets.

The cadet corps was called out as reserve in April and May 1862 during Jackson's McDowell Campaign and took to the field three times in 1863 to help resist Federal cavalry raids in southwest Virginia. Its most famous battlefield appearance was at the May 15, 1864, Battle of New Market in which a battalion of 247 VMI cadets commanded by Lieutenant Colonel Scott Shipp helped turned back a Federal force of over 6,000 men. Ten cadets were killed and forty-seven wounded in the battle. The monument "Virginia Mourning Her Dead" on the VMI campus honors these cadets. Following the Battle of New Market, the corps was ordered to Richmond, where it served briefly in the city's defenses. It returned to Lexington in June to resist Major General David Hunter's destructive advance in the Shenandoah Valley, but could do little to prevent the Federals from burning many of the VMI facilities. The corps was furloughed from July to October, when it was re-formed at Richmond to serve in the city's defenses. It was disbanded on April 2, 1865, on the eve of the evacuation of Richmond. The school reopened in October 1865.

SOUTHERN "VOLUNTEERS".

VOLUNTEERS

Volunteers flocked to the state regiments being formed in the early days of the war. The initial assumption that the war would be ended quickly created a desire in many to not miss this grand opportunity. Most enlisted because of patriotism, but others were merely looking for adventure or got caught up in the moment. There certainly was community enthusiasm for the new soldiers, who were often showered with attention from young ladies and other well-wishers. After the Confederate government began the draft, volunteering enjoyed

Above: *This cartoon depicts a less-than-flattering image of the Confederate soldier in the wake of the Conscription Act of April 16, 1862.*

renewed popularity as a means of avoiding the stigma associated with conscription.

The enthusiasm of volunteers was tempered once they were exposed to the rigors and routine

Below: *In a satirical scene, a reluctant civilian is presented with a musket and military coat by two veterans. The recruit is restrained from behind by another officer. In the background, left, a troop of recruits drill; on the right, two African American soldiers, one with rolled pants and military coat, look on with amusement.*

VOLUNTEERING DOWN DIXIE

Above: *Volunteer troops are familiarized with weapons stored at an armory in Charleston, South Carolina, in 1861.*

of military life. At first the new tasks seemed novel, but in short time the endless marching, drilling, parades, inspections, and camp duties grew monotonous. Volunteers found guard duty to be particularly mind-numbing.

Volunteers also had to come to grips with the reality of soldiering. The gaudy uniforms and accoutrements of the early days gave way to more practical items, and the volunteer learned that carrying extra equipment was physically demanding. The new soldiers learned to make do with the essentials.

Military discipline presented another challenge to the volunteer. Most entered the army with the individualism characteristic of the Southerner. The army's emphasis on uniformity, standardization,

and respect for authority warred against this value, but gradually the volunteer learned to accept, if not relish, his new environment. By 1862 he had become a soldier.

WALKER, LEROY P. (1817–84)

Leroy Pope Walker graduated from the University of Alabama and studied law at the University of Virginia. He was active in Democratic politics as a jurist and legislator and developed into an ardent secessionist.

On February 16, 1861, President Jefferson Davis appointed Walker to be his first secretary of war, a seemingly vital position for which Walker had little in the way of qualifications. Many observers felt Walker's selection indicated that Davis intended to minimize this office and for all practical purposes serve as his own secretary

of war. Walker had some success in focusing the Confederate effort to acquire weapons, setting up purchasing operations overseas, and equipping the newly formed units. However, he had almost no influence on formulating

Above: *Leroy Walker was the Confederacy's first secretary of war but wielded little influence.*

292

military strategy. A combination of health issues, a hostile Congress, and a domineering president conspired against Walker, and he resigned his position on September 16.

The next day, Davis appointed Walker as a brigadier general in the Confederate army. He served in artillery assignments in the Department of Alabama and West Florida but was unable to obtain the field command he desired. He resigned on March 31, 1862, and then served as a judge in a military court for the remainder of the war. After the war, he enjoyed considerable political power in Alabama and in 1875 presided over the Alabama constitutional convention.

WAR POWERS, CONFEDERATE GOVERNMENT

In spite of the emergencies of war, traditional Southern values of individualism and decentralization restricted the exercise of strong war powers by the Confederate government. Indeed, historian David Donald argues that the epitaph of the Confederacy might well read "Died of Democracy." President Jefferson Davis maintained a remarkably libertarian record, preserving freedoms of speech and press, as well as freedom from arbitrary arrest, even at the expense of his government. On only three occasions did Congress grudgingly permit Davis to suspend the writ of habeas corpus, and no Southern newspaper was suppressed for espousing views critical of the government.

Davis was decidedly apolitical. He never endorsed a political candidate, and he discouraged the formation of political parties. He even refused to silence his own vice president, Alexander H.

Stephens, who became one of Davis's most vocal critics. In contrast, President Abraham Lincoln enjoyed much broader wartime powers and was much more willing to limit civil liberties.

WATIE, STAND (1806–71)

Stand Watie was the son of a full-blooded Cherokee father and a half-blooded mother. Before the war he was a planter and newspaperman. Watie became unpopular with many Cherokees when he signed a treaty that surrendered their land in Georgia to the federal government and required them to move to Oklahoma. The three other members of the tribe who signed the treaty were killed the day it was signed, and Watie was also earmarked for assassination but escaped. When the Cherokee

Above: *A commander of Native American troops in the Confederate army, Stand Watie rose to brigadier general.*

Nation split into two factions, Watie became the leader of the smaller one.

When the Civil War began, Watie and other Cherokees at first tried to remain neutral, but Watie eventually signed an alliance with the Confederacy and convinced John Ross, the leader of the other Cherokee faction, to also support the Confederacy. Watie raised a company of home guards and was commissioned as a captain in early 1861.

Later that year he was appointed as a colonel of the Cherokee Mounted Rifles and mustered into the Confederate army. He fought at Wilson's Creek, Pea Ridge, and in many smaller skirmishes throughout the Indian Territory and Arkansas, earning a reputation as a daring cavalry raider.

In 1863 the majority Cherokee party repudiated the alliance with the Confederacy and began to side with the Federals. Watie remained with the Confederacy and became the principal chief of the tribe's Southern wing. He was appointed as a brigadier general in May 1864, and did not surrender until June 23, 1865.

WEST VIRGINIA

After Virginia voted to secede from the Union on April 17, 1861, dissenters from the western counties met in Wheeling in August to begin plans to separate from the state. These sentiments were encouraged by early Federal victories at Philippi, Rich Mountain, Carrick's Ford, and Cheat Mountain.

The Confederates enjoyed short-lived success during the Kanawha Campaign of September 6–16, 1862, when Major General William W. Loring captured Charleston, Virginia, but shortly thereafter the Federals regained control of the area. By 1863 the Confederates could only mount minor raids such as the one conducted by Brigadier Generals John D. Imboden and William Jones in April 1863. By then Federal control of the area was so strong that on April 20, 1863, President Abraham Lincoln issued a proclamation declaring the new state of West Virginia be admitted to the Union.

WESTERN THEATER

The Civil War's western theater certainly enjoys less popular renown than the eastern theater, but some historians argue it was there that the war's decisive battle, Vicksburg, was fought. Vicksburg controlled the Mississippi River, the western theater's defining feature. The Mississippi was not just the United States' most important transportation artery, it also divided the Confederacy in two. In order to maintain its national identity as well as ensure a continual flow of agricultural goods from its trans-Mississippi states, the Confederacy had to keep control of the Mississippi.

However, the Mississippi, like the other rivers in the western theater, offered an efficient Federal avenue of approach into the Confederate heartland. The Cumberland and Tennessee rivers posed the same risk to the Confederacy in Tennessee.

RUGGED TERRAIN

Mountains also played an important role in the western theater. The only significant east–west break in the region's rugged topography was by the Tennessee River Valley at Chattanooga, Tennessee. Defense

Right: *Joseph Wheeler commanded Confederate troops in the Civil War and then American troops during the Spanish–American War.*

of this area was critical to the Confederacy in order to protect its lower states.

The influence of General Robert E. Lee ensured the strategic primacy of the eastern theater. Nonetheless, there was a western bloc that argued that the Confederacy's true interests lay in the west. This informal group's members included General Joseph E. Johnston, General Pierre Gustave Toutant Beauregard, and Senator Louis T. Wigfall. However, in issues like the debate to reinforce Vicksburg or launch the Gettysburg Campaign, Lee's reputation, arguments, and record of success generally carried the day. In fact, the western theater became somewhat of a dumping ground for many generals who did not meet Lee's exacting standards in the Army of Northern Virginia.

WHEELER, JOSEPH (1836–1906)

Joseph Wheeler graduated from West Point toward the bottom of the class of 1859. He served as a dragoon on the frontier until he resigned from the U.S. Army on April 22, 1861.

He fought as the colonel of the Nineteenth Alabama Regiment at Shiloh and was promoted to brigadier general on October 30, 1862. He led a brigade at Murfreesboro and was promoted to major general on January 20, 1863.

On July 18, Wheeler entered the most important phase of his career when he was given command of all the cavalry of the Army of Mississippi. In this capacity, he conducted a series of raids against Federal communications, including

operations associated with the Chattanooga and Atlanta campaigns. He earned the nickname "Fightin' Joe" for his hard-hitting, aggressive tactics, but was more successful supporting a main army than in independent operations.

Wheeler was promoted to lieutenant general on February 4, 1864. He helped resist Major General William T. Sherman's March to the Sea and Carolinas Campaign before being captured in May 1865.

SPANISH–AMERICAN WAR

After the war, Wheeler entered politics as a Democratic congressman from Alabama, but was most well known for serving as a major general of volunteers during the Spanish-American War. Indeed, for many, the Spanish-American War marked a sectional healing in the United States in which the former Civil War antagonists united as Americans against a common enemy. Wheeler fought at San Juan Hill and in the Philippines, and retired from the U.S. Army in 1900 as a brigadier general.

WIDOWS, RELIEF OF

The ex-Confederate states began offering different pensions to widows of Confederate veterans at different times. For example, Virginia began offering widows' pensions in 1888, Tennessee in 1905, and Arkansas in 1915. States had to deal with younger women marrying older veterans well after the war had ended and claiming benefits. For example, in 1920, South Carolina revised its eligibility criteria to include only widows who had been married by 1900. In 1929 a further amendment extended eligibility to widows who had been married at least ten years.

Alberta Martin of Alabama was thought to be the last Confederate widow when she died on May 31, 2004, at age ninety-seven. When Martin married in 1927, her husband, William Jasper Martin, was eighty-one years old and she was only twenty-one. At the time of her death, Martin was receiving $2,500 per month from the state Confederate veterans' widows' pension, but the payments were sometimes seen as controversial and were even suspended for a short period of time. After her death, Maudie Hopkins of Lexa, Arkansas, emerged as another contender for the distinction of last surviving Confederate widow. She reportedly married William Cantrell in 1934, when she was nineteen and he was eighty-six. Hopkins died in 2008, but she did not receive widows' benefits after her husband's death.

WIGFALL, LOUIS T. (1816–74)

After graduating from the University of Virginia and South Carolina College, Louis T. Wigfall served as a volunteer lieutenant in the Second Seminole War before beginning a tumultuous law practice in South Carolina. He killed one man as the result of a political disagreement, and he both inflicted and received a wound in a duel with Preston Brooks. Wigfall moved to Texas in 1848 and served in the legislature and the U.S. Senate. A staunch advocate of secession, he delivered his "Southern Address" to the Senate in December 1860. He was an ardent believer in the power of "King Cotton." Wigfall resigned his seat on March 23, 1861, and went to Charleston, South Carolina, where he played an active role in the operations against Fort Sumter.

On October 21, 1861, Wigfall was appointed as a brigadier general in the Confederate army and led Texan troops in Virginia until resigning on February 20, 1862, to become a congressman. He advocated strong wartime measures, including conscription, impressment, and the suspension of habeas corpus. He was one of the most powerful members of Congress.

In spite of his brief military career, Wigfall considered himself something of a military genius, and he became an outspoken critic of President Jefferson Davis. He was a champion of General Joseph E. Johnston and an advocate of the importance of the western theater of operations. After the war, Wigfall fled to England before eventually returning to Texas.

Below: *Louis Wigfall pressed Jefferson Davis to place more emphasis on the western theater of operations.*

WILDERNESS, BATTLE OF THE

- ❖ DATE: May 5–7, 1864
- ❖ LOCATION: Spotsylvania County, Virginia
- ❖ ARMY OF NORTHERN VIRGINIA (C): 61,025
- ❖ ARMY OF THE POTOMAC (U.S.): 101,895
- ❖ CASUALTIES: 10,000 (C); 17,000 (U.S.)

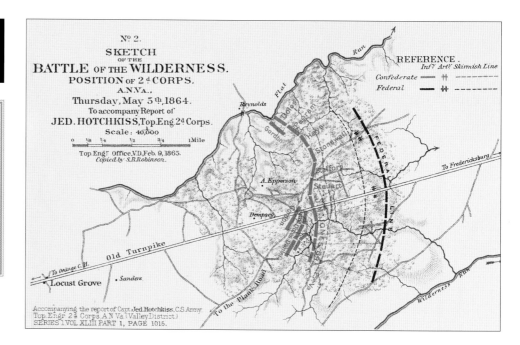

Above: *A map showing the battle positions on May 5, 1864. Even though he was defeated at the Battle of the Wilderness, Ulysses S. Grant continued to pressure Robert E. Lee.*

As part of his comprehensive strategy to press the Confederacy on all fronts, Lieutenant General Ulysses S. Grant crossed the Rapidan River on May 4, 1864, into an area of Virginia appropriately called the Wilderness. Grant outnumbered General Robert E. Lee by almost double the troop strength, but the restrictive terrain helped offset Lee's small numbers and negate Grant's superior firepower. Using this defender's advantage, Lee defeated Grant, but unlike previous Federal commanders, Grant did not withdraw. He continued to press Lee, bringing a new strategy of relentless attack that would ultimately grind the Army of Northern Virginia into submission.

The Wilderness was a tangled second growth of thick vegetation concealing a few roads that often led nowhere. The ground itself was compartmentalized by irregular ridges and crisscrossed by numerous streams that cut shallow ravines. It was a difficult place to maneuver a large army, and after crossing the Rapidan, Grant had hoped to clear the dangerous Wilderness as soon as he could. Instead, he was delayed as he waited for his supply train to catch up with his army. Grant and Lee were now in close proximity to each other, but neither knew exactly where the other was until May 5 when the Federals made contact with Lieutenant General Richard S. Ewell's corps and launched a hasty frontal attack that the Confederates stopped.

The fighting resumed at 5:00 a.m. the next day. The Federals gained the initial advantage, but as the battle wore on, the restrictive terrain caused Grant's units to dissolve into smaller and smaller groups. In one of the most memorable moments in Confederate lore, Lee rode to meet Brigadier General John Gregg's Texas Brigade as it arrived on the field, saying, "Ah! These are my brave Texans. I know you,

Left: *The dense terrain at the Battle of the Wilderness helped Robert E. Lee's numerically inferior army, since it made it difficult for the Federals to concentrate their forces.*

and I know that you can and will keep those people back!" Lee then prepared to personally lead the first counterattacking units, but passionate cries of "Lee to the rear!" dissuaded him.

Heavy fighting ensued as Gregg's men met stiff Federal resistance. Darkness and Federal reinforcements halted the Confederate effort, and during the night, both sides dug new lines. It was a terrible night, as brush fires burned many helpless wounded soldiers.

In spite of the superior Federal numbers, the Wilderness ended up a lopsided tactical victory for the Confederates, with Grant suffering 17,000 casualties compared to 10,000 for Lee. However, Grant knew that he could replace his losses while Lee could not. Thus, instead of retreating, Grant would keep the pressure on Lee by simply disengaging and continuing the effort to get around Lee's flank. Even after a tactical defeat, Grant would keep attacking, using the powerful Federal resources to grind away at Lee. In that sense, the Battle of the Wilderness marked the beginning of the end for the Army of Northern Virginia, and with it, the Confederacy.

Below: *These wounded soldiers recuperating following the Battle of the Wilderness escaped the nocturnal brush fires that killed many of their comrades.*

Above: *The Confederates take the field. Unlike previous Federal commanders, Ulysses Grant refused to retreat after the defeat at the Battle of the Wilderness.*

WILLIAMSBURG, BATTLE OF

❖ DATE: May 4–5, 1862

❖ LOCATION: York County and Williamsburg, Virginia

❖ FORCE UNDER LONGSTREET (C): 31,823

❖ ARMY OF THE POTOMAC (U.S.): 40,768

❖ CASUALTIES: 1,560 (C); 2,283 (U.S.)

On May 3, 1862, Confederate forces commanded by General Joseph E. Johnston abandoned Yorktown and withdrew up the Virginia Peninsula. Johnston's intention was to retreat rapidly to the vicinity of Richmond and negate the possibility of Major General George B. McClellan using the James River to outmaneuver him and get there first. A sharp delaying action at Williamsburg on May 4–5 helped Johnston make good his escape.

Johnston withdrew along two roads that came together eleven miles past Yorktown and two miles short of Williamsburg. For his retreat, he had his forces organized into four commands led by Major Generals James Longstreet, D. H. Hill, Gustavus W. Smith, and David Jones. Brigadier General Jeb Stuart's cavalry provided the rear guard. In the early afternoon of May 4, Federal troops pursuing Johnston caught up with Stuart's cavalry and began to push it in. Johnston ordered Longstreet to fight a delaying action to allow the remainder of the Confederate force to continue withdrawing along the single muddy road from Williamsburg to Richmond.

Williamsburg was a spot well suited for Longstreet's task. He would be defending an area between Queen's and College creeks that was only three miles wide. He was further assisted by a confused Federal pursuit that had a disjointed command structure and little knowledge of the terrain. The result was a piecemealed Federal attack.

LONGSTREET SUCCEEDS

In a sharp battle on May 5, Longstreet succeeded in halting the Federal advance, and then broke contact and rejoined his retreating comrades. When the Federals conducted reconnaissance the next morning, they found Longstreet gone. Thereafter, the Federals offered only token pursuit.

They were further hindered by primed artillery shells the Confederates hid in abatis as crude mines. Longstreet's successful delay at the Battle of Williamsburg was essential in allowing the Confederates to reorganize themselves to defend Richmond.

Above: *Union troops advance in closed ranks at the Battle of Williamsburg. The Battle of Williamsburg bought time for Joseph Johnston to continue his withdrawal up the Virginia Peninsula.*

Below: *This cartoon shows the controversy associated with the Wilmot Proviso, a measure that would have prevented any territory gained during the Mexican War from becoming a slave state.*

WILMOT PROVISO (1846)

On August 6, 1846, in the midst of the Mexican War, Pennsylvania congressman David Wilmot introduced a resolution that would prohibit slavery in any of the territory acquired from Mexico as a result of the war. This Wilmot Proviso was championed by the antislavery wing of the Democratic Party and cleared the House over vigorous Southern opposition. The Senate, however,

did not approve the measure. The proviso was reintroduced in February 1847, with the same result. Although defeated in this instance, antislavery forces continued their efforts to prohibit the expansion of slavery while many Southerners fought equally passionately against any further restrictions on the institution.

Above: *David Wilmot's failed proviso showed how divisive an issue slavery had become in national politics.*

WILSON'S CREEK, BATTLE OF

- ❖ DATE: August 10, 1861
- ❖ LOCATION: Greene and Christian counties, Missouri
- ❖ MISSOURI STATE GUARD AND McCULLOCH'S BRIGADE (C): 12,000
- ❖ ARMY OF THE WEST (U.S.): 6,000
- ❖ CASUALTIES: 1,095 (C); 1,235 (U.S.)

As Unionist and secessionist forces struggled to control Missouri, Captain Nathaniel Lyon moved 6,000 troops into the southwest part of the state. Sterling

Above: *One of the war's early battles, Wilson's Creek was part of the vicious struggle for control of Missouri.*

Price and Brigadier General Benjamin McCulloch had established a camp of some 12,000 Confederates along Wilson's Creek. Lyon attacked on August 10, 1861. He was killed, and the Federals retreated to Rolla while Price advanced to Lexington. Wilson's Creek was a small engagement, but it showed the intensity of emotions in Missouri.

WINCHESTER, BATTLES OF

- ❖ DATE: September 19, 1864 (Third Battle of Winchester)
- ❖ LOCATION: Frederick County, Virginia
- ❖ ARMY OF THE VALLEY (C): 15,200
- ❖ ARMY OF THE SHENANDOAH (U.S.): 39,240
- ❖ CASUALTIES: 3,610 (C); 5,020 (U.S.)

Winchester, Virginia, was the scene of a tremendous amount of fighting during the Civil War. Its location at the junction of several roads; its proximity to

Washington, D.C., and the Baltimore and Ohio Railroad; and its presence in the agriculturally rich Shenandoah Valley made it a very strategic location, and several engagements were fought near it.

The First Battle of Winchester was fought on May 25, 1862, as part of Major General Stonewall Jackson's Shenandoah Valley Campaign. After defeating the Federals at Front Royal on May 23, Jackson rapidly marched his "foot cavalry" to prevent the Federals from fortifying the critical heights around Winchester. In a skillful attack, Jackson routed the Federal force of Major General Nathaniel P. Banks.

SECOND WINCHESTER

The Second Battle of Winchester was fought on June 13–15, 1863, as part of the Gettysburg Campaign. Brigadier General Robert H. Milroy had begun an oppressive Federal occupation of the town on January 1, but he beat an inglorious retreat in the face of Lieutenant General Richard S. Ewell's attack. Ewell anticipated Milroy's withdrawal and cut off his route, inflicting 4,443 Federal casualties, including 3,358 who were taken prisoner.

The Third Battle of Winchester

Above: *Federal units attack Confederate troops defending a hill. The First Battle of Winchester was one of the highlights of Stonewall Jackson's Shenandoah Valley Campaign.*

Below: *During the Second Battle of Winchester, Richard Ewell cut off a Federal retreat from the town.*

was fought on September 19, 1864, as part of Major General Philip H. Sheridan's Shenandoah Valley Campaign. Major General Jubal A. Early had deployed his force in dispersed locations, and Sheridan took advantage of the faulty arrangement to feint to the northeast and move his main force from Berryville against Winchester.

Although Sheridan gained an initial advantage, Early's fast-marching veterans were able to elude decisive defeat and escape to Fisher's Hill.

In addition to these three major battles, there were enough smaller skirmishes and raids that Winchester changed hands over seventy times, of which fourteen represented formal changes of possession. This

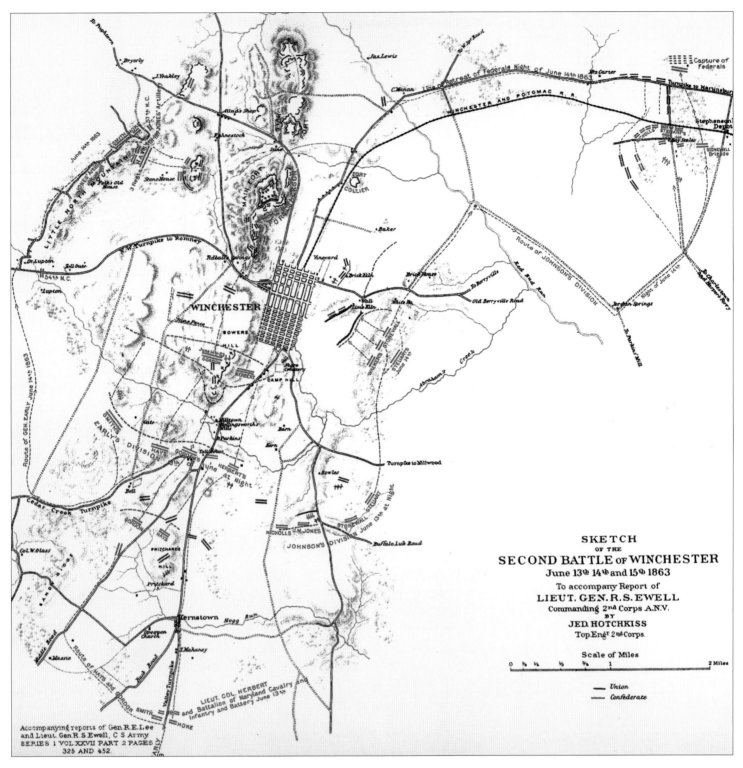

SKETCH
OF THE
SECOND BATTLE OF WINCHESTER
June 13th 14th and 15th 1863
To accompany Report of
LIEUT. GEN. R. S. EWELL
Commanding 2nd Corps A.N.V.
BY
JED. HOTCHKISS
Top. Engr 2nd Corps.

Scale of Miles

Union
Confederate

Above: *A map showing Confederate troop dispositions at the Second Battle of Winchester. The engagement was one of three major battles for the key location, which changed hands over seventy times during the war.*

continuous and disruptive activity left the town battered by the war's end. However, generous citizens from Baltimore donated farm animals, tools, seed, and money to help Winchester recover.

WINDER, JOHN H. (1800–65)

John H. Winder graduated from West Point in 1820 and served as an artillery officer before resigning from the U.S. Army in 1823. He returned to the army as a tactical officer at West Point in 1827 and fought in the Seminole and Mexican wars. In Mexico he served

as military lieutenant governor of Vera Cruz from December 9, 1847, to July 29, 1848. At the outbreak of the Civil War, Winder was on sick leave in his home state of Maryland. His absence from his post at Fort Pickens allowed Lieutenant Adam J. Slemmer to secure the valuable garrison for the Union when Florida seceded on January 10, 1861.

On June 21, 1861, Winder was commissioned in the Confederate army as a brigadier general and assigned command of Libby and Belle Isle military prisons in Richmond. By 1864 his responsibilities were expanded to include command of all prisons in Alabama and Georgia, including the notorious prison at Andersonville. In November of that year, he was given the additional responsibility of serving as commissary general of all prisons east of the Mississippi River.

On March 1, 1862, President Jefferson Davis declared martial law in Richmond and appointed Winder provost marshal general. Winder found this task of controlling his fellow Southerners—who greatly cherished their civil liberties—much more complicated than was his experience governing the defeated and compliant Mexicans at Vera Cruz. Winder became embroiled in controversies involving price controls, a pass system, the press, and alcohol consumption.

His tenure as provost marshal of Richmond was difficult and controversial. Even his critics conceded he got results, but many found his methods heavy-handed and indiscriminate. He was largely unpopular.

Moreover, Northerners accused him of abusing Federal prisoners, although given the scant resources available to him, he probably did the best he could under the circumstances. His death on February 7, 1865, is often attributed to anxiety and fatigue.

WISE, HENRY A.
(1806–76)

Henry A. Wise was a career politician, serving in the House of Representatives from 1833 to 1844, as minister to Brazil from 1844 to 1847, and as governor of Virginia from 1856 to 1860. He was appointed as a brigadier general

on June 5, 1861, and raised an independent legion to help defend the western part of Virginia. Wise lacked both military skill and the ability to cooperate with others. He has few champions, and most observers highlight his abrasive personality, poor judgment, and self-absorption. Even as governor, Wise was frequently at odds with the general assembly, and his programs were regularly vetoed.

These personality flaws contributed to a petty rivalry Wise played out with Brigadier General John B. Floyd in the Kanawha Valley in southwestern Virginia in

Above: *Henry Wise was a fire-eater as governor of Virginia, but was a disappointing political general.*

1861. He had similar problems later in North Carolina, where he had difficulty cooperating with Captain William F. Lynch, his naval counterpart, in the defense of Roanoke Island.

Wise was with General Robert E. Lee at Appomattox Court House and encouraged him to surrender, arguing that it was Lee's duty to save the lives of his men who, Wise argued, were at this point only following Lee.

WOMAN ORDER, BUTLER'S

On May 15, 1862, Major General Benjamin F. Butler issued General Order No. 28. It read, "As the Officers and Soldiers of the United States have been subject to repeated insults from the women calling themselves ladies of New Orleans, in return for the most scrupulous non-interference and

Below: Benjamin Butler's infamous "Woman Order," General Order No. 28, aroused indignation but also accomplished its desired effect.

courtesy on our part, it is ordered that hereafter when any Female shall, by word, gesture, or movement, insult or show contempt for any officer or soldier of the United States, she shall be regarded and held liable to be treated as a woman of the town plying her avocation."

Butler was decried throughout the South and vilified as the "Beast" for his heavy-handed military governance of New Orleans, but

his technique did have its desired effect. The provocative insults stopped without a single woman being arrested for violating the infamous order.

Above: Benjamin Butler was vilified throughout the South long after the end of the Civil War for his abusive occupation of New Orleans.

BUTLER'S PROCLAMATION

An outrageous insult to the Women of New Orleans!

Southern Men, avenge their wrongs !!!

Head-Quarters, Department of the Gulf, New Orleans, May 15, 1862.

General Orders, No. 28.

As the Officers and Soldiers of the United States have been subject to repeated insults from the women calling themselves ladies of New Orleans, in return for the most scrupulous non-interference and courtesy on our part, it is ordered that hereafter when any Female shall, by word, gesture, or movement, insult or show contempt for any officer or soldier of the United States, she shall be regarded and held liable to be treated as a woman of the town plying her avocation.

By command of Maj.-Gen. BUTLER,
GEORGE C. STRONG,
A. A. G. Chief of Staff.

WOMEN IN THE CONFEDERACY

The traditional image of the Confederate woman is the self-sacrificing Southern belle who proudly sent her man off to defend the cause and then supported him through varied patriotic and civic-minded activities on the home front. To be sure, some Confederate women met this description, but there were different types of Confederate women just like there were different types of Confederate soldiers.

As is the case in all wars, the role of Confederate women in the Civil War expanded based on the absence of men at home and the emergencies of war. Women executed the roles of heads of households and struggled to keep farms running, budgets balanced, and bills paid with their husbands gone. Others became involved in a variety of war-associated roles that included camp laundresses, nurses,

Above: *There were a few Confederate women, such as Loreta Velazquez, who disguised themselves and served as soldiers in the Confederate army. Velazquez went by the name of Lieutenant Harry T. Buford.*

and charity volunteers. For the first time, women replaced men as teachers in Southern schools. A small number even masqueraded as men and joined the soldiers' ranks. Some, such as Belle Boyd, served as spies.

HOME FRONT HARDSHIPS

Confederate women did the best they could to manage under the hardships of food shortages and inflation, but in 1863 a series of "Bread Riots" swept the South, the most famous occurring in Richmond. In several cases, women complained so bitterly of the hardships on the home front that they motivated their soldiers to desert and come home.

Women not only contributed in a variety of ways to life in the Confederacy, they also left a rich collection of diaries and letters that have made a significant impact on Civil War scholarship. Mary Chesnut, Mary Loughborough, and Judith McGuire are among those who left written records of their experiences.

YANCEY, WILLIAM L. (1814–63)

William Lowndes Yancey was a senator from Alabama and one of the South's most vehement fire-eaters. In spite of being a leading secessionist, he was not selected to be one of Alabama's delegates to the Montgomery Convention. His talents seemed to lie more in destroying the old Union rather than in constructing the new Confederacy.

Still, he was a force to be reckoned with, and President Jefferson Davis tapped Yancey to be part of the Confederacy's original set of three commissioners sent to seek recognition from England and France. When the mission failed, Yancey returned home. He was elected to the first Confederate Senate and served until his death in 1863. He was a vocal opponent of Davis and his efforts at centralization.

Above: *William Yancey's fire-eating rhetoric proved to be of little value to the Confederacy once the Civil War began.*

YELLOW TAVERN, BATTLE OF

❖ DATE: May 11, 1864

❖ LOCATION: Henrico County, Virginia

❖ FORCE UNDER STUART (C): 4,500

❖ FORCE UNDER SHERIDAN (U.S.): 10,000

❖ CASUALTIES: 300 (C); 625 (U.S.)

On May 9, 1864, Major General Philip H. Sheridan departed on a cavalry raid toward Richmond. Major General Jeb Stuart learned of Sheridan's move, and on May 11 he established a position at Yellow Tavern to block Sheridan's advance. Sheridan overran the Confederates, forcing some to withdraw north toward Ashland and some south toward Richmond. Sheridan, however, decided it would be unwise to continue to Richmond and instead went to the James River to link up with Major General Benjamin F. Butler. Stuart was mortally wounded in the fighting on May 11 and died the next day.

YEOMAN CLASS, SOUTHERN

Southern yeomen were skilled mechanics and tradesmen or small farmers who worked land they owned or rented. They formed an industrious and hardworking class, and few owned slaves. Consequently, yeomen often suffered from the prevailing social notion that white men who labored were not fully respectable.

For many Southern yeomen, the Civil War was the typical "rich man's war and poor man's fight." As the war progressed, many yeomen resisted centralizing efforts such as taxes and impressments, an indication of heightened class awareness and association of the planter class with an increasingly intrusive government. Especially irritating to the yeoman class were acts such as the Twenty (Fifteen) Slave Law that benefited slave owners, of which few were yeomen.

YORKTOWN, SIEGE OF
(APRIL 5–MAY 3, 1862)

After conducting an impressive amphibious move to the Virginia Peninsula, Major General George B. McClellan began a march to Yorktown, his first objective en route to Richmond. McClellan reports having 53,000 men available to move, although many authorities give a higher figure. Opposing him were the 12,000 men of Brigadier General John B. Magruder's Army of the Peninsula.

On April 4, 1862, McClellan sent one column marching up the Peninsula on the right toward Yorktown while another marched on the left toward Williamsburg.

This left column, commanded by Brigadier General Erasmus D. Keyes, was to turn Magruder's flank and push on to Halfway House between Yorktown and Williamsburg. However, late in the afternoon of April 5, Keyes's advance element came under fire from artillery and entrenched infantry at Lee's Mill, where the maps indicated only a harmless depot. Based on this small contact, Keyes reported that Magruder's

Above: *Rather than pressing his advantage, Major General George McClellan ceased to maneuver and subjected Yorktown to a siege.*

position was too strong to "assault without an enormous waste of life."

Magruder helped perpetuate this misconception by conducting a masterful ruse. He marched a couple of his regiments out of a thicket and into a clearing within view of the Federal advance guard. The Confederates then disappeared into another wood, doubled back around while still out of sight, and then repeated the process, giving the Federals the impression that the Confederate numbers were much greater than they really were.

McClellan then decided to forfeit his numerical advantage and reduce Yorktown by siege. The siege lasted until May 3, when the Confederates abandoned Yorktown and withdrew up the Peninsula on their own terms. The Federal delay had given the Confederates valuable time to rush reinforcements to oppose McClellan's offensive.

Left: *Abandoned fortifications and cannons at Yorktown, following the Federal capture of the city in May 1862. Rather than remaining at Yorktown, Joseph Johnston withdrew and foiled George McClellan's planned siege.*

LIST OF CONFEDERATE GENERALS

The Confederate army included the ranks of brigadier general, major general, lieutenant general, and general. The men occupying these positions were an eclectic group ranging from career professional soldiers to politicians. There were, however, some points of commonality. Of all the Confederate generals, 151 were products of the United States Military Academy at West Point, and 142 had served in the Mexican War. West Point and Mexico proved to be important formative experiences for Civil War generals, North and South. The following is a list of some of the Confederacy's most famous generals.

Adams, William Wirt *(1819–88)*	Brigadier General
Alexander, Edward Porter *(1835–1910)*	Brigadier General
Anderson, George Thomas *(1824–1901)*	Brigadier General
Armistead, Lewis Addison *(1817–63)*	Brigadier General
Armstrong, Frank Crawford *(1835–1909)*	Brigadier General
Ashby, Turner *(1828–62)*	Brigadier General
Baker, Laurence Simmons *(1830–1907)*	Brigadier General
Barksdale, William *(1821–63)*	Brigadier General
Bate, William Brimage *(1826–1905)*	Major General
Beall, William Nelson Rector *(1825–83)*	Brigadier General
Beauregard, Pierre Gustave Toutant *(1818–93)*	General
Bee, Barnard Elliott Jr. *(1824–61)*	Brigadier General
Bowen, John Stevens *(1830–63)*	Major General
Bragg, Braxton *(1817–76)*	General
Branch, Lawrence O'Bryan *(1820–62)*	Brigadier General
Breckinridge, John Cabell *(1821–75)*	Major General
Brown, John Calvin *(1827–89)*	Major General
Buckner, Simon Bolivar *(1823–1914)*	Lieutenant General
Buford, Abraham *(1820–84)*	Brigadier General
Cantey, James *(1818–74)*	Brigadier General
Chalmers, James Ronald *(1831–98)*	Brigadier General
Cheatham, Benjamin Franklin *(1820–86)*	Major General
Cleburne, Patrick Ronayne *(1828–64)*	Major General
Clingman, Thomas Lanier *(1812–97)*	Brigadier General
Cobb, Howell *(1815–68)*	Major General
Cockrell, Francis Marion *(1834–1915)*	Brigadier General
Colquitt, Alfred Holt *(1824–94)*	Brigadier General
Colston, Raleigh Edward *(1825–96)*	Brigadier General
Cooper, Samuel *(1798–1876)*	General
Cosby, George Blake *(1830–1909)*	Brigadier General
Cox, William Ruffin *(1832–1919)*	Brigadier General
Crittenden, George Bibb *(1812–80)*	Brigadier General
Dearing, James *(1840–65)*	Brigadier General
Dease, Zachariah Cantey *(1819–82)*	Brigadier General
Dibrell, George Gibbs *(1822–88)*	Brigadier General

Drayton, Thomas Fenwick *(1808–91)*	Brigadier General
Duke, Basil Wilson *(1838–1916)*	Brigadier General
Early, Jubal Anderson *(1816–94)*	Lieutenant General
Echols, John *(1823–96)*	Brigadier General
Elzey, Arnold *(1816–71)*	Major General
Ewell, Richard Stoddert *(1817–72)*	Lieutenant General
Fagan, James Fleming *(1828–93)*	Brigadier General
Floyd, John Buchanan *(1806–63)*	Brigadier General
Forney, John Horace *(1829–1902)*	Major General
Forrest, Nathan Bedford *(1821–77)*	Lieutenant General
French, Samuel Gibbs *(1818–1910)*	Major General
Frost, Daniel Marsh *(1823–1900)*	Brigadier General
Gardner, Franklin *(1823–73)*	Major General
Garnett, Richard Brooke *(1817–63)*	Brigadier General
Garnett, Robert Seldon *(1819–61)*	Brigadier General
Gary, Martin Witherspoon *(1831–81)*	Brigadier General
Gibson, Randall Lee *(1832–92)*	Brigadier General
Gladden, Adley Hogan *(1810–62)*	Brigadier General
Gordon, George Washington *(1836–1911)*	Brigadier General
Gordon, John Brown *(1832–1904)*	Major General
Gorgas, Josiah *(1818–83)*	Brigadier General
Govan, Daniel Chevilette *(1829–1911)*	Brigadier General
Gregg, Maxcy *(1814–62)*	Brigadier General
Grimes, Bryan *(1828–80)*	Brigadier General
Hampton, Wade III *(1818–1902)*	Lieutenant General
Hanson, Roger Weightman *(1827–63)*	Brigadier General
Hardee, William Joseph *(1815–73)*	Lieutenant General
Hatton, Robert Hopkins *(1826–62)*	Brigadier General
Hays, Harry Thompson *(1820–76)*	Major General
Heth, Henry *(1825–99)*	Major General
Higgins, Edward *(1821–75)*	Brigadier General
Hill, Ambrose Powell *(1825–65)*	Lieutenant General
Hill, Daniel Harvey *(1821–89)*	Lieutenant General
Hindman, Thomas Carmichael *(1828–68)*	Major General

Hoke, Robert Frederick *(1837–1912)*	Major General	Parsons, Mosby Monroe *(1822–65)*	Brigadier General
Holmes, Theophilus Hunter *(1804–80)*	Lieutenant General	Payne, William Henry Fitzhugh *(1830–1904)*	Brigadier General
Hood, John Bell *(1831–79)*	General	Pegram, John *(1832–65)*	Brigadier General
Huger, Benjamin *(1805–77)*	Major General	Pemberton, John Clifford *(1814–81)*	Lieutenant General
		Pender, William Dorsey *(1834–63)*	Major General
Imboden, John Daniel *(1823–95)*	Brigadier General	Pettigrew, James Johnston *(1828–63)*	Brigadier General
		Pickett, George Edward *(1825–75)*	Major General
Jackson, Thomas Jonathan *(1824–63)*	Lieutenant General	Pike, Albert *(1809–91)*	Brigadier General
Jenkins, Albert Gallatin *(1830–64)*	Brigadier General	Pillow, Gideon Johnson *(1806–78)*	Brigadier General
Jenkins, Micah *(1835–64)*	Brigadier General	Polignac, Camille Armand Jules Marie,	
Johnson, Bradley Tyler *(1829–1903)*	Brigadier General	Prince de *(1832–1913)*	Major General
Johnson, Bushrod Rust *(1817–80)*	Major General	Polk, Leonidas *(1806–64)*	Lieutenant General
Johnson, Edward *(1816–73)*	Major General	Preston, William *(1816–87)*	Brigadier General
Johnston, Albert Sidney *(1803–62)*	General	Price, Sterling *(1809–67)*	Major General
Johnston, Joseph Eggleston *(1807–91)*	General	Pryor, Roger Atkinson *(1828–1919)*	Brigadier General
Jones, John Marshall *(1820–64)*	Brigadier General		
Jones, Samuel *(1820–87)*	Major General	Quarles, William Andrew *(1825–93)*	Brigadier General
Jones, William Edmondson *(1824–64)*	Brigadier General		
		Rains, Gabriel James *(1803–81)*	Brigadier General
Kemper, James Lawson *(1823–95)*	Brigadier General	Rains, James Edward *(1833–62)*	Brigadier General
		Ramseur, Stephen Dodson *(1837–64)*	Major General
Lawton, Alexander Robert *(1818–96)*	Brigadier General	Randolph, George Wythe *(1818–67)*	Brigadier General
Lee, Fitzhugh *(1835–1905)*	Major General	Ransom, Robert Jr. *(1828–92)*	Major General
Lee, George Washington Custis *(1832–1913)*	Major General	Ripley, Roswell Sabine *(1823–87)*	Brigadier General
Lee, Robert Edward *(1807–70)*	General	Rodes, Robert Emmett *(1829–64)*	Major General
Lee, Stephen Dill *(1833–1908)*	Lieutenant General	Rosser, Thomas Lafayette *(1836–1910)*	Major General
Lee, William Henry Fitzhugh *(1837–91)*	Major General		
Lewis, Joseph Horace *(1824–1904)*	Brigadier General	Semmes, Raphael *(1809–77)*	Rear Admiral/Brigadier General
Longstreet, James *(1821–1904)*	Lieutenant General	Shelby, Joseph Orville *(1830–97)*	Brigadier General
Loring, William Wing *(1818–86)*	Major General	Shoup, Francis Asbury *(1834–96)*	Brigadier General
Lovell, Mansfield *(1822–84)*	Major General	Sibley, Henry Hopkins *(1816–86)*	Brigadier General
		Slaughter, James Edwin *(1827–1901)*	Brigadier General
Mackall, William Whann *(1817–91)*	Brigadier General	Smith, Edmund Kirby *(1824–93)*	General
Magruder, John Bankhead *(1810–71)*	Major General	Smith, Gustavus Woodson *(1821–96)*	Major General
Mahone, William *(1826–95)*	Major General	Smith, Martin Luther *(1819–66)*	Major General
Major, James Patrick *(1836–77)*	Brigadier General	Smith, William *(1796–1887)*	Major General
Maney, George Earl *(1826–1901)*	Brigadier General	Steuart, George Hume *(1828–1903)*	Brigadier General
Marmaduke, John Sappington *(1833–87)*	Major General	Stevenson, Carter Littlepage *(1817–88)*	Major General
Marshall, Humphrey *(1812–72)*	Brigadier General	Stewart, Alexander Peter *(1821–1908)*	Brigadier General
Maury, Dabney Herndon *(1822–1900)*	Major General	Stuart, James Ewell Brown *(1833–64)*	Major General
McCulloch, Benjamin *(1811–62)*	Brigadier General		
McLaws, Lafayette *(1821–97)*	Major General	Taliaferro, William Booth *(1822–98)*	Major General
Moore, John Creed *(1824–1910)*	Brigadier General	Taylor, Richard *(1826–79)*	Lieutenant General
Morgan, John Hunt *(1825–64)*	Brigadier General	Thomas, Bryan Morel *(1836–1905)*	Brigadier General
		Thomas, Edward Lloyd *(1825–98)*	Brigadier General
Northrop, Lucius Bellinger *(1811–94)*	Brigadier General	Thompson, Meriwether Jefferson *(1826–76)*	Brigadier General

INDEX